PORCELAIN
OF PARIS

1770–1850

Locré, Russinger.
So-called 'Etruscan' baluster-
vase. Decoration in the style
of Salembier. *Circa* 1780.
Sèvres, Musée National de
Céramique. Ht. 44 cm.
($17^1/_3$ in.).
Mark 143.

Régine de Plinval de Guillebon

PORCELAIN OF PARIS

1770–1850

Translated by Robin R. Charleston

WALKER AND COMPANY ✸ New York

This book has been published with the support of the Ceramica-Stiftung, Basle.

First published in the United States of America in 1972 by the Walker Publishing Company, Inc.

Published simultaneously in Canada by Fitzhenry & Whiteside, Limited, Toronto.

ISBN: 0-8027-0395-x

Library of Congress Catalog Card Number: 72-80541

Printed in Switzerland.

Contents

1 Dagoty.
Large urn-shaped cooler
with concave lid. The varied
techniques used point to a
consummate craftsmanship.
A wide underglazeblue band
is adorned with a broad
border of biscuit flowers.
The base is decorated with
medallions surrounding
antique scenes in contrast-
burnished gold, exquisitely
worked in relief.
Circa 1810.
Paris, Coll. Le Tallec.
Ht. 53 cm. (20^1/$_{10}$ in.).
Mark 62.

FOREWORD

Until now Paris porcelain has not been the subject of any special study. Any worthwhile information about it could only be drawn from either the *Histoire des Manufactures françaises de Porcelaine* which Comte X. de Chavagnac and the Marquis de Grollier published in 1906, or from a few specialized articles.

The origin of the present book is a thesis on *La Manufacture du Comte d'Artois, Faubourg Saint-Denis* which the writer presented at the Ecole du Louvre in 1956, and which started out from the very precise archive references supplied by Chavagnac and Grollier. Indeed, it must be emphasized that in spite of the limited sources available to them at the beginning of the century, they created a work that remains a paragon of scholarship for students of ceramics. Although some of their hypotheses have occasionally turned out to be inaccurate they are nonetheless of great interest on the subject since they are always conscientiously formulated. Furthermore, Chavagnac and Grollier had the enormous merit of never researching into archives without constantly relating this to a study of the porcelain which they collected. The framework of reference for this book is the large card index built up by the writer, on the basis of the items in the Grollier Collection bequeathed to the Musée national de Céramique de Sèvres. Although dedicated to ceramics in general, this museum may be regarded more especially as the repository of French ceramics and, as such, it has received many gifts and bequests from manufacturers and decorators in the early 19th century. This should be sufficient indication of how pre-eminently important it is in the preparation of a study such as the one that follows.

A host of new and hitherto untapped documents enabled the author not only to find a great deal of unpublished data relating to the factories' history, the objects themselves and their marks, but also made it possible to exceed the scope of a straightforward monograph or of a repertory of names. Indeed, it seemed feasible to trace the main outlines of the evolution of Paris porcelain production and to place it in a political, economic, social and artistic context.

Our knowledge of Paris porcelain actually derives from many historical sources. This is one of the factors which induced the author to prepare her latest thesis for the Ecole Pratique des Hautes Etudes at Paris, which aims specifically to enquire into *La fabrication et le commerce de la porcelaine à Paris, du Consulat à 1850*.

This book owes much to the guidance of M. Pierre-Henri Fourest, the head keeper of the Musée national de Céramique de Sèvres, and of M. Michel Fleury, principal of the 4th Division of the Ecole Pratique des Hautes Etudes.

In its eighteen years of preparatory research it has also benefited in various respects from advice and information, particularly the assistance given by Mlle Brunet, Bibliothécaire honoraire de la Manufacture nationale de Sèvres; Mme Felkay, Conservateur aux Archives de Paris; M. Hérold; Mme Jurgens, Conservateur aux Archives nationales; Dr Pecker; Mme Préau, Archiviste de la Manufacture nationale de Sèvres; Mme Pronteau, Sous-directeur d'études of the Ecole Pratique des Hautes Etudes; M. le Pasteur Paul Romane-Musculus, Mme X. Schoelcher; M. de Surirey de Saint-Remy, Conservateur en chef de la Bibliothèque historique de la Ville de Paris; M. Védère, Conservateur du Musée des Arts décoratifs, at Bordeaux; M. Verlet, Conservateur en chef du Département des Objets d'art at the Musée du Louvre.

Our thanks also go out to M. Ayrès de Carvalho, Director of the Palacio Nacional de Ajuda; H. Blois; Mme Brana, Keeper, Museo Arqueológico Nacional, Madrid; M. et Mme Broulard; The chairman of the Board of Trustees, Fundação da Casa de Bragança, Vila Viçosa; Mr Charleston, Keeper of the Department of Ceramics, Victoria & Albert Museum, London; Mme Chavonnet; Mr Conger, Curator of the White House, Washington; Mr Dautermann, West European Arts, Metropolitan Museum of Art, New York; M. David, Conservateur, Musée national du Château de La Malmaison; Mme Ducourtial, Conservateur du Musée de la Légion d'honneur; M. Fuertes de Villavicencio; Mlle Godefroy; Mr Hathaway, Curator of the Philadelphia Museum of Art, Philadelphia; Mme Herrenschmidt; M. Hubert, Conservateur en chef, Musée national du Château de La Malmaison; Mlle Jacob, Conservateur des Musées de Saumur; Mme James; Dr Lasserre; M. Le Tallec; M. Ludmann, Keeper, Palais de Rohan, Strassburg; Mme Lutterman, Keeper of the Department of Decorative Arts, Nationalmuseum, Stockholm; Mlle de Mendonça, Director, Museu Nacional de Arte Antiga, Lisbon; Mme Nast; M. Passerat; M. Pélichet, Conservateur du Musée de l'Ariana, Geneva; Mlle Popovitch, Conservateur, Musée des Beaux-Arts et de la Céramique, Rouen; M. Porfirio, Director, Palacio Nacional de Quéluz; Mr Tait, Keeper of the Department of Medieval and Later Antiquities, British Museum, London; M. Wilhelm, Conservateur en chef, Musée Carnavalet, Paris.   *R.P.G.*

The translator wishes to thank his father R.J. Charleston for his generous assistance which has been invaluable in the translation of this work.   *R.R.C*

INTRODUCTION

The definition of Paris porcelain in the 18th century is simple: hard-paste porcelain both manufactured and decorated in factories situated in Paris. It becomes more complex in the 19th century. We may now define it as hard-paste porcelain, generally decorated in Paris although not invariably manufactured there, and originating either from factories with at least an official Paris address or else from salesrooms located in Paris.

In the course of our survey we shall see how, over the first half of the 19th century, economic changes gradually transformed production methods, as well as the porcelain trade.

At present, items known to enthusiasts as 'Paris porcelain' are identified chiefly from the marks affixed to the back. By extension, the antique trade of today inaccurately describes as 'Paris porcelain' any unmarked piece appearing to have been manufactured and decorated in France at the end of the 18th, or in the first half of the 19th century.

From the end of the 17th century, porcelain factories had been set up in the vicinity of Paris. However, they manufactured pieces exclusively in soft-paste as kaolin had not been discovered in Europe. At the beginning of the 18th century an establishment was founded at Paris, in Rue de la Ville-l'Evêque, by manufacturers based in Saint-Cloud. Another factory was running in Rue de Charonne. Moreover, there is every reason to assume that the small-ware dealer Hébert turned his attention not only to the sale of porcelain but also to its manufacture.

The first French factory of hard-paste porcelain operated in Strassburg. It was created at the beginning of the 18th century but, even so, it must be pointed out that the china clay used came from Germany. After a few experiments conducted in France with kaolin found in the region of Alençon[1], the first noteworthy factories producing hard-paste porcelain were set up, following the discovery in 1769 of the kaolin deposits in the Limousin. Various centres, amongst them the Limousin and the eastern regions, were rapidly left behind by the Paris centre, where a good many factories were assembled, probably favoured by proximity to the Court, the plentiful supply of capital and the volume of commercial activity.

We shall restrict ourselves here to studying those establishments set up in Paris itself[2] mentioning only in passing those which operated in the outskirts of Paris: Boissette, Châtillon, Choisy-le-Roy, Conflans, Etiolles, L'Isle-Adam, Vaux, Vincennes and, of course, the royal factory of Sèvres, to which, however, we shall have many opportunities to allude. It is impossible to retrace the history of Parisian factories without referring to

---

[1] Experiments conducted by the Duc de Brancas, Comte de Lauraguais, member of the Académie des Sciences, in his mansion at Lassay. Other experiments were performed at Bagnolet by the chemist Guéttard, attached to the Duc d'Orléans.

[2] We are speaking of Paris as it was in 1859, before the integration of the adjoining communes, but including Clignancourt, a factory which in any case had salesrooms in the centre of Paris.

that of the royal factory, so closely were the two interconnected.

The appearance of factories producing hard-paste porcelain fits into the framework of immigration—temporary or permanent—of numerous artisans coming from the East, either from within France or from abroad. Just as in the art of furniture making, the fame of German cabinet makers is well known, so in the field of porcelain it is not surprising to find that, often, the best manufacturers originated from the East, since the discovery of kaolin in Europe occurred originally in Germany. Indeed, we find names of Germanic origin in Paris: Han-

nong, whose family were natives of Maastricht; Russinger, initially a modeller at Höchst, who had a factory Rue Fontaine-au-Roy, producing 'German porcelain'; Nast, who was born in Styria; Dihl, the 'Palatine modeller' who came from Lammsheim, and the Clauss dynasty which hailed from the small town of Traben, near to Treves. Other manufacturers originated west of the Rhine: the relatives of Marc Schoelcher tilled their lands near Colmar; Lassia, the childhood friend and cat's-paw of Pierre Antoine Hannong, was from Strassburg. Of course, there were also many Parisian porcelain manufacturers. Friendship and family ties drew the manufacturers closer together, also attracting the craftsmen of their country (Dihl brought in several members of his family), and they all tended to congregate in the quarter of La Courtille where the innkeepers, themselves 'Easterners', welcomed their compatriots.

Numerous marriages took place between families, directly or indirectly affecting porcelain: of Deruelle's two daughters, one married the modeller Moitte, the other the faience and porcelain dealer, Duban; Lebon became Halley's son-in-law, and Clauss married Odile Seeger, daughter and sister of porcelain painters. Some alliances were even decisive in the development of a factory, such as the remarriage of the porcelain manufacturer Guérhard's widow to his business partner Dihl. Family team work was eventually quite extensive; witness, amongst others, the Deruelle family, where eight children were involved in production, while their mother—like Madame Guérhard, later Madame Dihl—dealt with the sales. We should also mention the famous couple of porcelain miniaturists: Le Guay and his wife Victoire Jaquotot. Women proved

3 Jacob Petit. Rocaille candlestick. Polychrome and gold on turquoise ground. Imitation amethysts. Circa 1840.

Sèvres, Musée National de Céramique. Ht. 27 cm. (10²/₃ in.). Mark 125.

very successful at different stages of production.

One can roughly localise the early porcelain factories to the north-east quarter of Paris. From Clignancourt—at that time outside the city gates—and through the Faubourg Saint-Denis and La Courtille, one soon reached the thickest concentration in the Faubourg du Temple and the Faubourg Saint-Antoine. This was, in fact, an artisan quarter where the best cabinet makers and the faience dealers were already established. Nearly every street harboured a factory—sometimes two—producing either porcelain or faience. The parish of Sainte-Marguerite was one of those which drew together the majority of well-to-do artisans and it was not uncommon to see traffic jams due to the concourse of carriages bringing their wealthy clientele. In the 19th century the great urban upheaval changed this part of Paris when the Avenue de la République, Avenue Parmentier and Boulevard Voltaire among others were driven through, but it failed to separate the districts of Charonne, Reuilly, Popincourt, Pont-aux-Choux and Le Temple. It is still very easy to pick out on a modern street-map the Rue Fontaine-au-Roy, Rue des Trois-Bornes, Rue Saint-Gilles, Rue Crussol, and Boulevard du Temple. If most of them have kept their names or exchanged them for less poetic ones, the Rue des Amandiers (Almond Tree Street) has nevertheless become Rue du Chemin-Vert, (Greenway Street), a name almost as evocative. Besides the factories and many convents, there were also a certain number of 'follies' where eminent men such as Favart and Cagliostro resided.

In this context we must not think of the factories as resembling their modern counterparts, airless and joyless. The records of sale suggest some quite verdant scenes. Very often a door leading from the street took one through a long passageway, into a huge quadrilateral area around which were grouped the various buildings that were necessary for housing the manufacturer and his family (sometimes a few employees too), and for producing and selling the porcelain. In fact most manufacturers did not hesitate to put up new buildings according to their needs.

The factory of the Faubourg Saint-Denis prided itself on having a labyrinth and a well, essential for the production of the porcelain body. When Deruelle bought the buildings in Clignancourt they consisted of 'several blocks of buildings, a courtyard, farmyard, garden adjacent to aforesaid premises, walled-in, several sheep pens and shepherd's lodgings: the whole area being of two acres or thereabouts...'

Strangely enough, whereas the manufacturers from the eastern regions all gathered in the same area, the others did not have their quarters there; some of them clustered together at Clignancourt, or in the centre of Paris, in Rue Thiroux for instance.

Finally, to the outlying factories belonged numerous salesrooms located in the most central districts, but which shifted premises according to the fluctuations in their elegant clientele. They were first established in the Faubourg Saint-Germain near the Louvre, later at the Palais Royal and on the Grands Boulevards.

We find lastly that moves were frequent: not only did the shops change their premises or street, but the manufacturers themselves—Nast, Dihl, Guérhard and others—did not hesitate to transfer their establishments to bigger premises, better suited to the expansion of their business.

THE EIGHTEENTH CENTURY

General Remarks

PRIVILEGES. STRUGGLE WITH THE ROYAL FACTORY OF SÈVRES
One of the most characteristic features of the history of porcelain factories towards the end of the *Ancien Régime* is the struggle against the royal factory of Sèvres, especially against the privileges granted to it. As early as the 17th century, certain privileges had been accorded to private factories (Rouen and Saint-Cloud), this being the most effective support for these establishments, although they were already protected by important people. In 1745 an initial privilege was conceded to the factory of Vincennes, which was afterwards to set itself up at Sèvres but was at the time a private factory supported on the capital of financiers and powerful nobles. A decree of the King's Council allowed Adam, its nominal director, the exclusive privilege of making 'porcelain in the Saxon manner, painted and gilded...'—an especially extravagant privilege. Indeed, other factories such as Chantilly and Strassburg were already producing this type of porcelain. This decree was, therefore, not complied with and a second was issued two years later, in 1747, forbidding all private individuals, except those who had obtained letters of privilege, to set up factories producing porcelain or to construct or maintain kilns designed to fire porcelain. Adam further obtained the excessive right of inspecting any premises where he might suspect operations in contravention of these decrees. His successor Eloi Brichard, by a decree of 1753, obtained the monopoly on porcelain production in France, all other privileges previously granted being thereby revoked. After settling at Sèvres, the factory became the property of the King in 1759. Nonetheless, in the following year, the decree of February 17th 1760, although repealing previous decrees, relaxed the prohibitions which had hit the other establishments: 'His Majesty wishing to favour private privileges, small factories will henceforth be

4   P.A. Hannong. *Marabout* jug. Green monochrome touched with red and gold. *Circa* 1772.

Sèvres, Musée National de Céramique. Ht. 12 cm. (4³/₄ in.). Mark 25.

able to produce ordinary porcelain in white and painted in blue, Chinese style only...' This decree was strengthened in 1763 when the Lieutenant général de Police imposed a ban on production of flowers and items in relief 'other than for adhering to manufactured pieces'.

In 1766 a new and important concession was granted to private enterprise, namely to paint 'in monochrome with a single colour', provided that the contractor affixed his mark to the porcelain. He was, in addition, required to register himself officially with the Lieutenant général de Police. The use of gold and of three-dimensional ornaments remained prohibited. Shortly after the publication of this decree, *limousin* kaolin was discovered, and what the government did not allow in any positive ruling, it permitted by secret departures from the law, or by unspoken consent. In spite of a few confiscations for the sake of appearances, the general prohibition remained a dead letter, particularly for the factories that had been newly set up in Paris, which enthusiastically contravened the royal ban. So much and so successfully indeed, that M. de Sartine, then Lieutenant général de Police, proposed in 1773 the issuance of an order which would allow 'all Parisian factories six months' grace in which to sell off their painted and gilded pieces, after which time they would be seized'. However, the police inspector in charge of the visits to the factories thought up a clever expedient. He wrote circulars to the contractors who displayed them in their workshops, announcing to the craftsmen that they would in future be reduced to making nothing but ordinary porcelain, which would entail their dismissal. Demonstrations took place. Workmen came in bands to see the Lieutenant

5 P. A. Hannong. Handleless *cabaret*-cup. High-temperature blue. The 1766 decrees of the King's Council on porcelain-manufacture allowed only decorations 'in imitation of China porcelain, either in the white, painted in blue and white *[sic]*, or in mono-chrome using another colour' but forbad 'any further colour, especially gold...' This rather coarse piece is one of the few examples of early Parisian wares which has actually complied with the regulations. Items of this sort, including handleless cups and saucers of 'skull-cap' shape, were made at various times at Chantilly as well, in soft and hard paste. *Circa* 1722. Sèvres, Musée National de Céramique. Ht. 4.3 cm. (1²/₃ in.). Mark 24.

de Police and the manager of the royal factory. Amongst the Parisian manufacturers the one from the Faubourg Saint-Denis stood out particularly, by inciting the other porcelain makers to disobey the regulations.

The memorandum delivered to M. Bertin[1] by the administrators of Sèvres in

[1] Bertin, Henri Leonard Jean-Baptiste (1720–1792). Contrôleur général des Finances in 1759. Interim Foreign Minister in 1774. The Sèvres factory was under his administration until 1780.

6   P. A. Hannong.
Teapot. Handle of ribbed
wood. Polychrome and gold
sprigs. *Circa* 1772.
Strassburg, Musée des Beaux-
Arts. Ht. 10.5 cm. (4¹/₈ in.).
Mark 25.

7   P. A. Hannong.
Oval dish, scalloped rim, and
scroll motifs in relief.
Decorated with polychrome
and gold sprigs. *Circa* 1772.
Strassburg, Musée des Beaux-
Arts. L. 45 cm. (17³/₄ in.).
Mark 25.

8 P.A. Hannong. Basket embellished with branches in relief. Plain white. *Circa* 1775. Limoges, Musée National Adrien Dubouché. Diam. 21.5 cm. (8²/₅ in.). Mark 25.

March 1776 summarised their grievances against the Parisian factories, accusing them of enticing away the Sèvres craftsmen by paying them excessive rates, and of bringing down their sales prices after stealing moulds from the royal factory. This memorandum observed that their protection by the nobility encouraged the small factories to mock the royal privileges. It added that the Sèvres factory seemed to be in complete disarray and was rushing towards ruin, having been forced to raise the craftsmen's wages in order to face Parisian competition. This picture may have been wilfully blackened so as to improve the lot of the workmen in the royal factory. Whatever the case

was, a letter from Parent, the director of Sèvres, in 1777, discloses that the moulds of figures modelled by Boizot and intended for the King's appartments had been stolen and that these very figures were being executed in Locré's workshop and would be on sale even before the royal factory could present its own to the King. It also complains of the theft of gold and colours, resold to the small factories. All these complaints finally culminated in searches followed by confiscations.

One of the weapons used by the Parisian manufacturers was to procure for their establishments the patronage of a member of the royal family. At this time, many factories of all sorts, both in Paris and the provinces, were eagerly looking for princely protection. This is why, in a deed of partnership of December 21st 1776 concerning the factory in Rue Thiroux, an annual income of 2,400 *livres* was provided for during the life of the company 'in favour of any person who obtains for the said factory a privilege by which it may enjoy prerogatives resulting therefrom...'

Outside the possibility of powerful and effective intervention what were, then, the advantages of an august patronage? Firstly there was that of obtaining orders from the patron: the factory of the Faubourg Saint-Denis did some rematching of a service of Sèvres, covered with roses, for the Comte d'Artois, the Comte de Provence hired a large amount of tableware from the factory at Clignancourt when he gave a sumptuous reception to the King and Queen in his mansion of Brunoy, and it was porcelain from the Rue Thiroux which graced the travelling case that Marie-Antoinette carried off on her flight. Of course, the courtiers were bound to go and buy porcelain in such factories.

Furthermore, thanks to the patent granting protection, the manufacturer could affix his patron's coat of arms to the door of the factory or shop, print them on his invoices, have the illustrious livery worn by the porter of the establishment, and above all use a monogram formed from the patron's initials as a mark.

The Comte d'Artois patronized two porcelain factories, one at Limoges on his own domains, the other in the Faubourg Saint-Denis, Paris. His son, the Duc d'Angoulême, was the protector of Guérhard & Dihl in Rue de Bondy, but one may well wonder if he really appreciated

the porcelain, for he was hardly older than six when the factory assumed his name. The Comte de Provence, later Louis XVIII, conferred a diploma upon the factory of Clignancourt, as also to another one in Marseilles, while the Duc d'Orléans granted one to the factory in Rue Amelot. The best known of all these establishments was on Rue Thiroux, referred to as the Queen's factory. Balzac, a lover of porcelain, mentions a few products of this factory amongst the treasures admired by Cousin Pons, the prime example of an enlightened amateur.

The years 1779 and 1780 saw an early phase of great activity in the struggle between the Parisian factories and the

9 P.A. Hannong.
Dish with scalloped rim and shell-shaped motifs.
Blue band, garlands and gold bands. *Circa* 1775.
Paris, private coll.
Diam. 26.5 cm. (10²/₅ in.).
Mark 24.

royal factory. The privileged factories had for the most part obtained official or tacit authorization to depart from the decree of 1766. In the cases of the factories of the Queen, 'Monsieur' (the King's brother) Comte de Provence, and of the Comte d'Artois, respectively, the process had been very much the same. Let us take for example the Comte d'Artois' factory, whose successive managers were possibly more aggressive than those in other factories.

Since before princely patronage this factory had been petitioning Bertin not only for permission to paint, gild and make figures 'in the round', but also for an exclusive privilege. For his part, Bertin was reasonably inclined to vouchsafe it, for he saw a possibility of using it as a pretext for renewing Sèvres' privilege, but Parent, the director of Sèvres, was against it owing, he said, to the poor quality of the paintings and gilt. He also argued that Monsieur's factory as well as Locré's would have been 'revolted' at it, that the factory would have harmed the King's, and lastly that Barrachin, the contractor at the time, had gone bankrupt in Lyons. In fact, as early as May 17th 1777, Bertin had written to the Lieutenant général de Police 'that there was reason to depart from the Council's decree of February 15th 1766 in favour of the porcelain factory of Marquis Dusson, of the Faubourg Saint-Lazare, and that he may make porcelain in whatever manner he sees fit'.[2]

A search followed by confiscation was carried out on March 3rd 1779 at the domicile of two former craftsmen from Sèvres, Catrice and Barbé, who were decorating at home some white porcelain pieces originating from Sèvres and Paris. This touched off the explosion. Among the one hundred and seventy-five items seized, there was one from Rue Thiroux, one from Clignancourt and seven from the Faubourg Saint-Denis.

The growing audacity of the Parisian managers necessitated the order of the Lieutenant général de Police of April 21st 1779. He commanded the enforcement of the regulations relating to the exclusive privilege of Sèvres and empowered the royal factory's director to make domiciliary inspections in the private factories.

Alarmed by this return to strictness, the manager of the factory in the Faubourg Saint-Denis held a public sale of prohibited porcelain at the Hôtel d'Aligre in

10 P.A. Hannong.
Cup with rounded base and saucer. Polychrome birds, ungilded. *Circa* 1772.
Sèvres, Musée National de Céramique. Ht. 5 cm. (2 in.). Mark 25.

[2] Archives de la manufacture nationale de Sèvres, A⁴.

Rue Saint-Honoré on January 7th 1780, wishing thereby to prove his good faith. On the other hand, resorting to his authorization of 1777 'Bertin ordered proceedings against all Parisian factories'. Searches followed by confiscations took place: from January 24th to 27th 1780 in Clignancourt—because of the large number of pieces—on January 28th in Rue Thiroux, on February 10th on Locré's premises in La Courtille, and lastly on February 11th at the Faubourg Saint-Denis. The confiscations included 'works of porcelain, materials and utensils used in producing anything that may be found in contravention of the regulations...' Following the confiscations the director of the royal factory asked the Lieutenant général de Police to serve a summons on the owner of the offending factory so as to inflict upon him the sanctions laid down in the regulations.

In respect of the Faubourg Saint-Denis, the director of Sèvres required a fine of 3,000 *livres,* damages, the demolition of the kilns at the expense of the owner, the disqualification from producing any sort of porcelain and the prohibition of any subsequent establishment.

From then on, the struggle between Sèvres and the Duke of Artois' factory became fierce. On March 1st, Stahn the—incidentally fictitious—owner and the Marquis de la Salle—former owner but *de facto* responsible—received their writs. On March 2nd, La Salle contested a new search. On the 3rd, at the confiscation hearing in the presence of the Lieutenant de Police, La Salle pointed out that he was in no way offending, as no one had found a single craftsman working in the painters' workshop; and that the pieces were not completed. He thereby demonstrated his obedience to the order of 1779. On the

9th, Stahn requested the repossession of his goods and the annulment of the confiscation order. The latter request was sustained on April 1st and Stahn and La Salle were summoned to appear before the Lieutenant de Police. On the 4th the case was adjourned for a fortnight and La Salle started using the cunning ploy of

'fighting for time'. Consequently, on April 12th, he asked for a transcript and minutes of the confiscation proceedings, preparatory to the hearing on the 18th. The director of Sèvres, Régnier, withheld them, seeing in it only an excuse for delay, but his move was foiled; the case was once again postponed for a fortnight and Régnier received instructions from the Lieutenant de Police to forward the documents to the defendants. A new writ of Régnier's on April 20th was followed by a 'plea in abatement' of the confiscation, drawn up by La Salle on the 22nd. With supreme cunning La Salle declared, on April 27th, that the transcript sent by Régnier was inadequate and that he did

11 P.A. Hannong.
Double-lipped sauce-boat.
Polychrome sprigs.
Circa 1772.
Limoges, Musée National
Adrien Dubouché.
L. 25.5 cm. (10 in.).
Mark 24.

12 P. A. Hannong.
Chocolate-pot. Gold relief-
work. Attributes of
gardening, music, etc.
Insects. *Circa* 1775.
Sèvres, Musée National de
Céramique. Ht. 15 cm.
(6 in.).
Mark 25.

not know 'on what charge and what allegation to answer'. He concluded by asking for a copy of the regulations concerning Sèvres, to which Régnier had only been alluding. On the 29th, Régnier refused to transmit them, affirming they were common knowledge: 'there are nearly 500 facsimiles of them, posted up both at the factory of Sève [*sic*] and on the gates of the factories under injunction and elsewhere'. He ended up, however, by sending them. La Salle and Stahn countered a new summons of May 1st with a demurrer, pretexting once again their ignorance of the regulations. On May 17th defence council for La Salle, in a long review, explained the part played in the factory by the Marquis de La Salle, portraying him as victim of his own credulity. The barrister recalled the capital outlays ploughed into the establishment, then the tolerances—tacit and otherwise—which the factory had enjoyed. This fact was publicly known to all, particularly to the magistrate-judge of this lawsuit, who had signed the instrument allowing the advertising of products that were made there as well as of the shops that sold them. The minister in charge of Sèvres—Bertin—owned some of these pieces in his town house, while the King and his ministers 'glory in adorning their chambers with them'. He put forward the assertion that La Salle had no further interest in the factory, having found a purchaser. He forgot to say that Stahn was the leading painter in the factory and that its sale was purely fictitious. Officially, at the time of the confiscation on February 11th, no prohibited article was being produced any longer on La Salle's account: the impounded porcelain belonged to Stahn, and La Salle was even authorised to con-

tinue selling the porcelain already made at the time when he was the owner, and to dispose of the moulds and blocks. La Salle naturally declared that the sanctions only applied to Stahn and, going over to the offensive, arraigned the royal factory for its long silence. He declared that it was murderous to have let his factory

13 Comte d'Artois' factory. Ice-pail for bottles. Polychrome and gold. *Circa* 1785. Sèvres, Musée National de Céramique. Ht. 11.5 cm. (4½ in.). Mark 27.

14 Comte d'Artois' factory. Lobed plate, sprays of roses painted from life. This plate probably belongs to the 'replacers' for Sèvres porcelain, which the Comte d'Artois ordered from his factory, notably in 1784. They were intended for his residences of Maisons, Saint-Germain and Bagatelle, and for the priory at Le Temple, Paris. For this design, called 'roses and foliage', the Comte d'Artois was charged 18 livres, to which his major-domo objected: '…seeing that the offer from Monsieur Bourdon des Planches was to supply Monseigneur Comte d'Artois with wares copied from Sèvres patterns at a price lower than this factory's, it seems reasonable that he should make a reduction of ten per cent, having raised his prices to the level of Sèvres'…' However, a marginal note states 'the Major-Domo has decided against the reduction'. In addition, the Comte d'Artois' factory had produced quite a number of original moulds for pieces specially intended for its patron. *Circa* 1784. London, Victoria & Albert Museum. Diam. 24 cm. (9$^1/_2$ in.). Mark 29.

subsist like that: 'to allow the Marquis de La Salle lose a part of his fortune, and then afterwards to come and seize it'. He recalled the peaceful fraudulence of previous years, when Bertin had given Stahn 'the token of his satisfaction' and received 'the design for a breakfast set *(déjeuner)*…' on which was painted the portrait of Madame his niece. Lastly he played as much as possible on the fact that the order of 1779 did not forbid the possession or sale of the prohibited pieces of work, but only their manufacture.

No later than the following week Régnier replied that by registering himself La Salle had committed himself to following the regulations. He was indignant at his conduct: 'the presents which the Marquis de la Salle claims to have given to Monsieur Bertin the Minister are childish nonsense such as he should not talk, and nothing corroborates this assertion'.

This affair does not seem to have been followed up, nor for that matter were the confiscations from other factories.

From 1783 onwards the struggle with Sèvres was resumed. This time it was no longer a question of manufacturing prohibited wares, but of the private factories' enticing craftsmen away from the royal factory.

The decrees of the King's Council had concerned themselves with protecting the craftsmen of the royal factory, and above

15 Comte d'Artois' factory. Pair of baluster-vases, blue ground, decoration of translucent, opaque enamels on tooled gold leaf, gilt-bronze mounts. These vases bear the inscription *cuit au charbon de terre le 11 août 1783* ('fired by coal on August 11th 1783'). The crowned CP mark is accompanied by the name of Cotteau, the Genevan enameller at the royal factory of Sèvres who worked on the famous toilet-set given in 1782 to the Comtesse du Nord, wife of the future Tsar Paul 1st of Russia. These vases demonstrate the degree of perfection which this factory reached, and more especially the successful outcome of the early experiments with coal-firing at the Faubourg Saint-Denis. In 1783 the King was presented with a vase described as 'combining the size, relief, three-dimensional modelling, gold inlays and all the other embellishments which Sèvres claims to be the only factory competent to handle and use on its products…' In large characters and gold letters it bore the words *cuit au charbon de terre épuré dans la manufacture de Mgr le comte d'Artois le 8 février 1783* ('fired with refined coal in the factory of…' etc.).
Paris, Musée du Louvre.
Ht. 35 cm. (13²/₅ in.).
Mark 27.

23

all with obliging them to stay there. At the end of 1783 the manager of the factory in the Faubourg Saint-Denis— at that time Bourdon Desplanches—was summoned to restore to Sèvres one Rogé, a *répareur* (repairer) and his two sons. He did nothing about it; quite the reverse, for Rogé's elder son who was a painter enticed away a certain Martin. A report of 1785 confirmed that 'Rogé is at present working at enticing some craftsmen away'. One could mention many other Sèvres craftsmen working secretly and simultaneously for Parisian factories. This was so with Despréz, who sold cobalt to Le Dran, a painter in the Faubourg Saint-Denis, and with Gérard, a kiln-charger who supplied the private factories with models and facilitated their tests and experiments. Gérard was incarcerated at La Force, but we subsequently find him in the Faubourg Saint-Denis, where Albret, a second kiln-man, sold a pastoral group concealed in the modelling workshop at Sèvres.

It would be easy to multiply such examples, the situation being the same for all Paris factories.

The decree of May 16th 1784, signed by the Baron de Breteuil, was a fresh attempt by the royal factory to assert itself. The status of the factories is specially studied in his preamble which recalls the exclusive privilege granted in 1766 to the royal factory, and the restrictions imposed on private establishments (painting only in blue on white, or in monochrome with a single colour). The baron found that these obligations had not been entirely complied with, certain factories having obtained leave to decorate their work in gold and any colour; others having taken advantage of these authorizations to the extent of competing directly with the royal factory. Private establishments had enticed craftsmen away from Sèvres and actually forged its marks. From the propagation of these factories there had arisen a consumption of wood detrimental to the supplies for the capital, and an enormous amount of porcelain exceeding 'all possible retail sales'. Finally, despite these findings, the decree of 1784 positively reduced the privilege of Sèvres, leaving it with only the monopoly on luxury items (vases, pictures, bas-reliefs and groups), not without allowing the private establishments a year's respite for finishing and selling off any pieces of work begun. It recognized the right of the Parisian factories to continue producing 'all works of medium type intended as tableware or for general domestic use... to apply gilt to the rim only and to have painted upon them flowers in all shades of colour'. But this wonderful freedom was to cost them dearly, for it was then stipulated that 'at their own expense they must transfer their establishments within three years at most to a distance of at least fifteen leagues from Paris, and elsewhere than to provincial capitals'. This prospect of exile was due to provoke plenty of objections.

The decree of 1748 was communicated to the following manufacturers, which gives us an official list of factories sufficiently important to be involved:

- Advenier & Lamarre, at Le Gros Caillou
- Chanou, Rue de Reuilly, Faubourg Saint-Antoine
- Deruelle, at Clignancourt (Patronage of Monsieur, Comte de Provence)
- Dihl, Rue de Bondy (Patronage of the Duc d'Angoulême)
- Lebeuf, Rue Thiroux (Patronage of the Queen)

16 Patterns for cylindrical cups.
Four hundred decorative designs for cylindrical cups are assembled in a portfolio of illustrations in water-colour or gouache, by an artist who is unfortunately anonymous. He compiled this veritable repertory of porcelain-decoration at the very end of the XVIIIth century. Every type of decoration is represented: plants, with sprig-patterns or ingeniously arranged bouquets, and grasses from which hosts of more or less stylized borders issue forth: there are animals, landscapes, figures, swags of drapery and pseudo-antique themes. This is how many decorations are known to us which the actual porcelain has failed to hand down. Certain colour-contrasts come as a surprise to us even today. The decoration showing a goat is reminiscent of the Sèvres porcelain executed in 1788 for the dairy at Rambouillet.
Circa 1790–1800.
Paris, Bibliothèque nationale, Cabinet des Estampes.

- Locré, Rue Fontaine-au-Roy
- Mignon, at the Pont-aux-Choux
- Stahn, Faubourg Saint-Denis (Patronage of the Comte d'Artois)
- De Villiers, Rue des Boulets, Faubourg Saint-Antoine (Patronage of the Duc d'Orléans).

The successive infringements by the small factories had, therefore, induced the King little by little to give way over the privileges granted to the royal factory. This nibbling by private enterprise culminated in the emancipation of the most clamorous if not the most competent establishments.

The decree of 1784 did put an end to the objections set out by Bourdon, owner of the works at the Faubourg Saint-Denis. While the managers of the Queen's and Monsieur's factories proposed selling their establishments to the royal factory, which refused them, Bourdon went about things differently. Going on the sentences in the preamble dealing with the excessive consumption of wood by the factories, he did not omit to recall that he had experimented with firing by coal, an unrestricted fuel. He claimed the right to continue producing forbidden pieces, but although his request was endorsed by the Comte d'Artois in person, it was rejected. There were consequently six petitions in the course of 1784. The following year

17 Comte d'Artois' factory. Monteith with goats' heads. 'Picoted' lace ribbon coloured red, green and gold.
Circa 1778.
Geneva, Musée de l'Ariana.
L. 33.5 cm. (13^1/$_5$ in.).

18/19 Comte d'Artois factory.

Bust of Mirabeau. Biscuit. Moulded plinth bearing the gilded inscription: *Allez dire a ceux qui vous envoient que nous sommes ici par la volonté du peuple et que nous n'en sortirons que par la puissance des baïonnettes* ('Go and tell those who have sent you that we are here at the will of the people and that it will take the brute force of bayonets to drive us away'). There exist different versions of this bust, whose author is unknown. On the other hand the plaster cast has been preserved—an extremely rare phenomenon. It bears the same mark. There is little distinction between this original and its rendering in biscuit: only a few details —probably due to the 're-pairer'—are noticeable. The posture, the expression and the realism of this veritable portrait evince great crafts-manship. Sèvres issued this bust as well, on a larger scale but with less vigour.
A further model of the bust of Mirabeau, undraped, was produced by the Comte d'Artois' factory. *Circa* 1792. Paris, Musée Carnavalet. Ht. 27.5 cm. (10⁴/₅ in.). Paris, Assemblée nationale. Ht. 27 cm. (10³/₅ in.).

the Provost of Merchants himself requested that this factory be exempted. D'Angivillers[3] then wrote to Calonne[4] that he ordered the director of the royal factory to suspend for a time the enforcement of the provisions in the decree of 1784.

Bourdon having struck out again to obtain permission to stay in Paris while continuing to work on the forbidden pieces, d'Angivillers pointed out that the liberties granted to the small factories had to be compensated by shifting their premises elsewhere; he concludes thus: 'You see, Sir, how boldly these factories, and especially Seigneur Bourdon's, aspire to make exactly the same things as the King's factory. The number of craftsmen employed in this latter to work on modelling sufficiently reveals how little inclined is its owner to observe the conditions in the Council's decree of 1784 in this respect. It is time to enforce it rigorously, failing which the quantity of completed pieces will give new grounds for representation.' Bourdon kept quiet for a year, but resurfaced in June 1786. Monsieur de Montaran[5], invited to the factory, was won over by the coal-firing and Bourdon took advantage of this to claim exemption.

From July to December 1786 Bourdon signed no less than eight documents applying for the dispensation of his factory

[3] Angivillers, Charles Claude de Flahaut de la Billarderie, Comte d', (1730–1809). In 1774 he was appointed Director-General of the King's Buildings. The Sèvres factory was under his administration from 1780 onwards.

[4] Calonne, Charles Alexandre de, (1734–1802). He was appointed Contrôleur général des Finances in 1783.

[5] Montaran, Michaude de Jacques Marie Jérôme was Intendant du Commerce (Manager of Trade) in 1744, and was succeeded by his son.

from the requirements of the decree of 1784. After sending M. de Montaron to the Faubourg Saint-Denis, Calonne seemed to weaken; perhaps the sight of the 'sugar bowl and its lid' given by Bourdon had softened him, for on July 11th 1786 he concluded a memorandum relating to the factory by suggesting a decree interpreting the one of 1784 in favour of factories using mineral coal, together with an annuity of 2,000 *livres* for ten years 'for Seigneur Bourdon Desplanches by way of encouragement, and also to compensate for his non-exemption from costs'. Bourdon, who had not obtained the desired dispensation, then

20 Comte d'Artois' factory. *Cabaret*. Amorous scenes in the style of Watteau. *Circa* 1785. Stockholm, Nationalmuseum Tray: L. 38 cm. (15 in.). Mark 28.

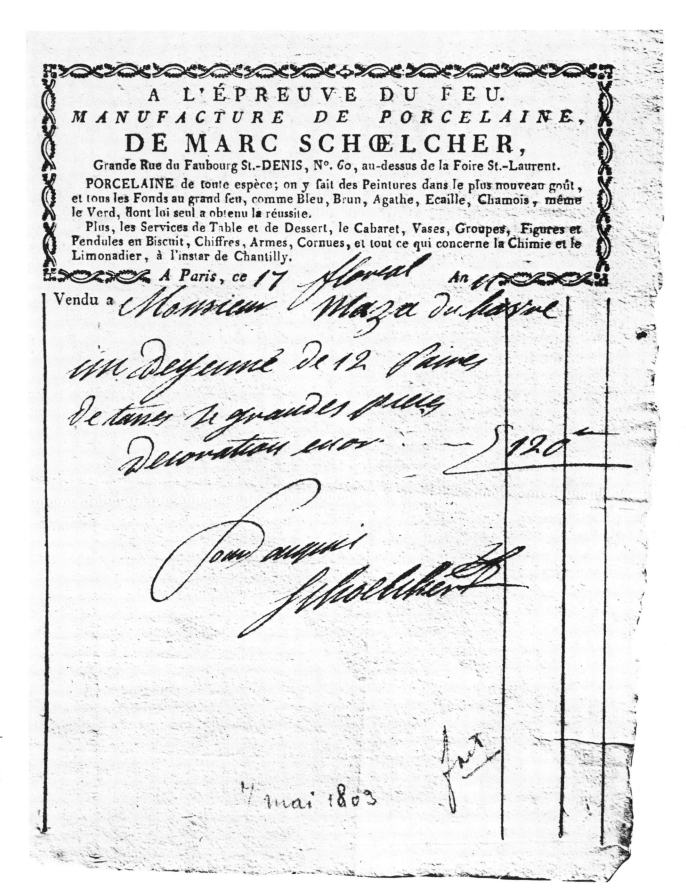

A L'ÉPREUVE DU FEU.
MANUFACTURE DE PORCELAINE,
DE MARC SCHŒLCHER,
Grande Rue du Faubourg St.-DENIS, N°. 60, au-dessus de la Foire St.-Laurent.
PORCELAINE de toute espèce; on y fait des Peintures dans le plus nouveau goût,
et tous les Fonds au grand feu, comme Bleu, Brun, Agathe, Ecaille, Chamois, même
le Verd, dont lui seul a obtenu la réussite.
Plus, les Services de Table et de Dessert, le Cabaret, Vases, Groupes, Figures et
Pendules en Biscuit, Chiffres, Armes, Cornues, et tout ce qui concerne la Chimie et le
Limonadier, à l'instar de Chantilly.
A Paris, ce 17 Floréal An

21   Schœlcher.
Invoice dated Floréal 17th,
Year XI (May 7th 1803).
The bill head lists the coloured, marbled and tortoiseshell grounds in which the
factory specializes. The
tortoiseshell, mauve-ground
plate shown on p. 37 is
identifiable with this
enumeration of skills.
Former coll. Chavagnac.

29

wrote to Calonne on September 2nd 1786: 'Respect forbids me to complain, but the cruel decree of May 16th 1784 still stands, I am not exempt from it despite your promises formally reiterated seven times in fifteen months, and each day it deals me further blows; every day and every instant it deepens the misfortune of my plight and makes me groan.'

Numerous other protests from Bourdon followed, until the publication of the Council's decree of January 17th 1787. The tenacity of the private factories, and in particular that of the Faubourg Saint-Denis, were thereby rewarded.

The decree of 1787 was the final test of strength for the royal factory: a strength that was in fact illusory, since through this decree the most censorious factories were emancipated. Let us quote Article IV of this decree: 'His Majesty similarly forbids all entrepreneurs of porcelain factories to manufacture any of the pieces of work reserved for the Royal factory by the decree of May 16th 1784, unless they have genuinely obtained permission so to do, which permission cannot be granted until after the perfection of their product has been ascertained at a concourse which will take place every year for this purpose, in the presence of the commissioners chosen by His Majesty, and nonetheless, the Factories of the Queen, of Monsieur, of Monsieur le Comte d'Artois and of Monsieur le Duc d'Angoulême, will be recognized as from now as having satisfied the aforesaid test, and will consequently enjoy the said permission save and except that the said factories, nor any established or which may be established hereafter, may not manufacture any works with gilt grounds nor any works of great luxury, such as porcelain pictures and modelled works, be they vases, figures or groups, exceeding 18 inches in height, not including the plinth; which works will remain reserved for the Royal porcelain factory of France, exclusive of any other.'

Other prohibitions hit particularly the jobs of 'outside decorators', working independently; the sale of unmarked wares, and the decoration of pieces deriving from Sèvres.

In fact it was the privileged factories, that is, the ones which had secured the patronage of a member of the royal family, that emerged from the struggle as the winners.

Facts having changed opinions, the manufacturers who had fought most bitterly against the royal privileges then had the insolence to complain of not being able to compel the smaller factories to respect their very recent prerogatives, which actually amounted to no more than an amnesty.

The managers of the factories respectively of the Queen, Monsieur the Comte d'Artois and the Duc d'Angoulême jointly demanded that the exportation of kaolin from France be forbidden, then finally asked for the repeal of the decree of 1787, to be replaced by an authorization to the managers of all porcelain factories in the kingdom to produce 'any articles which they shall see fit' (August 17th 1788). Once freedom of manufacture had been obtained for the bigger factories there were no further petitions or lawsuits.

With the Revolution came the abolition of privileges, but it was events themselves which then took in hand the rough job of selecting factories. Some came through the turmoil; those most firmly established and best managed survived to assume, under the Empire and the Restoration, a new lustre and new princely patronages.

22 Schœlcher.
Low baluster-vase. Poly-
chrome and gold. View of
La Malmaison after Garneray.
Circa 1820.
Sèvres, Musée National de
Céramique. Ht. 29.5 cm.
(11³/₅ in.).
Mark 34.

FACTORIES IN PARIS BETWEEN 1770 AND 1800

The decree of 1766 commanded the managers of porcelain factories to register themselves the Lieutenant général de Police or the Provincial Administrator, and to mark their products.

Between 1768 and 1781 eighteen registrations were recorded in the Paris Division *(Généralité),* thirteen of them for Paris itself, corresponding to eleven separate factories, including Clignancourt.

The first was that of Pierre Antoine Hannong, on May 26th 1773. In the same year four more factories in Paris completed this formality: Souroux of the Faubourg Saint-Antoine; Locré, Rue Fontaine-au-Roy; Morelle of the Faubourg Saint-Antoine; and Advenier & Lamarre at Le Gros Caillou.

The following years saw only one registration annually: in 1774 that of Lassia, Rue de Reuilly; in 1775 that of Deruelle at Clignancourt; in 1776 of Lebeuf, Rue Thiroux; in 1777 of the faience maker Mignon at the Pont-aux-Choux; and in 1778 of a certain 'Gamont, Boulevard de Rue de Grammon', to this day known solely by this formality. Finally Dihl, working at that time in Rue de Bondy, registered his trade-mark in 1781. Further registrations concerned the factories of: Etiolles, Sceaux, Mennecy, Bourg-la-Reine and Vincennes.

These texts yield a reliable list of the first Parisian factories producing hard-paste porcelain. It should be pointed out, however, that some of them were already in a position to manufacture and sell their products at the time of registration, whereas others by contrast were still only at an experimental stage.

A report submitted in 1774 to Monsieur de Sartine, Lieutenant général de Police by Police Inspector Buhot, specifies the activities of the most important establishments; these are the factories of: the Faubourg Saint-Denis, Souroux, Rue de la Roquette, Morelle in the same street, Le Gros Caillou, Rue de la Fontaine-au-Roy and Clignancourt.

The decree of 1784, as we have seen, was also communicated to all these factories except Morelle's, and to three more besides, of more recent creation: Chanou, Rue de Reuilly, Lebeuf, Rue Thiroux, and Dihl, Rue de Bondy.

On a list of factories probably contemporaneous with the decree of 1787, annotations indicate their importance. The comment 'worth keeping' appears before all the privileged factories (Rue Thiroux, Clignancourt, Faubourg Saint-Denis, Rue de Bondy), with the exception of the one in Rue Amelot, patronized by the Duc d'Orléans. Against this last is marked 'cannot support itself', which incidentally was borne out by the facts. Locré's works were considered worth keeping. Lastly, other factories were designated as 'doubtful': the one owned by Nast which experienced a difficult beginning, and another in Rue Albroisi, whose manager was a certain Lefevre.

Thus we see that the official number of these factories was greatly reduced under the *Ancien Régime.*

Paradoxically, while certain factories were having trouble surviving, new establishments were created curing the revolutionary period. A memorandum presented by Joseph Léon Julien, son of the manager of the Mennecy factory, to the Bureau des Arts in Year VII, specified that the number of factories had much increased over the previous ten years. There were those which had sur-

23 Schœlcher.
Cooler. Polychrome and
gold. View of the environs
of Lisbon: the Tower of
Belem. *Circa* 1800.
Palacio Ducal de Vila Viçosa,
Fundação, Casa de Bragança.
Ht. 36 cm. (14¹/₅ in.).
Mark 32.

vived the Revolution: Rue Fontaine Nationale, formerly Fontaine-au-Roy, Clignancourt, Faubourg Saint-Denis, Rue Thiroux, Rue du Temple (Guérhard & Dihl, the erstwhile Rue de Bondy), Rue des Amandiers (Nast), Rue des Marais (Toulouse, formerly Outrequin), Rue Pierre (now Rue Amelot—Josse & Le-

maire). To these Julien added the factories of Sauvel (Faubourg Saint-Denis), Pétry (Mesnil-Montant), Blancheron (Rue de Crussol), Despréz (Rue de Lancry), Battazerd (Rue Petite Pologne), Darte Frères (Rue de Charonne), Chevalier Frères (Rue de la Pépinière), Roger & Toussaint (at Mont Parnasse), Lefebvre (Faubourg Saint-Denis) and Lortz (Rue Saint-Gilles).

Two earlier factories, those of Guérhard & Dihl and Nast, are considered to be the most important, together with the more recent one owned by Despréz and specializing in porcelain cameos.

Several new factories were to become well known under the name of their re-

spective founders (such as Darte Frères or Blancheron), whilst others were not to rise to fame until the 19th century, known not by their founders but by their successors who were able to make them bear fruit: the Dagoty family would take over the establishment of Roger & Toussaint, Honoré that of Lortz, and finally the two factories would merge.

To these factories we must add the salesrooms:

– Firstly, many faience-makers and merchant-haberdashers were the factories' sole agents or anyway regularly forwarded orders. The same was true of certain goldsmiths or bronze-founders, and of inlay-workers, the former adding mounts of precious metal to the porcelain pieces, the latter wishing to use them to trim their *nécessaires* of wood.
The Queen's factory like that of Monsieur had its depot, called 'Petit Dunkerque', kept by Granchez. Furthermore, Duban, the merchant faience maker sold the Queen's porcelain, while the salesroom at the sign of the 'Bonnet d'Or' offered Monsieur's.

– Secondly, whenever the most important factories had been slightly displaced from the city centre, they had established salesrooms. The factory of the Faubourg Saint-Denis had a certain number of them, successively or simultaneously: in 1778 for instance, there was one at Le Carrousel, one in the Faubourg Saint-Germain, and others in the provinces, in Marseilles, Lyons, Caen, Avignon and Bordeaux. The oldest was in Rue Plâtrière and was transferred to Le Carrousel. The latter, in fact, was so exceptional that we shall study it further on. It was

24 Unidentified factory. Mortar for cosmetics. Gold ribbon with reserved panels containing alternately a polychrome rose or butterfly. *Circa* 1780. Paris, private coll. Ht. 4 cm. (1³/₅ in.). Unmarked.

sited in Rue de l'Echelle, near the Louvre, and having been the salesroom of the Comte d'Artois' factory it passed on to the Queen's, before its director became part-owner of the latter establishment. The salesroom called 'Le Petit Carrousel' also owned a subsidiary in Madrid and had its particular mark.

The same kind of sleeping partnership was most often adopted by the Paris porcelain factories, the partners sometimes moving on from one board to the next in spite of the successive disappointments. This was the case, for example, with the factory of the Faubourg Saint-Denis, several partners of which recon-

25 View of Schœlcher's salesroom on Boulevard des Italiens.
Reproduced from
La Promenade parisienne.

FINANCING
The foundation of the factory of Vincennes—which subsequently became the royal factory of Sèvres—was the work of Orry de Fulvy, Administrator of Finances and the brother of the Contrôleur général des Finances, around 1738 to 1741. Some years later, in 1745, Orry de Fulvy formed a board to run the factory. It was made up of seven 'sleeping partners', rich people belonging to the world of finance, who put up all the funds and on various occasions made good the standing deficit of the enterprise. The King bought a quarter share in the new company, founded in 1753, before taking it over altogether, six years later.

vened to found the factory in Rue Thiroux.

The process was always the same in these partnerships: the partners with personal fortunes would put up the entire capital that made up the registered funds and would subsequently respond to calls for capital, varying in number according to the particular instance.

We generally find, then, on the one hand the sleeping partners who contributed most of the funds, and on the other the *entrepreneur* who was in a way the manager of the concern, a title often confused with that of director. Usually the director, nominated by the partners, was salaried, whereas the *entrepreneur,* who sometimes put capital into the concern, had a share in the profits. The director was in charge of technical work and commercial transactions. Nonetheless, at the factory in the Faubourg Saint-Denis we find in 1776 two directors at once, the one technical who was salaried and the other commercial receiving a percentage on the sales. It must be added that these distinctions are often impossible to make: Hannong controlled all three posts at the Faubourg Saint-Denis, and later Barrachin in the same factory moved on from being joint owner to director. It is directors' names, following hard upon one another, that allow us to stake out the history of the factories, whereas the partners, not replacing one another all at the same time, play no preponderant personal role.

Most of the time the sleeping partners did not own the building in which the factory was established. The works were often set up in rented premises, sometimes bought up afterwards.

However, the capital outlays were generally considerable. Often, as in the case of Hannong or Dihl, the ceramists used to bring, besides 'their talent and their care', certain equipment consisting mostly of models and moulds. If this happened, the sleeping partners would only put up the capital needed to cover installation and running costs. These sums could vary widely. As far as Hannong was concerned, the first deed of partnership supplied him with 30,000 livres in 1772. He secured 18,000 of it in the following year and another 6,000 one year afterwards. In 1778, the liabilities reached the sum of 501,859 livres and 4 deniers, including a total borrowing of 142,400 livres. The sham sale of the factory in the same period was dealt with on the basis of 130,000 livres.

As against this, we witness the case of Guérhard & Dihl. The latter already had a large number of moulds and Guérhard contributed no more than 8,000 livres (1781).

These two cases seem extreme. Indeed, on the occasion of the partnership between Locré and Martin de Bussy in 1777, this latter put up 36,000 livres, and a few months later the sale of the factory by Locré to Russinger realized 50,000 livres. As for the factory in Rue Thiroux, the circumstances of its establishment are rather peculiar: an initial capital outlay amounted to 50,000 livres in 1777, but it was brought up to 300,000 some months later.

If they found themselves drawn together by the common concern to make their capital come into fruition, the sleeping partners belonged to quite different classes of society. We see for example the military nobility with 'High and mighty Seigneur Messire Adrien Nicolas Marquis de La Salle, Knight, Seigneur de Carrière, beneath the wood of Laye, Badouville, Broué, Saint-Crespin-aux-Bois, Comte d'Offémont, Major of the Provincial Regiment of Abbeville'; Claude Louis Comte de La Chastre, Gentleman of Honour to Monsieur, Lieutenant-Colonel of his Regiment of Dragoons, Seigneur de Malicorne; the Marquis d'Usson, who was notably the King's Lieutenant of the Province of Foix. Others were of recent nobility, such as Outrequin de Montarcy, whose father had been ennobled in 1761, or else were 'of the robe', such as Claude Martin Dormoy, a former King's Counsellor, Président de l'Election de Pithiviers; Martin de Bussy, Doyen des Substituts (King's Counsellor) to the Attorney General at the Grand Council; Lebeuf, son of an advocate in the Parlement, At-

26 Schœlcher.
Bold combination of marbled and lilac grounds, with antique subject, *La Marchande d'Amours. Circa* 1800. Limoges, Musée National Adrien Dubouché. Diam. 23 cm. (9 in.). Mark 31.

torney at the Châtelet. Still others were described as 'bourgeois': Guérhard was a burgher of Paris, and de Leutre (Véran de Leutre) a burgher of Avignon. Others were wholesale merchants, witness Barrachin, who had gone bankrupt in Lyons. It is interesting to note, moreover, that one sometimes meets these same people in other partnerships, centred on much less refined undertakings, such as this self-same Barrachin negociating for the trade in carriages and harness, or again Outrequin de Montarcy giving up his rights to certain reduced rents in return for the removal of Paris night-soil.

As to the ceramists themselves, almost all of them had a solid ancestry of artisans and their background was more modest: Edme Toulouse was the son of a master wheelwright, Nast of an Austrian master saddler. Locré's father was a wealthy Parisian dealer in fancy goods and Hannong was one of the last members of the dynasty of Strassburg ceramists. Deruelle was an architect and building contractor.

THE CRAFTSMEN

In the 18th century, there was a certain difference between the craftsmen respectively of the royal factory at Sèvres, and of the other factories. The decrees of the King's Council had laid down measures to force the Sèvres craftsmen not to leave the establishment, mainly because of the secrets of manufacture which they might possess. The decree of 1745 threatened to punish with imprisonment and a fine of 50 *livres* anyone leaving the royal factory without permission or dismissal, and inflicted a 1,000 *livre* fine on managers who received them. The decree of 1747 was aimed especially at the enticing away of craftsmen, who could not stay away for a single day without the permission of

the director, who had then to withhold twice their daily wage. Absence without leave for several days was punished with a fine and imprisonment. To secure their definitive dismissal, craftsmen had to undertake never to make use of the knowledge acquired at the factory, and Adam was entitled to reclaim them 'wherever they might be', in order to re-employ them. The enforcement of this decree resulted in the closure of Barbin's factory in Rue de Charonne. Besides this, some workers at the royal factory were arrested and incarcerated. Reinforcing the decree of 1747, another one in 1753 bound any workers wishing to leave the factory to give six months' notice and to obtain the

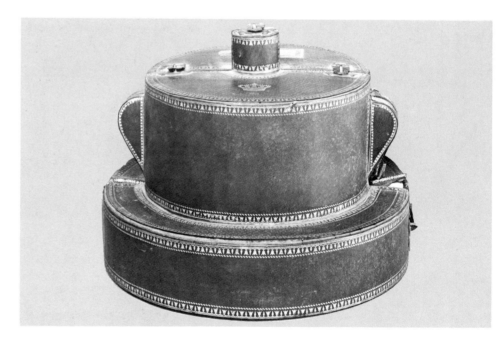

director's permission. It forbade them 'to make any use of models, pictures and drawing belonging to the factory other than in its service... to dispose of, or to copy them, or to employ skills thus gained in any other factory'. In return the private factories could henceforth take on Sèvres craftsmen holding a certificate of discharge.

27   See caption opposite.

27, 28, 29 Schœlcher. Covered broth-bowl and matching tray. Ground of contrast-burnished gold, with purple and green ornaments. Medallions and panels in reserve, showing 'a view of the environs of Lisbon' in particular, together with others of the Palais de Tuileries and the Château de Saint-Cloud. The tray is decorated on the bottom with a view of Lisbon signed by Freund and is stamped with the arms of King John VI of Portugal. This exceptionally sumptuous piece is set in a case of red morocco-leather stamped with a crown. It was probably a royal gift. King John VI, Regent of Portugal during the insanity of his mother D. Maria, left for Brazil in order to avoid the French invasion. He returned in 1821 and died in 1826. This piece is similar in shape to the yellow-ground bowl shown in ill. 40.

Circa 1825.
Palacio Nacional de Quéluz.
Ht. 18 cm. (7 in.).
Mark 33.

29   See caption page 39.

The Parisian factories did not fail to entice craftsmen away from Sèvres and the directors of the royal factory lodged many complaints. We have already seen this aspect of the struggle of the Parisian factories against the royal factory. Nonetheless, it is only fair to add that the factory of Sèvres, for its part, was not inhibited by scruples when it was signing on Parisian craftsmen. A petition presented to the King by the managers from the factories of the Queen, Monsieur, the Comte d'Artois and of the Rue des Boulets (Faubourg Saint-Antoine), concerning the decree of 1784, emphasized that 'the prohibition on receiving craftsmen leaving without authorization and the option of receiving only those craftsmen authorised to leave is something common to all factories, yet at this moment the royal factory of France has in its workshops at least six or seven craftsmen trained in private factories in Paris, Lorraine and Alsace'. Lamprecht, the one-eyed Viennese who invented the technique of painting in brown enamel, one of the triumphs of Clignancourt and Sèvres, was in Clignancourt in 1783. He later moved on to Sèvres, from 1784 to 1787, and was recalled to Vienna at the behest of the Emperor. La Branche, a painter in Rue Thiroux, asked to enter Sèvres in 1785.

However, there were not only private

factories to divert craftsmen away from Sèvres; many were working on their own account at home, and were called *chambrelans* (outside decorators).

The decree of 1787 forbade private factories 'to hand out any artefact to be handled in town' and forbade individuals to put up muffle kilns for firing colours; to make unmarked wares or to forge marks; to decorate any white ware from Sèvres or any other factory; or to fire 'figures imitative of biscuit ware'. We have seen how Catrice and Barbé, deserters from Sèvres, had been subject to prosecution as early as 1779. Joseph Cotteau, the famous Genevan enameller of clock-faces, is another case in point. He

by the other factories had, therefore, to be sufficiently high to attract them. Does not one of the opinions given by the Advocates of the Paris Parlement on April 10th 1785 reveal that the 'craftsmen of Sève [*sic*] have come to offer their services'?

From 1776 the business of enticing away

worked for Sèvres in 1782 where he decorated the famous toilet set of the Comtesse du Nord. For the factory of the Faubourg Saint-Denis he made vases in the same style, dated August 11th 1783. Chavagnac and Grollier quote a document of 1784 stating that he 'returned to join the private factories in order to find himself work, but of the forbidden type, intimating to them [*sic*] that, if carried out by him, they need have nothing to fear'.

The advantages conceded to the Sèvres craftsmen were particularly profitable; notably, they were exempted from taxes, billeting troops, and service in the watch, the guards, the militia. The wages offered

was, moreover, well organised: 'the throwers, *répareurs* and painters who have quit the King's factory come to Sèvres, and to Saint-Cloud on every public holiday to harass the craftsmen, magnificently attired for men of their station, and some of them affectedly show off their money, boasting they have earned more in one month than they earned in six at the [royal] factory'.

'Indeed, the rates that managers give their craftsmen have been investigated; they are twice and three times as much on some items, and even then the pieces are made with so little care that a craftsman can easily make twice as many. As to the increase, we had either to submit

to it or else close the factory [of Sèvres]. Not a week goes by without some craftsman, even one who has had an increment three months ago, coming insolently to ask either for an increase, or to be given work to do at home, at rates comparable to those they would obtain at Clignancourt, the Faubourg Saint-Denis, La Nouvelle-France, La Courtille, the Faubourg Saint-Antoine, Vincennes, etc...'
'The factory of Clignancourt has started on a porcelain set which had been ordered by Monsieur. The manager has boasted about it, he has had it proclaimed in the King's factory, and a first-rate craftsman, amongst others, has been enticed away to go and work on this set. It was necessary (because he is essential) to keep him back with money; his increase alone costs the factory 650 *livres,* although we are fortunate to have detected and kept him...'
A memorandum from Montaran to Calonne dated August 5th 1786 gives an overall order of importance in the matter of wages. In Paris, the painters and modellers 'earn up to a thousand *écus* even though wasting a lot of time in debauchery and sloth. The unskilled labourers earn thirty *sols* a day', while in the provinces the workmen's day-wages stand at only 15 or 18 *sols.*
In the first deed of partnership of the factory in Rue Thiroux (1776), the salaries are estimated as follows: the foreman, painters' supervisor and the head clerk: 1,200 *livres* a year; the second clerk 1,000 *livers,* and the third only 600 *livres.* The porter received no more than 200. Some years later (1781) the calculated salary for the best craftsman who can be taken on by Dihl is 2,000 *livres* a year, which hence seems to be a maximum.
As for the organisation of work, it had been formulated for Rue Thiroux in

1776 as follows: 'a manufacturer, a foreman, a painters' supervisor, a head clerk in charge of petty cash and the receipts and expenditure of the factory; of the entry and dispatch of goods; the sales to the main showroom; the inspection of the other clerks; the accounts; the goods; and the checking of the muffle-kilns: a second clerk in charge of the craftsmen's accounts; the entry and discharge from the store-room of top-quality white ware; of the accounts of all the labourers and those employed by the day, the week and the fortnight; of packing; of crates for dispatch; of book-entries except for the unfired products of painters and others; and of the registration of the

31 Schœlcher.
Plate. Polychrome and gold.
On the back, the inscription:
Vue de la place Louis XV à Paris. After Janinet.
Circa 1805–1810.
Paris, private coll.
Diam. 23.5 cm. (9$\frac{1}{5}$ in.).
Mark 35.

32 Schœlcher.
Plate. Wide band of gilt
scroll-work set off by a
russet stripe. Gold rosette.
Circa 1800.
Paris, private coll.
Diam. 22 cm. (8³⁄₅ in.).
Mark 33.

muffle-kilns; a third clerk in charge of the store-room for rejects, and the entry and dispatch of goods from the said store-room whenever he is not occupied; a fourth clerk who will always keep the store-room clean, will give assistance to whichever of the three other clerks needs it, will run errands in the town, will take into town small items without panniers or yokes: a porter...' Unfortunately, nothing is mentioned with regard to technical and artistic staff in the factory. The provisions of the 1784 decree on the removal or closure of factories posed the problem of an exodus of foreign craftsmen. A document of preamble said in particular: 'The private factories keep a prodigious quantity of craftsmen occupied, mostly foreigners. Is it not to be feared that, deprived of their livelihood by the abolition of these factories, they may leave the kingdom, taking their talents and their industry elsewhere...?' and further on: 'if Sèvres wishes to attain perfection let her fear competition'.

The number of craftsmen employed in a factory was never very stable. It depended on economic conditions in general, and on orders forwarded to the factory in particular. Nevertheless, let us give some figures: in 1775 the factory of the Faubourg Saint-Denis employed 38 craftsmen, to wit: 3 throwers, 5 moulders, 1 *répareur,* 1 modeller, 13 painters, 1 gilder, 5 kiln-men, 1 enameller, 1 woodcutter, 1 craftsman for the pastes, 1 saggermaker and 5 labourers. By 1785 this factory was employing 30 craftsmen for modelling alone. In the same year the factory in Rue de Bondy was giving work to only 12 modellers but 30 painters. Clignancourt had 80 craftsmen in 1780 and 94 by 1787. Before the Revolution, Russinger at La Courtille kept 50 to 60 craftsmen occupied. We have sadly miscalculated in the case of Sèvres which, in 1783, had a payroll of 274 of whom 71 were painters, 15 gilders, 83 *répareurs* but only 18 modellers.

More often than not, the artists were migrants. They remained only a short while in any one factory and occasionally came back to it.

Hannong was a lifelong traveller. Shortly after his departure from the factory of the Faubourg Saint-Denis, a list of craftsmen was drawn up, dated February 10th 1775. On it we notice names of craftsmen hailing from Venice, Austria, Alsace, Frankenthal, Amsterdam, from the States of Mainz, Berlin, Brunswick, Württemberg

and from Switzerland. Only the moulders, Vieilleville Senior and Junior come from France—from Limoges. From the notes we see that few of them were with the factory ever since its establishment. Some come straight from abroad, others have already been working in France at La Courtille, Nevers and Sceaux.

If we take the case of the Riehl brothers, both born at Strassburg in 1736 and 1738 respectively, one of them was in Kiel in 1767, and the other at Frankenthal in 1756, before being reunited under Pierre Antoine Hannong.

Teitscher, from Vienna, had been at the factory of the Faubourg Saint-Denis for a year, upon 'departing from Sceaux and Ethiol with leave'. We come across him again in Meissen by about 1780.

The same goes for the other factories. On May 4th 1784, Vergennes[6] mentions Nicolas Schouler, a native of Mannheim and porcelain modeller at present attached to a porcelain factory in St. Petersburg, as having previously been employed in that capacity at an establishment in Paris. In his reply to the Minister, Régnier revealed that Schouler had worked at Sèvres and that he had been dismissed in 1780 as a second-rate craftsman.

In another Parisian factory, La Courtille, one of the best modellers was Christophe Mô, who had earlier been working at Mennecy and Sceaux.

At first sight one might think these artists to be rather fickle. In fact, their journeys were what we would now call courses of training or self-improvement. In each factory they learnt and contributed something new. In this way, schools in their own right developed in the factories and particularly in those of Paris. At Clignancourt under the supervision of the modeller Moitte there were a few chosen pupils; Nast learnt the craft at Vincennes; Guérhard & Dihl had a whole workshop where painters were trained. Schoelcher and family were welcomed at La Courtille.

There were also indentures of apprenticeship as in the other professional bodies: in 1776 we find no less than six for the factory of the Faubourg Saint-Denis, amongst them that of Cœur Dassier who later owned the factory in Rue Popincourt, taken over by Darte Senior.

For the daily work-period we must refer to the documents of the royal factory. From an attendance of fourteen hours, minus two hours for meals, the length of the working day was brought down to twelve and a half hours (of which one

[6] Vergennes, Charles Gravier, Comte de, (1717–1787). Foreign Minister.

34 Schœlcher.
Covered broth-bowl and
stand. 'Rose-wreath'
decoration. Similar in shape
to bowl shown in ill. 40.
Circa 1820.
Paris, private coll.
Ht. 18 cm. (7 in.).
Mark 34.

hour and a half were for meals)—not out of humane concern but so as to avoid night-work, which was often sub-standard.

The plates to *L'Art de la Porcelaine,* published in 1771 by Count de Milly, illustrate perfectly the jobs of the craftsmen, grouped by workshops: those of the painters, the modellers etc., set up in accordance with the lighting most favourable to their respective tasks.

TECHNIQUE

The two main works in surveying porcelain making technique in the 18th century are: *L'Art de la Porcelaine,* published in 1771 by Comte de Milly, and the *Traité des Arts céramiques,* by Alexandre Brongniart, the director of the Sèvres porcelain factory from 1800 to 1847. The first edition of this work is dated 1844. *L'Art de la Porcelaine,* in the same way as Diderot's *Encyclopédie,* links the arts and the sciences. Nicolas Christiern de Thy, Comte de Milly, was renowned for his love of chemistry and the occult sciences. His work is made up of a 'Dissertation' that he read out in 1771 to the Académie des Sciences of which he was a member, and of a treatise on colours based on German methods and Montamy's work. He also studied the various reports of the Académie des Sciences, starting with Réaumur's at the beginning of the century. The plates, also in the spirit of the *Encyclopédie,* allow us to follow precisely all the phases of porcelain manufacture from the preparation of the clays right up to the decoration.

The *Traité des Arts céramiques* remains the paragon of technical works written by a scientist. It is impossible not to refer to it. It is, moreover, a great asset in our study. Published in 1844, his historical notes in particular contain elements of first-hand knowledge. We shall come back to them on many occasions.

According to Brongiart, the characteristics of hard-paste porcelain are its translucency and resistance to being scored by steel.

The body is essentially composed of two main elements: firstly, non-fusible clay, called kaolin, either alone or in combination: secondly, feldspar—dry and fusible, giving the translucency. Further petrous minerals such as quartz serve as binding materials.

The glaze *(couverte)* consists of quartzose feldspar, sometimes plain, sometimes mixed with gypsum, but without lead or tin.

This rule has been subject to many exceptions. Indeed, the manufacture of hard-paste porcelain in its early stages was often the outcome of empirical methods; no explanation given for this period can be absolute in character. Thus, recent analyses of fragments of hard-paste porcelain have revealed that the glaze could sometimes have had a lead content.

The materials of the body (paste) intended for porcelain require washing, pounding and mixing. Next the body is watered down, then 'dried and hardened' in tanks laid out inside sheds or in the open. It must also age, either by being kept for as long as possible in tanks or under water (sometimes for more than a year), or by being pugged. In the 18th century this operation was often performed by trampling, which may be compared to the treading of grapes.

The choice of kaolins is important: it must yield a fine white, workable body. Different strata of kaolin had been discovered in France in the 18th century: first near Alençon—which Guéttard used

35 Schœlcher.
Part of black-ground tumbler.
Polychrome and gold birds
and flowers. *Circa* 1830.
Paris, private coll.
Goblet: Ht. 10 cm. (4 in.).
Mark 36.

for his experiments—then near Limoges at Saint-Yrieix. At the end of the century a little was found in Normandy, just outside Valognes.

The Parisian factories either need clays coming straight from Limoges which they processed themselves in Paris, or else ready-made bodies from Limoges. Locré and Russinger personally prepared their bodies in Paris, and so did Dihl and Guérhard. The Clignancourt factory used clays from the royal Limoges factory, supposedly accepting the Government's offer out of sheer kindness, 'with a view to saving the King money on the return of H.M.'s wagons sent into that region to victual the province with powdered food-

stuffs'. This *limousin* clay was prepared by costly processes 'to imitate the fine texture of the porcelain of Saxony'.

It is probable that Hannong sent to Limoges for his clays and transformed them into porcelain bodies, for we note in the inventory of the Faubourg Saint-Denis factory of October 3rd 1774: 'To M.M. Grellet Brothers for clays, 1200 L. [*livres*]', and further on an account dealing with water-powered mills. It was mills of this type which were used by Grellet in Limoges for preparing the bodies.

According to the early factory stock lists of the Faubourg Saint-Denis, then, the clays originated from Limoges and were supplied by Grellet, but this factory also bought ready-made bodies and glazes. Agreements existed between the factory of the Faubourg Saint-Denis and Grellet on the one hand, and on the other, Poirier, a wholesaler in clay. Nonetheless, Chaussard, the director of the factory in the Faubourg Saint-Denis in 1776, soon objected that it was possible to 'procure

bodies at a rate of 25 *livres* per cwt. instead of the 55 *livres* which one has to pay Sieurs Grellet Frères in accordance with the agreement made with them; and glaze at a rate of 30 *livres* per cwt. instead of 65 *livres;* and that he has had both these substances tried out'. The shareholders decided to continue to honour the agreements made with Sieur Grellet 'subject to revision later' and in addition they authorized their director 'to make an agreement with the mercantile agent who is offering them bodies, as has just been stated, at a rate of 25 *livres* per quintal, and glaze at 30 *livres,* for whatever quantity he believes necessary, until he has managed to break off the

agreement with the said Grellet brothers'. In the same factory's inventory of January 12th 1778, we read 'Clays and pastes from Alençon as well as Houdan, 500 L.'

The scientist Berthollet, having gone to see Madame Guérhard on Rue de Bondy in 1786, wrote 'she did not think it right to confide in me the method of producing her procelain, but she showed me the clays which enter into its composition'.

Of course, each factory had its secrets, and the composition of bodies and glazes could vary when they processed them themselves.

Grellet was also selling clays and pastes to Russia, Holland, Denmark, etc.

A special body was used by certain factories for the production of 'porcelain for the fire' or 'porcelain resistant to the most intense heat'. Hannong had already conducted research along these lines at Vincennes under Laborde's patronage in 1770. Laborde forestalled the royal factory to test before the King a porcelain saucepan placed over a spirit-burner. For both factories the result of the experiment was identical; the saucepan broke. The attempt was renewed with a Sèvres saucepan and, success having been obtained, the King congratulated the chemists and the directors of Sèvres.

This special property in the porcelain of the Faubourg Saint-Denis was advertised in the *Mercure de France* of May 1773 'Manufacture of porcelain which goes on the fire... [this porcelain] has the property of suffering the most boiling viands, and of going on the fire without breaking or blackening...' The same was claimed for crucibles and retorts. At around the same period Lassia attempted similar experiments, and Cadet, Guéttard and Fontanieu, of the Académie des Sciences, signed the minutes supporting him.

36 Schœlcher.
Detail of a vase. Antique cameo in brown. *Circa* 1810. Paris, private coll.

Schoelcher was later to take up this tradition by inserting in the headings of his invoices 'Fire-proof'. It is true that, during his early days with Russinger at La Courtille, he might have learnt this technique which his host also practised. The factory in the Rue Fontaine-au-Roy had the same slogan as the Faubourg Saint-Denis: 'Fire-proof'.

Another slightly different formula was followed for biscuit figures.

The processes of manufacture require a lot of skill and are often rather complicated. We can pick out three principal methods: throwing, for round pieces, moulding for the other pieces, finished off by 'repairing', being the action of eliminating the defects due to moulding: for example, removing traces of seams or filling in the cavities formed by bubbles in the body; and lastly casting for plaques or small items such as handles. Casting was already being practised around 1790 at Locré's.

Next comes the addition of applied details by luting with 'slip' (liquid clay).

Firing is a single process although it appears to be twofold, for the first firing of the body which we call the *dégourdi* ('biscuiting') is only designed to stiffen and 'dessicate' the body enough for it to take its glaze more readily by dipping; at a pinch we could do without it. The paste and glaze are fired simultaneously, demanding the same temperature. This temperature rises to 1,300 degrees Centigrade. Naturally, we proceed most cautiously: the pieces to be fired are enclosed in 'saggers', objects like cases of different shapes, made of fire-clay, with the solidity and infusibility necessary for withstanding the high temperature. It is the saggers which are stacked in the kilns. Kiln charging is one of the most delicate operations; neglecting a few precautions means spoiling the whole batch.

The control of the fire also exacts a great deal of attention and care.

A further firing at less high a temperature —between 750 and 900 degrees—is now necessary for the painted decoration, and a final one at a still lower temperature for gilt. These two last firings can be done in 'muffles', a sort of small kiln built of fire-clay, rectangular in form and generally arched, which the outside decorators were able to use. The decoration is put on the fired piece by means of vitrifiable colours with oxide bases combined with fluxes which are thinned with certain oils that evaporate under firing. Ill. 38

Green is obtained from copper oxide, red, brown and purple from iron oxide, blue from oxide of cobalt as are also grey and black. Oxide of antimony yields yellow. Manganese oxide offers many possibilities: it comes into the make-up of the violets and blacks, replacing to advantage oxide of cobalt, which is more expensive and difficult to prepare. It may also be used in conjunction with iron oxide to obtain fine browns under high-temperature firing. Lastly, oxide of tin confers opacity. One of the most costly colours was 'purple of Cassius' containing a solution of gold. The fluxes—vitrifiable, colourless substances—are added to the metallic oxides or the metals to make them adhere and to obtain the glaze.

Some colours are robust enough to be fired at high temperature, while others can only withstand firing in a muffle.

The 'Report on the colours for Citizen Dihl's porcelain', delivered to the 'Classe des Sciences Physiques et Mathématiques' of the National Institute of France, on the 26th of Brumaire in the Year VI, was an event in the field of porcelain.

37 Schœlcher.
Plate with lobed edge. Polychrome and gold, raised rim of *beau bleu*. On the back, the inscription *Le Désabiller [sic]*. After Devéria.
Circa 1830.
Paris, private coll.
Diam. 24.5 cm. (9³/₅ in.).
Mark 34,
plus Perche mark 191.

Darcet, Guyton and Fourcroy, commissioned to investigate the colours invented by Dihl, went to his factory several times to examine them and subject them to various tests. The object was to find colours which resist deterioration and remain permanent when they vitrify.

Dihl presented, along with his pallet, pictures of a great richness of hue, painted by Sauvage and Le Guay using his colours. The findings of the scientists were very favourable to Dihl, both in respect of the 'hard colours' and of the 'soft colours'. That means: for high- and low-temperature firing respectively.

However, Brongniart subsequently pointed out that Dihl had not put onto his pallet the pinks, purples and violets which are made from the purple of Cassius and which change under heat whatever may be the vehicle that carries them; and that, besides this, he had kept silent about the influence of vehicles altogether. In Brongniart's opinion Dihl had spoken 'a part of the truth, but not the whole truth'.

Whatever the case may be, Dihl not only had his colours used in his factory, but also sold them successfully to other establishments. Drölling and Le Guay painted some magnificent portraits of him on porcelain with his own colours. Today these are kept by the Musée de Céramique de Sèvres.

The method of applying colours by dipping was chiefly practised in the 19th century.

Gold, which is brushed on, is prepared with sulphate of ferrous oxide or with mercury.

After firing, the gilt is mat. It is polished with burnishers, objects of differing shapes, most usually of agate. If the dull finish is to figure on the decoration, those parts are left untouched; this is called *brunissage à l'effet* (contrasted burnishing).

The number of kilns and muffles in a factory is a good indication of its activity.

When Hannong moved on from the Faubourg Saint-Denis he left behind two large kilns and a small muffle for colour-firing. In 1778 there were three kilns 'one for biscuit ware, very old' and two muffles.

If the heating of the kilns has always been an important problem for the ceramist, it was no less one for the municipal officials, who used to look upon the porcelain factories as greedy consumers who might bring about a depletion of fuel stocks and, above all, price increases. A trade inspector of around 1780 estimated the value of the wood burnt up by the faience works and porcelain factories throughout the kingdom, at 234,000 *livres,* that is, a twentieth of the value of the manufactured products. Not only was wood used as such, but also in the form of charcoal.

It was charcoal that Pierre Antoine Hannong would use for his third firing. For the others he took firs and very light wood.

Although burning nothing but whitewood and birch, the manufacturers could not stock up until after 'the pastry-cooks, bakers and plasterers were supplied'. They afterwards had exclusive rights to these fuels, and they kept them until 1796, in spite of the Revolution.

The fear of a fuel shortage was, incidentally, one of the causes of the 1784 decree. That very winter the cold had been so severe that the waterways were impassable. A Council decree of February 15th 1784 put up wood prices owing to the necessity to transport overland the wood left along the river banks. A provisional tax was set up and its duration extended by reason of the floods of February. Finally, a decree from the Cour de Parlement and then a declaration from the King ordered the use of a new measure for wood and fixed new prices.

This consumption was also one of the reasons for the desired exile of the private factories to fifteen leagues outside Paris. Discussions and debates between the manufacturers and the Lieutenant général de Police gave rise to the decree of 1787, the important point in these controversies invariably being the consumption of wood.

Thus, Dihl & Guérhard won a three-month reprieve on the implementation of the decree of 1784, by pleading that they could not burn coal without incurring considerable losses, whereas the types of wood they used could not be of any value either to the inhabitants of the capital or to the bakers. .

A draft decree elaborating the one of 1787 gave the Parisian factory-owners permission to stay there on condition that they used only coal, and did not resort to wood unless there was a scarcity of coal or unless repairs were to be done to the coal-fired kiln, 'and even then, subject to the provision that every contractor consumes annually, either in the above mentioned cases or for firing his colours, not more than 100 cords of wood and [a blank in the text] sacks of mineral coal'.

However, the decree of 1784 should not have been aimed at the factory of the Faubourg Saint-Denis. A protest from its managers dated August 17th 1784 pointed out that they had constructed a new kiln for burning 'desulphurized coal'. To a certain extent these experiments may be considered as being financed by the coal-producing companies. As early as October 1782, work on altering the kilns had begun and on December 13th of the same year, Mithouard, Macquer, Le Roy, Sage and d'Arcet signed 'minutes of an inspection of the porcelain kiln by M. Bourdon Desplanches'. The experts an-

38 Painters' and modellers' workshop. From *l'Art de la Porcelaine* by the Comte de Milly. (1771).
'Figure 1 shows the Furnace *[Fourneau]* and the Muffle-Kiln in which the colours are fused onto the porcelain.
'Figure 2 is the modellers' workshop.
'Figure 3 shows one Workman crushing up the colours, and another sifting them.
'Figure 4 is the Painters at work: we see three Artists busy painting various porcelain vases.'
Paris, Bibliothèque nationale.

39   Fay
Eight plate designs.
Flowers, palmettes, zigzag
patterns, assorted borders
(See also pages 44 and 66–67).

Fay inv. St

nounced that Bourdon had used one of the wood kilns without changing anything inside it. The brick-built kiln had the appearance of a tower flanked by four hopper-shaped hearths or 'bags' leading down to the kiln floor. Four ventilation shafts supplied air to these furnaces, each with a grating on an inclined plane. The portion on which the saggers were placed was about 2,50 metres in diameter and the same in height.

The advantages of this firing were clear: it took 29 hours instead of 38 or 40, requiring a quantity of fuel costing 310 *livres* 10 *sols* instead of 344 *livres* for firing with wood. Finally, last but not least among the advantages, the pieces were neither cracked, blistered, nor distorted. This batch of December 13th 1782 numbered 1140 items, of which 782 were of top quality, 127 'seconds', 131 'thirds', 76 pieces to be redone and 24 breakages. Many other batches were subsequently fired: in 1786 (July), Bourdon had 'fire set' to the twentieth batch of the year.

In Paris other experiments more official in character took place in Monsieur's factory. Indeed, having learnt of the experiments in coal-firing to which Leperre was applying himself in his factory at Lille in 1784–85, Calonne summoned the latter to Paris, in a letter of December 29th 1785. Leperre arrived at the beginning of 1786—pursued, incidentally, by his creditors. He had with him four craftsmen from his factory, and his foreman. He stayed for nineteen months. The place of experimentation was, therefore, the Clignancourt factory where, upon Leperre's arrival, the construction of the kiln had already been started. The un-

loading of porcelain from the kiln took place on May 30th, and the experiment failed. In a plea addressed to Calonne, Leperre justified his set-back by blaming it on the Parisian factories and more particularly on Bourdon Desplanches, reproaching them for bringing objects deliberately prepared from poor quality body to be fired.

In retaliation, Bourdon claimed that Leperre had copied his kilns—which the latter vehemently denied. It is nonetheless disturbing to note that Leperre had signed on one of his cousins, employed for a long time in the factory of the Faubourg Saint-Denis. Later on, Deruelle had a few changes made in the construction of the kiln and personally initiated tests, after Leperre had departed.

In 1785 several factories are thought to have staged comparable tests: Lassia, Faubourg Saint-Antoine in Paris; Pierre Antoine Hannong, believed to have been established in Verneuil (Marne) at the time; and Fauquez of Valenciennes, empowered by a decree of May 24th 1785 to set up a porcelain factory on condition that he fuelled it with coal.

We should also note similar experiments made by the faience maker Sturgeon at Rouen from August 1783 onwards, and in Bordeaux around 1799, by Alluaud and Vanier in their porcelain factory, following the methods that Vanier, according to Chavagnac and Grollier's account, had brought from Valenciennes. Thus the use of pit-coal towards the end of the 18th century was really beginning to spread, before becoming standard practice in the course of the following century.

Output and Evolution of Style

OUTPUT

We must return once more to the decrees of the King's Council regulating the manufacture and decoration of porcelain under the *Ancien Régime*

The decree of 1766 forbade any manufacture other than 'in imitation of Chinese ware, either in white and painted in blue-and-white, or in other monochromes: [it is forbidden] to make use of any other colour, especially gold, or to fashion any figures, flowers in relief or other modelled items unless they be for trimming or for attachment to the said artefacts manufactured by them'.

In fact, apart from a few signed pieces by Pierre Antoine Hannong, we know of no examples of blue-and-white pieces 'in imitation of Chinese ware'. They would, of course, probably be bowls and saucers Ill. 5 belonging to a *cabaret* (tea- or coffee-services).

This decree preceded by some years the creation—following upon the discovery of *limousin* kaolin—of factories for hard-paste porcelain. It does seem that, as soon as they were set up, Parisian factories ignored the prohibitions contained in this decree and produced polychrome pieces, sometimes even embellished with gold. We have seen, on the other hand, that certain factories had obtained special exemptions.

The decree of 1784 affirmed in its preamble that the restrictions ordered by the previous decrees had not been respected and that, in fact, every single factory had set its hand to 'every sort of work', not excepting things whose exclusive manufacture had constantly been reserved for the royal factory. This decree confirmed the privilege of Sèvres in the production of vases, the 'encrustation' [*sic*] of gold and the painting of pictures representing people and animals. Besides this, Sèvres retained the monopoly on manufacturing three-dimensional or bas-relief modelling. For their part, the private factories were granted the right to finish and sell off the prohibited works contained in their salesrooms. The decree of 1784 allowed them to 'continue making all other pieces of work of medium type, intended for the table and ordinary domestic use, such as olio pots, *terrines,* dishes and plates, *compotiers* (compote-dishes), sugar-bowls, cups and teapots, basins, pots, egg-cups, and other items of that type; to apply gilt to the rims only, and to have painted upon them flowers in all shades of colour'.

The greater part of Parisian production at this period does correspond to the concessions contained in the decree, being mainly composed of table-service pieces adorned with flowers in sprigs, *au naturel* (painted from life). The most common sort of border consists of a gold festoon, called *dent de loup* (wolf's tooth). Other Ill. 6 pieces are only edged with streaks of purple or blue, sometimes with monochrome scrolls or else perhaps with rich Ill. 50, 191 gilt borders.

But that does not mean that the decree of 1784 put an end to all production other than what was authorized. Many an example attests the opposite, such as the orders from the Comte d'Artois to his factory in 1784, for his residences of Le Temple (in Paris), Bagatelle, Maisons and Saint-Germain. They include table pieces in white and gold, or 'roses and foliage'; ornamental pieces, notably 'two *jardinières* (of the shape known as *hollandois*) and their bases with blue ground and decorated', together with numerous modelled biscuit-ware pieces of different sizes. Finally, the decree of 1787, by allowing the factories of the Queen, Monsieur, the Comte d'Artois and the Duc d'Angoulême to make whatever they deemed suitable, left practically none of the Sèvres privileges in existence. It was merely forbidden to decorate the outsides of white wares bought from the royal factory, and to counterfeit modelled work deriving from its workshops.

It is therefore not surprising to record that, from the 18th century onwards, the output of Paris porcelain was plentiful and varied. To study this production it is necessary at the same time to follow the evolution in style, with the help of the following:

– The marks, very often allowing one to date objects approximately, a given mark having been used by a given factory for a well-defined period

– The inventories drawn up either on the initiative of certain establishments or following confiscations, which similarly describe the output of a factory at one definite date

– The advertisements appearing at the time, which give some guidance

– The drawings by ornamentalists for use on porcelain, of which, unfortunately, only very few examples from the 18th century are still extant—apart from the sketches from the Sèvres factory, of course. The collections with which we are familiar give only sketches of plates and cylindrical cups, and we shall talk about them later in our study of decoration.

These different elements will allow us to examine firstly production itself, then the evolution of shapes and decorations respectively. In any case, we can specify straight away that this evolution comprises three fairly clear-cut divisions between 1770 and 1800:

– the end of Louis XV's reign, with the survival of the Rococo style

– the reign of Louis XVI

– the Revolutionary period up to the Consulate.

The output of Paris porcelain around 1775 is mostly made up of hollow wares, as we have already seen: plates, round and oval dishes, radish-boats (ancestors of our *hors-d'œuvre* dishes), soup tureens or *terrines* standing on their bases (soup-tureens are round whereas *terrines* are oval), salad-bowls, single- or double-lipped sauce-boats, egg-cups, salt-cellars, mustard-pots, butter-dishes, cruet-stands; then the olive-spoons and gravy-pots *(pots à jus)* for meat jellies, etc. The inventory for 1778 of the Faubourg Saint-Denis factory mentions hot-water plates and others for *hors-d'œuvre*.

For the dessert services we must add to the plates a host of compote-dishes varying in shape (bowls for strawberries or cream,

40 Monsieur's factory. Goblet and saucer, with inner foot-ring, flowers in relief touched with gold. The shape is reminiscent of Saint-Cloud and Chantilly soft-paste wares, themselves inspired from China porcelain in the white. This piece is somewhat unusual in the context of Parisian hard pastes. *Circa* 1775. Sèvres, Musée National de Céramique. Ht. 8 cm. (5¹/₁₀ in.). Mark 162.

for example), sugar-bowls (which tend, when they are without their lids, to be confused with sauce-boats, in spite of having no spout) and many recipients for ice. The latter vary in height and shape: ice-pails for bottles, phials, glasses ('monteiths') and liqueurs. A monteith, oval and crenellated in shape, is designed for putting glasses in, their feet remaining fixed in notches along the edge, while their bowls rest on the piled ice. One may include cheese-dishes with a perforated base to allow cream cheese to drain; jam-pots with two or three lidded compartments and ice-cups, 'frothy' or 'snowy'.

Ill. 57

Other pieces may match table services: 'boiling-pots', 'stew-pans' and saucepans, and also table burners.

Ill. 84

We should remember that at that time service in the French style meant putting all the viands of any one course on the table, whereupon everyone had himself served with whatever he wished. There were hence several (thick) soups, various *entrée* dishes, joints, etc.

Both the covered bowls—for broth—and the *cabarets* are less closely related to the table-service.

The *cabarets* or *déjeuners* (breakfast sets) consist of cups which may be used either for tea or coffee; a tea or coffee-pot, a milk-jug and a *pot à sucre* (sugar-pot). The term *sucrier* ('sugar-bowl') is reserved for receptacles that are put on the table for the dessert course. These *cabarets* are completed by a tray, sometimes of porcelain for the more costly sets, or just of varnished wood or painted tin.

Ill. 73, 193

Ill. 8

We must mention the *génieux* as well, which are large coffee cups; then the *marabouts* (hot-water pitchers), with a handle perpendicular to the lip, and fitted with a lid; the chocolate-pots with a side-

Ill. 4

handle of black turned wood, then the punch-bowls and tea-caddies.

Ill. 12
Ill. 57

Finally, many rather coarse bowls and saucers were manufactured for the *limonadiers* (literally lemonade-sellers: cafés). The toilet pieces are fewer than the items of crockery. Chiefly, we come across water-jugs or ewers and their basins, barbers' shaving-basins or dishes, soap- or sponge-holders, spittoons, cosmetic jars for pomade and rouge, a few small mortars for beauty preparations, eye baths, wash basins or *jattes à bidet* (bidet-bowls) and round or oval chamber pots. The term *bourdaloue* was not used in contemporary texts.

Ill. 5

Ill. 75

Ill. 86

Ornamental pieces are extremely varied. Firstly, there are vases which serve more for decoration than for holding flowers (some made of porcelain themselves). The richest or most perfect items are mounted in gilt bronze (ormolu). Sometimes these vases are set out on a pier-table or mantelpiece in series of three or five, like the earlier Delft ware. In such cases they are described as a *garniture de cheminée* (mantelpiece set) and the central piece is larger in scale than the others. The shapes and dimensions of the vases are as varied as those of the *carafes à fleurs* (flower-bottles) or *à oignons,* designed to take bulb-plants. Baskets intended for flowers, fruits or sweetmeats have always enjoyed wide popularity.

Ill. 15, 196

'Fountains' and kettles, together with candlesticks and chandeliers, mounted in bronze or unmounted, figure frequently in the documents of the Clignancourt factory, which by 1780 was already making bronze-mounted tables.

Ill. 63

References to pin-trays, watch-stands and inkstands are abundant, as they are to tobacco-jars. We even find at the turn of the century a *mouilloir à tabac* (tobacco-moistener). Le Petit Carrousel also sold more personal objects such as snuff-boxes and pipes.

Lastly, biscuit models were produced in plenty by the Parisian factories at the end of the 18th century, in spite of the monopoly of Sèvres and the consequent prohibitions.

Vases, figures and groups were intended not only for decorating suites of rooms, but also for embellishing the table. At the turn of the century busts and clocks were very fashionable.

SHAPES

The early 'Paris porcelains' dating from the last years of Louis XV's reign are still exposed to a Rocaille influence. Among the pieces which are datable as probably pre-1775, we should mention the ones bearing the marks of Pierre Antoine Hannong for the factory in the Faubourg Saint-Denis which he left in 1774, and the ones marked with the characteristic windmill of the Clignancourt factory.

Compared to subsequent Parisian ware all these pieces have a somewhat archaic appearance. There are for instance jugs with a low ample belly set on a plain foot-rim or 'flat-bottomed', just as Chardin
Ill. 4, 12 loved to paint them; teapots whose spout curiously simulates a rather weird bird's
Ill. 6 head; ice-cups with a distended belly set on a low *piédouche* (pedestal-foot), whose leaf-work handle comes half round in a ring. The pieces of flat-ware have waved rims, and often include ridging on their cavetto. The ones most fastidiously executed are adorned with shells and inter-
Ill. 7, 9 locking scrolls in relief. The cup-handles
Ill. 52 are auriform, and those of the *marabouts* or the teapots are frequently made of
Ill. 6, 12 black wood, with mouldings and fluting.

With the pieces dated between precise termini we may associate others, for instance an oval salt-cellar supported on four scrolled feet and bearing the mark of the factory in the Rue de la Fontaine-au-Roy.
Ill. 188

Nonetheless, we must not lose sight of the fact that the Rocaille style did not suddenly disappear on the very day of Louis XV's death. Its persistence is demonstrated, *inter alia*, by a piece bearing the factory mark of the Rue de Bondy, hence produced after 1781. It is a sugar-bowl consisting of a smooth ovoid shape resting in a matching stand which is fluted, indented and borne on four scroll-shaped feet. The whole thing is fixed to a tray, itself fluted and scalloped. The convex lid is topped with three shells whose shape has been specially prepared so as to allow an easy grip with three fingers.
Ill. 94

A very distinct influence of the gold-smith is undeniable in the forms of the early Parisian porcelains—an influence that we shall encounter throughout our survey, incidentally; for example in the 'goblet shaped like silver' which figures in the inventory of the factory in the Faubourg Saint-Denis in 1778. Perhaps it was similar to the goblet adorned with flowers in relief by the Clignancourt factory, in which we also find the characteristics of soft-paste porcelains from Saint-Cloud.
Ill. 40

In the reign of Louis XVI, whilst examining either the inventories of the confiscations carried out in private factories at the request of the royal factory, or else the objects still preserved, we notice that the products of these diverse establishments more or less resemble one another. The factories of Rue Thiroux, the Faubourg Saint-Denis, and La Courtille are hardly

distinct from each other. Clignancourt stands as the sole exception, by virtue of its manufacture of large-scale pieces—'fountains' or tables—and of the perfection of its modelled ornaments.

We encounter the most common objects whose shapes were gradually evolving. Dishes and plates for instance had lobed rims before becoming perfectly circular. The (cylindrical) cup progressively took the lead over the round-based models or the 'coated' ones *(à cotte),* or 'coated, handleless' *(à cotte sans hanse).* Already, 'sheathed' cups *(à gaine)* were appearing, probably of a tapering form. We also see numerous cups 'in the Queen's style' thought to be these same truncated-cone

cups having one or two handles, capped with a lid and set in a deep saucer. The cups of current form generally came in four sizes. The cylindrical cups are known as *mignonettes* (poppets) when they are hardly more than three to three and a half centimetres tall, whereas the usual size is six centimetres in height and in diameter. A cup which appears to be peculiar to Guérhard & Dihl is a large-scale cylindrical model fitted with a convex lid topped with a fruit and accompanied by a saucer with an angular profile.

Butter-dishes are shaped like moulded tubs, mustard-pots copy the form of a little cask, or are simply cylindrical with

Ill. 49

Ill. 10

Ill. 107

Ill. 59

Ill. 91

this evolution: roundish in the oldest pieces, they would flatten out to become angular, reminiscent of ancient Greek frets★. On broth-bowls which had abandoned the bulbous for the straight★★, flared shape as well, the side- and cover-handles no longer simulate knotty branches but have key patterns, square in cross section, rising from a bracket. The grip became a modelled button, often a pine-cone; the lids increased in height and became bell-shaped instead of convex.

The cylindrical shape became the rule for all *cabaret* items, just as it had already practically imposed itself on cups. More and more, teapot-spouts were faceted, and tapering sugar-bowls replaced the handleless sugar-pots with the rounded base. On this new shape of sugar-bowl we see embryonic handles and simulated rings appearing, and later on various masks. Milk-jugs have a slightly bulbous belly and invariably a wider lip.

For all that, some large-scale pieces such as *terrines* retained until late more complicated shapes closer to gold artefacts.

The forms and details of pieces from the Clignancourt factory at the time of Monsieur's patronage distinguish themselves from the models of other Parisian factories by genuine modelled work. In particular the handles shaped as myrtle- or laurel-wreaths were finely worked, and so were the acanthus leaves arranged at either end of a basin. Guérhard & Dihl, for their part, executed pieces adorned with details in the same vein.

One of the specialities of Clignancourt seems to be the manufacture of 'kettles for use on spirit-burners', mentioned in great quantity among the objects seized in 1780. The best-known model consists of a hemispherical kettle with a pivoted handle of turned wood mounted in metal.

attached tray and flat lid. Cream- or milk-jugs are often tripods or flat-bottomed, and come in different sizes. Handled *pots à jus,* with their low belly and convex lid, are the ancestors of the *pots à entremets* which every good 19th-century mistress of the house felt obliged to keep in her cupboards.

Generally speaking, then, we are witnessing a rapid sobering up of Rococo complexity, moving towards an antique simplicity. Curves were constantly being replaced by straight lines. The bellies of teapots and jugs, initially low and dumpy, would become elegant balusters, culminating in tapering shapes, sometimes even inverted cones. Handles would follow

42 Monsieur's factory.
Hercule Farnese. Biscuit.
Circa 1773.
Sèvres, Musée National de Céramique. Ht. 32 cm. (12³/₅ in.).
Mark 160.

★Ill. 89
★★Ill. 54, 90

Ill. 93

Ill. 44

43   Schœlcher.
Bulb vase. Underglaze blue
decoration heightened with
red and gold. Jacob Petit
and Schœlcher marks.
Circa 1832.
Paris, private coll.
Ht. 17 cm. (6³/₅ in.).
Marks 33 and 125.

Into this kettle is plunged a lidded, straight-necked infuser. The kettle rests on a raised circular base, having at the top a neck pierced with oval openings. The spirit-holder fits inside this base.

Ill. 63 There exist certain variations on this model. We find for example a double-spouted kettle in the form of swans with wings spread, issuing from its belly in the Ill. 48 middle of a clump of reeds. In this same inventory of confiscation in 1780 is an entry for 'fountains'. These are pieces nearly 50 centimetres high, pear-shaped, with a bulbous lid, and resting on a base

similar to that of the kettles. Being too heavy and too large to be handled easily, they are equipped with a metal tap and thereby assume the appearance of *samovars*, and were probably used for making tea. A certain process of transition may sometimes be observed in the change from round shapes to straight ones. A subtle blend of both gives an object unquestionable charm: witness a *confiturier à deux*, the containers of which are truncated cones fixed to a scallop-edged or lobed stand; or else a gadrooned monteith with handles in the form of key-patterns.

44 Monsieur's factory. *Terrine* and stand. Polychrome flowers, touched with gold. Probably came from the Château de Brunoy. *Circa* 1780. Paris, Musée du Louvre. Coll. Thiers. L. 46 cm. (14¹/₅ in.). Marks 161 and 164.

Ill. 57

Ill. 233

A few forms persisted despite everything —the shell-shaped compote dishes for example, which underwent only slight modifications in the form of the leaf-handle.

Among the table-pieces which have led to many fantasies, we are bound to remark upon the salt-cellars with one or two bowls. The inventories enter them as *panniers* at Clignancourt or 'with figures' in Rue Thiroux. A young girl, say, sits on two baskets, holding a cage.

We must remember that the client used to order the composition of his service or his *cabaret* as he himself fancied. He could, at will, mix the forms of his choice without being obliged to buy a set. Finally let us note that this sometimes resulted in effects of curious disparity. Thus, we have encountered a *cabaret* made up of cylindrical cups and teapot, accompanied by a tripod milk-jug with handle and feet shaped as branches. The bizarre group was completed by a straight-sided sugar-bowl flared at the top, standing on four goat's feet, the handles key-patterned and the lid topped with a fir-cone. A comparable sugar-bowl is in the Musée de l'Ariana at Geneva.

The toilet-pieces, although few, follow the same evolution. The barbers' shaving dishes or basins, once curvilinear, became more sober; the water-jugs and their bowls also underwent a simplification of outline, body shape and handle design.

Ornamental pieces gave rise to highly diversified forms. This is noticeable particularly in the case of vases, which we know either from written documents or from the objects themselves.

The inventory for 1778 of the Faubourg Saint-Denis factory gives 'urn-shaped' and 'swan-shaped' flower vases, and others to stand on corner-cupboards.

Should we connect this entry with the slightly later vases (being dated 1783) which may be found in the Musée du Louvre? A wide band in the centre separates a rounded bottom resting on a *piédouche*, from a long, incurving neck.

The following year, 1784, the Comte d'Artois bought vases for his sundry residences, some 'eared' or 'chalice-shaped', others *en écharpe avec colonne* (in sash with column). Some bore goats' heads, the moulds for which existed as early as 1778. Another was called modern, which is less helpful. Perhaps it was just ovoid on a pedestal-foot, like a vase in the Musée Adrien Dubouché in Limoges. Last of all came two 'Dutch'—meaning fan-shaped—vases. All these vases were delivered with their plinths or 'dice'.

The Clignancourt factory produced some very fine ornamental pieces, especially 'Medici' vases with moulded bases, magnificently sculpted handles or grips consisting of lion- or faun-like masks and wreaths of myrtle or laurel. This shape is also encountered in Rue Thiroux.

Ill. 72

Ill. 60

Ill. 15

45 Monsieur's factory. Tripod milk-jug. Gilt garlands. Before 1775. London, Victoria & Albert Museum. Ht. 6.5 cm. (2½ in.). Mark 157.

The inventories also tell us of sconces and candelabra, as well as candlesticks, few examples of which have survived. On the other hand we do know of a certain number of inkstands, usually round, with different holders for ink, pounce and Ill. 85 pens.

Certain models were reproduced in all the factories at the same time: the *jardinières demi-rondes* (half-round flower stands)—in half-moon shape—with fluted pilasters, were turned out just as much by Clignancourt and the Faubourg Saint-Ill. 73 Denis as by Rue Thiroux. The circular shape with pilasters was made in Rue Thiroux, whereas Guérhard & Dihl had models of square tubs with bevelled corners, miniature columns and artichoke capitals. These very artichokes reappear on a rounded *jardinière* in the shape of a Ill. 193 tomb, bearing the mark of La Courtille.

We have several guide-lines for identifying ware produced in the Revolutionary period, firstly the marks—for Clignancourt the name spelt out in full or M for Moitte; for the Rue Thiroux, the mark *Houzel*.

Furthermore, several inventories dating from this period provide us with vital information.

For the La Courtille factory we have the inventory drawn up in 1789, after the death of Catherine Behier, Russinger's second wife, and for the salesroom of Le Petit Carrousel, the inventory following the death in 1793 of Charles Barthélemy Guy. The latter, incidentally, is followed by another, drafted when the factory of the Rue Thiroux was sold (half of it entering Guy's estate).

From these documents one notes, besides the various common pieces belonging to table-services or *cabarets*, large numbers of bowls. Complete sets also figure in the inventories: *cabarets* of 17 pieces, dessert-services of 38, 64 or 88 pieces, the contents of which are unfortunately left unspecified. We may imagine them, going by pieces still extant which are in fact the same as those of previous services. We find sugar-bowls for the table, compote-dishes, jam-dishes, etc. Only the shapes change, for it was not until the turn of the century that various moulded pieces finally broke away from Rococo influence. The oval or semi-ovoid shapes are supported on *piédouches,* often raised ones: soup-tureens, broth-bowls, sugar-bowls for the table, urn-shaped coolers, Ill. 23 water-jugs and basins. Perhaps by way of Ill. 235 contrast other, squatter forms re-emerge, such as a ewer and its basin, signed by Moitte in Clignancourt. Ill. 67

In the inventories the references to 'sheathed' shapes predominate, and these are probably identifiable with many extant pieces of truncated-cone form. Ill. 89 Cylindrical cups continued, but others had a gently flared calyx, and we witness the emergence of a distinction between coffee-cups and tea-cups. The latter are semi-ovoid, low and flared. Ill. 87

The ornamental pieces are vases, either 'egg-shaped', 'lyre-shaped' or 'with dolphin', together with beaker-vases, *pots pourris* or flower- or bulb-'bottles', the shapes of which follow the general evolution.

The portrait of Dihl painted in 1797 by Le Guay displays the latest products from his factory: a spindle-vase on a *piédouche* together with a hemispherical cup likewise on a pedestal-foot, having on either side a vertical grip ending in a buckle. Ill. 97, 98 The Musée national de Céramique de Sèvres which houses this picture possesses

46 Monsieur's factory. Cruet-stand simulating wicker-work. Polychrome flower-sprays. The actual containers were always of cut glass. *Circa* 1780. Paris, Coll. Guy Passerat. L. 27 cm. (10²/₃ in.). Mark 162.

Ill. 101

in its collections a cup of similar form with vertical grips ending in female heads. The saucers that go with this shape of cup have lost the straightness of the previous years and become 'skull-caps' (rounded in profile).

While on the subject of the picture mentioned above, let us add that it was painted on a porcelain plaque, like others exhibited by the Dihls in 1789. They are the first examples of large-scale paintings to be executed on porcelain in a Parisian factory.

Clocks of this period appear to have been made exclusively of biscuit, so we shall discuss them in the chapter devoted specially to biscuit ware.

DECORATION

The early decoration of Paris porcelains, if they had followed the letter of the law in force at the time, would have lacked variety.

We have already seen that the only colours allowed before the decree of 1784 were blue-and-white only, 'in imitation of Chinese ware' or cameos in some other colour. The use of gilt remained forbidden.

The decree of 1784 did not authorize polychrome decoration except for 'shaded flowers' and permitted the application of gilt to the rim alone.

The investigation on the one hand of the

surviving objects and on the other of the texts—amongst them the official reports of confiscations—is consistent in demonstrating how little the regulations were obeyed from the earliest period (the end of Louis XV's reign) onwards.

The Clignancourt porcelains with the windmill mark and those of Pierre An-

of wildflowers or foliage; fruit is sometimes blended with the flowers.

Ill. 53
Ill. 41

The 1776 inventory of the factory in the Faubourg Saint-Denis also mentions decorations 'with birds', 'with figures' and 'with children'. Pierre Antoine Hannong had already marked a number of items embellished with birds or figures in polychrome.

Ill. 10

toine Hannong are more often than not embellished with polychrome decorations.

In all the Parisian factories floral decoration is predominant, with scattered sprays and sprigs painted from nature. It is obvious that manufacturers hesitated nonetheless to infringe the decrees in the matter of using gilt, for we are familiar with a certain number of decorated but ungilded pieces. This was perhaps due only to a wish to economize.

Floral decoration, when treated thus, was actually a great advantage: the choice and positioning of flowers and various other types of vegetation allowed the artist to cover up any defects in the porcelain body or the firing, which at the outset were very frequent in Parisian products.

Besides floral sprays, the contemporary plant decorations are made up of garlands

Ill. 6, 50
Ill. 191
Ill. 4
Ill. 50

Some Clignancourt porcelains bearing the windmill mark but whose decoration may be slightly later are adorned with amorous scenes in polychrome.

There remain from this period only a few items in monochrome. Let us cite, *inter alia,* a *marabout* decorated with small green leaves by Pierre Antoine Hannong (but with slight touches of red), and landscapes in blue or violet from Clignancourt (Victoria & Albert Museum, London).

The decoration of gold on white, for a long time the monopoly of the royal factory, was already being utilized—and most masterfully—by Pierre Antoine Hannong, on a chocolate-pot kept in the Musée national de Céramique de Sèvres. A wide lacy gilt border adorns the upper portion of this piece, while an oval medallion with rustic emblems decorates the

47 Fay.
Cup-designs. Imbricated patterns (1), monograms (2), garlands (3), birds and butterflies set in medallions framed by foliage (4, 6), strewn sprigs, ornaments in style of Salembier (5).

Ill. 12

body. Some insects are scattered over the medallion.

During the ensuing period, under the reign of Louis XVI, the decorative motifs multiply.

The decorations familiar on Parisian wares from the start (which were to last a long time) such as flowers after nature, roux for the *nécessaire de voyage* (travelling-set) that Marie-Antoinette took with her on her flight to Varennes.

The cups, teapot, cosmetic-jars, spittoon and eye-bath are of porcelain from the Queen's factory, while the many other objects in the round are of chased silver. A large number of ivory and crystal

birds, figures, cupids, Chinese emblems, and so on, are joined by many others.

The inventory drawn up in 1778 at the factory of the Faubourg Saint-Denis gives a few classifications for polychrome decorations: landscapes, ribbons, Chinese, as well as a decoration 'with blue band' which is enriched by a gilt garland. This decoration is probably quite old as it adorns a dish bearing Hannong's Ill. 9 mark.

The monogram decorations *(à chiffre)*, mentioned in 1778, were equally common. Here, the initials were formed from polychrome sprigs—painted on in gold— painted in freehand with different colours, alternatively in gold accompanied by garlands, drapery and various other ornaments. One of the most touching examples is probably the monogram composed by the factory of the Rue Thi-

objects complete this set, enclosed in a rectangular mahogany chest with brass mounts, signed *Palma ébéniste et faiseur de nécessaires* ('Palma, cabinet maker and manufacturer of *nécessaires*') in Paris. The total weight is 50 kg. nearly 9 kg. 300 g. of it being silver.

Certain floral decorations ceased to be formed from anything but a single species of flower. In 1784 the Comte d'Artois ordered from his factory a dessert-service 'with roses and foliage' which in fact consisted only of items rematched from a Sèvres service. Another floral motif the Ill. 14 popularity of which never waned is a rendering—or rather, various renderings —of the cornflower, which is most often painted in blue, with a few touches of red or yellow, accompanied by green leaves. Ill. 61 More rarely, it is combined with purple flowers or even entirely painted in pink Ill. 70

and green. The cornflower appears in bouquets, sprigs, borders, and medallions, ornamenting the simplest and most complicated forms alike. By tradition it was Marie Antoinette's favourite decoration, and was made for the first time in Rue Thiroux specially for her. However, the cornflower figures in the decorative repertoire of Sèvres as early as 1774, that is, before the Rue Thiroux came into being. The cornflower is mentioned as a common decoration in the official report of confiscation from the Clignancourt factory in 1780.

Ill. 195 Scattered sprays of flowers were equally popular. Roses, cornflowers and pansies were strewn about in profusion by all the porcelain makers. The Clignancourt factory invented a particular type of spray, consisting of various straight-stemmed polychrome wildflowers. These flowers, separated by fine gilt leaves, are arranged horizontally in three-dimensional pieces or laid out in concentric circles on flat-Ill. 57 ware.

Ill. 192 We likewise encounter a lot of bouquets composed of assorted flowers, enclosed in medallions hung on ribbons.

Flowers open out again in the ribbon-decorations which were amongst the most prized at the end of the *Ancien Régime*. If the influence of the goldsmith is manifest in connexion with shapes, decoration on porcelain has on many occasions borrowed ideas from the textile arts. On many pieces the decorative friezes and borders are made up of 'picoted' ribbons, or ribbons with a plain rim, adorned with flowers on a contrasting ground which Ill. 17 is often dotted and striped. Occasionally the goffered ribbon covers the entire sur-Ill. 231 face of a cup. Similarly, a striped material Ill. 13 may be simulated on a teapot or a cooler. Decoration with fauna becomes more

48 Monsieur's factory. 'Kettle with spirit-burner'. Polychrome and gold. One of the original pieces occurring most frequently in the inventory of confiscation from the Clignancourt factory, instigated by Sèvres in 1780, is the kettle. A great many of them are estimated at between 96 and 200 *livres* when they come complete with burner. They are generally made up of a round burner having circular openings pierced in the top, over which is set a hemispherical kettle with a pivoted handle of turned wood: into this kettle is plunged a lidded infuser. The one reproduced here displays exceptional characteristics in having two spouts and modelled decoration. The two swans facing outwards, emerging from clumps of reeds, are not without their parallel in the 'swan' service which in about 1740 Count Brühl had ordered from Meissen. *Circa* 1780. Rouen, Musée des Beaux-Arts et de Céramique. Ht. 30 cm. (11⁴/₅ in). Mark 162.

49 Monsieur's factory. Deep plate. Gold on white, speckled ground. *Circa* 1780. Lisbon, Museu Nacional de Arte Antigua. Diam. 23 cm. (9 in.). Mark 162.

50 Monsieur's factory.
Ice-pail. Sprays of flowers,
ungilded. Probably from
the Château de Brunoy.
Circa 1776.
Sèvres, Musée national de
Céramique. Ht. 12 cm.
(4³/₄ in.).
Marks 162 and 164.

and more frequent, especially birds grouped in a medallion against the background of a landscape. Sometimes a single exotic animal decorates an object. We see many goats as well, perhaps because of the propagation of sheep-folds and dairies in the manner of Marie-Antoinette's at Rambouillet.

Ill. 73
Ill. 51

Ill. 16

One of the most skilful decorations includes figures; it is equally the decoration that costs the most. Whether they are contemporary with the end of the 18th century or belong to Antiquity, men, women and children are to be treated more and more like miniatures. The children's games and *chinoiseries* are going to be joined by figures in Antique style, scenes of domestic life and portraits.

Ill. 20, 198

Often the figures animate landscapes which at first are enclosed in oval or circular medallions, then in frames with truncated corners. The richest decorations using panoramas are harbour scenes and those completely covering objects.
Coloured grounds lend porcelain a par-

Ill. 90
Ill. 58

ticular richness and brilliance. Both the commonest and most sought after is the fine blue *(beau bleu)*, in imitation of Sèvres. Various factories made use of it, particularly Guérhard & Dihl for their richest products. *Beau bleu* is unequalled in setting off a medallion with polychrome decorations of flowers, landscapes or animated scenes. Of the yellow grounds—quite often used at the end of the *Ancien Régime*—few examples are left.

Ill. 90

Instead of being plain, the ground may be covered by an unobtrusive, ceaselessly repeated pattern such as *l'œil de perdrix* (partridge-eye), used on borders as well. It is generally handled in a pale colour-tone; pink or blue dotted with a darker shade, sometimes wholly gilt, or else it changes to imbricated work which Clignancourt often executed in gilt or pale green.

Ill. 192

Ill. 52

The pebbled and new marbled grounds to which, incidentally, it gave rise, come simultaneously into evidence. Their uses differ slightly: pebbled decoration aims

Ill. 16

51 Monsieur's factory. Hemispherical cup and saucer. Gold garlands, medallion decorated with a panther. *Circa* 1790. London, Victoria & Albert Museum. Ht. 4.5 cm. (1³/₄ in.). Mark 162.

52 Monsieur's factory.
Cylindrical cup and saucer.
Blue, green and gold imbri-
cated patterns. *Circa* 1780.
Lisbon, Museu Nacional de
Arte Antigua.
Ht. 6.3 cm. (2¹/₂ in.).
Mark 162.

Ill. 113

Ill. 111

*Frontispiece

primarily at setting off polychrome decorations contained in medallions in reserve: marbled ground sometimes covers
the whole piece.

Another type of decorated ground is the
trompe-l'œil simulation of wood. It was
actually seldom resorted to by the Parisian factories and served chiefly as an
imaginary background for finely drawn
reproductions of prints in sepia, black or
carmine.

The multiplicity of fancy decorations, all
more or less indefinable, claim kinship
with the drawings and prints of ornamentalists. One of them in particular,
Salembier[1], published in and after 1777
various books on decoration. His com-
positions of arabesques, trophies, garlands
and draperies are exceptionally elegant.
They have often inspired decoration on
porcelain but were probably somewhat
modified in the course of time. Salembier
subsequently worked for Dihl: he is too
often forgotten among the 19th-century
figures although he did not die until
1820.

It does not seem obligatory to date pieces
decorated in the style of Salembier before
1785. Sèvres and all the Parisian factories
took hold of this abundance of ideas of
'Etruscan' inspiration: pieces dazzling in
their technique and execution have come
down to us. Witness the vase from the La
Courtille factory, marrying the semi-
ovoid long-necked antique form on a
pedestal-foot, with a clever decoration of
polychrome arabesques enhanced with
grisaille and animated by subtly coloured
birds. Areas variously tinted mauve, buff
and orange are laid out with an admirable
grasp of adapting decoration to shape★.
This decoration can also be used for borders and bands.

The whole ornamental repertoire of the
turn of the 18th century is to be found
on the borders and friezes of many pieces.
There are the strings of piastres or pearls,
the ovolos, leaf motifs and ribbons
which discreetly enhance a polychrome
decoration or a coloured ground.

The pattern in monochrome known as
grisaille had an enormous success in the

[1] Salembier, Henri. Draftsman and engraver, born in Paris,
circa 1753, deceased in Paris on October 1st 1820.
He exerted an overwhelming influence on the Louis Seize
style by virtue of his designs and ornaments.

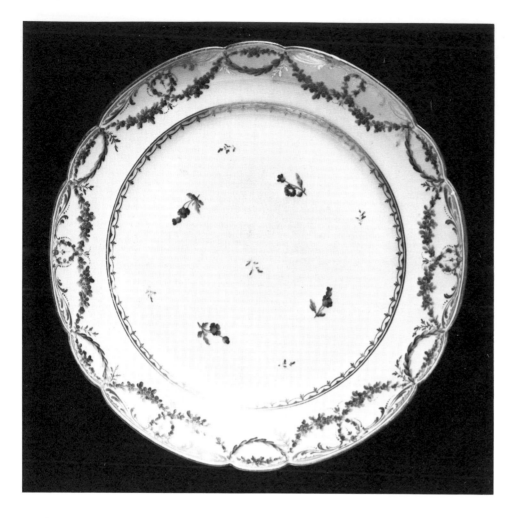

53 Monsieur's factory. Lobed plate. Red, green, blue and gold. Garlands of forget-me-nots, sprigs of wildflowers. *Circa* 1775. Paris, Coll. Guy Passerat. Diam. 23.5 cm. (9¹/₅ in.). Mark 162.

18th century and the fashion for it extended well into the next century.

Although the regulation governing the decoration of porcelain before 1784 allowed decorations of this kind, we know only a few examples, mostly from Clignancourt.

Indeed, the arrival of Lamprecht at Clignancourt *circa* 1783 was to give this monochrome technique new impetus. Handled in bistre, this celebrated monochrome painting was imitated by all the factories, including Sèvres. Several known pieces bear Lamprecht's signature together with the Clignancourt mark LSX. One of these is painted with figures in the manner of Callot. The broth-bowl in the Musée national de Céramique de Sèvres is decorated with sheep-folds and bears the inscription: *Georges Lamprecht pinxit à Paris 1783*.

The bistre monochrome painting which allows for great delicacy of stroke and shaded relief, is also exploited for allegories, amorous scenes, floral *décors* and trophies. Dihl and Guérhard adroitly executed such monochrome paintings not only for whole decorations but for enhancing polychrome decorations as well. It was the bistre monochrome painting which occasioned the grisailles that were used so much in decorations of classical inspiration; they are usually set on a white ground. Some cups by Chanou—of

Ill. 56

54 Monsieur's factory.
Covered broth-bowl.
Diaper of gold peas.
Circa 1780.
Paris, Coll. Guy Passerat.
Ht. 12 cm. (4³/⁴ in.).
Mark 162.

around 1784, therefore—are decorated with landscapes in grisaille on a yellow ground.

Ill. 58 It was likewise at Clignancourt that Lamprecht did decorations with black, a colour which until then had been missing from decorations on hard-paste porcelain and was mainly used in this factory and in Dihl & Guérhard's.

Black and gold are often combined for decorations of sentimental mottoes, simply composed of words written in running script, occasionally accompanied by an emblem. *Fidélité* (Faithfulness), *Souvenir d'amitié* (Souvenir of Friendship), *Venez au secours de mon cœur* (Come to the Aid of my Heart) are the commonest. They are related to the rebus on an amorous theme.

Gilt decoration on white is the supreme triumph of any factory, for it demands faultless pieces.

We have seen how Hannong and Deruelle had already decorated many pieces solely with gilt on white—more or less illegally, one might add.

In 1784 the Comte d'Artois did not hesitate to order from the Faubourg Saint-Denis some matching items for services painted in gilt on white.

If it served principally to set off coloured decorations, gold was increasingly used on its own. The Clignancourt goblet decorated with flowers in relief is touched

Ill. 212

Ill. 40

73

PORCELAINE DURE.

MANUFACTURE
DE MONSIEUR,
ÉTABLIE A CLIGNANCOURT.

Du Magasin rue Neuve des Petits-Champs, au coin de celle de Chabannois, A PARIS, *Le 2 f.. 1779.*

		Liv.	Sols.	den.
Suivant Monsieur le Marquis de Montesquiou				
4 Douzaines d'assiettes à bouquets détachés à	48	192	"	"
4 Verrières à	60	240	"	
		432	.	
Avance de 10 p%0		43	4	.
Reste net		388	16	.

Pour acquit du present Memoire
p.. M.. Deruelle en C..

55 Monsieur's factory.
Invoice dated 1779. The
monogram of Monsieur –
from his initials LSX – was
long used as a mark as well.
Paris, private coll.

74

56 Monsieur's factory. Covered broth-bowl with lobed tray. Painted in sepia – sometimes simply referred to as 'monochrome' *(camaïeux)* – which was invented by Lamprecht, the one-eyed Viennese painter attached to Monsieur's factory. These shepherd-scenes are signed *Georges Lamprecht pinxit à Paris 1783.* The following year Lamprecht went over to the royal factory. Nonetheless, in 1785 its manager Hettlinger wrote to the Comte d'Angivilliers '…the cup which was painted here in sepia, copying the ones which were received from Clignancourt, is now finished…' Further pieces painted by Lamprecht at Clignancourt are known to us, in particular a cup decorated with figures in the style of Callot, also dated 1783. Sepia monochromes allow for great delicacy of stroke and shading. Sèvres, Musée national de Céramique. Ht. 11 cm. Mark 162.

with gold. The report of the confiscation at Clignancourt in 1780 lists cups with gilt bouquets and we know of plates, the raised rim of which is wholly decorated with ornamental foliage in gilt, on a gold-flecked ground. With an elegant simplicity the gilt sprays of sweet pea entirely cover certain pieces. The sprigs of tiny leaves are more original.

Apart from a few exceptions, gilt appears on all decorated pieces: it forms the simplest wolf- or rat-tooth borders, the garlands or lines of foliage and the sumptuous borders copying the braid of *passementerie* work.

A separate place must be accorded to decoration using the translucent or opaque

Ill. 49
Ill. 54
Ill. 236

Musée du Louvre and dated very precisely August 11th 1783, are profusely embellished in this ingenious manner. One does not know which to admire more: the enamels on the neck, bottom and pedestal-foot, shining with a thousand fires from the dark blue grounds or the border of alternately blue and red palmettes, touched with green, that glitters on the band left in reserve.

In order to have an overall idea about Parisian porcelain in 1784, let us imagine ourselves for a moment in the shoes of a ceramic-lover at this date.

At the factory in the Faubourg Saint-Denis he can admire the wares ordered

polychrome enamels by Cotteau to which we have already alluded on many occasions. In fact, these drops of enamel in relief are placed on gold-leaf sunk in the porcelain glaze and worked in relief, adding a complementary decoration that sets off the colours. The vases from the Comte d'Artois' factory, which are kept in the

Ill. 15

by the Comte d'Artois: services adorned with roses or decorated in gilt on white, vases of different shapes and in particular the two blue-ground *vases hollandais*, each one worth 300 *livres*. He is dazzled by the vases (likewise with blue grounds) that Cotteau decorated the year before with translucent or opaque enamels in

57 Monsieur's factory. Tea-caddy (*boîtte à thé*) and 'jam-dish for two'. Polychrome and gold. This pattern of wildflowers is peculiar to Clignancourt. *Circa* 1780.
Paris, private coll. Caddy: Ht. 9 cm. (3$^{1}/_{2}$ in.). Jam-dish: L. 25 cm. (9$^{4}/_{5}$ in.). Marks 162 and 165.

58 Monsieur's factory. Lidded water-jug. Perfectly simple in shape, this baluster-jug displays decoration painted with great competence. The family scene unrolls around the body of the piece, and its subtle poly-chrome colour-scheme is enhanced by decorative motifs on a black ground, one of the triumphs of this factory which the Sèvres craftsmen vainly tried to imitate. The grisaille orna-ments are another of the factory's specialities. The relief-work on the lip and handle is no less refined. Very much a luxury item, this piece bears the LSX mark painted in gold. *Circa* 1785.
Geneva, Musée de l'Ariana. Ht. 24 cm. (9²/₅ in.).
Mark 162.

relief set on gold leaf and further enriched by a gilt bronze mount. The figures, groups and vases in biscuit are so many that he does not know which one to look at. A topical *décor* attracts his attention: it is the 'balloon' decoration, commemorating the experiments in aerostatics performed by Montgolfier, Blanchard and their emulators. If he goes to visit the factory in Rue Thiroux he will find hot-air balloons on the cups. At Clignancourt he is told that Lamprecht's pupils execute to perfection both bistre monochrome paintings and those items with borders touched in a fine thick black. Out of curiosity our porcelain lover will proceed further, to the re-

cently opened but short-lived factory owned by Chanou where he will admire a cooler entirely painted in *trompe-l'œil*★ and simulating marble, and cylindrical cups with yellow or buff grounds enlivened with unfolding landscapes and joyful peasants★★. A new decoration, light and witty, taken from the decorator Salembier's compilations, will hold his attention. Our enthusiast will not omit to finish his tour with a visit to the young but famous factory of the Rue de Bondy where, two years previously, Guérhard and Dihl received a visit from the Comtesse du Nord—but, like most of his contemporaries, he will probably not venture into Nast's workshop, set up in

59 Monsieur's factory. 'Toy' breakfast-set (*déjeuné mignonette*) and cup of normal size. Polychrome and gold. *Circa* 1780. Paris, Musée du Vieux Montmartre. ('Toy') cup: Ht. 3.5 cm. (1²/₅ in.). Mark 162.

★Ill. 113

★★Ill. 115

60 Monsieur's factory.
Sugar-bowl borne on four
feet ending in goats' hooves.
Cornflowers. *Circa* 1785.
Geneva, Musée de l'Ariana.
Ht. 13 cm. (5¹/₈ in.).
Mark 162.

cramped quarters where he is still work-ing single-handed, although on the point of attaining a prominent position amongst his colleagues.

By various means we are able to date precisely the decorations of the last decade of the 18th century.

The inventories of the Rue Thiroux fac-tory and of the salesroom called Le Petit Carrousel, as well as the latter's ledger, together with the inventory following the death of Madame Russinger, consti-tute veritable repertories of *décors,* which are joined by the various designs from the collection of 400 cylindrical cups, each of them decorated differently (Paris, Ill. 16 Bibliothèque nationale).

Floral decorations still predominate. Strewn flowers have by now given way to garlands—a frieze of flowers assembled contiguously—generally of a single va-riety of flower set against a contrasting coloured ground. Hence, one sees gar-lands of roses on gold or yellow grounds, and daisies or cornflowers. Let us no-tice, too, the profusion of newly intro-duced poppies. Amongst the flowers the Ill. 197 small pink roses and cornflowers recur most often in the texts. Sweet peas and crowns of laurel are also to be found.

Butterflies flit hither and thither on nu-merous decorations, either alone or on a background of gilt foliage or even Ill. 235 green-painted peas. Decorations with figures are increasingly subjected to the Antique influence. New renderings follow a transient fashion, like the cup 'with black figure', a term which probably denotes decoration with a silhouette.

On reading inventories one is struck above all by the abundance of grounds in bright colours and even black. The col-

polychrome decoration of landscapes, or by 'antique' cameos, by portraits, domestic scenes or bouquets of flowers ingeniously arranged in a vase.

Ill. 16

Marbled or pebbled grounds are akin to coloured grounds, and Dihl's research results in remarkable mottled or variegated grounds.

Ill. 97, 98, 101

ours most often mentioned in connexion with these coloured muffle-fired grounds are yellow, green, red and blue, but the whole spectrum has been used. These coloured grounds themselves are decorated in black or gilt with figures, animals or landscapes which are continuous unless interrupted by medallions in reserve with

61 Monsieur's factory.
Cask-shaped mustard-pot affixed to tray. Cornflowers. *Circa* 1780.
Geneva, Musée de l'Ariana.
Ht. 8 cm. (5 1/5 in.).
Marks 162 and 165.

62 Monsieur's factory. Monteith, undulating notched rim. Polychrome and gold. *Circa* 1780 Geneva, Musée de l'Ariana. L. 26 cm. (10¹/₅ in.). Mark 162.

Ill. 87

In design, straight lines supersede curves; round or oval medallions are supplanted by square reserves with truncated corners or by lozenges or hexagons. Whole pieces are covered with juxtaposed lozenges in plain gold and in white. Occasionally the lozenges left in reserve are adorned with flowers or tiny polychrome themes.

In themselves, the borders often constitute the sole decoration on items for a table service or a *cabaret*. Wide or narrow, they draw on all the resources of the ornamental repertoire in vogue at the time. Be they polychrome, with or without gold, exclusively gilded, or in reserve on pieces with coloured grounds, these braid-like patterns were the object of studied care on the part of the decorators. On flat-ware the borders are often accompanied by fine matching rosettes painted in gilt or grisaille. Almost all types of decoration may be borrowed for the borders: landscapes, animated scenes, flowers, strap-work, scrolls, trophies, geometrical patterns.

Many other examples, in the case of shapes as much as decorations, could be given. The ones cited above undoubtedly suffice to demonstrate that, within hardly thirty years, the Parisian factories had attained the mastery of their art, and that the very diversity of the products was a measure of their success.

Ill. 16, 92

Ill. 231

63 Monsieur's factory. Cistern ('fountain'). Decoration with Chinamen, blue, red and gold. A number of cisterns are entered in the inventory of confiscation from Clignancourt, on the orders of the royal factory in 1780: a cistern with tap, worth 216 *livres*; some 'footed' cisterns valued at between 72 and 288 *livres*; and a 'cistern and its burner' at 180 *livres*. This latter probably resembled the piece illustrated. Once again we should observe the exquisitely detailed relief on the handles, feet and even around the aperture of the metal tap, which characterizes Monsieur's factory. *Circa* 1780. Geneva, Musée de l'Ariana. Ht. 47 cm. (18²/₅ in.). Mark 162.

Frontispiece of
Art de la Porcelaine
engraved in 1771 by
Comte de Milly.
(See page 41)

THE NINETEENTH CENTURY

General Remarks

Industry and the luxury trade are particularly sensitive to political events and are the first to be affected by their economic consequences.

The repercussions of the Revolution on the porcelain trade in Paris were extremely far-reaching. Thus, for instance, the abolition of privileges allowed complete freedom for setting up a factory, and in addition the profusion of promissory notes permitted rapid and numerous financial transactions. From this there ensued a proliferation of porcelain factories in Paris—most of them, however, unable to sustain themselves for very long. Before the Revolution there had been fifteen private factories in the kingdom, which propagated themselves to forty-one, but by 1814 only half of them were left.

In Paris itself twenty-nine factories had been constructed. Some of the oldest ones had difficulty in carrying on, vegetated, then closed down; Moitte at Clignancourt, for example. Others, which were endowed with a robust organisation and had kept at their head the stalwart men who had founded them, such as Dihl and Nast, took the lead at the beginning of the 19th century. Furthermore, under the *Ancien Régime,* porcelain wares had been luxury items intended chiefly for a wealthy clientele, whose brutal suppression was a disastrous blow to the factories until the emergence of new customers.

The Report presented by Joseph Léon Julien to the Bureau des Arts in Year VII (1799) examined those factories that had attained a peak of perfection and whose trade was the most extensive. They are those of: Dihl, 'now the leading house in this field, thanks to the sustained will-power of the managers and their good administration'; Nast, accomplished in all aspects of his profession; Lemaire & Josse whose knowledge was acquired through sheer experimentation and lastly the cameo factory owned by Despréz.

The manufacture of porcelain ran into the problems firstly of man-power (craftsmen were scarce owing to the Revolutionary wars) and secondly of the transportation of raw materials.

The *coup d'Etat* of Brumaire 18th (1799) gave Parisian trade a new impetus.

The economic situation in Paris shortly afterwards (1801) is well known, thanks to the report of Frochot, the Préfet de la Seine, in reply to an inquiry entitled 'Sources of National and Individual Wealth', resolved upon by General Lacuée, the commander of the military region. According to the epithet of M. Bertrand Gille who published these docu-

64 Unidentified factory. Thimble. Polychrome flowers. *Circa* 1840. Sèvres, Musée National de Céramique. Ht. (⁴/₅ in.). Unmarked.

the creation of the Banque de France (1800) brought the bank rate down, and the Treaty of Amiens (1802) restored confidence.

In its Bulletin of Thermidor 25th, Year XII (1804), the Ministère de la Police générale indicated a resumption of work in porcelain factories employing a great number of craftsmen. This act was probably tied up with the advent of the Empire which, with its Court and its pomp, produced large orders for the trade in luxuries.

But two great economic crises, partly due to the Napoleonic wars, shook the Empire: the first in 1805–06 when speculating merchants put the young Banque de France in straits, and the second in 1810–13. Neither was without its effects on the trade of porcelain.

The situation of porcelain factories particularly preoccupied the authorities, and Costaz, on behalf of the Bureau des Arts et Manufactures, made a report to the Minister of the Interior on May 8th 1806, in which he investigated ways of increasing the sale of porcelain. He was assisted by Madame Dihl whom he had asked for advice. The latter, who had so dearly wished for freedom of manufacture under the *Ancien Régime,* now asked for certain limitations on the free practice of such work, among other things the compulsory marking of wares and the control of work done by outside decorators. She recalled that before the Revolution there had been ten factories in Paris, Sèvres *(sic)* amongst them, out of which only four used to mark their wares. She noted that there were now thirty-three factories and more than four thousand outside craftsmen which made competition hard. In his report Costaz deplored the state of war for closing French outlets to coun-

ments, the balance-sheet is 'uneasy': 'Everything leads us to suppose that consumption has dropped, that revenues have greatly declined and that consequently companies are making an annual loss or at best breaking even.' Trade was stagnant everywhere. Amongst the most important manufacturing enterprises in the Département of the Seine, Dihl's porcelain factory alone is mentioned, although out of the one hundred and thirty craftsmen formerly employed the count had fallen to sixty. Other factories, like Nicolet and Greder in Rue du Rocher, had discontinued activity. In the depths of the slump, two events quite different in character brought about an improvement in trade:

tries 'beyond the seas'. The blockade weighed heavily on French exports. Nonetheless, it had a stimulating effect, witness the porcelain imitations of Wedgwood done by Nast or Despréz in response to the demand from enthusiasts. Costaz also insisted that the foreign powers, for their part, were imitating French ceramics, 'naturalizing in their own countries the products that we were once exclusively qualified to supply'.

Confronted with the difficulties with which the factories were contending, Napoleon decided to grant them loans and forward orders to them. A formal command was signed by the Emperor in

Ostend, on March 27th 1807, to 'come to the aid of those factories of our Empire which, through force of circumstances and lack of retail sales of merchandise manufactured by them, are suffering from shortage of funds'. Dagoty, supplier to the Empress, and Dihl were amongst the first beneficiaries, together with Darte Frères and Caron & Lefebvre. Further loans were withheld, notably from Revil and from Lebourgeois.

It was certainly necessary to find subsidies, and when a second loan was granted to Dihl in 1809 it came out of funds raised from fines imposed upon the critics in Belgium...

Large orders for the Imperial palaces were likewise forwarded to these factories: Dihl and Dagoty each supplied more than 20,000 francs' worth of porcelain to Compiègne and Versailles in 1807.

New loans had to be granted following the crisis of 1810–13, which in Napoleon's view was very serious. 1811 had been the year of bankruptcies, and 1812 saw famine in three-quarters of Europe.

In the early stages the loss of overseas outlets caused by the Continental Blockade had been offset by the growth of trade with countries invaded by the French armies. But as the Napoleonic troops fell back, the field gradually shrank and commerce found itself reduced only to transactions conducted on home ground. A number of industrialists and traders found themselves in straits, such as Caron & Lefebvre who had been exporting mainly to Russia and Spain, and who went bankrupt with liabilities of 793,700 francs.

The conscription of 1813, the taxes, and the return to France of people who had settled in the vassal kingdoms weighed heavily upon industry and trade. Then came the campaign in France and the collapse of the Empire. In his *Histoire de Paris sous le Consulat et l'Empire,* Monsieur Tulard displays the weakness of the young Parisian industry, wilfully slowed down by Napoleon on the advice of Frochot, partly out of a fear of rioting and of violent working-class reactions.

The return to peace was followed by the reopening of the Continent to British trade and precipitated the ruin of a portion of Parisian industry. It was necessary to await the consolidation of the monarchical régime, restored to witness a new rise in fortunes.

Indeed, the peaceful years of the Restoration were to favour the stabilization of particularly profitable innovations, and the appearance of new techniques.

At the close of 1814 the principal manufacturers in Paris had signed a memorandum on the causes of the decline of the porcelain trade in France. They pointed to the halving of the number of French factories, which had dropped to a score, and insisted once again on curbing the outside craftsmen. These independent decorators sometimes kept shops which they did not hesitate to call *fabriques* (works) and they were removing craftsmen from the factories. Taking up the decrees of 1784 and 1787, the manufacturers of Paris called for a restriction on the number of factories, a ban on keeping muffle-kilns outside the factories, compulsory marking and a prohibition against removing craftsmen from the factories and against counterfeiting models. Besides this, they demanded the twofold prohibition against giving up a factory without authorization and exporting clays or glazes. Finally—a particularly

66 Designs for two coffee-
pots, a cream-jug, sugar-
bowl and large bowl, of
matching shapes but differing
decorations. Taken from the
*Album de références d'une
manufacture de céramique,
Epoque Restauration.*
Paris, Library of Musée des
Arts décoratifs.

interesting feature—they claimed that it should be forbidden to paint any items coming from elsewhere. This memorandum was signed by Baruch Weil, Dagoty, Darte Senior, Darte Frères, F. M. Honoré, Lefebvre, Lebourgeois, Lhote, Nast, Trégent and Pouyat Frères. The answer from the Comité des Arts et Manufactures dated January 17th 1815 referred to the reply to the previous memorandum of 1806 and, deeming that there were laws protecting marks and craftsmen, added that nothing was preventing the manufacturers from enforcing them. It was nonetheless proposed to raise Customs duty on exported clays.

Being careful to appease, the Restoration changed nothing in the regulations which had been issued since the Revolution. But commerce was still haunted by the spectre of war, to the extent that, on the occasion of the Spanish expedition in 1820, the manufacturers trembled. Fleury announced to his labour force that if war with Spain broke out he would be forced to dismiss them.

In spite of the Revolution of 1830, the advent of Louis-Philippe and the chronic riots that were rife at this time, people unanimously agreed by 1831 that peace had enormously developed industry since 1816. The growth in consumption following the lowering of prices on a

67 Moitte.
Pitcher and basin. Polychrome and gold. One of the few pieces actually signed by Moitte. *Circa* 1795. Geneva, Musée de l'Ariana. Ht. 24 cm. (9²/₅ in.). Mark 166.

68 Monsieur's factory. Covered dish affixed to its tray, hybrid shape – a cross between a *terrine* and a covered dish. Polychrome and gold. *Circa* 1795. Paris, Musée du Vieux Montmartre. Diam. 29 cm. (11²/₅ in.). Mark 170.

number of manufactured articles had stimulated production; in many branches overproduction was even reached.

Nevertheless, in the long run political upsets gave rise to misgivings amongst capitalists and tended to obliterate credit; this was a grave danger to enterprises too deeply committed which were bound to fail. It was necessary to revive security and confidence, quell disorders in the streets, and foster trade abroad.[1] In the ensuing years, the general tendency towards a recovery in business became pronounced. Despite the cholera epidemic of 1832 which greatly affected life in Paris, business was not slow in picking up. Later on some workers'leagues again

had a troublesome effect, but, thanks to plentiful harvests which brought a drop in the price of foodstuffs, business managed to make headway.

With the Revolution of 1848 and the events following it, the crisis broke out forthwith, assuming a character more serious than any that had preceded it. After four months of slackness and dejection, activity picked up again at the end of 1848. The Paris Chamber of Commerce took the initiative in conducting a statistical investigation into the City of Paris, using new methods: investigators went out to explore a definite area, whereas previous investigations had been based on answers given either by the

[1] Oral inquiry conducted in 1831 by the Président de la Commission du Commerce et des Colonies, in the Chambre de Commerce de Paris. *Statistique de l'Industrie... 1847–1848.*

interested parties themselves, or by members of one association.

Thus we learn that in 1850 there were no more than seventeen porcelain producers left in Paris, only four of whom had craftsmen exceeding ten in number, and eight were working alone or with a single craftsman. On the other hand, one hundred and fifty-eight porcelain decorators are enumerated. The investigation recorded that business connected with the trade in porcelain had been reduced by sixty-four per cent by 1848 and that fifty-nine per cent of the craftsmen had not been kept on during the four critical months.

In fact, the total number of porcelain factories had not ceased to decline rapidly since around 1820. The high cost of labour and raw materials was one of the chief reasons for this, as was the difficulty in obtaining cheap fuel. Some factories shut their gates, having failed, through ignorance or incompetence, to adapt themselves: the Dihls, now too old, had seen their factory decline and been forced to go into liquidation in 1828; others transferred production of their white wares to the provinces to benefit from the low wages of craftsmen and to have clay and fuel at hand: Honoré, for example, moved the production of his white ware to Champroux (Allier) in 1824, keeping in Paris only his decorators'

workshops. Merlin-Hall, successor to Lefebvre, was Jeanne's partner, and they owned jointly the factory of Noirlac in Le Cher. Still others had transformed themselves into salesrooms and were giving work to *chambrelans:* such was Schoelcher's case, whose factory in the Faubourg Saint-Denis had ceased operating after 1810. A further reason may also have been the legislative control over unhygienic workshops and kiln-mouths, from 1810 onwards.

By 1819 there were only fourteen factories left in Paris: Dihl, Pouyat, Nast, Trégent—or rather his successors—Cadet de Vaux and Deruelle, Choste Lebourgeois, Dagoty & Honoré, Darte Senior,

Darte Frères, Flamen-Fleury, Merlin-Hall, Despréz and Baruch Weil. As from this period we must distinguish manufacturers from decorators, which is no easy task. Moreover, certain provincial factories had set up depots in Paris with a view to selling white-wares intended for the decorators. A list of 1838 gives us the names of 21 decorators who stocked up in porcelain colours from those famous chemists the brothers Desfossés. Some employ as many as 18 craftsmen like Dutertre, 15 like Darte Junior or 12 like Parcheminier; these were 'master decorators'. A note specifies that MM. Bernard-Jacob, Mayer and Pelletier 'make exclusively rich ware *(du riche)*—the others make the first half rich or semi-common, and the other half semi-common or common'. Shortly afterwards, in 1839, Clauss, the *doyen* of the porcelain makers of Paris, certified that there were only eight porcelain factories in Paris—even then, two that he mentions are in the suburbs. The ones in Paris were Clauss, Coulon, Déséglises, Margaine, Sobre, Talmours and Discry. He himself stated that his society-funds amounted to 100,000 francs and that he employed 30 craftsmen 'inside' and 10 'outside'. He was probably not counting any artisan working alone or assisted by a single craftsman as a manufacturer, whereas in 1850 the Chamber of Commerce was taking these into account.

By this last date there were, according to the *Almanach du Commerce,* twenty-seven depots in Paris belonging to provincial factories situated chiefly in the Parisian region, but also in the Limousin, Cher, Allier, Marne, Mièvre and the southwest of France. There was a depot for the Meissen factory as well, and another on Toy's premises for English porcelain.

Business turnovers fan out in diversity.

In 1807 Lefebvre, with 60 craftsmen, had a turnover of 350,000 francs, or 5,833 per craftsman, but Dagoty with 90 craftsmen was only making 300,000 francs (3,333 francs per craftsman); Nast with 83 craftsmen had a gross product of 200,000 francs (2,170 per craftsman), whereas

71 Queen's factory. Lobed plate. Large cornflowers painted from life. *Circa* 1780. Paris, Coll. Guy Passerat. Diam. 23.5 cm. (9$\frac{1}{5}$ in.). Mark 209.

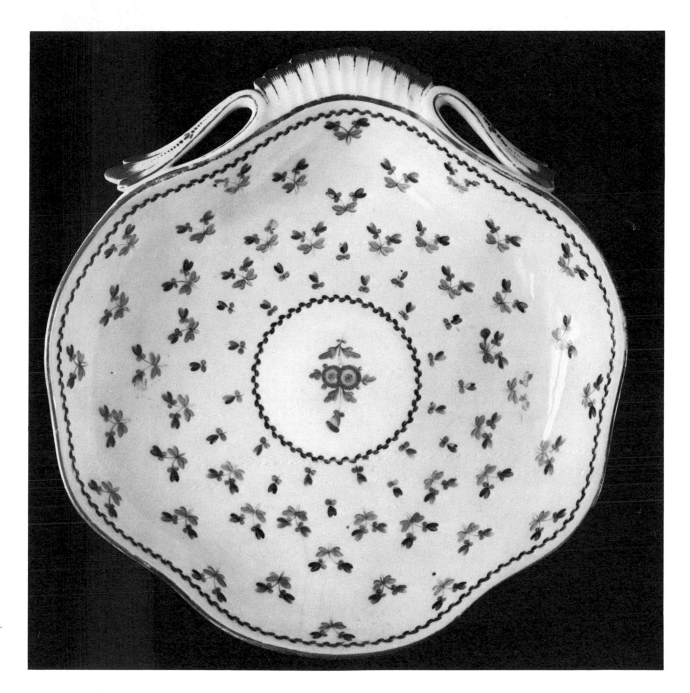

72 Queen's factory. Shell-shaped bowl. Polychrome and gold. *Circa* 1780. Paris, Coll. Guy Passerat. Diam. 24.5 cm. (9³/₅ in.). Mark 209.

Darte Frères, with 150 workmen, totalled only 70,000 francs.

By themselves alone, the decorators and gilders achieved a turnover of 4,369,200 francs, giving an average of 32,606 francs per workshop. Seven industrialists only reached a turnover of somewhere between 100 and 200,000 francs.

The capital was sometimes supplied by sleeping partners: we still find deeds of sleeping partnership—the Baronne de Plessen put up 112,000 francs for Merlin-Hall in 1820—but most of the deeds relate to family or commercial associations: Darte Frères, or Schoelcher and his son. Occasionally this partnership is part of the marriage contract: for instance Guy had taken his son into partnership through a marriage contract, and Louis Joseph Darte entered into partnership with Auguste Remi under the same circumstances.

We also see two enterprises amalgamate to form a more powerful one, for instance Dagoty and Edouard Honoré, the latter supported by his father as a sleeping partner.

We likewise notice dynasties of porcelain manufacturers or craftsmen. Some, their fortunes made, left the profession and offered their experience in the service of the partnership: Henri Nast was to become deputy mayor of the 8th Arrondissement and under this title was decorated with the *Légion d'honneur*. Others stayed with their craft to become great industrialists. Honoré belonged to the Conseil général des Manufactures (General Council of Factories), and his opinion was sought on any decisions of an economic character.

The importance of partnership funds is extremely variable. In the course of the first half of the 19th century we have picked out only two 'millionaires'. In 1816 Pouyat & Lebourgeois brought their partnership funds up to 1,200,000 francs, 500,000 francs of it from collective funds (manufacturers' contributions) and 700,000 francs from the funds of sleeping partners, represented by shares. Then in 1839 Auguste Decaen, who had factories for porcelain—and also faience—close to Lyons, plus a decorators' workshop in Paris, likewise reached 1,200,000 francs with his partnership funds, but twenty years later. Next come Deruelle and Leullier with 400,000 francs in 1837, then on a much more modest level Revil and Merlin-Hall, having in 1814 and 1826 respectively 200 to 250,000 francs. The factory of Talmours & Hurel ran perfectly on 160,000 francs in 1841, and the decorator André—subsidized by the banker of the same name—climbed to the 100,000-franc level in 1832. A single partnership fund of 100,000 francs in 1839 was controlled by the factory-owner Clauss and by Margaine, while the decorator Francisque Rousseau did not exceed 70,000 francs.

In another connexion, we have seen that the fortunes of manufacturers' wives were often important in serving to swell the finances of the establishment. If a premature death occurred the factory was sometimes in straits. In such cases various solutions were envisaged. We have, for example, seen Charles Barthélemy Guy enter into partnership with his son so that the latter might assert his claim to his mother's estate without capital being withdrawn. One of the causes of Flamen-Fleury's bankruptcy was the death of his wife.

According to statistics from the Préfecture de Police in 1807 there were 92,000 workmen in Paris, only 1,200 of whom were in the ceramics sector: porcelain, faience and earthenware. This second figure calls for caution; we have seen, after all, that Madame Dihl in 1806 put the number of outside craftsmen at 4,000. We think that the number 1,200 needs to be interpreted as the total number of ceramics craftsmen working in factories.

Those craftsmen aged between eighteen and forty represented only half the 1,200 craftsmen, because of the decimation caused by wars. In the porcelain factories the number of craftsmen fluctuated, as in the 18th century, in sympathy with

73   Queen's factory.
Half-moon *jardinière* (flower
stand).   One of a pair.
Circa 1780.
Geneva, Musée de l'Ariana.
L. 30 cm. (11⁴/₅ in.).
Mark 209.

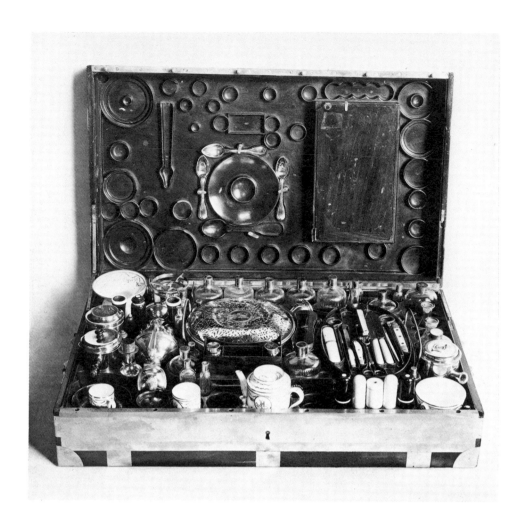

74–75 Queen's factory. Spittoon, rouge-jar and eye-bath. Polychrome and gold decoration: contained in Marie Antoinette's travelling-case *(nécessaire de voyage)*. The case itself bears the signature of Palma in Paris, and the gold artefacts the hall-mark of Chappenat and those of Paris for 1787 and 1788. Besides the toilet items the casket holds a teapot and two cylindrical porcelain cups. All the porcelain and silver objects have the Queen's monogram. It weighs altogether 50 kg. (111 lbs), more than 9 kg. of which consists of gold arte-facts. Mme Campan notes in her *Mémoires* how fond the Queen was of this *nécessaire*. When in 1791 she ordered it to be cleaned, the wardrobe maid instructed to do so perceived that it was effectively a preparation for the royal family's departure, and raised the alarm. The case left France in circumstances that are still mystifying, for ever since the Revolutionary period the gold items have shown the official Milanese stamp, dated 1794. *Circa* 1787. Paris, Musée du Louvre. Spittoon: Ht. 12 cm. (4²/₃ in). Mark 209.

either the general economic situation, or with the situation in the enterprise itself. In that year of 1807, Fleury showed a pay-roll of 20 to 60 craftsmen. Numerically the most important factory was that of Darte Senior, with 150 craftsmen. Next, comprising 90 craftsmen, came: Dagoty, Pouyat-Russinger and Neppel. Nast had 83, Dihl hardly more than 30 to 40 and Revil only 14.

By 1844 the situation had shifted, because most of the factories had been moved out into the provinces leaving behind nothing but decorators' workshops in Paris. Pétry and Ronsse were employing 500 craftsmen at Vierzon and from 100 to 110 in Paris; Honoré had 160 craftsmen at Champroux and 40 in Paris, but 'outside'. Clauss, staying on in Paris, had 25 craftsmen; Talmours & Hurel with 70 craftsmen in their factory counted as two of the most important Paris manufacturers, yet were easily outdone by Louis André who employed 300 craftsmen in his *usine* (works) and 200 more 'outside'. Although overshadowed by such enterprises, the craft was still at the stage where the decorators worked in numerous small workshops by themselves or with a single assistant.

The inquiry by the Paris Chamber of Commerce in 1850 disclosed a total of nearly 4,000 craftsmen working on porcelain, more than 1,000 of them being

women. But amongst them there were nearly 1,400 outside craftsmen, including 800 women but not counting children under sixteen years of age. The craftsmen were designated as: ornament-painters, landscapists, painters of letters or labels, monograms or coats of arms, muffle-operators, gilders, grinders and their helpers; the women were burnishers, a few of them painters or gilders.

The wage-earners were paid by the day or by the piece. Men's wages in factories varied between 2,50 and 15 francs per day, and in the decorators' workshops from 2 to 12 francs. Women earned between 1,50 and 2,50 francs with the manufacturers and 1 to 3 francs with the decorators. Only three women, exceptionally, earned more. One alone, an artist, earned 20 francs a day. The women, most of whom worked at home, incidentally, were usually remunerated by the piece (870, as against 126 payed by the day). Lastly, the off-season was not the same for the manufacturers as it was for the decorators; January to May in the latter case, June, July und August for the manufacturers. The work schedules were 'from 7 till 7' in winter and 'from 8 till 8' in summer. Of these twelve hours of daily attendance—six days a week—one hour was set aside for lunch.

Finally, as in the 18th century, the Parisian craftsman under the Empire enjoyed only very relative freedom. The law of Germinal 22nd, Year XI had instituted a compulsory *livret* (booklet) for the working class. An order of Year XII stipulated that when signing on, the craftsmen had to give his booklet to the employer, who would return it to him on his departure. Without the booklet the craftsman could be arrested for vagrancy. In 1821 Pouyat Frères asked the Minister of Justice to have eight of their apprentice craftsmen punished for vagrancy: they had left despite committing themselves for five years and incurring debts. The Minister referred it to the tribunals. In another affair, the Minister's refusal to intervene was due to the absence of any conspiracy between the workers. Indeed, sometimes strikes did break out, principally on public building-sites. There was one in September 1807 in Lefebvre's factory. Evidently the shortage of labour was great and the booklet must have brought the enterprises a certain guarantee of stability.

Concerning the localization of factories or workshops, the findings of the Chamber of Commerce in 1850 inform us that the porcelain-decorating industry centred on the 5th Arrondissement of that time, with 75 industrialists employing 1,227 craftsmen and a turnover totalling 2,194,800 francs. Heading the list were the districts of the Porte Saint-Martin, Le Temple, the Faubourgs Saint-Denis and Poissonnière, and the Porte Saint-Denis. It is interesting to observe that the locality of the porcelain trade—or rather its manufacture actually reduced to its decoration—had hardly shifted since the days of the *Ancien Régime*.

On the other hand, the salesrooms are almost always in elegant districts which change at the whim of fashion. It was chiefly the quarter of the Boulevards, in particular the Boulevard des Italiens where Schoelcher kept his salesroom from the beginning of the century. Balzac wrote: 'the Boulevard des Italiens is today what the Pont Neuf was in 1650. Everybody in the public eye crosses it at least once a day...' It is close to the quarter of Antin-Poissonnière, the home of financiers like Ouvrard and marshals like Ney or Lefebvre. It was near to the 'Nouvelle Athènes', where numerous personalities from the theatre were moving in—Mademoiselle Mars, Talma, Mademoiselle Duchesnois. All these people received, bought and gave one another presents, and congregated at the Café de Paris, the Café des Arts or even at the famous 'Bains Chinois' (Chinese Baths). Schoelcher was not alone as a dealer in porcelain, for Dagoty, supplier to the Empress, had a delightful shop on Boulevard Poissonnière. It is not uninteresting to observe that this district to this day contains many shops selling ceramics, as do the Rue de Paradis and the Rue Bleue, both nearby.

Ill. 137

Another fashionable place was the Palais Royal, renovated under the Restoration. The Dartes already kept a shop at the Palais du Tribunat. The Escalier de Cristal was installed there. If Schoelcher was paying a high rent (7,000 francs in 1816), those in the Palais Royal who received payment were in the same situation. The *Almanach historique et commercial du Palais Royal ou le Conducteur de l'étranger dans cet édifice pour l'année 1827* lists the price of hiring an arcade in 1823: 8,000 francs. It adds 'but today their rents must be greater still by reason of the fact that dealers have imagined that a shop at the Palais Royal was a pedestal for ascending to Fortune. In the brilliant shops occupying the back of the galleries is the tasteful assembly of all the richest and most elegant things that Man has been able to invent in which to indulge his love of luxury and his pleasures… Fashion has established its empire here: its priests and priestesses have sovereign rule; from here it spreads into all departments…' The famous 'Escalier de Cristal' actually did owe its name to a crystal staircase, and exhibited crystal glass, bronzes and porcelain wares. The courtyard of Les Fontaines where Bondeux had set himself up was annexed to the Palais Royal.

Other commercial centres collected in the *passages*. Around 1826, Parisians witnessed a proliferation of *passages* where shops were springing up. Some of them, by the way, have survived. They were mainly sited in the district of the Opéra and the Boulevards. The Passage de l'Opéra was particularly favoured by customers[2]. With its various galleries it was a very important trading complex. Baruch Weil ran a salesroom in the Galerie de l'Horloge (Clock Gallery), between a seller of hat-silks and a tailor, not far from 'Polichinelle Vampire' where toys were sold. Gaillard had settled in the Galerie du Baromètre.

Lastly, other salesrooms such as Feuillet and Rihouët stood on the Rue de la Paix.

76 Nast.
Succeeding their father, the Nast brothers won the highest award at the Exhibition of 1819, as well as personal congratulations from Louis XVIII. They had been displaying some outstanding pieces: a clock in biscuit, *l'Amour fait passer le Temps*, tall colums, table-service pieces with modelled ornaments including a tiered tray *(guéridon)* for sweetmeats (fig. 7) and monumental vases. The left-hand one (fig. 1) measured no less than 1 m m.50. Figure 2 shows a smaller vase, some undecorated specimens of which have been preserved: they measure 67 cm. (29²/₅ in.). Along with these luxury pieces the Nast brothers exhibited porcelain clock-faces (fig. 8), costing much less to manufacture than the enamel dials previously used. The print is taken from the *Annales de l'industrie*, published by Le Normand and Moléon.
Paris, private coll. Ht. 67 cm. (29²/₅ in.).
Unmarked.

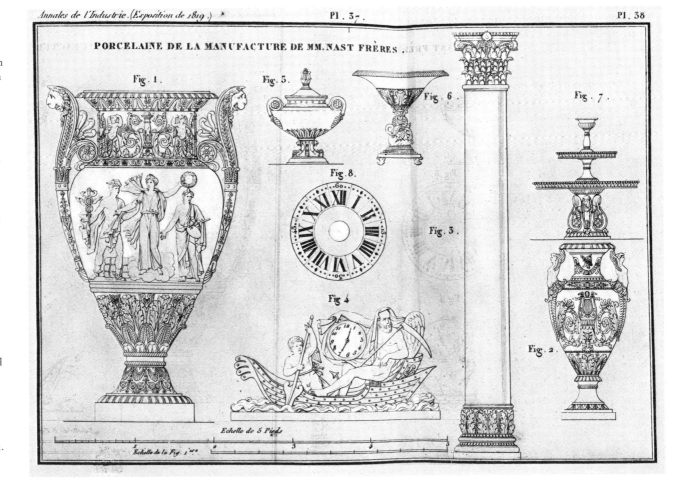

[2] We might explain that we are speaking of the old Opera-House—where the singing was in Italian—which, of course, was close to the Boulevard des Italiens.

101

77 Nast.
Vase of plain undecorated
porcelain, resembling the
ones displayed at the 1827
exhibition (see previous
page). These exquisitely
executed, large-scale vases
show modelled details that
are exceptionally becoming.
The absence of decoration
emphasizes its purity of shape,
as do the reserved panels in
biscuit which were to have
been finished with a bronze-
like matt gold.
Paris, private coll. Ht. 67 cm.
($29^2/_5$ in.).
Unmarked.

Industrial and Commercial Exhibitions

A particularly interesting source of documentation is supplied by the industrial and commercial exhibitions which were held in Paris.

Today, such exhibitions no longer bring us so much of interest and curiosity as the first manifestations of their kind, which mark out the economic history of France from 1789 onwards. Those we shall discuss are innovations which, by virtue of their rarity, their importance and the quality of their exhibits, allow a latter-day reconstruction of the technical, artistic and economic evolution of French industry.

Besides this, it is of great interest to study in the Official Reports the opinions of the best qualified men of the time. The juries were made up of the most eminent personalities and were originally presided over by the Minister of the Interior and Commerce. Notables such as Costaz, Baron Dupin, Brongniart, Ebelmen and Salvétat guaranteed the reliability of official documents—the important reports in particular.

The industrial exhibitions of the first half of the 19th century had an unquestionable influence on the emergence of the big factories, for the distinctions were handed out not only on the strength of the products' quality but also their quantity and inexpensiveness, the special object being to promote exports.

In order to stimulate the manufacturers of France as a whole, François de Neufchâteau organised the first 'Exhibition of the Products of French Industry'. It was held on the Champ-de-Mars on the last days of Year VI (1798) and was surrounded

jacob Petit

Cheminée en Porcelaine de M.ʳ Jacob Petit.

L'INDUSTRIE

78 Jacob Petit.
Design for a mantlepiece of
solid porcelain, executed for
the Exhibition in 1834. An
all-round artist, Jacob Petit
himself engraved this illustrative plate. About 1830 he
had published a *Recueil de
décorations intérieures* in which
his imagination had been
unleashed onto all sorts of
techniques. He did not make
table-service items for long,
but concentrated instead on
ornamental pieces, reviving
the Rococo style by infusing
into it an exuberance such
as France had never known
before.
Although challenged by
certain of his contempo-
raries, on 'the weird outlines' which he gave to his
shapes, he met with stupen-
dous success – and a dramatic
bankruptcy, caused primarily
by the competition of
plagiarists against whom he
had been winning costly
lawsuits.
From *L'Industrie, description
pittoresque de l'industrie
française,* published by
Stéphane Flachat in 1834.

by a pomp worthy of the ceremonies celebrating the goddess of Reason.

Of the sixty-eight manufacturers enrolled, five producers of ceramics (including two Paris porcelain-makers) exhibited their wares in company with the first pencils by Conté and watches by Bréguet. Alone out of the five, Dihl won for his porcelain pictures one of the twelve distinctions awarded on this occasion.

The Cour du Louvre housed the next two exhibitions in Years X and XI (1801 and 1802).

If some of the manufacturers from the *Ancien Régime* were still in evidence, such as Russinger, Potter or Fourmy, they had changed their style of manufacture and were exhibiting utilitarian objects: ordinary crockery, crucibles or sanitary fitments *(hygiocérames)* made of a hybrid porcelain related to stoneware, and resistant to great temperature changes. Of the other participants, some were short-lived factory owners, whilst others watched their establishments soar in the 19th century, as Baignol did in Limoges. Yet we should note that the champions in these exhibitions were chiefly the faience makers: Villeroy (from Vaudrevanges), Boch (from Septfontaines) later to become Villeroy & Boch; or Ulzschneider of Sarreguemines.

We shall confine ourselves to studying those national exhibitions which were of a commercial nature, excluding special exhibitions for State-run factories and of course any which were organized in the provinces.

When François de Neufchâteau was appointed Minister of the Interior under the Directory, after the *coup d'Etat* of Fructidor 18th, Year VI, he was confronted with a disastrous financial situation, partly due to difficulties abroad: the expedition to Egypt and fight against England. Alone amongst her allies England had not signed the peace treaty with the French Republic and soon built up a second coalition against her.

France, therefore, saw no option but to provide for her own needs and develop her industries intensively. She equally had to withstand the competition from foreign goods coming from various countries.

As the first trade fair of the Empire, the exhibition of industrial goods in 1806 assembled for twenty-four days more than fourteen hundred exhibitors arranged on the promenade of Les Invalides, which was invaded by specially erected constructions of papier mâché.

Particularly noticeable were the abundance and excellence of items made of pipe clay.

Dihl and Guérhard, who enjoyed a new lease of glory under the Imperial pomp, were decorated with a gold medal, while Nast, Caron & Lefebvre, Dagoty, Darte Frères, Despréz and Gonord won silver medals. Honourable mentions were shared between Pouyat and Russinger, Neppel and Bertrand.

Pouyat & Russinger had displayed a group in biscuit showing an appropriate subject: 'the Victor of Austerlitz brings to Europe the Olive-Branch of Peace'. Nast displayed busts of the Emperor and Empress as well as some monumental vases. The most noted innovation was a new colour, chrome green, discovered by Vauquelin, the famous chemist attached to the Nast factory.

The economic aspect of these manifestations was emphasized by three instructions to the exhibitors; they were to mark items during production so as to prove their French origin, give the standard price of each object and finally to fix to each piece a certified declaration stating whether the article was in common production, an object for trade or an isolated creation made expressly for the exhibition.

After 1806 the political upheavals postponed the organization of a new exhibition and it was not until thirteen years later that such a trade fair could take place. In choosing his name-day for a visit to the exhibition, Louis XVIII intended to demonstrate the store he set by this first exhibition under the Restoration. It was held once more in the Palais du Louvre and was paired with a display of fine arts. In this way Louis XVIII officially asserted the vitality of French industry under the monarchy.

The Press did its best to attract the inquisitive, and by way of itinerary for the visit recommended the route followed by the King. The royal tour took five hours! In order to add splendour to this fair the royal manufacturers figured amongst the exhibitors. The Sèvres factory, therefore, took part in this exhibition, although it had its own private exhibitions with the other royal factories. If its presence made it an object of emulation by the other factories, it does not seem that Sèvres benefitted from having its goods compared with those of the private factories. Indeed, a contemporary opposed the admission of Sèvres as 'utterly futile and even harmful to trade', since Limoges did just as well and even better. Was it diplomacy on the part of the members of the jury that, when the awards were made, Sèvres won an honourable mention, Schoelcher and Alluaud (of Limoges) a silver medal, and Nast a gold medal?

But let us return to August 25th 1819.

When the King entered the hall reserved for the most precious exhibits, he was greeted by the following sight: 'On a great table set in the middle of the hall were placed porcelain wares made by Parisian industry. All around, one perceived a collection of alabaster, some artificial eyes, articles of spun glass, lamp-globes with transfer printed decoration, paste jewellery, instruments of navigation... a brass skeleton for use by painters, pictures painted on glass...' What would one think today of such an assembly? The hall was decorated with Gobelin hangings, looking-glasses both engraved and with portraits and prints— everything Parisian in origin.

His Majesty halted especially in front of the Nast brothers, the successors to their father, and said to them pleasantly: 'I am glad to see talent passing on from father to son: I conjure you to cultivate it.' We must imagine the King's admiration before the (admittedly commonplace) feats performed by the House of Nast. It had exhibited biscuit-ware Corinthian columns more than four feet tall, a clock likewise in biscuit *Amour fait passer le* Ill. 76 *Temps* (Love makes the Time pass), a soup-tureen a foot in diameter, and huge, skilfully painted vases.

To judge by the descriptions of the objects shown, it would seem that the manufacturers were determined, as in 1806, to outdo one another in virtuosity. Most of the vases exhibited had a height of one or one and a half metres and were painted and gilded in the richest fashion. Schoelcher reproduced on his vases some contemporary or Classical pictures by Poussin and David. The other Parisian manufacturers to be officially rewarded were Darte, together with Dagoty and Honoré. These last mentioned displayed 'Wedgwood'-type vases after the bas-reliefs of the Fontaine des Innocents by Jean Goujon.

A new class of artist was represented for the first time—the decorator of porcelain. Louis Pierre Froment had painted *Amphitrite portée sur les Eaux* after Lucas Giordano on a tray by Nast, and Legort had decorated two vases by Lefebvre.

Some porcelain makers had already specialized in the manufacture and sale of colours. Besides producing porcelain, Dihl was leaning in this direction as well, successfully exploiting his talents as a chemist. A newcomer who was subsequently much talked about, Mortelèque, had ingeniously painted an old man's head, using the entire range of colours that he had made available to porcelain painters. A few years later, Mortelèque had become one of the main suppliers to French decorators and was exporting colours for considerable sums of money.

The new factories for transfer printing on ceramics also demonstrated their growing importance at this exhibition in 1819. Gonord, whose workshops were operative no later than 1806, received an order for reproducing the portraits of the royal family, as well as for decorating a service, each plate of which was to be adorned with the map of a Départment.

Two further transfer printing factories

79 Escalier de Cristal. Porcelain and crystal-glass displayed at the Exhibition of 1844.
From *Exposition de l'industrie française, année 1844*, published by Jules Barat.

set up in Paris were also in evidence: Sponner's and—more important—Frémont's, who was none other than the collaborator with Legros d'Anisy, a specialist in transfer printing on ceramics and other mediums for ten years or so. Frémont, a forward-looking man, had not been ashamed to proclaim his prices, and on the occasion of this exhibition had even arranged what we would call an 'advertising sweepstake', something that had tremendously surprised and almost shocked the public.

The improvements introduced into the ceramics industry after the exhibitions held under the Empire and the Republic were shown off at the 1819 exhibition. On the technical side 'jiggering' by machine was particularly noteworthy, as were the relief-ornaments and transfer printing, together with the new chemical colours resistant to high temperatures.

Economically speaking, the developing production of pipe-clay ware or 'semi-porcelain' grew at such a prodigious rate that porcelain makers had to make every effort to hold their own. 'Semi-porcelain', usually decorated by processes of transfer printing, reached an enormous output and huge outlets because of its moderate prices, and competed seriously with the porcelain market. The factories for creamware (*faïence fine*) belonging to Saint-Cricq-Cazeaux which had been set up in Creil and Montereau employed respectively three- and four hundred craftsmen and turned out annually the considerable figure of twelve to fifteen hundred thousand ceramic items apiece. The large number of craftsmen as well as the quantity of pieces produced was a new factor which marked the transition of these establishments from the status of handicrafts to that of mass production.

The exhibition of 1823 only served to stress the main features of the one held in 1819.

More and more, the porcelain factories were withdrawing from Paris. New patents were registered which allowed the use of machines designed to turn out and to decorate ceramics.

At this exhibition Honoré displayed pieces decorated in accordance with the two patents taken out in 1822, dealing firstly with the application of lithography to porcelain decoration, and secondly with the production of coloured grounds at high temperature in the first firing, a process that dispensed with refiring and all the risks that it entails.

Seventy-three Départments took part in this exhibition, which was held at the Louvre. Brongniart, the director of the royal factory of Sèvres, was a member of the jury.

For the first time the jury members defined two categories for the exhibitors of porcelain: the manufacturers and the decorators. The general movement towards lowering prices was strongly encouraged by the authorities.

Among the manufacturers Nast once again found himself awarded a gold medal, while Denuelle received a bronze for his tortoiseshell grounds.

As for the decorators, the jury differentiated between those who decorated by hand, such as André of Rue Notre-Dame-de-Nazareth, who was accorded an honourable mention, and those who used mechanical aids, like Legros d'Anisy who received a silver medal.

Nast, Denuelle, André and Legros d'Anisy were the only Parisian ceramists to win awards. The other distinctions went to provincial factories.

An amusing and significant detail is that

PORCELAINES-HONORÉ

80 Honoré.
Porcelain displayed at the Exhibition of 1844. The relief-work and fancy outlines are growing, aided by new techniques whereby hitherto impossible feats of audacity become feasible. This exhibition drew together objects with a maximum of decoration. Sèvres exhibited some improbable pieces: amongst other things a *jardinière* having columns, caryatids and arcades which some claimed 'would have been suitable for supporting, not a few flowers, but the gardens of Queen Semiramis herself'. This accounts for Jules Burat's comment that 'the pieces by Honoré retain their simplicity'.
From *Exposition de l'industrie française, année 1844,* published by Jules Burat.

documents state that the royal factory of Sèvres exhibited 'some fine wares', including cups 'imitated with great care' by Pillivuyt of Foëscy (Cher).

Exhibitions in the provinces succeeded one another at a fast rate. Caen, Bordeaux and Toulouse also organized trade-fairs which were not limited in scope to their particular region.

In Paris, Charles X personally decorated Baruch Weil on the occasion of the 1827 exhibition. For all that, Baruch Weil won only an honourable mention for 'his varied goods'. In fact commercial and economic considerations had always been amongst the Government's criteria.

Nast, 'always at the forefront', received yet another gold medal. The other Parisian manufactures to be distinguished won only honourable mentions. Besides Baruch Weil these were: Flamen-Fleury; Discry; Honoré and Boilleau et Cie. The one silver medal awarded to a ceramist was given to Saint-Cricq-Cazeaux for his creamware from Creil.

The exhibition of 1834, together with that of 1819, was one of the greatest trade fairs of the first half of the 19th century. For sixty days nearly two thousand five hundred exhibitors occupied the Place de la Concorde.

The provinces near and far were assuming ever more importance to the detriment of Paris. Creamware asserted its supremacy in the ceramics field: two of its chief producers received a gold medal, to wit Saint-Cricq-Cazeaux at Creil and Lebeuf at Montereau. However, Nast had his previous gold medal confirmed, while Mortelèque and Legros d'Anisy received silver medals. The other distinctions conferred upon Parisian manufacturers were bronze medals to: Denuelle, not for his unpopular porcelain but his money-saving method of *encastage* (stacking); and to Honoré, whose partner Grouvelle had invented a mechanical press for 'drying out' pastes. Finally, two honourable mentions were handed out, one to Discry for 'the perfection of the ridges, corners and straight parts' of his pieces, and the other to Jacob Petit who was exhibiting for the first time. Incidentally, this caused a furore at the exhibition. The jury did not omit to specify that this distinction was awarded solely on technical and economic grounds. In fact, the 'three champions' of ceramics in 1834, according to official reports, were still Sarreguemines, Creil and Montereau. Their products were constantly improving and their cost prices were dropping on an impressive scale.

The headway made by creamware on the national ceramics market was to assert itself once more at the exhibition of 1839. The improvement of the transfer printing was one of the factors involved.

The Parisian porcelain manufacturers won only bronze medals or honourable mentions; Honoré, whose factory incidentally was at Champroux (Allier), Jacob Petit who sold in Paris the white ware made at Fontainebleau, and Clauss, the sole producer having an establishment in Paris itself, and only one at that.

On the other hand the superiority of Paris triumphed in the field of porcelain decoration.

Discry and Talmours received a gold medal. A silver medal was conferred upon Francisque Rousseau and another upon Halot. Several honourable mentions were awarded to the decorators Chapelle, Julien-Moureau and Vion. Lastly, the suppliers of colours were not forgotten: Dubois-Mortelèque (successor to his father-in-law Mortelèque), and Defossés Frères received a silver medal and an

honourable mention respectively. We shall not mention here the participants left unrewarded.

Technique was becoming increasingly refined and Parisian decorators seemed to vie with one another in richness.

Material, shapes and decorations evolved further and the 1844 exhibiton offered various examples of this.

Among the Parisian ceramists, Talmours & Hurel (Successor to Discry) was once again awarded a gold medal, and Honoré a silver medal, as were Pétry and Ronsse. These manufacturers with a factory at Vierzon (Cher) employed not less than one hundred craftsmen in Paris, working on decoration. Bronze medals were similarly awarded to Halot, and Louis André et Cie—the latter being manufacturers at Foëscy (Cher) and decorators at Paris. Two Parisian decorators alone received honourable mentions: Edmond Corbin who was employing not less than two hundred outside craftsmen, and Lebourg. But it was principally the colour manufacturers who were encouraged by the jury: Discry and Rousseau received gold medals, Colville, Binet and Desfossés silver medals, and Chapelle an honourable mention.

Decorators thus had the possibility of executing the most varied and difficult decorations that their fertile imaginations suggested to them.

The last exhibition of this half-century was in 1849. The porcelain trade was struggling to recover from the severe upset it had suffered in 1848. The toughest establishments kept running. Some were mentioned for the first time: among them Lachassagne, a decorator in Paris, partner to Ruaud of Limoges, Tinet, a manufacturer at Montreuil, decorator in Paris, Gille and Grenon.

---

[1] The operation of putting pieces on supports or into saggers prior to firing.

81 Unidentified factory.
Basket borne by two biscuit
figurines. Early 19th
century. Palacio Nacional de
Queluz. Ht. 41 cm. (16²/₅ in).
Unmarked.

After discussing these numerous national exhibitions we could not pass over the first international exhibition, which was held at London in 1851, in the famous Crystal Palace (which was later destroyed by fire) constructed specially for the occasion. The Victoria & Albert Museum was built from the proceeds.

The official report on the 'ceramic arts' had been drawn up by Ebelmen and Salvétat, of Sèvres. It surveyed the state of porcelain in France in 1850. More than forty factories had a total annual output worth more than ten million francs, and to this one needs to add two or three millions realized by the decoration of porcelain.

The French hard-paste porcelain industry was represented in London by the Sèvres factory in particular but also by several manufacturers from Limoges (Gorsas & Périer, Jouhanneaud & Dubois), by Honoré (still based on .Champroux and Paris), by Gille (of Paris) and finally by Jacob Petit whose two establishments were sited in Fontainebleau and Paris. Besides this, the Nast brothers had been asked to exhibit a few of their pieces, even though their factory was no longer in operation. Their renown abroad and the quality of their goods deserved such a tribute.

Several Parisian manufacturers were rewarded: Gille, and Tinet & Talmours. The Sèvres factory won the grand medal of honour.

Paris accommodated the second universal exhibition in 1855, but by that time the era of mass production had really begun.

Technique

We shall not repeat here the principles of porcelain-making technique that we have briefly described above. We shall confine ourselves to giving information on the inventions brought about in the course of the first half of the 19th century, basing this both upon the reports of industrial exhibitions and on the patent registrations. Let it be noted, however, that inventions were sometimes not covered by a patent until some time after being put into use.

The first half of the 19th century turned out to be especially fertile in innovations of all kinds for refining every aspect of ceramic technique. At every stage of porcelain production, discoveries, either French or else foreign but used in France, and often sanctioned by patents, introduced improvements or procedures that reduced man-power.

Thus, in the grinding of porcelain bodies —a very delicate operation—first Alluaud and then Parent, both from Limoges, took out patents in 1826 and 1847. By the middle of the 19th century Sèvres was grinding clays using pan mills known as 'American' mills. They had first been tried out in England.

The very important operation of pugging and drying out the bodies was subjected to new processes. The first of these, published in Paris by Grouvelle and Honoré in 1853, consisted in pugging the body (reduced to slip after the surplus water had been poured off), by putting in into very closely woven bags which were left to drain before being pressed. A second principle was based on an actual filtration process induced by atmospheric pres-

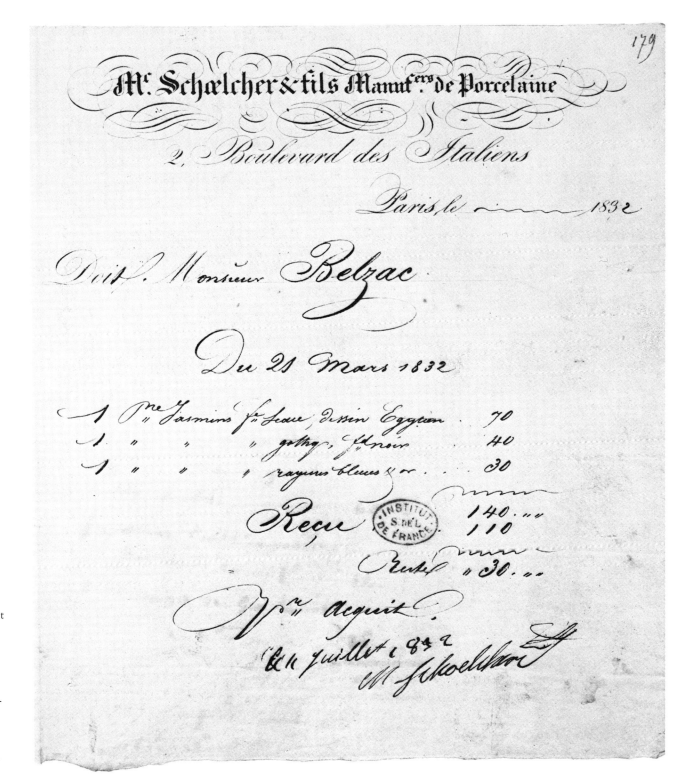

82   Schœlcher & Son.
This invoice is interesting in
several respects: Balzac, a
friend of Victor Schœlcher's
and a porcelain-lover, bought
from him some 'vases with
Egyptian designs' and others
'Gothic with black ground',
as late as 1832. The co-
existence and the longevity
of these two types of decoration is hereby established.
In the second place Balzac's
biographers note that this
invoice was duly settled – an
extraordinary occurrence in
view of the writer's notorious husbandry.
Paris, Bibliothèque de
l'Institut.

sure. Talbot Frères of Paris had an apparatus for this purpose set up at Alluaud's Limoges factory in 1834. Various tests at Sèvres in 1843 involved laying the unpugged body on a cloth resting on dry and very thick plaster. Unfortunately the filtration was not strong enough.

Throwing, as an isolated job, had nothing more to gain, but in combination with moulding it made for versatile and effective methods such as skin-mouldings[1] and various methods of jiggering.

Amongst the new techniques for moulding (although the subject slightly exceeds our terms of reference), we must mention dry-moulding, exploited for the manufacture of buttons by the industrialist Bapterose in about 1849. His process differed from Prosser's which had been applied in England for ten years or so. Bapterose struck his buttons in batches of five hundred at a time. No later than 1809, Potter had successfully press-moulded a large number of coat buttons and, since 1837, Madame Matelin of Paris had been attempting to manufacture *petits creux* (pomade jars, saucers, etc.) by compressing clay into metal dies, but success in the case of plates had not been complete. In 1838 the same idea prompted Delpech to experiment in Cahors. Both testers were held up by the difficulty of subjecting all the points of an item to an even pressure, which cannot be achieved by the impact of a press.

By way of ingenious adaptations of modelling by hand we must mention the rouletting and engine-turning practised by Nast for decorating porcelain, which antedate the registration of his patent in 1810. One of the peculiarities of these techniques is that they may be applied either to the raw or the stoved body, or even to fired pieces. Up till then porcelain had not undergone the process of engine-turning such as was employed by Bougon & Chalot of Chantilly under a patent of 1815; this is a combination of moulding and turning, the piece to be decorated being rotated. The same operation of rouletting and engine-turning is for finishing off.

In 1817, Baudet Junior of Fleurines suggested an eccentric wheel, and different methods of jiggering to be applied to round and oval shapes respectively. These were being practised in Vienna as early as 1812, and also at Sèvres and Chantilly. As a result the calibration, especially of plates, offered a tremendous advantage which Sèvres generalized about 1834.

Although the idea of fashioning an object by casting goes back to around 1790, at Tournay for soft paste and Rue Fontaine-au-Roy for hard paste, (thanks to one of its craftsmen, Tendelle), it is Ferdinand Régnier, overseer of kilns and porcelain bodies at Sèvres until 1848, who took credit for almost all the refinements derived from it. After 1814 the process allowed plaques to be produced, the dimensions of which by 1833 might reach 1 metre by 1,33 metres; and similarly from 1848, vases 92 cm in height as well as bowls 83 cm in diameter appeared.

Ronsse and Pétry of Paris patented a sagger-design in 1837, under the name of *encastage à bâte et à contre-bâte*. It described a sort of sagger that allowed the craftsman to dispense with the lute-bob[2] joining the cases. Two years later, Régnier at Sèvres succeded in modifying the *encastage à cul de lampe* (consisting of superposed rings), invented in about 1800.

Equipment for firing was greatly refined in form and in the quality of fuels used. Notable improvements related principally to kilns with 'bags' which appear to

[1] Skin-moulding (*moulage à la housse*), a cross between 'roughing out' on the wheel and moulding. The thrower roughs out the piece, endeavouring to achieve the desired shape and thickness as far as possible: the piece is now called a 'skin' (*housse*). Still soft, this skin is placed in a hollow plaster mould and made to assume its exact shape by being pressed on with a sponge.

[2] 'Lute' is an argillaceous paste with which piles of saggers are fixed to ensure that they stay properly upright throughout the firing.

have been first constructed in France by Guéttard at Sèvres *circa* 1769 in the early stages of hard-paste porcelain production. They originally had neither a second chamber nor a second arch. From 1804 to 1851 we count no fewer than twenty-six patents of invention registered in France for improving kilns and firing-processes, not including the refinements introduced by Dihl & Guérhard in Paris, Alluaud in Limoges and by Sèvres factory. Most of these kilns were used for differing sorts of ceramics. Finally, in 1842, Sèvres constructed a two-tiered kiln for hard-paste porcelain.

As for fuel, efforts were directed towards burning mineral coal: we have seen experiments with this in the 18th century. As early as 1804, Revol (Lyons) took out a patent for a kiln designed to fire faience with coal, but it was only in 1846, after many refinements, that it was at last possible to derive substantial advantages from it: Laurent & Money (Bourg-la-Reine) thereby realized a saving of fifty per cent, and the patent of Vital-Roux &

Merkens (Noirlac) definitively established in France the firing of hard-paste porcelain with coal.

However, to mitigate the inconvenience due to the smoke deposited during combustion onto certain high-temperature grounds such as blue, attempts were made to fire 'with the combined flames of wood and pit-coal' (Chavandier, at Cirey [Marne], 1851). While this fuel was widely used in Great Britain, others were advocated in France, especially gas extracted from peat or the coke-gas used in blast-furnaces. When in 1822 Dodé rented a site on Rue des Trois-Bornes from Baruch Weil, there stood on it a 'gas-kiln which the said S. Weil has had constructed'.

Much progress was achieved in hard-paste porcelain production by means of polishing. The technique adopted came from lapidary work, using a wheel for polishing inevitably lustreless areas as well as blemishes. If Brongniart appears in about 1806 to have introduced this operation, (which had been practised in Germany as early as 1798), into France, it seems that Bougon of Chantilly was the first to set up polishing wheels driven by high-speed motors. Amongst the most highly skilled polishers of the mid-19th century, contemporaries cited Boquet of Sèvres, Bossin of Quai-aux-Fleurs, and Langry of Impasse de la Pompe, the last two being in Paris. Paris was renowned for the great dexterity of her polishers, and it was in Paris, too, that other methods were sought for giving the foot-rims of plates or vases a glaze-like sheen: first Denuelle in 1840, then Hébert in 1846, glazed these parts by having the pieces to be fired taken to the kiln on a collar concealed beneath the base; others would cover the lustreless parts with a more fusible glaze, for firing in the muffle.

83 Thanks to one of the prints in Brongniart's compendium, *Traité des arts céramiques,* it is easy to visualize the workings of the studios in a porcelain-factory in the mid-XIXth century. For details see the following pages.

P. ASSELIN, Editeur

Imp. Ch. Chardon ainé Paris

Les actions dans les principales opérations des arts céramiques.

1. Moulage et garnissage — 2. Trempage en couverte — 3. Ebauchage et tournassage — 4. Transport au four.

The procedures in the main operations for making ceramics, and porcelain in particular, by Ch. Devely, painter at the Factory of Sèvres:

Some operations cannot be described because they depend in some way on the movement of the body and limbs. Others are closely interrelated, although very different in kind, and cannot be grasped until they have been seen in the workshop where they are performed. I wished to convey an overall idea of these operations, and of those which are peculiar to the ceramics industry, by assembling them in four pictures. An artist at the factory who has the greatest capacity for capturing, perceptively and accurately, the gestures that characterize each craftsman's job, is M. Ch. Devely: from the workshops he has selected and rendered with his habitual talent, the phases in the four main operations of porcelain making.

Fig. 1. This shows moulding and 'handling', in other words the fitting on of an item's accessories, such as the spout or handle.

The moulder A rolls out the 'bat' b or sheet of porcelain body which is to be laid onto the mould m. Craftsman B has transferred this easily-torn bat b onto the mould m, which will give him a bowl with broad flutes. When he has set it down as skilfully as possible he presses it on hard (C) with the sponge, so as to force it down into the tiniest recesses of the mould. To handle easily any point on the circumference of the piece, the mould m is placed on a plaster disc P whose iron spindle f may be turned at will by craftsman B. Craftsman G has just moulded the handle a of sugar-bowl s: he 'repairs' it by removing the seams (a) and cleaning out the recessed portions.

Fig. 2. This is the operation of applying glaze by dipping. Glaze-dipper A immerses a biscuit plate in the glaze, holding it in his right hand and plunging it in, starting with the portion of the rim diametrically opposite his thumb. He moves his left hand towards it, ready to catch it by the rim. Glaze-dipper B dips the plate holding it in his left hand, plunging it vertically and withdrawing it with the same hand and in the same plane. The unabsorbed glaze is seen dripping off: this is called the 'drip' *(la chute)*.

The craftswomen C and D are 'touching up'. One of them, C, is using a blade to remove any excess thickness or any drops of glaze which may be left on the body of the milk-jug which she is holding. The other, D, is brushing or (with felt) wiping the glaze off the foot-rim of a plate, so that it shall not stick to the support, known as the disc *(rondeau)* on which it will be placed for firing. This illustration shows several of the implements of what is generally called the glazing-shop: *g* the wooden rack on which the pieces are put after coming out of the tub; *t* the strainer that is used for removing the scum or the foreign bodies floating on the glaze-bath; P, the paddle or spatula which serves to stir up the glaze at frequent intervals in order to maintain its consistency; *b* the bottle containing the vinegar for mixing into the glaze; next to the craftswoman D is the small cup *c* holding the glaze and brush used for touching up the edges of plates or cups, or indeed any part where the glaze is too thin or altogether lacking.

Decorative processes were also the subject of much research.

As far as modelling was concerned, Dodé & Frin of Paris registered a patent in 1820 taking over the Chinese process of brushing ordinary, well-ground body onto the unfired piece. The relief was thus built up layer upon layer, and the process yielded a truly sculptural effect. It does not appear, however, that any really interesting results were obtained by inventors after this time. But, as from 1848, the Sèvres factory used this method of *pâte sur pâte* to make very sizeable pieces, particularly ones ornamented with white reliefs on a celadon ground.

The introduction into France of the transfer printing process long in use in Great Britain, started at the beginning of the century. By 1802 Potter had taken out a patent for transfer printing on earthenware, followed in 1808 by Stone, Coquerel & Legros d'Anisy in Paris. In 1809 Neppel of Paris applied the colour transfer print to underglaze porcelain decoration, then in 1818 Gonord found an ingenious process for increasing or diminishing the scale of the 'pulls' from intaglio engravings. Four years later Honoré of Paris was using a lithographic technique. Later in 1843, he even entered into partnership with one Ducoté, a 'porcelain engraver' who had invented a technique for engraving and transfer

printing porcelain, which he put into operation at Champroux. Further patents relating to transfer printing on porcelain were also registered by Roussel of Paris (1850), by Lebeuf & Milliet of Creil, and by Percheron of Paris, in 1851.

The first half of the 19th century in France witnessed great improvements in

of Marlborough House immediately after the international exhibition at London in 1851. At this time Sèvres had a reputation for reproducing meticulously the pictorial masterpieces kept in the Musée du Louvre, which demanded a very extensive range of colours.

The superiority of the products by Morte-

Fig. 3. The main operations in throwing. The thrower A has been brought a ball of porcelain body, big enough to rough out into the vase v; he has put it on a plaster disc covering the revolving table or wheel-head and is roughing it out. Notice the position of his arms, hands and fingers, and the sort of leather apron which catches the wet clay that flies off during the operation.
B. Shows the vases v being turned or finished off with the iron tool which he holds in his right hand. c is a pair of callipers; d the drawing of the vase he is making, whose outlines must be measured with the callipers to correspond exactly to those on the drawing.

the field of colours, stimulated by Dihl's discoveries at the very end of the previous century.

If the factory at Sèvres in 1806 had asked its counterpart in Vienna for a complete set of its colours, which were renewed in 1838 and 1842, it was conversely Sèvres that lent its palette to the English school

lèque, a Paris dealer in porcelain colours, guaranteed him sales outlets throughout Europe. Colville and Desfossés (a former colour mixer at Sèvres) were likewise renowned as the worthy successors to Dihl and later to Bourgeois.

Amongst the new colours we should mention:

Fig. 4 This picture shows the unfired but dry pieces from the workshops where they have been shaped, being taken to the kiln in the biscuiting department. Such pieces are very fragile, having yet to be toughened: they can neither be packed up, put in a hamper nor even carried by two workmen on a stretcher. A board placed on the upturned palm (as we see with workman A) is used for moving objects from a ground-floor workshop to the biscuit-kiln, which is perforce at a higher level. Few accidents occur. Incidentally, the Chinese have a similar way of carrying their wares, which seems to demand even greater dexterity.

P. is the door of the biscuiting chamber of the kiln. Piles of saggers already stacked there are visible, and a workman B is lashing the saggers c together, meaning that he is tying up, with string and a tourniquet, the pieces of a broken sagger which must continue use. They can then be taken – along with their contents – into the kiln without fear of their falling apart. The string is easily removed by loosening the tourniquet. (From Brongniart: *Traité des Arts céramiques*, 1844).

ultramarine blue by Mortelèque, in imitation of Vienna's (1808)

turquoise blue as a ground-colour on hard-paste porcelain, by Mortelèque

meadow green and blue-green, by Pau, a chemist in Paris (1833)

reds, by Pannetier

light yellow, invented in 1819 by J.F. Robert, a landscapist at Sèvres

platinum grey, prepared for the first time at Sèvres (it was being used there by 1814)

the 'pink colour', a British invention studied in 1836 by the chemist at Sèvres, Malaguti.

This period also witnessed important innovations in high-temperature colours.

One of the earliest was chrome green, invented in 1802 by Vauquelin—some say for Sèvres, others say for Nast, who was a friend of Vauquelin's. In 1822 Honoré of Paris took out a patent for some new shades and an economical way of producing them. In about 1831, Bunel and Paul Noualhier at Sèvres obtained coloured grounds on stoved porcelain by dipping, and in 1837 Halot of Paris used 'slipping' to achieve, in one operation, varied underglaze colourings with reserves. About 1836, Discry & Talmours of Paris invented some new colours, which were further enriched and added to in 1844 by Fouques & Arnoux of Toulouse, exploiting comparable methods.

Hard, muffle-colours, fired at medium temperatures *(de demi-grand feu)*, were discovered in 1839 by Francisque Rousseau of Paris. This discovery caused a sensation. Indeed, they obviated the need for reserves or the costly scraping-out process required for superimposing gilding on ordinary muffle-fired colours.

Gold-, platinum- and silver-based decorations were also subjected to research. As early as 1818 the Marquis de Parois and Guédet, of Paris, registered a patent. Rousseau in 1844 tried to give gilt more solidity by applying it on top of a layer of platinum, while Grenon superimposed two layers of gold, the first fired at a very high temperature.

It was Rousseau again who applied metal —especially silver—onto porcelain (1844), while Gille of Paris had been using it on biscuit ware since 1836.

But if chemists were seeking to strengthen the resistance of gold, silver and platinum, they were searching no less for economy measures. The patents of Dutertre Frères of Paris for thin gilding (1850: a Meissen invention), and of Jacob Petit in the following year, reflected this tendency. In an appendix to the *Traité des Arts céramiques* by Brongniart, Salvétat mentions 'Paris gilding' as being economical.

Finally, the application of gems and enamels on to metal foil, a technique neglected since Cotteau's time, was brought into fashion again by the processes of Rousseau (1844) and of Marceaux (Paris, 1846).

We should also mention lithophany, a technique which gives transparent effects in porcelain; invented by M. de Bourgoing in 1827, it achieved great popularity in Berlin.

Another equally fashionable technique was that of setting biscuit cameos, in-

84   Queen's factory.
Casserole with black wooden
handle, turned. 'Picoted'
ribbon, polychrome and
gold. *Circa* 1780.
Lisbon, Museu Nacional de
Arte Antigua. Diam.
29.5 cm. (11¹/₂ in).
Mark 209.

correctly called 'sulphides', in crystal glass—a practice originating in the 18th century. Despréz Junior of Paris took out a patent for a new porcelain body in 1812. Lastly, a curious process was devised by Jacob Petit which consisted of dipping lace into an extremely fluid slip and putting it straight onto biscuit sculptures, in order to 'clothe' them.

The new processes also often required new body-formulae containing kaolin: Nast took out a patent for a new body intended for rims, medallions and figures in relief (1810), and then further patents were registered by Cerf Weil & Baruch Weil of Paris (1820), Jacob Petit (1843 and 1849), Burguin at Crécy (Cher), etc.

Output and Evolution of Style

The turn of the 18th century had seen the transition from Rococo complexity to Antique simplicity. By a sort of counter-movement the first half of the 19th century was going to witness, in shapes as much as *décors,* antique sobriety giving way to a prodigious luxuriance that was all the more exaggerated for being in fact no more than a pastiche of the preceding ages, especially of the previous century. The years marking the transition from the first to the second third of the 19th century must be thought of in various respects as an important point in the history of Paris porcelain.

On the economic plane big industry came to stay, and we now see two of the oldest Paris factories close their gates. Rather than reorganize their establishments in accordance with the new industrial and financial imperatives, Schoelcher did not renew his commitments at the end of 1834 and Henri Nast stopped production in 1835.

On the artistic plane the evolution was no less important.

The Antique style had gradually become bastardized to such a point that by 1833 Victor Schoelcher was exclaiming in the *Artiste;* 'Enough of Antique things! *Do* make something French!' He criticised the shapes and decorations of Sèvres, an act which would have appeared sacrilegious half a century earlier. Schoelcher even deemed that the factory was useless and suggested its downright abolition. His admiration went out to Nast, his unequalled rival, and to Jacob Petit from whom he used to buy white ware.

The uproar caused by the appearance of the new Rococo-style shapes created by Jacob Petit dates from the 1834 exhibition. One is almost tempted arbitrarily to divide the first half of the 19th century into two periods: before and after Jacob Petit. Indeed, Jacob Petit was making a name for himself at a time when the desire for change was being itself felt. The quest for a new movement had already been stimulated a few years before, by the growing clumsiness of antique shapes and *décors,* and also by the infatuation with the 'Cathedral style'. Except for the early years of the 19th century, shapes seldom regained the simplicity of the late 18th century.

We should observe, however, that contrary to the ideas of Jacob Petit, other porcelain makers were turning out extremely simple shapes by 1834 which subsequently became Classical. Clauss for example displayed some twelve-sided cups accompanied by teapots, sugarbowls and milk-jugs which were rectangular with chamfered corners. Discry Ill. 169, 170 put out a tea service of a model with globular bellies and scalloped edges, which was more complicated but had a lasting success. Ill. 157

With the multiplicity of shapes and decorations, there was much confusion which was only heightened over the following years. On the subject of the exhibition of 1834 Flachat wrote: 'Where are the styles, where are the schools, where are the masters? Are we at the Greek, Roman or Gothic phase? Are we adopting the style of the Renaissance. or of Louis XIV or of Louis XV or of the Empire? Do we have our own?... At present, art is being dissipated and industry is enslaving it to its own needs before even discerning its laws.'

An excess of inspiration now flooded in.

86   Queen's factory. Oval chamber-pot, known in 19th-century France as a 'Bourdaloue'. *Circa* 1780. Paris, Coll. Dr. Pecker. L. 23 cm. (9 in.). Mark 209.

Let us note firstly the preponderant influence of large-scale sculptures and of paintings by old masters, the synthesis of which is achieved with the tall monumental vases.

Previous styles were plundered. Incidentally, it is strange to record the chronological sequence in which the characteristics of each one reappear: Classical and Egyptian antiquity, the Middle Ages with the 'Cathedral style', the Renaissance, the 17th century, and finally Rococo even more than *Rocaille*.

To this enthusiasm for bygone ages we must add the fascination for faraway countries, particularly the Far East.

In fact, we are observing nothing other than a tendency of the Romantic school. A phrase of Théophile Gautier's, quoted in the Goncourt brothers' *Journal* defines the Romantics thus: 'What sets us apart is the Exotic. There are two interpretations of the Exotic: the first gives one a taste for women who are yellow, green, etc. The more refined taste, a more supreme corruption, is a taste for the Exotic throughout Time.'

Certain styles and tastes persisted both in shapes and decorations, and one sometimes finds it hard to imagine their longevity.

The 'Cathedral style' and the Egyptian influence in particular survived side by side for many a long year. We see these two types of decoration figuring in the inventory after Madame Nast's death in 1811 and we encounter them again in the contents of an invoice for porcelain bought by Balzac from Schoelcher in 1832. Indeed, by 1811 certain of Nast's pieces were ornamented either with 'Gothic arcades' or else with Egyptian patterns. More than twenty years afterwards Schoelcher was still selling to Balzac—both of them reputed for their refined taste in porcelain—some 'Gothic vases with black grounds' and others having 'Egyptian designs'.[1]

As far as Egyptian *décor* goes, it is permissible to explain its perenniality not so much in terms of a reminiscence of the Egyptian Campaign, but rather as one of the side-effects of the enormous interest aroused by Champollion's deciphering of the hieroglyphics. His *Précis du Système hiéroglyphique* was published in 1824.

As for the Gothic style which reached its apogee between 1820 and 1830, it undoubtedly owes its appearance partly to the interest excited by the old monuments that Lenoir had assembled in the Paris convent called the Couvent des Petits-Augustins, with the object of removing them from the destructive fury of the Revolutionaries[2]. Even for the coronation of Napoleon, the decorations in Notre-Dame were pseudo-Gothic and, in 1811, Joséphine had a Gothic gallery for her pictures constructed at Malmaison. But the honourable reinstatement of the Middle Ages and the Gothic style was to turn into an out-and-out craze with the advent of Romanticism. The Duchesse de Berry appeared as a mediaeval queen at a festival organized by the banker Greffulhe in 1819, and as Maria Stuart in a quadrille which was the grand finale of the ball which she gave ten years later in 1829.

All this confusion, all these pastiches, could only end in mis-shapen ugliness. The exhibition of 1844 bore out these anticipations, and after visiting it Théophile Gautier declared in *La Presse* that ugliness was a modern phenomenon against which artists were fighting as best they could.

[1] Invoice of Schoelcher & Son, settled by Balzac, July 4th, 1832. Paris, Bibliothèque de l'Institut.
[2] It bore the title of 'Musée des Monuments français'.

OUTPUT

The various table-service items already mentioned in the 18th century continue into the 19th. We should, nevertheless, note the slow disappearance of common entrée services in favour of dessert services. This phenomenon, moreover, tallies with the evolution of Paris porcelain towards a luxury trade centred more upon the decoration of white ware than upon its manufacture. Let us observe, nonetheless, the birth of a new shape: the *légumier* (vegetable dish), which undoubtedly only succeeds the *casserole* (saucepan).

Nevertheless, the concept of a table service did not disappear. By 1826 Pouyat could offer his customers a service 'with bouquets of roses and flowers', composed as follows:

6 dozen flat plates
1¹/₂ dozen soup plates
4 round soup tureens No. 4
2 round 11-inch dishes
4 oval 12-inch dishes
4 oval 15-inch dishes
2 oval 18-inch dishes
4 lidded casseroles
1 10-inch salad bowl of new shape
4 round sauce boats on paw-feet

The set was priced at 459 francs 95.

Dessert services are often made up of 60 to 72 pieces and more. The highest number seems to have been reached by the set that belonged to Bernadotte, which comprised no less than 600 plates and 82 other items.

Still in 1826, at Pouyat's, here is the composition of a dessert service:

2¹/₂ dozen 8¹/₂-inch plates
4 shell-shaped compote dishes
4 square compote dishes
4 oval compote dishes
2 coolers of new shape
1 cheese bowl
2 sugar bowls of new shape, for the table.

This dessert service, decorated with sprigs of flowers in varied colours with *petit fileté* (spiral pattern), was reckoned to be worth 977 francs 25, which is more than double the price of the previous table service. The *guéridon* (tray) had already

Ill. 80, 89

been very successful. Initially intended for cream pots, it was later made up of two or three tiered trays joined by a central shaft. It was then used for *pâtisseries* and sweetmeats.

Ill. 81

The term *cabaret* is still used—simultaneously with the appellations of tea- and coffee-services, we might add. These services often match the dessert services and are generally made up of seventeen pieces, sometimes even of thirty. A verbatim description from Pouyat's inventory of 1826 reads: 'Tea-*cabaret* of 17 egg-shaped pieces, cavalier on terrace, silver-gilt neck and foot, cup with gilt base. Composed of: 1 coffee pot, 1 teapot, 1 milk jug, 1 sugar pot, 1 bowl with raised foot, 12 pairs of cups of new shape, 83 francs.'

It is odd to observe how at this time no precise distinction seems to be drawn between tea- and coffee-services.

In the 19th century, we encounter the standard toilet items as well, including *bourdaloues*. Let us also remember the washstands composed of a large basin accompanied by a water-jug and fitted into a special piece of furniture. Fancy goods occupied an important place in the output from Parisian factories. They now become extraordinarily fashionable, invading all the rooms and cluttering all the furniture. Among the objects most in demand were the *veilleuse* and the writing set, and in addition spill-holders, ring-stands, flasks, etc.

We have mentioned elsewhere the incredible range of objects that Nast was making for furnishings by 1817—lamps, snuffers, candlesticks, frames, curtain-pulls, 'bed-finials and attachments', thermometers, clock-dials (less expensive than enamel ones), plaques, etc.

We must also stress the importance of the output of drug jars. In the 19th century they became the object of special care on the part of the decorators, thanks to whom they enjoyed a great rise in popularity.

We know all too little about the production of religious objects, which may be traced in the various inventories of factories and salesrooms *circa* 1820–50: statuettes, crucifixes and particularly holy-water stoups.

The vogue for paintings on porcelain did not abate during this period, while the production of plaques for decorating furniture and mantelpieces was still exceptional. It did not really reach its climax until the second half of the century.

We should finally draw attention to the

88 Duc d'Angoulême's factory.
Biscuit group, *L'Automne*.
Circa 1785.
Lisbon, Museu Nacional de Arte Antigua. Ht. 37 cm. (14³/₅ in.).
Mark 10.

manufacture of items destined for exportation, to the Near East in particular.

Just as we have already done for the 18th century, we shall study the shapes and decorations of this first half of the 19th century, with evidence from contemporary texts and from the examination of marked objects.

We shall use in particular the inventories taken after the deaths of Madame Nast (1811), of Nast himself (1817) and of Jean Pouyat-Duvignaud (1826). We shall also resort to two other inventories of slightly later date, since they were both drawn up in 1828 when the seals on Jeanne's and on Flamen-Fleury's premises were removed. The minutes of sale, recorded in 1837 and 1838 following Monginot's bankruptcy, and the inventory appended to the balance sheet of Jacob Petit's bankruptcy petition in 1848, give us valuable information on the last period in our survey.

Naturally, we shall also turn to the documents assembled by the various national exhibitions of industrial products.

Finally, the marks will be of great help to us. Some of them, by their exactitude, may allow us to date objects: for example the mark *P. L. Dagoty, Manufacture de l'Impératrice* was only used between 1804 und 1814; that of *Schoelcher et Fils* indicates a date between 1829 and 1834.

SHAPES

The early years of the 19th century did not bring any significant novelties in comparison with the last decade of the 18th century. Thus, the style which was to predominate beyond 1800 was already well defined by about 1798. Over the following years it simply asserted itself. In the course of the last years of the 18th century the edges of flat-ware pieces had become perfectly smooth and regular without any indentation, and the names for shapes were borrowed from Antiquity. The type of shape most commonly mentioned—as it will continue to be until about 1830—is 'in Etruscan style'. It corresponds to the Sèvres 'Paestum' shape, that is to say an ovoid belly on a pedestal-foot. Tea- and coffee-pots usually have an overarching handle. Dagoty's rendering of this shape offers a slight variation: the belly is semi-ovoid and the shoulder is surmounted by a collar. Milk-jugs are now shaped like antique helmets and sugar bowls are semi-ovoid supported on three paw-like feet. In about 1830 the scalloped shapes reappear, along with the 'English' services and *Rocaille* influence. As from the end of the 18th century cup-shapes had begun to diversify. During the first half of the 19th century a host of new shapes were discovered: more and more, indeed, the cup became a trinket and followed the general trend towards over-refinement. The number of different cup-shapes given in Pouyat's inventory of 1826 is surprising: with paws, with paws and beading, second *jasmin,* flared with ornate base, Etruscan, fluted Etruscan, square, square with everted rim, shaped as a swan, a shell, an oval shell, a snail, teacup, fluted teacup, with low foot, goblet-form, *bouillarde,* 'Berlin with straight rim', 'Berlin with everted rim', egg-shaped with relief, 'with relief-work and with paws', 'so-called roses', *mignonnette,* toy *jasmin,* jewel, 4/4, for milk, for chocolate, Etruscan for chocolate, duchess-form for chocolate, English, and so on.

Most of these shapes, incidentally, recur in many Parisian factories, for example swan-shaped cups bearing the marks of Dagoty or Darte.

Ill. 124

Ill. 169

Ill. 120

Ill. 143

89 Duc d'Angoulême's factory.
Footed tray (guéridon) carrying seven gravy-cups. Polychrome and gold, 'chain-pattern' decoration in grisaille. Circa 1790. Palacio Nacional de Quéluz. Pot: Ht. 10 cm. (4 in.). Tray: Diam. 25 cm. (9½ in.). Mark 9.

The general trend in the first quarter of the century is towards richness of modelled *décor*, particularly of detail. Often the items are mounted on paw-feet; handles, both for vases, cups and other service pieces, are clad with modelled patterns. They are almost always emphasized by a high loop. They emerge from a modelled shaft or a palmette and end in a woman's bust, a monster or an animal-head. Often they curl round at the top and enclose a leafy volute, a rosette or human mask.

Nast distinguished himself particularly in his modelled patterns. We have seen in another connexion how he had taken out a patent in 1810 for applying relief decoration by means of a mechanical process using a roulette. The patent was complemented by the invention of a new paste suitable for the manufacture of moulded ornaments. By this process Nast Ill. 2 decorated rims with leaf-borders. The richest porcelains from his factory, about 1810–20, are adorned with single- or double-faced female heads, with winged lions, ibexes, paw-feet, lyres, fleurons, palmettes or rosettes, using a dazzling technique further enriched by contrasting the matt gold of the reliefs with the glossy gold of the flat areas. The service of the King of Spain Ferdinand VII and Queen Isabel is a brilliant demonstra-Ill. 220 tion of this work (*circa* 1816).

Other Parisian factories similarly looked to large-scale modelling for their inspiration. We know too little about production in the factory on Rue Amelot, under the management of Lefebvre, perhaps because his wares were mainly exported to Spain and still more to Russia. We might nonetheless mention a cup in the form of a human head, its handle shaped Ill. 108 by the lifted plait of hair. This cup must be dated between 1806 and 1819—the dates marking either end of Lefebvre's presence in the Rue Amelot factory.

The handles or knobs to every vase, be it ovoid or Medici, are likewise little mas-Ill. 77 terpieces of modelling. At the exhibition of 1819 Nast and Schoelcher had both exhibited monumental vases of the same style. They both displayed ovoid forms on a pedestal foot with a long flared neck, flanked by winged female busts or by lion-heads emerging from shafts with Ill. 76 palmettes. Besides this, Schoelcher was exhibiting a straight-sided vase flanked by sphinxes.

To these, the most frequent shapes, we must add numerous trumpet-vases or *jasmin*-vases, and others having a flattened profile resting on an oval plinth or on paw-feet; still others were tapered Ill. 22 with a neck like a cylindrical collar. Ill. 138 Some factories, like Dagoty's, would adorn their vases with flower garlands in biscuit relief. Ill. 1

By about 1840, thanks to Jacob Petit's influence, the number of vase-shapes was considerable. A new rendering of the lidded vase of the *Ancien Régime* was very fashionable; under the Second Empire it would be given the name of *potiche*. Ill. 79

In addition, the influence of the Orient inspired globular vases and *rouleau*-vases. Ill. 80, 156 With the fashion for green plants scattered in profusion through one's suite of rooms, the flower-pot holder *(cache-pot)* appears. They are mostly of tapering shape, sometimes slightly ovoid, and rest on a moulded plinth. *Jardinières* (flower stands) as-Ill. 112 sume a growing importance and the gilt-bronze mounts which enrich them are as complicated in conception as they are disarmingly difficult to describe succinctly. Ill. 79

In the middle of the century lighting appliances account for a lot of porcelain: chandeliers, hanging lamps and oil-lamps are made up of different components in which porcelain plays the leading part. Ill. 79 Let us also note, around 1830, the short-lived use of lithophanes for lamp-shades and sick-bed lights.

Decorated porcelain invades rooms more and more. The clock in particular becomes indispensable to the decoration of any mantelpiece. Simple or complicated, looking like a vase or trimmed with Ill. 80, 140 brightly coloured relief or with scroll-work, the clock is most often flanked by matching sconces or candelabra. The Ill. 78 mantelpiece itself may either be adorned

90   Duc d'Angoulême's
factory.
Covered broth-bowl and its
tray. Harbour scenes.
Circa 1785.
Paris, Musée des Arts déco-
ratifs. L. 24 cm. (9²/₅ in.).
Mark 9.

with porcelain plaques on jambs and lintel—Gille manufactured them regularly around 1844—or may itself be of solid porcelain like the one that Jacob Petit had displayed at the exhibition of 1834, a dazzling demonstration of technical dexterity harnessed to a fertile imagination.

Ill. 78

The multitude, and the fancy appearance, of shapes devised for trinkets defies all description. They obey the constantly renewed current of fashion and by turns undergo its various influences.

We shall give some examples of these in the case of writing-sets and *veilleuses* (or drink-warmers), borrowed from the inventories (see above) of the years 1826 and 1828.

The ordinary writing sets or inkwells, and the writing sets known as 'aerostatic' (which, by a system based on the equilibrium of air, provided a constant ink-level), assumed the most diverse features. By 1828 Flamen-Fleury was offering a choice of writing sets, described as follows: columnar, triangular, with Egyp-

tian figure, fish, ram's-head on three feet, basket-shaped, slipper-shaped, shell-shaped, surmounted by a dog, a fawn, *mondes* (world-maps), tortoise-shaped, 'Homer', fruits on vine-leaves, 'Cupid as a merchant', barrel-shaped, 'apple', square, 'sentry-box', helmet, with paws, with hand-bell, as portmanteau, 'with American fruit', thick-sided, with diamond points, as grave, 'with Gothic handle', 'cup-shaped'. Elsewhere we reproduce one of the illustrative plates from the album of models by Dagoty & Honoré, devoted to writing sets and in particular to the Russian-style model directly inspired by the contemporary models being manufactured at the Imperial Factory of Saint-Petersburg.

We might add that the writing sets were often accompanied by a matching paper-weight, and sometimes even by a magnifying-glass mounted in porcelain.

As for the drink-warmers *(veilleuses)*, cylindrical, oval, square, lozenge-shaped, triangular, hexagonal, etc., they can assume the most diverse appearances and owe much to the 'Cathedral style'. They also sometimes simulate a tower, a dome, a 'shanty', or else are simply surmounted by a bowl. Jacob Petit unleashed his zest upon this item, often giving it the appearance of a statuette. Who could guess that this Louis XV marquise holding in her hands a little teapot with truncated corners, or this Madonna admiring the Infant Jesus resting on her lap, or even this Catherine de Medici embracing her favourite dog, are in fact nothing but agreeable recipients for herbal tea?

We have already underlined the importance of drug jars. The commonest form is cylindrical, moulded at the base and the top and covered with a bell-shaped lid.

Ill. 121

91 Duc d'Angoulême's factory.
Large lidded cup and saucer with purple ground.
Circa 1795.
The same shape is reproduced in Ill. 92.
Paris, Coll. Guy Passerat.
Ht. 12 cm. (4²/₃ in.).
Mark 16.

Ill. 209, 145

Ill. 163

Ill. 181

Ill. 177

Ill. 154

92 Duc d'Angoulême's
factory.
Large green cup and saucer.
Grisaille and gold decoration.
The same shape is reproduced
in Ill. 91. *Circa* 1800.
Sèvres, Musée national de
Céramique. Ht. 12 cm.
(4²/₃ in.).
Mark 16.

A further model takes on the shape of a
semi-ovoid urn on a pedestal-foot.
Let us remind ourselves at this point that
there are items of glazed porcelain which
are accompanied by various components
in biscuit. We shall speak of them at
greater length in the chapter devoted to
biscuit sculpture.

Decoration

The albums of decorations and the isolated designs from the first half of the 19th century which have come down to us, in particular the model book of Dagoty & Honoré, plus the designs from the factory on Rue Fontaine-au-Roy, run by Pouyat, allow us to discern several currents from among the influences which were rife at that time.

Various types of *décor* deriving from the 18th century survive, but gradually they evolve in sympathy with the new forces brought to bear either by technical discoveries or by fashion. In this latter respect let us emphasize the preponderant

well to the use of coloured grounds or of gilded and contrast burnished grounds, entirely covering some objects. More and more often in the early years of the 19th century, the decoration spreads out to 'envelope' an object such as we have already seen at the end of the 18th century. Veritable pictures—generally rectangular—adorn the three-dimensional pieces and wholly cover the bottoms of the richest plates.

It does not seem that the colours chosen allow us to date Paris porcelain exactly. Under the Empire as much as in the ensuing reigns the colour-schemes are greatly varied, from the strong colours—such as the famous chrome green or brick

93 Duc d'Angoulême's factory.
Teapot and sugar-bowl.
Polychrome and gold.
Circa 1785.
Paris, Coll. Guy Passerat.
Teapot: Ht. 10.5 cm.
(4¹/₅ in.).
Mark 9.

influence of Romanticism which, linked with a certain encyclopedic spirit orientates artistic decoration towards a quest that is actually more documentary than scientific.

The importance of decoration becomes progressively obvious as the surfaces able to accommodate it expand, and thanks as

red—down to the mildest tones: pink, mauve, water green, agate and nankeen. The use of all these colours together characterizes Jacob Petit's work, involving the most striking hues such as black to set off the softest colour-schemes.

The multiplicity of colours and the discovery of the various mechanical pro-

94   Duc d'Angoulême's
factory.
Rocaille sugar-bowl and its
tray. Cornflower decoration.
Circa 1785.
Paris, Musée du Louvre.
Coll. Thiers. Ht. 15 cm.
(6 in.).

cesses which we have been studying gave the 19th century the chance to achieve a technical perfection never attained before in the field of decoration on porcelain. The ceaseless growth of the range of colours available enriched the decorator's palette to the extent of attracting many painters to this particular art form which

ries absorb and in a sense lure away the talents of MM. De Marne, Droling, Sweback, Mallet, etc.'[4] Further on, the author takes pity on the 'deplorable condition' of Drölling, who is 'today attached to a porcelain factory', but he ends by acknowledging the interest in porcelain painting: 'Let us nonetheless applaud

95 Dihl & Guérhard. Portrait of Bonaparte. Polychrome. Inscribed: *Drölling pt 1803 M^{tre} Dihl et Guérhard*.
Paris, private coll. Ht. 57 cm. (22¹/₂ in.).

some still considered to be a minor art. *Le Pausanias français,* reviewing the *Salon* of 1806, comments on this in the style befitting the period. The article devoted to the painter Demarne[3] opens thus: 'Let us begin by lamenting that such a brilliant brush should be obliged to hire itself out to manufacturers... Thus do the facto-

such efforts, and the steadfastness that M. Dihl has exhibited, in giving porcelain wares a prestige that owes nothing to their industrial origins, and in augmenting their price by the value of the painting. This *genre* is definitely not to be disdained, opening, as it does, new outlets to industry and the arts, giving luxury

[3] Demarne, Jean Louis. (1744–1829). *Genre* and landscape painter.
[4] Drölling, Martin. (1752–1817). Painter of interiors and *genre*. Sweback, Jacques Jose. (1767–1823). Painter of military subjects. He worked at Sèvres from 1802 until 1813. Mallet, Jean-Baptiste. (1759–1833). *Genre* painter and engraver.

the character of good taste and elegance, and enlarging the realm of art.'

In that same year of 1806 Dihl displayed various pictures at the industrial exhibition, and amongst them a moonlight scene which had been described as 'magic'. Let us recall that he had already attained much success with the pictures ex-

Nast, Schoelcher, Darte, etc.—or of such-and-such a decorator. Drölling, Demarne, La Guay and later Lachassaigne enjoyed a well-deserved success and even enthusiasm: 'Copying like that is creating!' exclaimed Baron Dupin in his report of the 1834 exhibition.

Reproductions of pictures by Old Mas-

96 Dihl & Guérhard. Plate. Sprig decoration in blue. *Circa* 1798. Paris, private coll. Diam. 22.5 cm. (8⁴/₅ in.). Mark 18.

Ill. 95, 100, 104

hibited in 1798. He remained unrivalled in this field until the end of his active life. During the first half of the 19th century, copies of famous pictures, old or contemporary, whether they were reproduced on rectangular plaques, on plates or on three-dimensional pieces, were the triumph of such-and-such a factory—Dihl,

ters are often masterpieces in their own right, particularly the copies of Flemish painters. At the Tuileries, Joséphine owned a 'water-jug and basin, porcelain by Schoelcher, white ground, painted with Flemish figures and subjects…'

But copies of pictures of the Classical or contemporary schools also achieved great

97, 98 Dihl & Guérhard. Dihl's portrait, painted by Le Guay in 1797 on a porcelain plague. At 44, Dihl was now a happy man. For sixteen years he had been managing the factory he had created with the two Guérhards, which – unlike other factories – did not apparently suffer unduly from the Revolutionary period. Dihl devoted himself to research into colours, on which he made a report to the Institut the following year. His palette is shown here, together with the jars in which he stored the various substances needed in his research. From amongst the successes on which he prided himself he had selected a large-scale biscuit piece, a mottled spindle vase embellished with bas-reliefs by Sauvage; and a yellow-ground hemispherical cup on a pedestal foot, fitted with two overarching handles. These objects are akin to a pair of mottled spindle vases and an agate-ground cup, reproduced on pp. 101–104. Le Guay, one of the best porcelain-painters, who executed this portrait, also witnessed Dihl's marriage to the widowed Mme Guérhard a year later. In 1800 Drölling painted a further portrait of Dihl. Porcelain with simulated gem-stone decoration bears the Dihl mark in underglaze blue.

Sèvres, Musée National de Céramique.

Picture: Ht. 48 cm. (19$\frac{1}{3}$ in.): signature on the left, towards the bottom.

Vase: Ht. 36 cm. (13$\frac{4}{5}$ in.). Mark 18.

Cup: Ht. 9 cm. (3$\frac{1}{2}$ in.). Mark 18.

success, whether in the case of works inspired by Antiquity: Poussin (*Moïse sauvé des Eaux* by Schoelcher, 1819), Luca Giordano (*Amphitrite portée par les Eaux* by Legort, 1819), Guérin (*Enée chez Didon* by Schoelcher et Fils, therefore between 1829 and 1834): or from especially renowned canvases such as Raphael's *La Belle Jardinière* (Schoelcher, 1806), *La Vierge à la Chaise* (Denuelle, 1819): or even from works evincing a certain domestic sensibility, as in *La Barque d'Isabey,* showing the painter and his family taking a walk (Schoelcher).

Portraits also enjoyed an unquestionable popularity and were normally contained in medallions. Contemporary personages, notably the members of the ruling families in France and abroad, were just as prized as the illustrious figures of antiquity or of French history—and so were famous women, like Madame de Sévigné, Madame de Montespan, Henrietta Maria
Ill. 141 of England, or Dante's Beatrice. But the most picturesque works of the Romantic school were of no less value. Devéria[5], one of the most conspicuous painters of this school, saw his canvases transposed
Ill. 37 on to porcelain: scenes like *Le Désabiller* or *La Prude* (Schoelcher, *circa* 1830) usher us into the intimacy of a woman's bedroom.

Ever since the beginning of the century anecdotal themes, indoor scenes and children's games had appealed to enthusiasts by their more human and less frigid atmosphere than the subjects inspired from Antiquity. *L'Enterrement de Grand-Mère* (Pouyat, 1826), *Les Promenades familiales*
Ill. 132 (Dagoty, *circa* 1815), and *Un Enfant jouant*
Ill. 165 *de la Flûte* (Gaugain, *circa* 1810) are only a few examples out of many.

Finally, we should note the persistence of a taste for landscapes and especially for seascapes, which, in turn, were often copied in pictures or prints of that time (*Vues des Côtes de France,* by Garneray, published in 1823, for instance). Very often the landscapes are no longer anonymous, as before. They, too, reproduce the coloured prints and the watercolours of Garneray[6] or of Janinet[7]. The familiar landscapes of the environs of Paris, e.g. La
Ill. 22 Malmaison and views of all the cities in
Ill. 23, 29 the world, from Lisbon to Philadelphia and from Saint-Petersburg to Constantinople, were repeated on many occasions, either by hand or by the process of
Ill. 31 transfer printing. The views of Paris are of course the most numerous, but we must give special mention to a complete set signed by Rihouët showing the most important monuments in Philadelphia
Ill. 241 after prints made between 1800 and 1840. The fashion for Antiquity manifested itself particularly in *décors* with figures. Whether they were full of vitality and painted in polychrome colours, or wheth-
Ill. 2 er by contrast they imitated ancient ceramics, it does not seem that their success extended much beyond the second third of the 19th century. Amongst the most attractive decorations let us remember Dagoty's, whose toned-down shades may be of different colours according to the
Ill. 124 service. Let us mention, too, some reproductions of Etruscan vases with black or dark-brown grounds adorned with brick-
Ill. 153, 169 red figures such as those exhibited by Denuelle in 1834.

Folk-costumes, inspired by the illustrated accounts of contemporary travellers, make picturesque subjects that were especially popular. Amongst those most often reproduced, in bright, gay polychrome colours, let us point out the natives of Spain and Russia (Honoré & Dagoty, *circa*

---

[5] Devéria, Eugène. (1805–1865). He was the representative for painting in the Romantic 'Cénacle' (coterie).

[6] Of the three Garneray brothers the youngest, Auguste (1785–1824), instructor of drawing to the Duchesse de Berry, painted landscapes which his brother Ambroise (1783–1857) then used to engrave.

[7] Janinet, Jean François. (1752–1814). Refined the technique of aquatinting.

99 Duc d'Angoulême's
factory.
Breakfast-set on openwork
tray. Polychrome and gold.
Pastoral themes. *Circa* 1785.
Paris, Musée des Arts décoratifs. Tray: L. 21.5 cm.
(8²/₅ in.). Teapot: Ht. 10 cm.
(4 in.).
Mark 9.

1820) and those of the Alpine region, discovered therefore by the first tourists (Schoelcher, Pouyat, 1826).

The publication of historical novels around 1840 gave rise to a rendering of coloured scenes worthy of Alexandre Dumas' descriptions in *The Three Musketeers,* which appeared in 1844.

Floral *décor* was still popular in the 19th century. The cornflower, a survival from the previous century, had become classic, almost trite, as it continues to be in our day, together with sprays of wildflowers. Bouquets of flowers, if they still existed, were swiftly replaced under the Restoration by two different species of flower, then by the big single flower inspired from

the illustrative plates to botanical books. Nast owned all fifteen volumes of *La Flore des Environs de Paris* and borrowed ideas from it on many occasions. Schoelcher, Feuillet and Darte are past masters in floral art★.

Even the choice of species has changed. If it were possible to term them 'bourgeois', one would be tempted to say this of the flowers the public preferred between 1830 and 1850—the hollyhock, snapdragon, poppy, mint and nasturtium. Beside these rustic varieties the traditional roses and tulips remain. The colour-schemes are extremely fresh, the roses are of the most natural pink, but as for the lilies, narcissi and guelder roses (or 'snowballs'), their transparent purity and whiteness against a white ground are well-nigh miraculous. Only the foliage brings a touch of colour, as does the border when it is not confined to a single 'braid' or band of gilt.

The garlands have given way to 'crowns' by the turn of the 18th century. The sprigs are now tightly bunched, heaped together, arranged in thick friezes and usually standing out against a coloured ground. Principally it is the forget-me-not, convolvulus, sweet-pea and the rose which are in favour. Schoelcher likes to set them on a straw-coloured ground. Halley creates some bold contrasts, for example brown flowers touched with gilt on a mauve ground, whilst Feuillet, not a wit his inferior in originality, sets the flowers and leaves of the strawberry plant against a uniformly pink ground.

Flowers in relief, standing completely free of the basic shape, remain one of the triumphs of Jacob Petit, who builds up different species of flower (but especially guelder roses) on pieces frequently of monumental size★. At the exhibition of

101 Dihl. ▶
Cup with high-temperature ground simulating agate. *Circa* 1797. Sèvres, Musée national de Céramique. Ht. 9 cm. (3½ in.). Mark 18. (see page 136).

★Ill. 151, 152

Ill. 139

Ill. 34

Ill. 161
◀100   Dihl & Guérhard. Rectangular plaque. *Amour et Psyché enfants* ('Cupid and Psyche as children'), after Prud'hon. *Circa* 1810. Sèvres, Musée national de Céramique. L. 22 cm. (8⅗ in.
★Ill. 179

141

1849 he displayed tall vases decorated in this manner. By the time he went bankrupt in 1848 he was employing no fewer than seven floral artists *(fleuristes)* in his factory at Fontainebleau—six young ladies known by their old-fashioned Christian names of Caroline, Coelina, Emélie, Hortense, Joséphine and Scholastique, and a male artist, M. Isaac.

Besides the floral decorations, other plants were introduced for ornamental patterns: Nast in 1811 was using wreaths of hay and also spinach, laurels, palm-trees, pine-cones, etc.

Nast likewise composed decorations derived from certain fruits, in particular clusters of gooseberries or grapes, while vine-shoots were often used by other factories.

By the 19th century fruits were seldom combined with flowers any longer. The manner of rendering them follows the same evolution as floral embellishment: one or more fruits of one or of two varieties are painted in detail on the bottom of a plate or, more rarely, on a three-dimensional item. The same choice of colours recurs, demanding great virtuosity from the painter in the art of the *trompe-l'œil* (witness the pear cut into pieces with almonds by Feuillet, or chestnuts by Darte).

Ill. 148

Just as floral *décor* is inspired by herbals, so decoration with animals faithfully copies the illustrative plates of contemporary naturalists. Here too it is the concept of the specimen which is adopted, particularly in the case of birds, which continue the tradition of the so-called 'Buffon'

*Ill. 32

services which were, however, made prior to 1811 by Nast, following Sèvres' lead. It is noteworthy that, besides reproducing the birds of France perched on a branch or rock, decorators—Darte

among them—often chose the *Oiseaux d'Afrique* ('African Birds'), after Levaillant. Other animals enjoyed short-lived popularity, such as the famous giraffe which was given to Charles X by the Sultan of Egypt, in about 1830.

Ill. 150

One of the most widespread decorations on table-service items at the beginning of

the 19th century consists simply of a border occupying the whole surface of the raised rim on plates, often accompanied by a rosette in the centre★. This border reappears around the lip of the cups, and forms a matching band on the other pieces.

To this day there still exist whole reper-

102 Dihl & Guérhard. Cylindrical cup and its saucer. Tulips painted from life on a gold ground. *Circa* 1810. Paris, Musée des Arts décoratifs. Ht. 6.5 cm. (2¹/₂ in.). Mark 16.

103 Dihl & Guérhard. Drop-front secretaire, mounted on ormolu legs extending into the corner-columns of the carcase. Green marble. Ascribed to Weisweiler. It is adorned with porcelain plaques and medallions. The black-ground plaques are decorated with cameos in reserve accompanied by polychrome garlands. Small medallions, set notably in the corners of the flap, imitate the Wedgwood style. Others have a reddish-brown ground. In the centre of the flap a broad circular medallion is decorated with a gold-painted antique scene: the *Triomphe de Cérès*. The style of these plaques is similar to Sauvage's This piece of furniture was bought in Paris between 1805 and 1807 by Marie-Louise of Parma, Princess of the Asturias, later Queen of Spain. Early 19th century. Madrid, Palacio de Oriente.

toires of such early 19th century borders, in the form of specimen plates or even a plaque that derives from Nast's workshops. It features all the patterns from the decorative repertoire. Most of them consist of borders of flowers, sometimes accompanied by ribbons and stylized foliage.

It is not unusual to encounter other decorations as well—swags of drapery, fleurons, scrolls, sundry emblems and landscapes. All these motifs are painted either in polychrome or in monochrome, or even in contrast burnished gold.

Of course, the style of the borders follows the general tendencies in decoration; some of them, using the Cathedral-style decoration, are especially successful. In about 1830 the purple or dark-blue grounds were the most highly prized, and for the most lavish pieces they were additionally embellished with reserves bearing decorations either of intricate miniatures with trophies, or of flowers or birds. Later, the influence of the Renaissance—particularly of Limoges enamels—manifests itself in black grounds adorned with delicate foliated scrolls in relief, painted in white.

This border decoration is put to its proper use on services bearing monograms or coats of arms, which became widespread in the middle of the century and which Deroche and Couderc promoted as their speciality.

Coloured grounds are not a 19th-century innovation. At the end of the 18th century some became very fashionable, but apart from *beau bleu* all were obtained by means of muffle-firing.

A bill head from Schoelcher's factory, dated Year XI, announces: 'We make pictures in the latest style, firing all the grounds at high temperature: blue,

brown, agate, tortoiseshell, buff *(chamois)* and even green with which we alone have achieved success.' Nonetheless, the brown grounds of certain pieces of this period leave room for doubt as to whether high-temperature technique was applied, since they flake off easily. They are chiefly used for items decorated with Antique cameos. Of the rest of the grounds mentioned in this document, 'agate' is a shade that is difficult to determine, but it may be akin to 'nankeen', that pale pinkish beige so popular at the same period. At Sèvres the name 'agate blue' denotes a very light blue, produced from a base of cobalt blue. Buff, a darker beige colour, was most successful. Nearly twenty-five years after this invoice of Schoelcher's, Baruch Weil was exhibiting a tea service with a buff ground (1827).

A further document that postdates Schoelcher's invoice by a few years, to wit the Nast inventory of 1811, mentions a decoration of a 'blue band fired at high temperature', several items with chrome-green grounds, and others with grounds

Ill. 65
Ill. 210, 217
Ill. 240
Ill. 37, 241
Ill. 21

104, 105 Dihl & Guérhard. Marquetry table with ormolu mounts. Hexagonal porcelain top, divided into hexagons and lozenges. Each hexagon encloses a large circular miniature in polychrome, the central one showing *Le Triomphe de Galatée,* surrounded by six episodes from the story of Psyche after Lucius Apuleius' *Metamorphoses.* Every medallion bears the inscription: *Le Guay. 1804. Mfre de Dihl.* In the corners six lozenges contain oval cartouches in reserve. These cameos are signed by Sauvage. A completely unsubstantiated tradition has it that this piece of furniture was presented by Napoleon to King Charles IV of Spain and Queen Marie-Louise, whose interlaced initials appear in the ormolu angle-pieces. The arms of Spain are also inlaid in this occasional table.
Madrid, Palacio de Oriente.

Ill. 36
Ill. 216

105

of matt green, matt yellow or matt blue. These lustreless grounds were extremely popular from 1810 onwards.

The neo-Rococo *décors,* appearing around 1830, mainly comprised grounds of harsh hues; purple, green and black. At the exhibition of 1839 Discry displayed four high-temperature colours—brown, blue,

flesh-tone and chrome green—whereas by 1844 decorators had at their disposal all the greens, yellows and blues, plus a 'celadon green'. Other grounds made it possible to simulate different materials, like bronze, iron and even ivory.

In 1838 a dispute over the turquoise ground broke out between Desfossés and Colville, each claiming authorship. By way of proof Desfossés then brought out the list of twenty-one master decorators who were using his colours. The minutes of Monginot's sales (1837 and 1838) enumerate many objects with turquoise grounds.

Following the coloured grounds a place must be accorded to the marbled grounds

which, as in the previous century, enjoyed public favour. Tortoiseshell grounds were principally used in the Empire period, yet as late as 1823 Denuelle won another prize for his 'unequalled' tortoiseshell grounds.

The mechanical transfer printing processes that were stupendously successful in the field of creamware by virtue of their low costs and excellent performance seem not to have enjoyed so much popularity amongst porcelain lovers. There remain but few pieces decorated by Gonord and Legros d'Anisy. However, such examples as we know of are of very high quality. Their decoration may be monochrome or polychrome, sometimes heightened with gold. The subjects are from popular prints: scenes from mythology, or from ancient or modern history, views of cities or portraits. We should observe, too, the survival of the decoration on a sentimental theme such as this note 'issued' by the 'Banque d'Amitié' (Bank of Friendship), by Gonord, and—more prosaically—the calendars or the commercial puffs. We have, for example, come upon a cup decorated with an advertisement for a reputed optician.

The application of these diverse processes was carried out on a larger scale for ornamental borders decorating the rims, and for rosettes.

When, from 1822 onwards, lithographic techniques were put into practice (principally by Honoré) decoration reached the stage of industrialisation★.

The use of gilt plays an increasingly important part in decoration during the first half of the 19th century. The rims, backs and areas in relief are, on the most sumptuous pieces, completely gilded. Cups, for example★★, are 'lined' with gold. Besides the exclusively gilded decora-

Ill. 108

Ill. 168

Ill. 26

106 Duc d'Orléans' factory. Cylindrical teapot. Green ribbon decorated with mauve roses. Touches of gold. *Circa* 1785. Paris, Coll. Guy Passerat. Ht. 10.5 cm. (4¹/₅ in.). Mark 182.

Ill. 186
Ill. 185

Ill. 164

Ill. 200

★Ill. 36
★★Ill. 130

107 Duc d'Orléans' factory. ▶ *Trembleuse* cup called *à la Reine* ('Queen's style') and its saucer. Two hearts burning on the marriage-altar. Sepia and gold. *Circa* 1790. Sèvres, Musée national de Céramique. Ht. 15 cm. (6 in.). Mark 184.

tions on a white ground which continue,

Ill. 102 and the polychrome decorations on a gilt ground which had already appeared in the 18th century, two further *décors* solely in gold make their appearance shortly after 1800.

The less frequent is a reserve decoration on a gilt ground. In this manner Schoelcher decorated service pieces with vine shoots and bucranes.

The second uses the technique of contrast-burnished gilt, which we have already described. This decoration first served to enrich the rims with ornamental patterns which initially surrounded the medallions before being used for the central panels themselves. Subsequently it spread to the undersides and on the more sumptuous porcelains covered the entire surface area. Certain items executed with especial care are hence gilded all over. We could cite as examples a clock by Darte with a back embellished by a sunburst, and a pair of monumental vases by

Ill. 140 Dagoty, made between 1804 and 1814 and decorated with medallions showing antique figures constituting pictures in their own right, executed with a peerless virtuosity.

From 1811 onwards silver was used by Nast in landscapes of 'grey and blue with silver figures': so, later, was platinum.

The *chinoiserie* decorations of the 18th century survived into the early years of the following century with the same richness. A cup by Dagoty painted in gold

Ill. 130 on a bright lacquer-red ground illustrates this continuity, but right through the first half of the century, and even more in decorations than in shapes, the oriental influence will be present.

After 1830 two tendencies stand out simultaneously: Firstly, copies, claiming to be perfect, of Chinese or Japanese porcelain, particularly with floral decorations and celadon grounds. By 1844 Honoré Ill. 156 and the 'Escalier de Cristal' salesroom were exhibiting various vases quite distinctly inspired from Cantonese wares. Ill. 80 Let us also mention the vases executed in 1827 by Flamen-Fleury for a temple in Peking.

Secondly, a pseudo-Oriental taste which shows an elegant delicacy so long as it keeps to traditional designs, such as some decorations by Schoelcher or Perche, Ill. 35 painted in blue with touches of gold, or again with polychrome birds on a black Ill. 43, 229 ground.

The taste for the Exotic sometimes has its amusing side when the decorator pretends to parody Oriental themes, or still more then he 'orientalizes' a French subject. It makes figures seem disguised. This Ill. 112 fantastic decoration, generally handled in brillant colours, is one which contributes gaiety to the wares of this period.

Biscuit ware

Models in the round occupy a major place in the output from Parisian porcelain factories.

After the manner of the Sèvres factory which was the innovator in this field, modelled pieces—essentially statuettes and various ornamental items—are left in their 'biscuit' state, that is, fired but unglazed.

The technique employed for statuettes and complicated pieces is moulding. Finishing off the piece demands meticulous work, and this is entrusted to the *répareurs*. In *Art de la Porcelaine* the engraver Ransonnette has illustrated perfectly the care required by the various operations that are carried out in a modelling work- Ill. 38 shop.

THE EIGHTEENTH CENTURY

From the earliest years of their existence and in spite of the regulation which reserved the monopoly on modelled porcelain for Sèvres, the Parisian factories turned out an abundance of decorative pieces in biscuit.

Some renowned modellers managed several of the factories: Russinger, for instance, settled in 1777 on Rue Fontaine-au-Roy and surrounded himself with modellers and sculptors, such as Mô who hailed from Mennecy and Sceaux; or again Deruelle, the architect of plastic design, who had composed groups of angels to crown the holy-water stoops for his parish of Montmartre, and whose son studied to be a modeller under Jean Guillaume Moitte[1]; and lastly Dihl who, before partnering Guérhard and setting up the business with him in Rue de Bondy, had been making busts and figures which he sold on the miniaturist Meyer's premises in Rue Saint-Martin (1780).

Around the 1780's two factories, in the Faubourg Saint-Denis and Rue Fontaine-au-Roy, seem to have specialized in the large-scale manufacture of work in the round left in biscuit form. The Clignancourt factory, with a lower output, has bequeathed us some high-quality objects. The number of modellers working in

108 Lefebvre.
Cup in the shape of a human head, the hair bound with a scarf, and its saucer. Matt gold and matt blue.
Circa 1810–1815.
Paris, private coll.
Ht. 7.5 cm. (3 in.).
Mark 188.

---

[1] The painter Alexandre Moitte, brother of Jean Guillaume, married one of Deruelle's daughters and became his successor.

Parisian factories could be considerable; by 1785 about thirty craftsmen were employed on modelling in the Faubourg Saint-Denis. There were twelve of them in Rue de Bondy, whose recent appointments as such did not antedate 1781.

Output chiefly consisted of ornamental pieces for suites and for the table. We are apt to forget nowadays that table-settings called for numerous decorative items amongst which models in silver or ceramics were very well represented.

On January 16th 1777 the *Annonces, affiches et avis divers* notified the public that the Rue Fontaine-au-Roy factory was selling 'figures in biscuit, for ornamenting drawing-rooms and for dessert-courses...'

The items most frequently mentioned in the reign of Louis XVI are divided between (single) figures, groups, busts and vases. The figures and groups sometimes make a pair, for example a gardener and his wife, or constitute a series such as the Elements, the Parts of the World, etc.

The models were provided by the greatest designers and sculptors—Boucher or Falconet—from whose portfolios of designs the factories borrowed their subjects, unless they commissioned them direct. The Parisian workshops found yet another source of inspiration by unashamedly copying the products of Sèvres, and we have already related the protests of Parent over the moulds for 'six charming figures modelled by Boizot' stolen from Sèvres in 1777 on Locré's behalf.

The themes are in keeping with the taste of the period for antiquity and allegory blended with the charm and lightheartedness of pastoral subjects. The *genres* may be arranged under several headings: the *Cris de Paris*—probably after Lemire or

109 Darte Frères.
Model of a circular temple, partly of coloured biscuit.
Circa 1810.
Private coll. Ht. 37 cm.
(14$^1/_5$ in.).
Mark 77.

Cyfflé[2]—*Enfants* after Boucher and Falconet; cupids, divinities and mythological groups, allegories, pastoral scenes and animals. The art of portraiture was not neglected, as numerous references to famous people can attest.

The documents dealing with the Comte d'Artois' factory have enabled us to draw up a list of one hundred and twenty-five subjects. They comprise various figures and groups executed in the factory before the end of the 18th century.

The inventory of 1776 itemizes the 'painted pieces, white ware, gold and figures' in the store-room, and the same year one of the partners partly paid himself in kind by taking 'two groups of chimney-sweeps' which we may assume to have belonged to the series of *Cris de Paris*[3].

The inventory for 1778 of this same factory includes in this extensive series sellers (male and female) of dogs, of bouquets, of pencils, pins, stoneware, herbs, *plaisirs* (a kind of cake), ribbons, canaries, etc., totalling more than forty-five subjects of dealers in different things, plus subjects from other itinerant trades—the boot-black or the hirer-out of umbrellas. The children and cupids are fewer but provide some charming *ensembles,* such as *Groupe de Polissons* or *L'Amour rémouleur.* Mythological figures, together with a host of divinities, especially Venus— *Vénus au Bain, Vénus fouettant l'Amour*— are frequently to be found, and so are a score of pastoral subjects such as: *Le Berger chéri, La Chasse aux Oies, Le Jardinier* and *La Jardinière.* Amongst the varied allegorical subjects we might pick out *L'Anglais à Cheval, L'Espagnol, Les Quatre Saisons, L'Homme à la Perruque, Le Père de Famille* and *Le Jaloux.*

The busts of Louis XVI and Marie-Antoinette, of Henri IV and Sully are also mentioned in 1778, along with a tall figure of Christ, some 'swan vases' and a watch stand.

Similar subjects may be discerned in all the factories in which confiscations were carried out in January and February 1780. Be it in Clignancourt, Rue Thiroux or Rue Fontaine-au-Roy, all the important factories of Paris at that time manufactured more or less successfully: the *Cris de Paris* (Rue Thiroux), *Enfants* (Rue Fontaine-au-Roy), mythological figures and groups, Bacchantes, Hercules (Clignancourt), Perseus and Andromeda (Rue Fontaine-au-Roy), pastoral subjects (Clignancourt), antique figures, Belisarius (Faubourg Saint-Denis, Rue Thiroux), Henri IV (Faubourg Saint-Denis, Rue Thiroux), and animals, such as goats and marmots (Rue Thiroux).

Ill. 42

Slightly later, when the Comte d'Artois sent a large order to his factory of the Faubourg Saint-Denis in 1784, he bought several examples, varying in size, of a good many models, including *L'Amour piqué par une Abeille, La Conversation espagnole* and *Enfants* after Boucher and Falconet.

The La Courtille factory executed a bust in biscuit of Madame du Barry, after a plaster by Pajou. This bust occasioned grave misapprehension. The model for it had been executed at Sèvres as early as 1771 and sold for six *louis* (18 *livres*). Now, Locré was asking the enormous sum of 12,000 *livres.* The considerable discrepancy between the prices was no doubt explicable in terms of the very different dimensions of the two objects, as is evident from Locré's entry in the accounts of Madame du Barry as published by Davillier[4]: 'Instead of the one at 12,000 *livres* previously supplied and delivered

[2] Charles Gabriel Sauvage, called Lemire (1741–1827) Modeller. Cyfflé, Paul Louis (1724–1806). Plastic artist to Kings Stanislas at Lunéville: modelled statuettes and groups in *terre de Lorraine.*
[3] In French, *savoyards:* young boys from Savoy were for a long time the chimney-sweeps of Paris.

[4] Davillier, Ch. *Les Porcelaines de Sèvres de Madame du Barry.* According to Ph. Dally this bust was signed *Russinger 1776,* and in 1912 belonged to the Vicomte d'Arlincourt's collection (cf. Ph. Dally, Belleville. *Histoire d'une localité parisienne sous la Révolution.* Paris, Schmit, 1912).

to Madame la Comtesse du Barry by the factory of German porcelain established at La Basse-Courtille in the month of December 1773: 'A life-size porcelain bust executed after the plaster which has been submitted to it by M. Pajou, in accordance with the orders of Madame la Comtesse, worth 3,000 *livres. L. 3,000*' Signed: *Locré*.

The success of busts derives from the contemporary taste for portraits—a taste which will remain pronounced during the ensuing decades.

Prud'homme in *L'Ancien et le Nouveau Paris* notes that in the course of the Revolution one witnessed the appearance on mantelpieces of the bust of the latest idol: busts of Necker, the Duc d'Orléans and La Fayette were succeeded by the effigy of Mirabeau,[5] then Bailly (Mayor of Paris) and finally Marat and Robespierre.

The inventory drafted in Year VI at the factory of Rue Fontaine-au-Roy gives details about the biscuit ware of the Revolutionary period which in reality does not differ from that made in the reign of Louis XVI. Divinities, mythological groups, allegories and pastoral scenes are the subjects most frequently mentioned. We may nonetheless note that many figures are described as being 'on a column' so as to raise the subject.[6] Finally, in a text, we record the first reference to a clock. Its subject is a group from 'Pygmalion'.

Although this reference dates from Year VI, we should not deduce from this that Parisian factories had produced no biscuit clock cases prior to this date. We know of a certain number of examples of them, but nonetheless it does not seem that these monumental pieces were commonly manufactured before the end of the century.

Nast in particular was about to excel at creating clocks whose allegorical subjects (Astronomy) or mythological ones (Mercury and Hebe) were realized in blue and white biscuit, coloured in the mass in imitation of Wedgwood.

Ill. 213

The fashion for imitations of Wedgwood ware, created by the impossibility of importing any because of the Blockade, is reflected in vases, including one signed by 'Citizen Nast' *(Citoyen Nast)* (Musée national de Céramique de Sèvres): it is also attested by plaques and medallions, the body for which Despréz boastfully claimed to have discovered as far back as 1783, and, too, by the clocks turned out by the Dihl & Guérhard factory.

For the sake of refinement the blue is occasionally replaced by grey or mauve. In 1797 Dihl, wishing to have his portrait painted, had a biscuit model of exceptional dimensions placed beside him. It was of a naked child reading★. He had to be a past master of this technique in order to obtain so sizable a piece.

110 Bringeon.
Cylindrical cup and saucer. Brown and mauve landscape touched with gold.
Circa 1805.
Geneva, Musée de l'Ariana.
Ht. 6 cm. (2¹/₃ in.).
Mark 46.

★Ill. 98

[5] We know of two different models of Mirabeau's bust, both executed at the Faubourg Saint-Denis factory, one of them being datable to 1790.

[6] A group called *Vénus et l'Amour* perched upon a column is kept in the Palacio Nacional da Sintra, Portugal and is reproduced in the *Cahiers de la céramique,* no. 38, p. 109.

111 Blancheron.
Cylindrical cup and saucer.
Decoration simulating red-
wood with black veins, on
which is set – in Niderviller
style – a grisaille print. At
the bottom of such prints,
the inscription *Fait chez
Blancheron* serves to identify
the gold-painted EB mark

underneath the cup, entered
by Chavagnac and Grollier
as unexplained.
Circa 1800.
Paris, Coll. Le Tallec.
Ht. 6 cm. (2¹/₃ in.).
Mark 40.

At the same time the factory that he was
managing attained further success by dint
of making bronzed biscuit wares which
deceptively simulated patinated bronzes.
In the inventory after Dihl's death we
find old stock such as Sauvage's[7] bronze-
painted bas-relief showing cupids at play,
which was exhibited in Year VI, together
with a 'bull in bronzed biscuit on a gilt
plinth'; some goblets 'with bronzed
heads'; and 'two candelabra with figures
of Egyptian women in biscuit; bronzed
and bearing girandoles of gilt brass for
four candles. Sea-green marble plinths
mounted in brass'. Busts and baskets were
also produced using this technique, but
few examples have come down to us. A

rather austere style was no doubt more
in keeping with Revolutionary ideas than
the biscuit flowers previously made in
the 18th century. By 1793, however, we
observe in the trade register of 'Le Petit
Carrousel' 'a bouquet in biscuit and its
bocal'—meaning its glass globe. In Year
VI Russinger was selling a Medici vase

with a biscuit garland. It will be mainly
in the 19th century that Dagoty and
Honoré stand out in this form. In this
context it is not superfluous to recall that
Honoré at the beginning of the 19th century had bought up a factory producing
biscuit flowers, on which he had founded
his business.

THE NINETEENTH CENTURY

The output of biscuit ware in the 19th
century is only a continuation from the
preceding century, although models grow
more complicated and dimensions more
imposing.

If we are to cite some innovations let us
point to the factories at the beginning of
the century which blended biscuit ware
with glazed porcelain—Lefebvre and
Dagoty, for example.

The latter more exploited this process,
with a virtuosity whose excesses sometimes gave rise to artefacts in dubious taste,
such as the egg-cups made up of a cupid on
all fours supporting a gilt holder, a faintly
ridiculous variation upon another, more
successful type of egg-cup borne by a
kneeling cupid. The writing sets are   Ill. 134
better illustrations of this union whereby
a biscuit statuette is integrated into a
setting of painted or gilded porcelain★.

Dagoty evinces the same dexterity with
a service entirely of biscuit adorned with
reliefs, palmettes and rosettes, some of
which are touched with gold. This serv-
ice★★ is very similar to a porcelain *cabaret*
from Sèvres, given by Napoleon in 1813   ★Ill. 121, 122
to the Maréchale Augereau, Duchesse de   ★★Ill. 117, 118
Castiglione (Musée national de Céra-
mique de Sèvres).

Darte, too, produced decorative pieces in
biscuit and glazed porcelain, such as the
circular colonnaded temple, inspired from   Ill. 109
Antiquity.

112 Cassé-Maillard.
Cache-pot (flower-pot case).
Polychrome decoration on
black ground, psuedo-
Chinese. *Circa* 1835.
Paris, Coll. Le Tallec.
Ht. 30 cm. (11⅘ in.).
Mark 49.

---

[7] Sauvage, Piat or Pieter Joseph (1744–1818). Painter of flowers
and still life, painter on porcelain and enamel, and modeller.

Under the Empire Nast made some biscuit wares that were remarkable in their
quality and their size. The busts of Napoleon and Joséphine (1806) and the groups

Ill. 232 such as a Bacchanal, after Lemire, reached
exceptional proportions.

An allegory of the Emporer, entitled *Le
Vainqueur d'Austerlitz apportant à l'Europe
l'Olivier de la Paix* ('The Victor of Austerlitz bringing to Europe the Olive-Branch
of Peace'), was exhibited by Russinger
and Pouyat in 1806, and by 1819 Nast
was causing a sensation with his tall Corinthian columns of faultlessly executed

Ill. 76 biscuit.

Beside these outstanding exploits ordinary wares still consisted of figures and
groups with 'bespectacled' clocks (*à lu-
nettes*—with a circular opening into which
the movement is fitted), and vases.

A large proportion of the figures act as

Ill. 81 foils to the fruit baskets which complete
the dessert services and are sometimes
very delicately made. Still more are found
in the inventory taken after Madame
Flamen-Fleury's death in 1826: 'kneeling
figures for baskets' and in Pouyat-Duvignaud's records for 1828: 'a winged figure on a column for a basket'.

Until around 1830 the most diverse subjects are still handled in the tradition of
the 18th century. We find scenes from
Antiquity and mythology such as *Diane
et son Chien, Narcisse se mirant dans l'Eau*,
allegories such as *La Guerre, L'Espérance*,
and busts including Louis XVIII or Emperor Alexander of Russia (Pouyat 1828).
We must add to these the highly sentimental family scenes: *Le Premier Pas de
l'Enfant* and its companion-piece *Dites
s'il vous plaît* (Pouyat, 1828).

The themes of many clocks are related to
the groups: *L'Amour gardé par la Fidélité*
or *L'Attrapeur d'Ecureuils* (Pouyat, 1828).
Other clocks have subjects in gilded biscuit (Flamen-Fleury, 1826).

As from this period, however, we notice
the general public's dislike of biscuit
ware. Such, at any rate, was the opinion
of the manager at Sèvres. By 1828 Dihl,
winding up what remained of his once
brilliant factory, was offering to sell
Brongniart his collection of pseudo-antique models executed by Lemire. Brongniart declined this offer with the excuse
that 'the taste for biscuit ware has faded
so much that we have a great deal of
trouble occuping even the two modellers left in the factory, and if it were
not for the ornamental pieces and busts
of the royal family, a single craftsman
would suffice'.

About 1850 Jacob Petit attempted to
rejuvenate the biscuit art by covering the
statuettes of brides or children with lace,   Ill. 182
by means of an ingenious process already
described above, whilst Gille kept to
tradition with statuettes that met with
much success. Jacob Petit produced cups
and other pieces in the round, glazed
inside and having an outer surface adorned with pseudo-antique bas-reliefs.   Ill. 183

114 Chapelle.
Clock of 'milestone' shape.
Polychrome and gold on
green ground. Allegorical
representation of the Arts.
White porcelain by Jacob
Petit. *Circa* 1834.
Paris, Coll. Le Tallec.
Ht. 38 cm. (14³/₅ in.).
Mark 125, and on the dial
Chapelle à Paris.

115 Chanou.
Cylindrical cup and saucer.
Polychrome decoration on
nankeen ground. *Circa* 1784.
London, British Museum.
Ht. 6.5 cm. (2½ in.).
Mark 48.

Historical Account of the Factory

Introduction

Any classification of the Paris porcelain factories runs into numerous difficulties as no one system is entirely satisfactory. The chronological order would be hard to lay down, as the foundation date of certain establishments cannot always be ascertained with sufficient accuracy.

The topographical order would be still less convenient to adopt, since many factories had several successive sites and the exact address of some of them is unknown.

The purely alphabetic order, proceeding by the names of the porcelain makers would still seem the best, but it poses no less of a problem, as the same establishment was often passed on from owner to owner in the course of its existence.

Finally, it seemed a wise course to adopt a compromise between these possible classifications. At the beginning we have arranged the privileged factories in chronological order, considering them as making up a separate category as much by their fame and age as by virtue of the princely protection from which they benefitted. Moreover, their respective histories have many points in common.

In a second category we have classified in alphabetic order the rest of the establishments, designating each one by the name of its best-known owner or manager. In addition, an index allows any essential cross-references to be made.

Privileged Factories

116 Map of Paris before the outlying communes were annexed. The solid white frame encloses the area in which most of the earlier porcelain-factories gathered, in other words primarily the districts of Le Temple and the Faubourg Saint-Antoine, or roughly the north-eastern quarter of Paris (Rues du Faubourg Saint-Denis, des Récollets, de Bondy, Fontaine-au-Roy, Pierre-Levée, de Crussol, des Trois-Bornes, Popincourt, des Amandiers, de Charonne, de la Roquette, de Charenton, Amelot des Boulets, de Reuilly, etc.). The factories which settled outside this area were few, but such was the case with Clignancourt (to the North, beyond the gates), and Rue Thiroux (today part of Rue Caumartin).

THE FACTORY OF THE COMTE D'ARTOIS

Faubourg Saint-Denis

The Faubourg Saint-Denis factory was founded by Pierre Antoine Hannong in 1772. Pierre Antoine was the grandson of Claude François, a native of Maastricht who settled at Strassburg in 1709, bringing into France the secret—jealously guarded by Saxony—of hard-paste porcelain. He was the son of Paul, who is referred to elsewhere.

Pierre Antoine was born at Strassburg in 1739 and, as soon as his father died, took charge of the negotiations for the sale of the family secrets to the factory of Sèvres. In fact, the seller himself was not entirely acquainted with these secrets and was just living on his wits, together with his friend Lassia whom we shall meet again later as the manufacturer in Rue de Reuilly. 'There is nothing of which Lassia and Hannong are incapable...' said a police report.

Meanwhile Hannong set up a faience factory in the Château de Vincennes, on the premises formerly used by the royal factory; then, at Vaux near Meulan, he established a second works for producing porcelain. It is highly likely that he made porcelain at Vincennes as well. It was out

In the 18th century the salesrooms were located in the residential districts near the Louvre and the Faubourg Saint-Germain. The dotted frame corresponds to the area where decorating-workshops and salesrooms were later – mainly after 1820 – to be set up. Indeed, the 19th century saw a shift towards the West which may be accounted for as follows: the post-1820 exodus into the provinces of most factories (apart from a few which kept to their original sites) occasioned the creation of many decorating-workshops, generally in the districts of La Porte Saint-Martin, Le Temple and the Faubourg Saint-Denis – therefore to the West of the first rectangle, in the zone where the two rectangles overlap. Hence, these workshops stood near the northern factories: Rues des Vinaigriers, Corbeau, du Faubourg Saint-Denis, des Petites-Ecuries; then, further South, Rue de Poitou, Rue de l'Arbre-Sec, Rue Jean-Jacques Rousseau.

For their part the salesrooms sprang up still further West, in the elegant districts of the Grands Boulevards and the Palais Royal. Boulevard Poissonnière, and Boulevards des Italiens and des Capucines were particularly busy, as were the neighbouring streets: Rue Vivienne, Rue Neuve des Capucines, and Rue de la Paix.

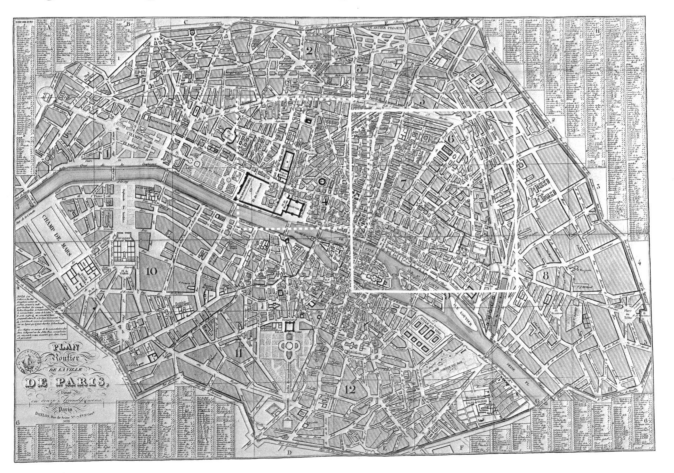

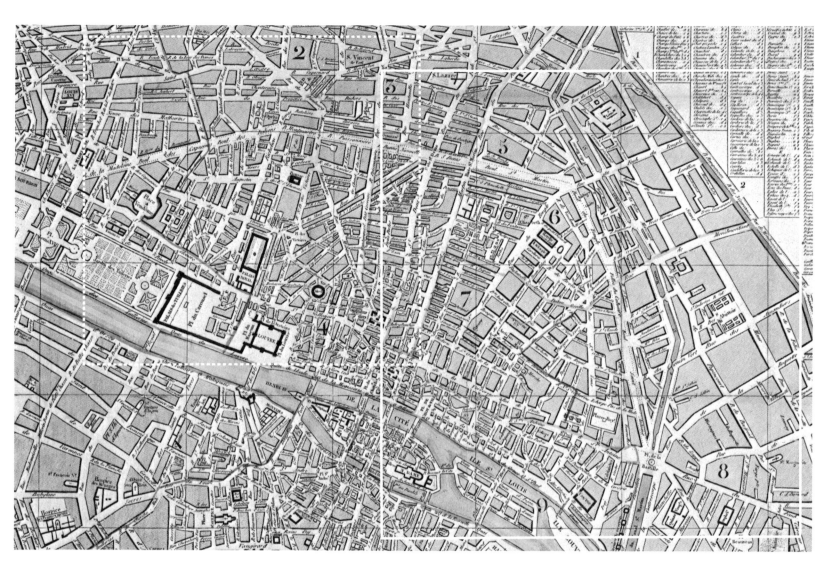

The *passages* (arcades), where the elegant shops stood side by side, were especially popular – Passage de l'Opéra, for instance. Lastly, we should note a few anomalous factories in the district of Le Roule, west of Rue Thiroux (Rue du Rocher, Rue des Grésillons), and finally on the left (south) bank of the Seine, Dagoty's factory at Montparnasse, and some salesrooms in Rue du Bac or Rue Grenelle-Saint-Germain. Plan de Paris, Danlos, 1833. Paris, Bibliothèque historique de la Ville de Paris.

of the debris of the Vaux and Vincennes factories that he built up the one in the Faubourg Saint-Denis. The fresh capital which he now invested was put at his disposal by a deed of partnership of June 6th 1772, signed by Louis Victor de Fusée, Comte de Voisenon, and by Claude Martin Dormoy. They thus agreed to become partners 'in the venture of a factory for porcelain from which there are grounds to hope for the most glorious success'. The funds that were put up amounted to 30,000 *livres* and Hannong who had contributed nothing (with good

reason, too) reserved for himself as author of the enterprise two-thirds of the profits. He did, however, supply all the working plant, which was valued by him at 32,000 *livres*. He could therefore pay off his debts forthwith. On the same day the sleeping partners had mortgaged off some of their properties for 1,250 *livres* in annual income so as to raise the requisite outlay of 30,000 *livres*. Six days later the lease for the premises was signed. Over the first six months Hannong swallowed up the capital and claimed to have manufactured more than

24,000 *livres*' worth of porcelain. However, he was always being pursued by his creditors.

On May 26th 1773 he enrolled with the Lieutenant général de Police and registered his trade mark, the capital letter H. Expenditure became heavier and heavier and his sleeping partners hastened to give up their rights as from October 13th 1773 to the Marquis d'Usson. In order to acquire them the Marquis had borrowed 24,000 *livres*. Almost always away from Paris—d'Usson was at the time colonel of the provincial regiment of Montargis and Lieutenant de Roi of the province of Foix—he appointed proxies and accumulated deeds signed by the interested parties and their 'men of straw'.

The second partnership deed, signed by Hannong with Aubourg, d'Usson's 'man of straw', is dated October 18th 1773. Other people joined d'Usson and Hannong, beginning with Jacques Pascal Barrachin in 1774 who supervised the factory's trading affairs. He had become insolvent in Paris earlier that year and had gone 'scandalously bankrupt' at Lyons as a corn merchant. On June 30th an agreement between the partners stated that, since the factory's business was daily growing more extensive and active it therefore needed funds, and Barrachin was instructed to borrow a sum not exceeding 20,000 *livres* on behalf of the factory. Two months later Hannong, d'Usson and Barrachin acknowledged

117 Dagoty & Honoré. Designs for a teapot, cream jug, sugar bowl and cup in biscuit. Between 1804 and 1814.

From *Recueil de modèles de porcelaine peinte et dorée de la manufacture de Dagoty et Honoré*.
Paris, Library of Musée des Arts décoratifs.

118 Dagoty.
Cup embellished with biscuit palmettes in relief. An almost identical piece, belonging to a *cabaret*, is illustrated in the factory's portfolio of designs. Depending on the decoration, the price varied between 16 and 22 francs. The technique used was moulding – the seam here being quite conspicuous. A tea-set in the same vein, from the imperial factory of Sèvres, was executed in 1813 for Mme Augereau, Duchess of Castiglione. Between 1804 and 1814.
Lisbon, Museu Nacional de Arte Antigua. Ht. 10.5 cm. (4¹/₅ in.).
Marks 57 and 64.

that they owed 4,500 *livres* to Sieur Boutet who had lent them this sum to pay the craftsmen. At the end of August Barrachin addressed certain complaints against Hannong to the Marquis d'Usson, who at the time was commanding his regiment at Montauban. Alarmed, d'Usson instructed his notary to check the justification for the complaints and to commence legal proceedings. The nomination of Balthazar Byellard (or Byellert) from Haguenau as foreman of the factory came shortly before the dissolution of the company. An out-of-court settlement of October 1st 1774 set Hannong free but made d'Usson and Barrachin liable for the factory's debts. The preamble stated

that the venture, instead of yielding a profit, 'was becoming onerous owing to the funds which continually had to be sunk into it'. Hannong received a sum of more than 3,000 *livres,* part of which was to be used for redeeming the chattels belonging to the factory which he had pawned at the baker's, in particular three clocks and eight pieces of muslin.

A comprehensive schedule of the factory, drawn up on October 3rd 1774, reveals that the establishment was in debt to the tune of 104,887 *livres,* giving a net loss of more than 4,000 *livres.* Hannong vacated the premises as he had undertaken to do, before November 1st 1774. We come upon him two years later at Vinovo

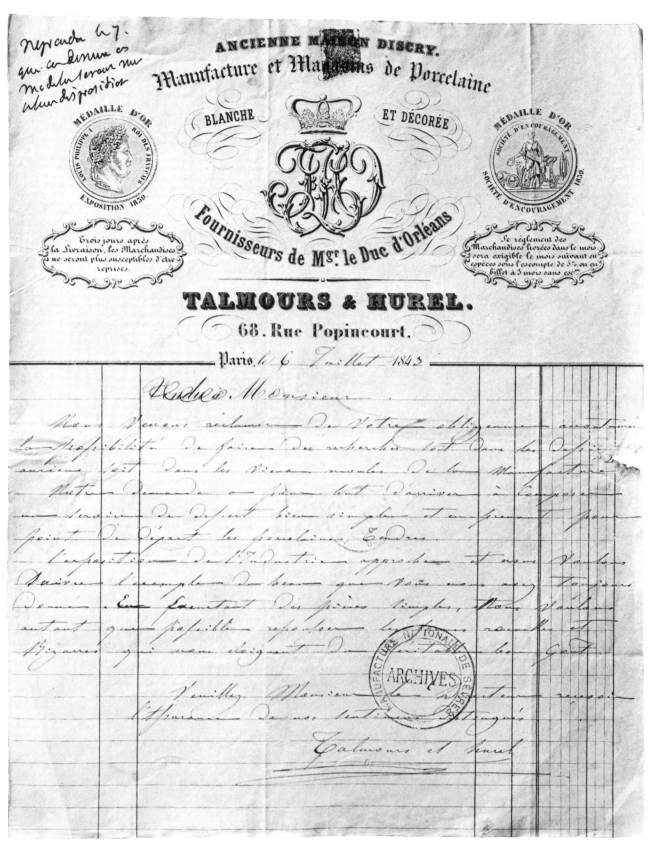

119 Letter from Talmours and Hurel, Discry's successors, addressed to Brongniart and dated July 6th 1843. They are requesting his permission to conduct research into the superannuated designs and old moulds belonging to Sèvres, with the object of 'drawing up a perfectly simple dessert-service derived from soft-paste wares'. The manufacturers were planning this service for the Exhibition of 1844 and hence were thinking of 'rejecting the bizarre Rococo shapes which are divorcing us from truly good taste'. The letter bears the following annotation by Brongniart: 'Replied on 7th that the drawings and models would be made available to them'. This document illustrates the spirit of trust and co-operation established between Brongniart and the Parisian manufacturers during his 47 years of office as head of the Sèvres factory. Sèvres, Archives de la manufacture nationale.

120   Dagoty & Honoré.
Designs for various sorts of
cups and decorations. Taken
from the *Recueil de modèles de
porcelaine peinte et dorée de la
manufacture de Dagoty et
Honoré. Circa* 1815.
Paris, Library of Musée des
Arts décoratifs.

near Turin. He then returned to France. He was in Haguenau in 1780 to contest a lawsuit. He died in 1794, after vainly attempting to sell some new techniques to Sèvres.

After Hannong's departure there were two co-managers at the factory: Barrachin, in charge of the commercial section

and Byellard on the production side. A new deed of partnership dated October 7th 1774 names three sleeping partners: the Marquis d'Usson, the Marquis de la Salle and Barrachin. They were to supply an outlay of 62,000 *livres*. The capital in question not being in the partners' possession, they gave up their rights the very same day, borrowed from various people and had their rights restored to them a few days later. On February 9th 1775 a further partner, Bénard (or Renard) joined them upon payment of a 10,000-*livre* contribution in the form of loans. Eventually, because of the size of the debts (79,000 *livres*), which was shown up in a factory-schedule drafted by

Barrachin on April 18th 1775, and in spite of a favourable balance for the first time ever, the partners decided upon an augmentation and redivision of the company's capital. It was henceforth composed of one hundred shares *(sols),* a portion of them being equally divided between the four recognized partners, the re-

maining shares to be distributed among people wishing to invest in the venture. We now witness an incredible trafficking in the shares making up the company-funds. A certain Ricard actually received a 1,000-*livre* reward 'for having brought along' a new dupe, the Baron de Lunar, to whom ten shares were handed over. By April 1st 1776 the partners were seven in number[1]. The most sharp-witted ones extricated themselves speedily. The Baron de Lunar got rid of four shares on May 2nd, the direct result of which was to reduce Ricard's reward to 600 *livres,* and on May 31st he demanded to be refunded the 12,000 *livres* left to him in the factory. The documents do not state

121 Dagoty & Honoré. Drawings for various writing-sets. Together with food-warmers or night-lights *(veilleuses),* writing-sets met with a great deal of success between about 1820 and 1850. The designs vary widely, often incorporating components in biscuit and painted or gilded porcelain. 'Snails' and conchshells were also frequently used for cups in questionable taste (ill. 127). Further designs, with cupids or pseudo-antique statuettes in biscuit, keep to the tradition of statuettes (ill. 121). It is, however, simply astonishing to behold Ceres flanked by two life-like snails (ill. 127[b]). The 'Russian-style' writing-sets, although more original, are merely derived from the successful Saint-Petersburg designs of 'male and female water-carrier' (ills. 126 and 126[a]). The only change is in the position of the pails, for the sake of their functional purpose which now replaces their anecdotal relevance. Curiously enough, the water-carrier has also been exchanged for a cupid (ill. 126[a]). This writing-set cost 20 francs, whereas the Ceres model was priced at 60 and a straightforward 'snail' inkwell at only 10.
Circa 1830–1835.
Paris, Library of Musée des Arts décoratifs.

(See pages 170–172 and 175.)

[1] Usson, La Salle, Lunar, La Chastre, Millon d'Ainval, Barrachin and Fleury Gombault.

122 Dagoty.
Writing set.
The eagle is of gilded biscuit.
Between 1804 and 1814.
Musée national de La Mal-
maison. Ht. 23 cm. (9 in.).
Mark 62.

also involved the Marquis d'Usson and Boutet de Monvel.

The factory of the Faubourg Saint-Denis, however, did not founder. Chaussard became its manager from June to November 1776, Byellard staying in charge of the technical side. Chaussard's first report severely criticized the management of his predecessors, citing wares entered in the inventories at far-fetched prices, excessively burdensome agreements reached with agents and salesrooms, and goods bought at inflated prices. In his conclusion he insisted on the need to find new sales outlets. Chaussard, with the partners' authorization, distributed handbills on which his name alone figured, which occasioned vehement protests from Byellard and then a lawsuit between himself and the company. Jean Antoine Laurent Deleutre, a burgher of Avignon, took over from Chaussard on December 23rd 1776 and did not leave until May 12th 1779. The inventory of March 1st 1777 brought to light a deficit of 66,000 *livres,* explained largely in terms of 'the previous bad administrations' and 'the defects of early products'. Deleutre took precedence on a new partnership-deed of April 26th 1777 on which only La Salle, La Chastre and Millon d'Ainval appear. A certain Houdeyer was appointed as auditor and was immediately empowered to raise 30,000 *livres.*

The situation was precarious and owing to the accumulated borrowings La Chastre and La Salle decided upon the *pro forma* sale of the factory, on January 24th 1778, to Deleutre who in reality was only acting vicariously for La Salle himself. A letter from Parent declared that 'La Salle, d'Usson and others are losing 160,000 *livres* on the factory, without counting

whether Ricard collected any of his commission. The summer of 1776 saw the number of partners dwindle further. Barrachin left the apparently sinking ship. He handed over his shares to La Salle and La Chastre and gave up the managership of the establishment. Taking possession of some of the factory's equipment for his own use he departed, lured away by new and more fruitful ventures in which he invested the 60,000 *livres* that Parent accused him of carrying off. The first in question was the trade in carriages and harness, then an opthalmic elixir. On October 31st 1776 he signed the deed of partnership which created the Queen's factory on Rue Thiroux in which he the first outlays which come to more than 200,000 *livres'*. Deleutre resigned on May 12th 1779 and his liabilities were not discharged until legal proceedings had been commenced against him.

At the same time the Lieutenant général de Police was obliged to issue an order concerning the enforcement of the regulations laid down about the exclusive privilege of the Sèvres factory. The confiscation that followed the search at Catrice and Barbé's house, which we have already discussed above, probably motivated La Salle's sale of the factory to Stahn on October 29th 1779—undoubtedly a sham transaction. Since 1772 Stahn had been attached to the factory as a painter and it was he who registered the new mark CP on September 5th 1779, disclosing that the company enjoyed the protection of Charles Philippe, Comte d'Artois.

It is in this period that the incidents in the struggle against Sèvres occur, but we have already discussed them.

La Salle, left alone after Stahn had departed (probably for Russia), quit in his turn, after sinking more than 300,000 *livres* into the factory and after selling up his estates of Carrières and Badanville for this purpose.

Louis Joseph Bourdon, Seigneur des Planches, settled at the Faubourg Saint-Denis in 1782[2]. Born at Alençon in 1723, he became a King's Counsellor and then first clerk to an administrator of finances *(intendant des finances)*. He died at Paris in 1800. It seems that initially Bourdon was the owner and director of the factory. Later he took on some managers: Josse, a chemist, was a works' supervisor *(chef des travaux)* from 1787: Houël in 1793 officially joined the board.

The era during which Bourdon Desplan-

ches ran the factory was marked by two events: the tests with firing by mineral coal in 1782, and the resumption of the struggle against Sèvres in 1783 which was punctuated with protests and petitions to the Administration.

The decree of 1787 finally rewarded Bourdon's perseverance in his fight; his

factory was exempted from the concourse. Thereupon he changed camp and subsequently complained to M. de Tolozan of the difficulty of detecting contraventions by other *entrepreneurs*.

The two years that followed must have been prosperous since their history is unknown. Then came the dark days of

123 Dagoty.
Cylindrical cup and saucer. Pompeian-red ground with violets and dark-green palmettes. *Circa* 1810.
Paris, Coll. Guy Passerat.

[2] Bourdon belonged to the Conseil des Subsistances in 1789 and became *administrateur* of the Commune. One of his sons was the head of a porcelain factory at Orléans; another, Léonard, was dubbed the Leopard of the Revolution for his sinister deeds; Marc Antoine the third, was Ministre de la Marine under the Directory.

124 Dagoty.
Tea- or coffee-service. The
shapes and decorations are
characteristic of this factory.
Circa 1810.
Geneva, Musée de l'Ariana.
Teapot: Ht. 20 cm. (7⁴/₅ in.).
Mark 57.

the Revolution. It was probably in Year II that Bourdon left the Faubourg Saint-Denis.

In the lease of Brumaire 17th, Year II, Louis Houël is described as the factory's *entrepreneur*. He declares himself to be perfectly familiar with the premises 'through the experience which he has of them as nominee of Citizen Bourdon des Planzes'. He was probably the works overseer. Houël was still in office when the property was sold off in Years III and IV, the purchaser being this time the Benjamin family. Was there any partnership between Houël and Benjamin? This is quite probable. A table of the factories, of much later date, notes that Houël and Benjamin have gone bankrupt, but we have recovered no balance-sheet. Then again, it is Benjamin who figures on the Memorandum of Julien of Vendémiaire 7th, Year VII. Now, the Benjamin family had already sold the property to Schoelcher on Floréal 9th, Year VI. On the other hand Houël is mentioned in the *Almanach du Commerce* of Year VII as a faience

maker, and the next year he is named as one of the porcelain manufacturers on Rue des Blancs-Manteaux. It is probably the same Benjamin whom we encounter in 1801 running the salesroom of the Fontainebleau porcelain factory.

Of all the manufacturers who succeeded one another in the Faubourg Saint-Denis only the last two, Benjamin and Schoelcher, actually owned the grounds, buildings and factory funds: the other men who ran the concern owned only the capital and rented the property. This had belonged to the Huet family since 1753 and passed into the possession of Quinibert le Roux, a sculptor, on Floréal 7th, Year II, for 100,000 *livres,* plus 3,000 *livres* as dower for the widowed Madame Huet. It was re-sold on Thermidor 5th, Year II, to Citizen Saint-Cricq for 603,000 *livres* in promissory notes. On Thermidor 29th, Year IV, the Benjamin family acquired it at a cost of 200,000 francs, and resold it on Floréal 9th, Year VI, to Marc Schoelcher for 35,000 francs, plus Madame Huet's dower.

125 Schœlcher.
These bill heads display the arms of the King and of the Duchesse de Berry. Harking back to the tradition of the *Ancien Régime,* Schœlcher was hereby recalling that the factory he had bought after the Revolution had previously enjoyed the patronage of the Comte d'Artois, who became King Charles X. Paris, Library of the Institut d'Art et d'Archéologie; formerly Coll. Haumont.

◀126 Dagoty & Honoré. Design for a writing set. See also caption on page 166, and pages 171, 172 and 175.

126ᵃ Dagoty & Honoré.
Design for writing sets.
See caption on page 166,
also pages 170, 172 and 175.

The whole complex consisted of a passage way leading into a vast square-shaped site from which there arose various blocks of buildings separated by gardens.

SCHŒLCHER

Marc Schoelcher was born at Fessenheim (Haut-Rhin), where his father was a farmer, on April 26th 1766. He died in Paris on October 14th 1832. In about 1789 Marc came to Paris. He was apparently intending to pursue his studies at the seminary, but the Revolution forced him to change course. He had been received in Paris by a cousin of his mother's (Jeanne Hoffmann). This cousin, Christiana-Caritas Hoffmann, was the wife of Locré who had just given up his factory at La Courtille to Russinger. Marc Schoelcher was thus quickly initiated into the secrets of porcelain and, when he married 'Citizeness Victoire Jacob Marchande, a linen-draper' on Messidor 1st, Year VI, the signing of the contract took place in the presence of Laurent Russinger, a wholesale merchant, his son Christophe, Jean Baptiste Locré, a former merchant and his wife. This union lasted but a short while, for Madame Schoelcher asked for a separation of their property on June 21st 1806. This separation had extremely far-reaching consequences for the factory.

One of the three sons born of this

union, Victor (July 22nd 1804 – December 26th 1893), helped his father in his business as soon as he had left college in 1819, and simultaneously launched himself into politics. However, by a deed of partnership of December 21st 1828, Marc Schoelcher took Victor into the business, under the trade name of Schoelcher et Fils. Soon afterwards Marc Schoelcher sent Victor off to Latin America to sell his father's porcelain, while his brother Jules was dispatched to the Orient on the same mission. No one could depict Victor Schoelcher better than his friend Legouvé: 'I cannot help laughing when I think that Schoelcher began life as a travelling salesman and porcelain merchant. His father, the founder of a fine salesroom on the corner of Rue Grange-Batelière, had the odd idea, knowing *him,* of sending him off to Mexico for twenty years with a job-lot of goods. Schoelcher as canvasser. Schoelcher waiting in an antechamber! Schoelcher unpacking his merchandise and buttering up his clients!... He would

have suffered a hundred deaths rather than resign himself to such a role. Thus he returned in eighteen months' time with an immense cargo of trinkets, costumes and curios of every kind, having lost his hair through dengue, having learnt Spanish with the Mexicans—chiefly the women—thoroughly knowing the country

through which he had travelled on horseback, but as to the goods, he would have been most abashed to give news of them, having left them to do their own business, that is to say having posted them to all the addresses given him without sparing them a further thought apart from one letter which someone obligingly undertook to deliver...'[3] After visiting Mexico, Havana and the United States, Victor Schoelcher on his return to Paris published his impressions, in the form of letters, in the *Revue de Paris.* A born artist—for he had never touched a brush or pencil—Victor Schoelcher observed and invented; everything which he used had been conceived by him—his furniture, his door-knobs, etc. A friend of Chopin, Berlioz and Pleyel, one would meet him at Liszt's home, at Eugène Sue's, Legouvé's and Marie d'Agoult's, where he made the acquaintance of George Sand: she speaks of him in *Histoire de ma Vie,* whilst Victor Hugo later admired him on the barricades of July, in *Histoire d'un Crime.*

129 Dagoty.
Cylindrical cup and saucer.
Frieze of polychrome birds on black ground.
Circa 1810.
Musée national de La Malmaison. Ht. 6.3 cm. (2½ in.).
Mark 57.

127–127a
Dagoty & Honoré.
Designs for writing sets. See caption on page 166, also pages 170, 171 and 175.

[3] Legouvé, Ernest. 'Soixante ans de Souvenirs', Paris, no date.

130   Dagoty.
Cup and saucer. Chinese-
style decoration in gold on
lacquer-red ground.
Between 1804 and 1814
Musée national de La Mal-
maison. Ht. 5.5 cm. (2¹/₅ in.).
Marks 57 and 64.

Balzac speaks of the Mexican vases that Schoelcher sold him. A writer himself, Schoelcher was an art and music critic, wrote a life of Handel but chiefly a number of works on the abolition of slavery in 1833. On his journeys he had seen slavery at first hand and, as Legouvé says, 'he had left as a commercial traveller; he came back an abolitionist'. From now on porcelain was the last thing he bothered about and he devoted himself to politics. It was he who, in 1848, in his capacity as Under-Secretary of State at the Naval and Colonial Offices of the provisional government, signed the decree abolishing slavery. It was for his good offices on behalf of slaves that his ashes were transferred to the Panthéon in 1949. As he had asked in his will that they should never be separated from his father's, the manufacturer and merchant of porcelain both rest in the Panthéon.

When Marc Schoelcher bought the factory in the Faubourg Saint-Denis he was already established as a faience seller on Rue de la Monnaie and he remained entered as such in the *Almanach du Commerce* until 1808. Perhaps he had two irons in the fire. In 1804 he rented a salesroom on Boulevard des Italiens at the junction of Rue de la Grange-Batelière. When his wife asked for the separation of their property she was living above the salesroom and Schoelcher in the factory. For the purpose of repaying his wife's dowry Schoelcher suggested to her that he should sell her *inter alia* the house in the Faubourg Saint-Denis. Madame Schoelcher assumed ownership of it on October 1st 1806. The *Almanach du Commerce* continues to attribute this address to the factory until 1816, whereas a schedule of factories asserts that it was already closed by 1810.

Ill. 25

At all events, production had certainly stopped by 1823 when Madame Schoelcher sold the property.

Marc Schoelcher, then, ceased manufacturing the porcelain ware which he had been selling in his salesroom on Boulevard des Italiens. On the occasion of the signing of the partnership deed between Marc and Victor Schoelcher on December 31st 1828 they both declared that they were forming privately 'a company under a collective name for trading with wholesale and retail porcelain merchants in the salesroom of M. Marc Schoelcher, Boulevard des Italiens no. 2, which shall be the headquarters of this company'. The agreement was fixed

131 Darte Senior.
Plate. Portrait of Louis XVIII, transfer-printed. *Circa* 1820.
New York, Metropolitan Museum of Art.
Diam. 22 cm. (8³/₅ in.).
Mark 53.

to run for two years as from January 1st 1829 but was prolonged by verbal consent for two years and four months as from September 1st 1832. One month later Marc Schoelcher died in the lodgings above the salesroom.

The salesroom on Boulevard des Italiens became highly fashionable, as much for political gatherings as for the sale of porcelain. By 1816 it was decorated with moulded pilasters having capitals and astragals 'of oak, oil-painted in a chocolate colour... both inside and out'. The pigeon-holes in which the wares were displayed were lined with blue paper and the heating was provided by a tall faience stove. But let us allow Legouvé to speak again: 'One could fill a volume with his [meaning Victor's] eccentricities as a merchant. One morning, there comes into his salesroom one of his colleagues from the Passage de l'Opéra with whom he had some business or other. Treating him as an equal, the merchant loses his temper and permits himself some rather heated words. "Monsieur", Schoelcher says to him, "I wish to point out to you that you are not being polite." Exacerbated by this softness of tone the merchant carries on, whereupon Schoelcher administer a sharp slap, and when the merchant tries to charge at him Schoelcher kicks him backwards, sends him rolling to the back of the salesroom and then, turning to his assistant, blandly says "Pick Monsieur up". This story filled us with mirth. "But my friend", I would say to him, "you have no idea about what is called transition! Heavens! One prepares things, one warns people. There was no connexion between that slap and your phrase". "What?" Schoelcher calmly replies, "my phrase was 'Monsieur, you are not being polite': what could I have

127[b] Dagoty & Honoré. Design for a writing set. See caption on page 166, also pages 170–172.

said to him that was stronger than that?" Legouvé saw another obstacle to Schoelcher's commercial prosperity: 'Any shop presupposes a counter; any counter presupposes a shopkeeper sitting behind it, selling. Now, Schoelcher's self-esteem was revolted at the idea of sitting at a counter—an absurd scruple with Republican principles, such as his,

but he was twenty-eight years of age [so we are in 1832]; he had not yet managed to change his vanity into legitimate pride. He therefore took it into his head to replace this counter with a little glass-fronted office at the back of the salesroom from where he could see without being seen, and appear at the right moment. Unfortunately, after four o'clock this office served as a rendezvous for his friends from the Press. It was like a newspaper-office. People came to bring news, to discuss painting and music, slate the *députés,* suggest that some minister be put on trial, to outline here and there some little plan of conspiracy and on occasion to comment on the purchasers and their wives. The latter would look askance at the office from which hoots of laughter were escaping, and would go off saying 'What a peculiar porcelain shop!'

The lease of this 'peculiar shop' fell in on October 1st 1834, and the company of Schoelcher et Fils closed on December 31st. It was most likely, then, that at the end of December 1834 Victor Schoelcher wound up his porcelain business. According to Legouvé again, he lost around fifty thousand francs of his inheritance on it, a tidy sum for that period.

Different marks were affixed to the wares of the Faubourg Saint-Denis factory.

In the 18th century, as we have seen, Hannong registered the mark of a capital A in 1773. Incidentally, it is only found in a cursive script, painted in underglaze blue, with a few variants, for example the occasional accompaniment of crossed pipes—the founder of the Hannong dynasty having first been a pipe maker. In 1779 Stahn registered the mark CP, proclaiming the protection of Charles Philippe, Comte d'Artois, the King's brother and the future Charles X. These initials are usually surmounted either by a prince's coronet or else a closed crown stencilled on in red. It is also to be found painted in gilt.

The Schoelchers signed their name in full. The early marks, the ones which are definitely from the Faubourg Saint-Denis factory, are painted in underglaze blue. The rest are painted in red or gilt cursives, or otherwise stencilled *Schoelcher,* or *Schoelcher à Paris.* Between 1829 and 1834 the later marks are *Schoelcher et fils* with certain variations. These marks may accompany other underglaze marks: Ja-

cob Petit's, for instance, the maker of white ware, or that of Perche. They confirm that the Schoelchers by then were no more than porcelain sellers employing specially appointed decorators.[4] According to the advertisements appearing in the almanacs and journals of the 18th century the Faubourg Saint-Denis was manufacturing 'everything that relates to serving and embellishing: also, some of the figures and other works are produced in biscuit'.[5] We must add the toilet-items, of which hardly any have survived, apart from the water-jugs *(pots à l'eau)* and their basins.

Amongst the ornamental pieces figure a quantity of vases: vases for flowers or for

132   Dagoty.
Tea- or coffee-service.
Purple ground. Polychrome scenes of family life.
Circa 1815.
Montargis, Musée Girodet.
Coffee-pot: Ht. 20 cm.
(7⅘ in.).
Mark 57.

See also page 178.

[4] Schoelcher's certificate, February 17th 1821. 'Sieur François Blanchard, residing at 46, Rue des Marais, is a craftsman employed in my service and a booklet-holder, as a painter and gilder employed by the day...' Paris, Bibliothèque d'Art et d'Archéologie, Fondation Doucet.

[5] Gournay, 'Tableau général du Commerce', Paris, 1789-90.

corner cupboards, and vases with ears, no doubt inspired from Sèvres ware.

We have already mentioned elsewhere (see p. 58) both the models enumerated in the inventory of 1778 and those bought six years later by the Comte d'Artois for his sundry residences.

It was in 1783 that King Louis XVI received the gift of a vase 'which combined the height, relief, depth of detail and encrusted gilding and all the other embellishments with which the factory of Sèvres, alone and exclusively, claims to decorate its products...'

In gilt capitals it bore these words:...*cuit au charbon de terre épuré dans la manufacture de Mrg le Comte d'Artois le 8 février 1783...* ('fired by purified coal in the factory of Mrg le Comte d'Artois on February 8th 1783...')[6] A comparable inscription is inserted beneath two vases adorned with enamels by Cotteau and mounted in gilt bronze: *cuit au charbon de terre le 11 août 1783.* It accompanies Cotteau's name and the CP mark, crowned.

Ill. 15

132 Dagoty.
See caption on page 176.

We must also draw attention to the square flower tubs with truncated or concave-chamfered corners. Round or oval openwork baskets are noted in the inventories, but early examples are scarce. Lastly let us mention the writing sets, watch stands and candle-holders.

Ill. 8

A very complete list of table-pieces is furnished by the inventory of 1778 which we have been using extensively above (see p. 58). The two most common shapes are 'Sèvres-type' for the compote-dishes, trays and salad-bowls; and 'Saxon-type' for trays, cruets and sugar-bowls for the table.

As at Strassburg, shapes are also made to simulate gold artefacts, such as a 'silver-shape goblet'. Many pieces are of diminutive *(mignonnette)* size: coffee-pots, broth bowls, milk-jugs, teapots and cups: they were assembled to form little *cabarets*.

The earliest designs are bowls resting on a foot-rim; and 'cupels' *(coupelles)*. They are often called *bols de cabaret* or *bols de limonadier*. Their blue-and-white decoration was the only one allowed under the regulations in force. Other factories—Chantilly for example—made some as well. The inventory of 1778 gives many shapes for cups: cylindrical, *à cotte sans hanse,* round, Queen's-style, and no less than four different sizes.

Ill. 5

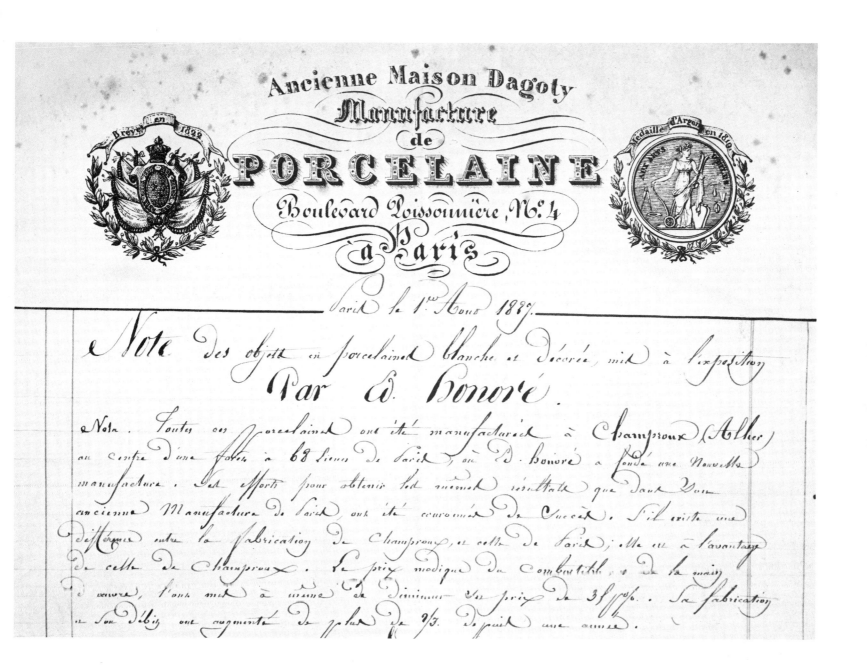

133 Honoré.
The headed note-paper shows in the left-hand corner the arms of Louis XVIII and the date 1832, when Honoré was specially appointed supplier to the King: in the right-hand corner is the silver medal won by Honoré and Dagoty in 1819. The document, dated August 1st 1827, is a 'record of the plain and decorated porcelain wares exhibited by Ed. Honore'. This description is preceded by a laudatory justification of the porcelain of Champroux where Honoré had started production of white wares in 1824. 'If there is any difference between manufacturing at Champroux and manufacturing in Paris, it favours Champroux. The reasonable price of fuel and of labour have enabled [Honoré] to lower his prices by 35%. His output and retail sales have increased by two-thirds over one year'.
Sèvres, Musée national de Céramique.

The most ordinary pieces are the round
or oval plates and dishes, but Hannong
Ill. 9 adorns them with pleasing relief scroll-
work. The sauce-boats and sugar-bowls
have shapes highly influenced by gold
work, and the same applies to the barrel-
shaped mustard-pots or the butter-dishes,
and the large three-dimensional pieces.
The covered broth-bowls standing on a
tray are bulbous and their handles formed
out of twigs.

To make up *cabarets* the cups are supple-
mented by teapots of various shapes,
marabouts, milk-jugs mounted either on
a foot rim or on three feet, and by sugar
pots. Other charming items include egg-
cups.

Despite the prohibitions polychrome or
gilt decorations are numerous. Descriptions of these figure in two deeds of 1776
and 1778 (already mentioned on pp. 66, 67),
the only documents giving us an idea of
the richest among them: 'yellow monochromes, landscape, with ribbons, purple
and gold, flecked with gold, Chinese'.
The decoration using (single or double)
garlands often occurs, as do the mono-
grammed pieces. The floral decoration,
which definitely predominates among
the pieces still in existence, does not appear
in the texts; this is the one which is encountered in all the factories. Let us also
include the sprays of flowers and the
bluebottles. Other pieces referred to by

134 Dagoty.
Pair of egg-cups supported
by a cupid in biscuit. Matt-
black plinth heightened with
gold. *Circa* 1810.
Sèvres, Musée National de
Céramique. Ht. 8 cm.
(3$^{1}/_{5}$ in.).
Mark 57.

135 Honoré.
Pot-pourri. Turquoise-blue ground with polychrome garlands. *Circa* 1830. Paris, Musée des Arts Décoratifs. Ht. 23.5 cm. (9¹/₅ in.). Mark 71.

the inventory of 1778 as 'with a blue line' are also adorned with gilt garlands. It was this gilt, painted on or in relief, which attracted the attention and envy of the private establishments, in spite of the prohibitions. The Comte d'Artois' factory was no exception and even quite early on produced some pieces decorated solely in gold. Broad lace patterns and trophies constitute the richest *décors* (Hannong mark). One generally finds gold combined with colours for decorations with flowers or animals, especially birds (often poultry, as in the Hannong period), butterflies, figures, sometimes children, or the many amorous scenes, renderings of

Ill. 12

contemporary pictures and portraits. At the end of the century a topical subject arrests our attention—the decoration 'with Balloon' of about 1784.

The output of biscuit ware from the Faubourg Saint-Denis was prolific, and more than one hundred and twenty-five references to groups or figures have been picked out from the inventories—children after Boucher, others after Falconet, 'L'Amour piqué par une Abeille', etc., and above all the important series of the 'Cris de Paris'. We also notice a figure of Christ, and later some busts of Necker and Mirabeau.

Ill. 18, 19

Whether or not the porcelain sold by the Schoelchers was also manufactured by them, it is certainly of very good quality. To the exhibition of 1806 Schoelcher dispatched 'some tall, highly ornate vases'. In 1819 he received a silver medal. A most laudatory report observes that 'the modelling is perfectly executed, and decorated with a great many artistically arranged gildings, and adds that the ornaments are in excellent taste. Schoelcher mostly sold

luxury articles and in particular a number of dessert services, one of which, tradition has it, was presented by the City of Paris to Bernadotte when he acceded as marshal.[7]

The services for tea or coffee often match the dessert services. The cups are of differing shapes. They were frequently presented singly or in pairs as gifts, and so were the broth-bowls★—a survival from the 'accouchement cups' (écuelles d'accouchées) given to the young mother as far back as the Renaissance. Comfit-dishes, watercups or veilleuses, all of them elegant objects, were sold in the 'peculiar shop'. Very fine coloured, marbled or tortoiseshell grounds had become a speciality of the factory by Year XI. One of the later coloured grounds was black, circa 1830. Many decorations were inspired by Antiquity, while others are composed of rosettes and decorative elements which later adapted themselves to the 'Cathedral style'. Decorations of flowers and birds abound. As soon as the water colours and prints of Garneray and Janinet appeared the Schoelchers decorated numerous porcelain pieces with views of Paris or of estates in the vicinity of Paris (such as La Malmaison). Others show the harbours of France or Portugal. The faithful reproductions of paintings are executed with particular care—Moïse sauvé des Eaux by Poussin, or Le Déshabiller by Devéria. The same applies to portraits painted in miniature. The examples of the fashion for folk-culture and the Orient are among the most colourful.

★Ill. 35

136 Honoré.
Plate with transfer-printed decoration of blue arabesques in the Byzantine manner. Exhibition of 1844. Sèvres, Musée National de Céramique. Diam. 22 cm. (8³/₅ in.). Mark 71.

Ill. 26

Ill. 32

Ill. 31
Ill. 22

Ill. 23

Ill. 37

Ill. 35

MONSIEUR, COMTE DE PROVENCE'S FACTORY
Clignancourt

The buildings of the Clignancourt factory were still standing at the beginning of this

[7] Now kept in the Nordiska Museets, Stockholm.

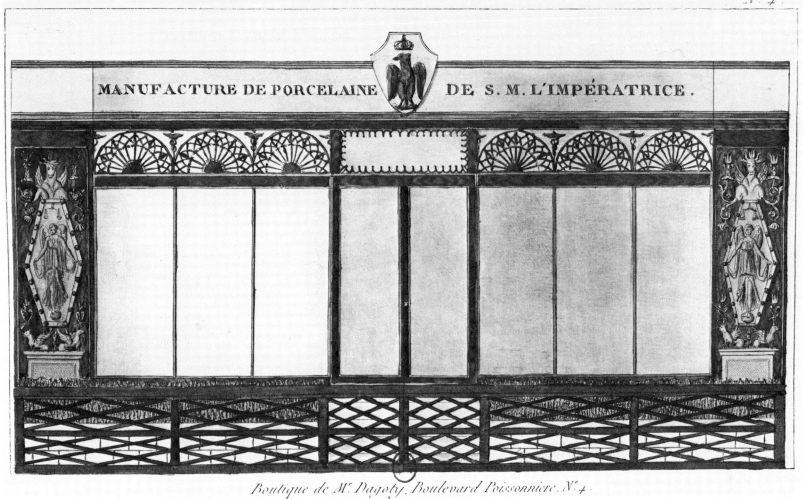

MANUFACTURE DE PORCELAINE DE S. M. L'IMPÉRATRICE.

Boutique de M.ʳ Dagoty, Boulevard Poissonnière, N.º 4.

137 Dagoty's shop in Boulevard Poissonnière, No 4. *Circa* 1810. From *Collection des maisons de commerce de Paris les mieux décorées,* published by Mixelle.

century, at the junction of Rue du Mont-Cenis and Rue Marcadet, right in the heart of Montmartre. At the time when it was set up, this establishment was sited 'within musket-shot' of the city gate, and the advertisements proudly proclaimed how pleasant it was to walk there. On May 12th 1767 Pierre Deruelle, at that time architect and building contractor, bought from his mother-in-law separate blocks of buildings connected by court-yards and gardens. It is possible that Deruelle waited four years before selling his porcelain. According to Thiery's *Guide des Amateurs,* the factory existed in 1771. It was controlled as a joint-stock company, Deruelle receiving the yearly fixed sum of 10,000 *livres* for the manage-ment of production and sales, plus a third of the profits, which was extremely high in comparison to other factories. But, unlike other establishments, Deruelle of-fered only profits to the share-holders. There was general agreement that people worked hard at Clignancourt, where the whole family was occupied: 'The sale of wares is entrusted to the wife of Seigneur Deruelle; she combines a perfect knowl-edge of the prices with a great aptitude for selling, which she performs with the meticulous honesty that typifies this worthy family.' One of the daughters married the painter Alexandre Moitte, the son of the engraver to the King and brother of the modeller. In order to keep his industry running, Deruelle was obliged to take part in 'civic' functions, and in 1790 became attorney (*procureur*) of the newly-created municipality of Montmartre. Two years later Moitte succeeded his father-in-law as the manager of the concern, but he had to shut down in the month of Ventôse, Year VII (1799). The factory together with its equipment was then put up for public auction, and Moitte resumed his profession as drawing instructor. He died in 1828, after being elected a member of the Institut. The personality of the first manager and the very high quality of the porcelain won the factory the patronage of Monsieur, Comte de Provence, who bestowed his diploma upon it on October 25th 1775. The following year Deruelle hired out to Monsieur the hollow ware required for the reception at Brunoy given for the King and Queen.

This princely protection turned out to be most useful at the time of the struggle between Sèvres and the private factories. On September 20th 1779 a search followed by confiscation was carried out on Deruelle's premises. In a workshop, six painters were discouvered to be painting 'in different colours' and gilding. In his verdict of September 27th the Lieutenant général de Police ordered the factory to abide by the regulations. A few months later Deruelle applied for a post at Sèvres as sub-manager, and, on his wife's behalf, for a post in the porcelain warehouse of Sèvres which it was proposed to set up at the Louvre. This petition, drafted on January 23rd 1780 was followed the next day by a search. Drafting minutes of the confiscation took four days, both at the factory and in the salesroom at the sign of the 'Bonnet d'Or' ('Golden Cap'), Rue

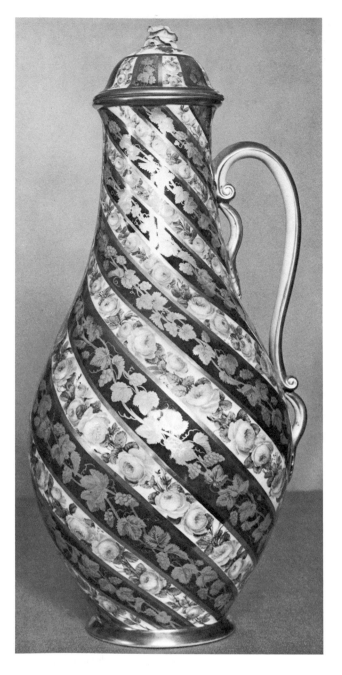

138 Honoré.
Large beakless cooler. Spiral *décor* on white ground with pink roses on high-temperature blue ground decorated with gold vine-tendrils. The lid is adorned with a rose on the top and the handle is terminated by vine-leaves. This type of object was intended for the Near East. Honoré boasted to be known in Constantinople as well as in Paris. Similar pieces, of the same shape and *décor,* were also exported to the Near East by Meissen and Vienna.
Circa 1844.
Paris, Coll. Le Tallec.
Ht. 50 cm. (19 in.)
Mark 70.

139 Honoré. ▶
Plate from the service of James Polk, President of the United States between 1845 and 1849. A border of pale green, interrupted by an oval panel bearing the arms of the United States, sets off a huge flower painted from life – in this case a poppy. The moulded shapes, embellished with interlocking scrolls in relief, were specially executed for export, from designs supplied by the American clients and inspired from English services. Commissioned in 1848. Washington, The White House. Diam. 24 cm. (9²/₃ in.).
Unmarked.

Neuve des Petits-Champs. For the next three months the petitions and summonses succeeded on another. Régnier even visited the Clignancourt factory which Deruelle was offering to sell him as he was no longer able to work under such unfavourable conditions, but nothing definite materialized for him from this

184

visit. It was then that one of the leading shareholders, Jolivet, applied for a respite of three years to modify the operations of the workshop to comply with the royal decrees. Deruelle received notification of the decree of 1784 and forwarded through d'Arcet in 1785 a new offer to sell the factory; then Monsieur himself intervened to ask for permission to carry on with the prohibited manufacture until 1787. This ingenious solution allowed Deruelle to await the decree of 1787 whereby his factory was exempted from the mythical yearly concourse. Later, times having changed and Sèvres lacking petuntse, Deruelle supplied it to the royal factory, repeating the gesture of Monsieur, who had already made a gift of cobalt from his mines at Allemont, in the Dauphiné.

At the outbreak of the Revolution many factories were established and the work of outside decorators began to disturb the existing factories. It was then that Alluaud, the director of the royal factory at Limoges and friend of Deruelle suggested to him that he should 'make porcelain for marketing in Paris'. One of Deruelle's sons left Clignancourt 'with a collection of the moulds of that time' and directed operations for nearly six months of 1791 in the Limoges factory, supported at that time by the Civil List. The results showed a 'profit' of one third. But Deruelle sold the factory to Moitte on July 28th 1792, and his son found himself out of work.

The state of the factory was less than brilliant, and although Moitte offered discounts to buyers who personally came to Clignancourt he was obliged to close down the factory in Ventôse, Year VII. Several salesrooms were affiliated to the factory of Clignancourt, the two biggest being the 'Bonnet d'Or' on the corner of

Rue Neuve-des-Petits-Champs and Rue Chabanais and Madame de la Fresnaye's shop at the Palais de Justice. By 1775 Clignancourt porcelain was also available from 'Le Petit Dunkerque', and lastly, in 1798, Moitte set up a storehouse on Rue Feydeau, while Guy at 'Le Petit Carrousel' ensured a steady sale of his wares. In the provinces a storehouse was established on Descat's premises in Bordeaux, and it is highly likely that competition from Clignancourt porcelain was a threat to the factories of Limoges on the occasion of the Bordeaux Fair of 1787, to judge by the complaints that were lodged. Many sales were made abroad as well. Among the tradesmen who resold wares after

140 Darte Brothers.
Clock in the form of a vase.
Contrast-burnished gold.
Dial by Angevin of Paris.
Circa 1825.
Palacio Nacional de Ajuda.
Ht. 28 cm. (11 in.).
Mark 77.
See back of the clock opposite
page.

mounting them we pick out the name of the trunk- and case-maker (gainier) Prieur.

The clientèle of such a factory was bound to be a select group, a fact which did not preclude difficulties over payment. After Monsieur, we might cite the Duc Charles de Lorraine, and the Marquis de Louvois who ordered a cornflower service, some cups with gilt bouquets, etc.

In the course of its lifetime the factory saw the number of its workshops and kilns wax and wane. In 1775 two extra kilns were constructed. Important experiments in firing with coal took place at the Clignancourt factory, similar to those conducted in the Faubourg Saint-Denis, which have already been mentioned. The number of craftsmen was high; eighty were employed in 1780, and ninety-four in 1787, without including the outside craftsmen. One of the most famous painters of Vienna, Lamprecht, worked there before he was enticed away to Sèvres. Among the modellers there was Deruelle Junior and his instructor Moitte. Monumental pieces were created, such as the 'two holy-water stoups imitating on a smaller scale those of Saint-Sulpice. They are surmounted by groups of angels . . .' Various marks were attached to Clignancourt wares. From the outset, it seems, Deruelle took a windmill as his mark. More or less stylized, this silhouette represented one of the famous windmills of Montmartre which to this day evoke a whole district of Paris. This mark, usually painted in underglaze blue, can only have been used for a few years, for it was replaced on January 24th 1775 by the monogram LSX, from the initials of the Comte de Provence's Christian names, Louis Stanislas Xavier. Nonetheless, the *Mercure de France* of December 1775 asserts

that Clignancourt porcelain bears the mark M, supporting the fleur-de-lys crown of the Prince of the Blood, thus referring to the King's younger brother by his title of 'Monsieur'. Whatever the case may be, these two last-named marks may be found together on a single item and are sometimes accompanied by a B, surmounted by the same crown. Chavagnac and Grollier have not explained this last mark which presumably denotes the country-house of Brunoy. These marks, as symbols of a régime which it was wished to forget, disappeared in the Revolutionary tumoil, although an attempt was made to remove only the crown and to look upon the M as the initial of Moitte's name. This, however, remains somewhat obscure. These marks are usually brushed on in red or stencilled; they are seldom to be found painted in gilt. To Moitte are attributed items marked with an M in underglaze blue, or again the name *Clignancourt* stencilled on in red.

Like all contemporary factories Clignan-

court sold ornamental pieces, toilet items and above all hollow ware. An advertisement in the December 1775 issue of the *Mercure de France* is fully borne out by the objects which have come down to us: 'The porcelain from this factory is singularly recommendable both for its strength, greater than any known, the fine white texture of the biscuit ware and for its glaze, comparable to the artefacts of Old Japan, as also for the elegance of the shapes and the tastefulness of the ornaments. All pieces suitable for use at table and for decorating interiors are made there, together with perfectly modelled figures, either single or grouped, large or small. Lastly, it is possible to order any artefacts of this type which one may wish.' Decorative pieces are numerous—sets of mantelpiece ornaments, vases of varying shapes and sizes, sometimes reaching a height of fifty cm., sconces, 'perpetual inkwells' (*écritoires perpétuelles*), 'fountains' (cisterns), baskets, medallions, no doubt for decorating furniture and even tables. All this proves to us that the factory was successfully turned out large-scale pieces. The greatest diversity of shapes, often inspired from the work of goldsmiths, asserts itself over these different models. The handles, masks, knobs, fruits and feet are particularly pleasing; one would be almost tempted—were it not for the material concerned—to say that Ill. 44, 62 they are chiselled.

The sumptuous decoration further enhaces the finish and delicacy of the shapes. It is often painted on solely in gold, in a thick coat that resists deterioration, for-Ill. 49 ming interwoven or pendant garlands, or animated scenes of Chinese figures. Otherwise it is simply applied in the form Ill. 54 of sprays of wild pea, as at Sèvres. One of

the oldest pieces is undoubtedly a cup decorated with sprigs in relief, heightened with gold and reminiscent of the soft-paste wares from Saint-Cloud and Chan- Ill. 40 tilly. Polychrome decoration occurs most frequently of all. One of Clignancourt's specialities was rematching Dresden services; the service of the Comte de Provence for Brunoy was adorned with big flowers after nature. A floral decoration Ill. 50 peculiar to Clignancourt, a sort of regular diaper (*semis ordonné*), blends polychrome sprigs with fine gilt leaves. The bouquets Ill. 57 and landscapes are very becoming, and so are other monochrome decorations in blue or violet, but often in pale green for imbricated patterns. Ill. 52 But the triumph of Clignancourt is to have introduced into France the celebrated sepia *décor* called simply *camayeu* (monochrome) and painted by Lamprecht. The broth-bowl in the Musée national de Céramique de Sèvres bearing the date 1783 is decorated with animated Ill. 56 scenes of remarkable quality. It is Lamprecht once again who takes credit for the thick, smooth black used by Monsieur's factory for making linear decorations of lozenges, stripes, etc. Being a difficult Ill. 58 technique, it caused despair among the painters of Sèvres who complained they had not yet 'got the hang of it'.

A certain number of biscuit models are known to us: theatrical figures or children, mythological groups or seasons, sentimental allegories in imitation of Dresden figurines, 'Cris de Paris' and even *Père Système*. The magnificent Hercules Farnese of the Musée de Sèvres is perfect in its modelling and shows supreme confidence of technique. The biscuit ware of Ill. 42 which we know is marked with the windmill.

142 Darte Brothers.
Religious scenes in poly-
chrome after Raphael or
landscapes with animals after
Potter embellish four vases
from Nast's works: two of
these vases were exhibited in
1819.
Sèvres, Musée National de
Céramique. Ht. 40 cm.
(15³/₄ in.).
Mark 79.

QUEEN'S FACTORY

Rue Thiroux

The history of the factory in Rue Thiroux appears to begin with the registration of the mark A with the Lieutenant général de Police, performed by André Marie Lebeuf on September 9th 1776. Three weeks later Etienne Moreau de La Brosse, a wholesale merchant of Paris, handed over the freehold of a site at Les Porcherons adjoining Rue Thiroux which had a surface area of 30 *toises*, 5 feet 4 inches square. The recipients, at a cost of 14,000 *livres*, were Marie Madeleine Gruel, widow of Jean François Nicolas Lebeuf, attorney at the Parlement and Jacques Pascal Barra-

chin, a wholesale merchant residing in Grande Rue du Faubourg Saint-Denis. In fact Dame Lebeuf declared that she was only acting by proxy for her son André Marie 'to please him, because he has been unable to stipulate or acquire anything himself owing to his being a minor'. This status being due to end on January 17th 1780, André Marie was then only twenty-one years of age. This purchase was followed by another on October 21st 1776, of a site of 45 *toises*, also on Rue Thiroux. Rue Thiroux was located in the quarter of La Chaussée d'Antin and corresponds to a fraction of the modern Rue Caumartin, between Rue des Mathurins and Rue de Provence.

143 Darte Brothers. Swan-shaped cup with oval saucer. This model, which was very popular, was also made by Dagoty, at Sèvres, and in a number of foreign countries, for example the Portuguese factory of Vista Alègre. Note here the contrast of the matt, biscuit finish on the outside of the cup and the palmettes on the saucer, against the lustrous effect of the gold. The inside of the cup is adorned with a rosette in contrast-burnished gold. *Circa* 1810. Musée National de La Malmaison. Ht. 10 cm. (4 in.). Mark 78.

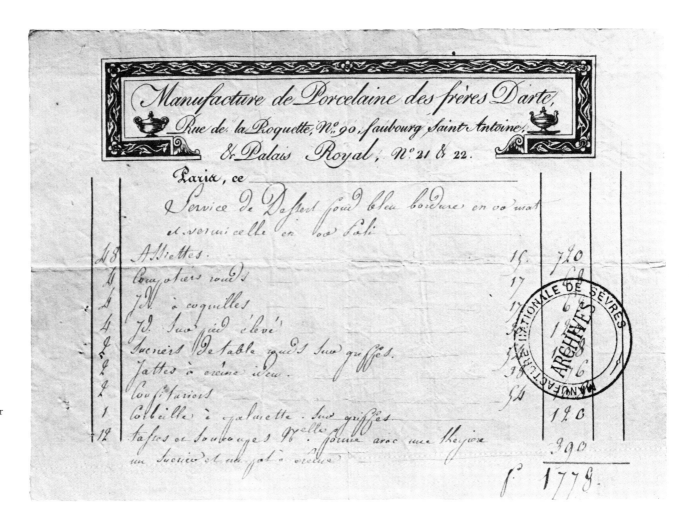

144. Darte Brothers. Invoice for a blue-ground dessert-service with a border in matt gold and with 'vermicelli' (vermicular motifs) of polished gold. Undated. Sèvres, Archives de la manufacture nationale.

What, then, did Barrachin do for a living? We have come across him among the shareholders of the Faubourg Saint-Denis factory in which he had been actively interested for two years. He had been skilfully extricating himself by signing a new deed of partnership, for the trade in carriages, harness and horses, on July 13th 1776, then another one for a sort of sale-room where furniture could be brought to be displayed and sold. He did not disclose his projects when, on October 31st 1776, he set up with André Marie Lebeuf 'a company dealing in every type of business, acting either through commission agents or on its own account, operating from the different establishments and concerns which they are creating or may subsequently create'. This company, entitled Barrachin Lebeuf et Cie., had a projected term of eighteen years and funds amounting to 50,000 *livres* supplied in equal proportions. Barrachin's share could be collected from the 27,078 *livres'* worth of goods belonging to him in the shop set up on Rue Saint-Nicaise, whilst Lebeuf had to contribute 25,000 *livres*. Barrachin put his house in the Faubourg Saint-Denis at the company's disposal, pending the construction of offices and salesrooms on one of the sites that he had just acquired in Rue Thiroux. Article 22 of the partnership deeds laid down that 'by common consent, the said partners shall give to the neediest amongst the poor the yearly sum of 100 *livres*, that God may bestow his blessing upon their works'. This was a wise precaution in view of the position of the Faubourg Saint-Denis factory. Some months later, on December 31st, further deserters from that establishment came to partner Barrachin, namely the Marquis d'Usson, Aucanne, Donzé de Verteuil and Boutet de Monvel. Madame Lebeuf and a certain Claude Barrachin, known as Barrachin the Younger, joined them. It was left to Barrachin and Lebeuf to manage the business. In this new deed the company's objectives were made quite specific; the parties expressed the wish to 'form amongst themselves a company for running a porcelain factory established on Rue Thiroux, Chaussée d'Antin by the efforts of the said Messrs Barrachin and Lebeuf.' The company assets were then brought up to 300,000 *livres* 'both in porcelain goods kept at present in their salesroom in Rue Saint-Nicaise and in ready cash'. It would be interesting if we could be certain that this saleroom on Rue Saint-Nicaise whose porcelain belonged to Barrachin had in fact been stocked by the factory of the Faubourg Saint-Denis before becoming his property when he left that factory. This being the case, not only the financiers but also the wares from the Faubourg Saint-Denis would have contributed to the founding of the factory in Rue Thiroux.

Barrachin withdrew rapidly, or, was perhaps, supplanted by Lebeuf; June 2nd 1777 marked the dissolution of the partnership between Barrachin and Aucanne on the one hand, and André Marie Lebeuf and his mother on the other. Since the deed of association on December 31st 1776 was followed by a deed of sleeping partnership, we may infer that the Marquis d'Usson, the Abbé de Verteuil and Boutet de Monvel remained passive associates. Lebeuf, however, retained the raw materials, implements and moulds. What did Barrachin do next? We find him in the shop on Rue Saint-Nicaise when he filed his petition of bankruptcy on April 11th 1778; he had been selling champagne, almonds and prunes. On this balance sheet the Marquis d'Usson was entered as being worth more than 2,300 *livres*.

Meanwhile, Lebeuf was left as sole master of the factory, assisted by specialists. The *Affiches, annonces et avis divers* of June 23rd 1777 published the following statement: 'There is in Paris, on Rue Thiroux (which leads into Rue des Mathurins) Chaussée d'Antin, a factory producing porcelain that withstands the most intense heat. The owner notifies the public that his workshops, set up at the end of last year, are now in a position to execute any type of order which may be given them: firstly, any items for the table or domestic use, styled and decorated in the most solid, convenient and best-designed shapes; secondly, the most fashionable and pleasing biscuit groups. The underside of every piece is marked with the letter A in blue. S. Balzé who holds the post of works manager (*fabricant*) continues, by the success of his labours and by his daily progress, to maintain the reputation which he has acquired in other factories. The proximity of the new establishment and its ease of access having dissuaded the owner from opening a saleroom inside Paris, S. Vieusse, the chairman of the board, will receive at the factory itself any commissions from the capital or the provinces.' The same publication informs us that, on December 16th 1778, the Queen had granted the factory her patronage.

The time had come. Carried out on March

145 Darte Brothers. Triangular *veilleuse*, decorated in polychrome and contrastburnished gold. The subject is drawn from contemporary history: on each of the three faces are reproduced the outstanding episodes of the *Trois Glorieuses,* the days of the uprising in Paris (July 27th–29th 1830) which saw the departure of Charles X and the accession of Louis-Philippe. The tricolor, flown over the barricades as the emblem of the Republicans now replaces the royalist flag with the fleurs-de-lis. 1830
Paris, Musée Carnavalet.
Ht. 25 cm. (9¹/₂ in.).
Mark 77.

3rd 1779 by the Lieutenant de Police, the confiscatory search at the home of the painters Catrice and Barbé brought to light an item from the Rue Thiroux factory. Two confiscations took place in Rue Thiroux, on September 27th 1779 and January 28th 1780. In the case of the first, the Lieutenant général de Police recorded that—'having entered the painters' studio, there were found six work-benches loaded with merchandise and six craftsmen painting and gilding, notably a chamber-pot (*vase de nuit*), two coffee-cups and -saucers, and three plates'. The confiscation on January 28th 1780 yielded a list of a considerable number of items. A long lawsuit arose between the royal factory and the factory protected by the Queen. Lebeuf fought for time. The Lieutenant général de Police ordered the demolition of the kilns, notified Lebeuf that he was disqualified from manufacturing even blue-and-white or monochrome wares, and forbade him to set himself up in business again or to work as a craftsman. (He was probably incapable of this in any case.) On April 13th Lebeuf's appeal, lodged on March 13th, was quashed. He then countered the Lieutenant général's successive summonses with passive resistance. The balance sheet dated October 20th 1788 of a merchant-haberdasher of Paris, Martinet of Rue du Coq Saint-Honoré discloses that he had been selling wares from the Queen's factory. Things quietened down; a correspondence of the period records a conversation in 1783 between the Comte d'Angivilliers and the Comte de Grais, the King's envoy at Cassel, in the course of which the products of Rue Thiroux were mentioned as being reasonably priced. At the close of that same year the factory did not fear advertising its clearance sales in the *Affiches, annonces et avis divers.*

The decree of 1784 was communicated to Lebeuf, who joined the manufacturers in addressing a petition to the King, asking to be kept in business. Moves and counter-moves multiplied, culminating at the beginning of 1785 in a suggestion from Lebeuf that he should sell his factory to Sèvres. Giving the Comte d'Angivilliers his opinion, Hettlinger told him that he saw in this no advantage for Sèvres apart from 'bringing about the extinction of a privately owned factory which will probably suffer this fate of its own accord'. On March 12th a negative reply was delivered to Lebeuf.

In the decree of 1787 the Queen's factory was exempted from the concourse.

Did business run less smoothly? Certain reports list problems: 'on entering into the details of the manufacture and the administration of this factory it comes as no surprise to witness the prevailing disorder and the huge losses which the interested parties are making: there is no coherence except in the words of Sieur Lebeuf who is the cat's-paw of Madame Farnera, a shareholder... The aged manager in charge of sales has told Monsieur du Four that they have been reduced to accepting the first offer that comes along of wood, candles and other urgent things ... that he is parting with goods at any old price, in spite of which Sieur Lebeuf is propagating the news that he is making a considerable profit ... which does not exist beyond his speeches...'

Yet again, the history of the factory in Rue Thiroux was about to enmesh itself with the factory of the Faubourg Saint-Denis. By 1789 salesroom of 'Le Petit Carrousel' was selling porcelain supplied by Lebeuf. Payment was taken by Houzel, probably the factory manager. It was on

146 Darte Brothers. Hemispherical bowl with protuberant base, borne by three caryatids ending in lion's paws. Three oval panels contain views of the factory: the entrance, 'View or the porcelain-salesrooms [*magasins*] from the courtyard' and (illustrated here), 'View of the porcelain-salesrooms from the garden.' This factory was located at 90 Rue de la Roquette, in a building previously known as the Hôtel Montalembert but taken over in 1804 by Darte brothers to accommodate their factory as well as their families. There was also a salesroom at the Palais du Tribunat. *Circa* 1805. Sèvres, Musée National de Céramique. Diam. 20 cm. (7³/₄ in.). Unmarked.

Pluviose 30th, Year v that Lebeuf sold to Charles Barthélemy Guy and Marie Antoine Houzel 'the stocks and goodwill of the porcelain factory heretofore known as the Queen's'. It was indeed Lebeuf's property, set up in a house belonging to him at 661, Rue Thiroux. Moreover, Lebeuf granted Guy and Houzel a lease.

The sale was concluded for the sum of 25,500 *livres* 'in ringing [*sic*] metal currency of gold and silver and in no other form'. It was clearly specified that there were no debts. This sale had been anticipated by a deed of partnership between Guy and Houzel on Pluviose 17th, Year v, whereby each took an equal share. After Guy's

147 Darte Brothers. Cup and its saucer. Polychrome decoration reminiscent of cathedral style. *Circa* 1815. London, Victoria & Albert Museum. Ht. 10 cm. (4 in.). Mark 77.

death the half-ownership of the factory included in his estate was put up for auction on Vendémiaire 14th, Year VII. On Vendémiaire 24th Houzel bought Guy's share to become the sole owner. An invoice of Germinal 28th, Year IX is headed *Manuf^{re} de porcelaine du citoyen Houzel, rue Thiroux No. 661*. When, on Fructidor 29th, Year X, Lebeuf married the daughter of Boissy d'Anglas, Membre du Tribunat, he possessed amongst other assets the house in Rue Thiroux.

As far as the factory was concerned, judging by a survey of porcelain factories kept in the Archives de Sèvres, Houzel appears to have gone bankrupt before 1810. Did he have successors in Rue Thiroux? This is not proven, although research has identified one Julienne as such; he was a dealer in porcelain and crystal glass of number 8, subsequently 12, Rue Thiroux, whose very name, incidentally, does not appear till 1825. Also, Léveillé who succeeded Julienne in 1836 was still entered in the 1850 issue of the *Almanach du Commerce.*

The wares from Rue Thiroux were sold in various salesrooms as well, in particular at 'Le Petit Dunkerque', one of the Queen's favourite shops.

The early porcelain wares bear the mark A in blue, registered on September 9th 1776. Two years later the *Annonces, affiches et avis divers* contained the following information: 'the owners of the Queen's factory, established in Rue Thiroux, hereby notify the public that, since the Queen is willing to honour their establishment with her patronage and to allow it to bear her august name, every newly-manufactured item will henceforth be marked

underneath with a crowned A, the initial letter of Her Majesty's name . . .'
It is hollow wares and toilet items that are most often encountered. We find cups, sugar-pots, chocolate-pots, teapots, monteiths, stew pans (*cocottes*), salt-cellars with two or three compartments, mustard-pots, broth-bowls and olive-spoons.

The toilet items are numerous—pitchers with basins, pomade-jars, and spittoons. Marie-Antoinett's travelling-case (*nécessaire*) contains a set of pieces bearing the Queen's monogram.
Amongst the decorative pieces we might mention the writing sets, mantelpiece ornaments and *pots-pourris*. Chavagnac and Grollier assumed that the factory had produced no biscuit ware. It does, however, appear in an advertisement of 1777, and we can also find some biscuit items in the inventory of confiscation of 1780.

The porcelain is of a beautiful quality, its decoration fresh and attractive. Floral decorations predominate, in particular the cornflower which is regarded as having been the Queen's favourite flower. Most often seen are flowered ribbons, either alone or accompanied by flowers, by vividly coloured birds or by vertical stripes.
We must remember that some wares from this factory were sold under the mark of 'Le Petit Carrousel'.

Later pieces bear the Houzel mark or *Guy et Houzel* spelt out in full. The ones which have come down to us are more elaborate in decoration, being often embellished with polychrome animals.
The porcelain bearing the Léveillé mark is of very fine quality, mostly in the style of the late 18th century.

DUC D'ANGOULÊME'S FACTORY

Rue de Bondy, later Boulevard du Temple

The deed formally creating the factory of Dihl & Guérhard is dated February 25th 1781. An initial deed of partnership bound Christophe Dihl, a modeller, to Antoine Guérhard, a burgher of Paris and his wife, Louise Françoise Madeleine Croizé 'who have laid down as follows the articles of the company which they wish to set up together to handle the manufacture and marketing of any porcelain that may come from the factory which Sieur Dihl proposes to establish'. Whilst the latter brought his diligence and his talents the Guérhards supplied a capital outlay of 8,000 *livres* and in addition undertook to 'pay from their personal resources the wages and salaries of the most expensive artist or craftsman whom Sieur Dihl may deem it necessary to employ during the term of the said company'. The company had a projected lifespan of nine years from April 1st 1781, and the lease on a house in Rue de Bondy commenced on the same date. This, then, was the creation of a factory in its own right, because the deed of partnership further provided: 'in the garden of the said house shall be built workshops and a kiln for the manufacture and firing of goods'. The Guérhards were in charge of administration, Madame Guérhard being solely responsible for sales, while Dihl was the technical expert. Christophe Erasimus Dihl, the 'Palatine modeller' born at Neustadt in 1753, arrived in France in 1778. By 1779 he was settled in Rue du Temple turning out advertisements for 'vases with flowers of 19 inches'. The following year (October 26th 1780), he signed an agreement with Augustin Meyer, a miniaturist on Rue Saint-Martin, whereby he conceded exclusive rights for three years on 'all porcelain medaillons worth 12 *livres* and above, which are to be made and manufactured on his premises to be exhibited for sale by Sieur Meyer in his shop'. Besides this, Dihl was permitted to leave any of his wares with Meyer, busts, figures, flowers, etc. In return for a ten percent commission on sales Meyer advanced Dihl the sum of 3,000 *livres*. Later, Dihl distinguished himself by a number of feats in the field of chemistry, in particular the discovery of colours for painting on to porcelain. He subsequently invented a mastic with extraordinary properties which could be used either for filling in cracks in roofing materials or for works of art such as busts and bas-reliefs. He even took out an English patent on this invention.

The Guérhards were the administrators. Although termed a burgher of Paris by the first partnership deed, Guérhard had ties with the Germanic countries. In 1782 he presented the Académie des Sciences with a monograph on the mining of cobalt in Saxony and Silesia for use in porcelain manufacture, which attracted much attention. Madame Guérhard herself displayed some remarkable qualities. When a second partnership deed was signed in 1782, it was additionally stipulated that she should draw the same monthly salary as Dihl, and both of them committed themselves to running the factory unaided, although she had previously undertaken to manage only the sales and the book-keeping. She was a capable woman whose advice the Administration heeded, particularly on the formulation of the 1787 decree, or later in 1806 on economic

148 Darte Brothers. Plate. Dark-blue raised rim. Chestnuts painted in *trompe-l'oeil*. Circa 1820. Paço Nacional de Vila Viçosa, Fundação Casa de Bragance. Diam. 23.5 cm. (9¹/₅ in.). Mark 77.

questions about the situation of the factories and their trade.

Dihl then created and opened up his factory on April 1st 1781 and registered his mark with the Lieutenant général de Police on November 28th of the same year. He soon procured the protection of the Duc d'Angoulême. The company was ratified in 1782 with a few alterations to the management, but its expiry-date, originally set for April 1st 1790, was postponed on November 1st 1787. Although Dihl had until then had the option of taking over the company's factory and goodwill in the event of his marrying, the parties nevertheless agreed that the company should continue as it stood until April 1st 1790, and that on that date it should be prolonged for a further eighteen years. In this deed of partnership plans were also made to acquire more spacious premises to which to transfer the business —which was expanding rapidly by then— at the not inconsiderable maximum cost of 432,000 *livres*. This purchase was concluded on March 7th 1789; it was a large mansion to which were annexed various buildings, gardens and a number of adjacent houses. It stood at the junction of Rue and Boulevard du Temple and Rue Meslée. Further properties were subsequently added, particularly some grounds and sheds, in Year IV.

Right from the start this factory ran very well: they were 'overwhelmed with orders' and they sold 'a considerable amount'. The decree of 1784 was communicated to Dihl, in response to which 'Sieurs Dihl et Cie' declared in a memorandum that they could not burn coal without running the risk of sub-standard results and that 'they undertake not to make any item worth above ... 1,200 *livres*'. The decree of 1787 exempted the

factory from the concourse, and as business grew still more in volume, Dihl and Guérhard signed an agreement with the London agent Thomas Flight in 1789, thus guaranteeing a sales' outlet worth at least 50,000 *livres* annually.

Guérhard, however, died on April 28th 1793, and on Nivôse 4th, Year VI, the partnership which had continued between Guérhard's widow and Dihl was extended for nineteen years until April 1st 1829. The next day Catherine Guérhard, only daughter of Antoine, who resided with her mother in the factory, signed a contract of marriage with her cousin Bernard Guérhard whom she had known at the factory where they were

both working. She had a sizeable dowry of 130,000 francs 'in metallic tender', although Madame Guérhard apologized for this amount, enumerating the difficulties and hardships of the time. Finally, the day after her daughter's contract had been signed, Madame Guérhard in her turn signed her own with her partner Christophe Dihl. Legally, they opted for a joint estate, but the bride had complete freedom to draw the revenues from her realty. One cannot help but be amused in retrospect at one of the articles in the earliest partnership deed whereby Dihl had 'the option of dwelling with Sieur and Madame Guérhard upon paying them 800 *livres* yearly, but if he should happen to marry he will be compelled to set up his household separately'. The witnesses to this contract were the painter Joseph Sauvage, Etienne Charles Le Guay, who painted a portrait of Dihl shortly afterwards, Le Guay's wife Marie Victoire Jaquotot, one of Sèvres' greatest miniaturists on porcelain;[8] and lastly a nephew of Dihl's, Allovis Hoffmann. The wedding was held on Nivôse 7th, Year VI.

In the meantime the factory was still enjoying a great deal of success, which was rather exceptional in this difficult phase.

Dihl's experiments with colours were ratified by the Académie des Sciences et des Beaux Arts. Julien's report (Year VII) rated the establishment as the leading porcelain factory, by virtue of its sound administration and of the first-class artists which it had assembled. They year before, at the exhibition of Year VI, Dihl and Guérhard had displayed pictures on porcelain and had been the only manufacturers of porcelain to receive an award: this was the equivalent of the gold medal that they won in 1806, their factory being by then

considered one of the most prosperous in Europe.

Problems arose from the consequences of the European economic situation and from Dagoty's competition. Both applied the Emperor for loans and for orders. In 1807 Dihl secured an initial loan of 150,000 francs. In his survey of the situation he stated that he had made it a rule not to sell anything but decorated pieces and was releasing onto the market a million francs' worth of products annually, 300,000 to 400,000 francs' worth of this for export. He said that he was at present holding 800,000 francs' worth of unsold wares commissioned from England and Russia and that, instead of the labour force of two hundred to two hundred and fifty which he used to employ he had only forty men left, albeit the best in Paris. He was granted a second loan of 50,000 francs in 1809. Simultaneously the real estates were mortgaged off; by September 1st they were encumbered with no fewer than eighteen mortgages totalling nearly 350,000 francs. In 1811 it was the turn of his lands of La Cristinière close to Houdan (bought for the sake of the sagger clay which he was mining). They were mortgaged off, and he offered to sell Sèvres his factory for use as a warehouse (1810).

Meanwhile Dihl continued with his research into various fields, as a result of which one of the curious sights in Paris *circa* 1809 was a gallery in his factory whose windows were embellished with 'paintings on glass of amazing perfection and extraordinary size. Each window is a picture on a single pane. The paintings, executed by artists of outstanding merit, produce the most amazing and lifelike effect'. The members of the Consultative Board for the Arts and Manufactures (*Bureau consultatif des arts et manufactures*),

Ill. 98

149, 150   Darte Brothers. Plates. Dark-blue raised rims. African birds in polychrome. *Circa* 1820. Paço Nacional de Vila Viçosa, Fundação Casa de Bragance. Diam. 23.5 cm. (9¹/₅ in.). Mark 77. See page 204.

[8] LE GUAY, Charles Etienne (1762–1846). *Genre*-painter. He studied drawing at Sèvres, where he worked on several occasions.

Montgolfier, Ampère and Molard, were unanimous in praising their beauty. Prince Charles de Clary et Aldringen who came to Paris for the wedding of Napoleon and Marie-Louise, relates how he visited Dihl's immense and magnificent porcelain salesroom, which in his opinion rated far above Sèvres', and he adds that Dihl 'for a long time showed visitors—at a price—a gallery that is unique in the world. He chooses no longer to do so. I saw it thanks to Nesselrode's influence'. Dazzled by the landscapes painted on glass which replaced the windows, the Prince de Clary then wished to take his friends Madame Alexandre Potocka and Flore de Ligne round the gallery. On Dihl's refusal, he recounts: 'Finally I turned with honeyed words to old Madame Dyle [she was fifty-eight years old at the time], and by dint of cajolery and wheedling we obtained leave to see the gallery'. When Madame Potocka asked if she might order a madonna for her chapel at Natioline she was greeted by Dihl's retort of 'it is too expensive'. Nonetheless, the day ended pleasantly enough with the appearance of Comte Marescaldi, Italian Envoy to Paris, who gave each of the ladies a cup.

The factory lasted until 1828. Over the previous ten years the estates had been sold off, one after the other. In 1828 Dihl offered to sell Sèvres his collection of pseudo-antique models. Soon afterwards, on June 23rd 1828, Dihl asked that the partnership between his wife and himself be dissolved. The couple, almost in their eighties, were suing one another. Dihl stood accused of mismanaging both the factory and his wife's fortune, and of making irresponsible claims on the factory funds for developing his mastic. He countercharged his wife with giving her

daughter Catherine Guérhard an enormous dowry out of the monetary resources of the partnership. He declared that the partnership, weighed down with debts, 'ceased being effectual long ago' and demanded the return of various very large sums of money. The Tribunal of Commerce, in its verdict of July 8th 1828,

announced the dissolution of the partnership between Dihl and his spouse and nominated him as liquidator. This settled nothing, for Madame Dihl no longer had anything to live on, being cut off from the proceeds of sales. She complained bitterly of her accommodation which was attached to the factory buildings. Dihl

150 Darte Brothers.
see caption page 203.

acknowledged that he should provide every month for his wife's needs, but added that as the building which she inhabited had been put up for sale the inconvenience to her would soon be over. A sum of one hundred and fifty francs a month was allocated to Madame Dihl by the court of arbitration on August 5th 1828. On November 30th 1829 the Dihls were still living in separate lodgings on Rue Meslée. Madame Dihl summoned her husband to appear before the arbiters, charging him with failing to fulfil his mission as liquidator, although the building in which she was living had by that time been sold. She insistently demanded that the furniture and merchandise be sold off and claimed the right to use a horse and gig which Dihl was monopolizing. Dihl kept quiet at first, then replied that he had honoured his obligations by selling almost the total stock of porcelain wares, and pleaded that no one was available to purchase the surplus at a reasonable price. He obstinately refused his wife the use of the horse and gig as he continually needed them for going about the business of liquidation. Chavagnac and Grollier published a poster advertising the sale of porcelain and furniture after the dissolution, dated February 2nd 1829. On December 28th the arbiters recorded that Dihl had neither fulfilled his mission as liquidator nor indeed gone through any formality. He was, therefore, disqualified from this function which was entrusted to Monsieur Rousse, a notary in Paris. Six weeks later, on February 12th 1830, Dihl died 'in his house on Boulevard Saint Martin, number 5'. On the cards announcing his death are entered the names of Madame Dihl his widow, Madame Hoffmann his sister, Monsieur Hoffmann his nephew, Monsieur and Madame Guérhard and their children, his sons-in-law, daughter-in-law and their offspring.

After the seals affixed by the magistrate had been broken. Dihl's study was found to contain some pictures on porcelain, others on mastic, framed plates, checks painted on plate-glass, a medal from the Société d'Encouragement and, in his laboratory, 'a large number of pots, jars, vases and boxes containing residues presumed to be necessary for making mastic and colours'. Among his papers, besides his patents on mastic and painted panes there were reports, some to learned societies, and one on a new cosmetic. Being unwell, Madame Dihl could not be present at the closure of the post mortem inventory. She died on July 10th 1831, aged eighty.

In fact the organization had been resting entirely on one couple. Growing old and incapable of adapting themselves to the new economic conditions they let the factory die of old age.

Achieving the highest quality was always the aim of the factory. The artists working there included Le Guay, Sauvage and Salembier, all three of them renowned painters. Dihl himself was both modeller and chemist. As early as 1786 he was pointing out how—unlike Sèvres—he had managed to apply durable coloured grounds to hard-paste porcelain.

This assemblage of artists constituted a veritable 'studio' and the painter Blondel, a friend of Ingres', joined it at the age of about fourteen to learn drawing and the crafts of a porcelain painter. Le Guay used to teach figure-drawing: 'five days out of ten were devoted to the study of this and the other five to ornament-painting'. After the Revolution, when the drawing classes were cancelled, the pupils had to keep up with the orders flooding in, mainly from abroad, by replacing the craftsmen working on the commissioned paintings.[9]

The factory's output comprised many items for the table, the toilet and for decoration that are common to all such establishments. The quality is perfect. The shapes are often original; one sugar-bowl for the table exemplifies the tenacious *Ill. 94* survival of the *Rocaille* style. The Guérhard & Dihl factory excelled in especially meticulous and sumptuous decorations; those of Salembier are very fresh in colouring, his sepia monochromes being of figures or flowers. Often these two *décors* are fused, as in the 'chain-decoration' (*décor à la chaîne*) in which decorative *Ill. 89* patterns are heightened by a sepia chain. When Le Guay painted Dihl's portait in 1797 he placed beside his subject the things which were dearest to his heart— his palette, jars filled with the colours he had invented, a hemispherical cup with a bright yellow ground, a spindle-vase with a mottled ground decorated with a bas-relief by Sauvage, a large-scale biscuit *Ill. 98* model of a child reading, and his favourite dog dozing under the desk.

The coloured grounds are definitely one of Dihl's triumphs: brilliant yellow, green, purple, pink and the blue called *Ill. 90, 91* 'Sèvres blue'. Together with a single gilt-pattern border in reserve they often constitute the only decoration on a piece. The few specimens of mottled grounds of which we know are remarkable in their *Ill. 98, 101* quality, which never becomes excessive. But the pride of the factory is undeniably the copious output of pictures on porcelain. Some early plates were even painted by Drölling. Dihl jealously kept some of them in his study, mounted in gilt frames like pictures. There are large portraits by *Ill. 95, 98,* Drölling or Le Guay, and also landscapes, *100* children's games, flowers, etc. By Year VI

Dihl was already exhibiting specimens. They are plaques painted by Sauvage or Le Guay which embellish the sumptuous furniture kept in the Royal Palace of *Ill. 103, 105* Madrid. In 1806, the report on the exhibition spoke enthusiastically of 'pictures on porcelain' painted in this factory [which] are of the greatest beauty: one moonlight

scene in particular has a magical effect. The portrait of the Emperor is also a perfect likeness'. The biscuit ware is also of a very fine quality. It consists of vases, models of naked children, alone or grouped, or else clock-cases with allegorical themes, often supported on plinths in imitation of Wedgwood ware.

151, 152 Darte Brothers. Plates. Dark-blue raised rims. Polychrome wildflowers. *Circa* 1820. Paço Nacional de Vila Viçosa, Fundação Casa de Bragance. Diam. 23.5 cm. (9¹/₅ in.). Mark 77. See page 209.

⁹ GUILLAUME, Germaine. 'Merry Joseph Blondel and his friend Ingres'. *Bulletin de la Société de l'histoire de l'art français*, 1936.

Various marks were used by the Guérhard & Dihl factory. The earliest, registered with the Lieutenant général de Police in 1781, is composed of the monogram GA. It is usually inserted in an oval cartouche and surmounted by the crown of a Prince of the Blood. This mark is sometimes accompanied by the address in Rue de Bondy. It is stencilled in red or painted on in gold and accompanied by decorators' initials.

A further mark likewise alluding to the protection of the Duc d'Angoulême is stencilled on in red: *Manuf^re de Mgr le Duc d'Angoulême a Paris*. It was probably used until the Revolution.

A third mark, stencilled on in red, runs thus:

Mre de Dihl et Guérhard, Paris. It was undoubtedly applied from the Revolution until production ceased. A much scarcer variant transposes the names to *Guérhard et Dihl*.

Ill. 98, 101

Finally the mark in Dihl's name alone, painted in underglaze blue or in red, is rather unusual. It is mainly found on high-temperature pieces.

The biscuit ware bears an incised mark, either *Manufacture du Duc d'Angoulême Paris* or *Dihl*.

DUC D'ORLÉANS' FACTORY

Rue des Boulets; later Rue Amelot
On April 22nd 1784 Louis Honoré Delamarre de Villiers Esquire, presented himself to the Lieutenant général de Police and 'expounded to him that, being disposed to establish one of these factories [for producing porcelain], he had to this end rented a sizeable site; he besought him to receive his declaration, the mark which he wished to put on his wares, and his oath. The Lieutenant de Police acceded to his requests and once the formalities were over, Sieur Delamarre de Villiers turned his attention to the costly establishments which were necessary for his venture'.

As from the first of May following he entered into partnership with Jean Baptiste Augustin Outrequin de Montarcy, Esquire, 'to exploit the privilege or concession granted by His Majesty in respect of a porcelain factory established in Paris, on Rue des Boulets, Faubourg Saint-Antoine'. Outrequin de Montarcy was the son of Pierre Outrequin, the Director-General of schemes for beautifying Paris. Two years later, on June 26th 1786, Delamarre de Villiers acquiesced to Outrequin's requests by handing over his share in the factory in return for a life annuity of 2,400 *livres*, 'payable at all times and in any circumstances'. Outrequin took over all the wares, the clays, kilns, implements and fittings, kept both in the factory-buildings and in a salesroom on Rue Saint-Honoré, together with the usufruct of current leases. A joint declaration by Outrequin and Delamarre acknowledged that all the capital needed to work the factory had always been put up by Outrequin. The latter, however, 'being ill-versed in this aspect of commerce entered into another partnership, with Sieur Toulouse... and from then on Sieur Toulouse was put in charge of the whole operation'. Toulouse was made an equal partner on June 23rd 1786.

Edme Alexis Toulouse was the fifth child of Edme Toulouse, a master cartwright in Rue de Charonne, Paris. When his father died on January 23rd 1768, Edme Alexis was seventeen years old. Later, in 1779, he was 'employed in a porcelain factory on Rue Fontaine-au-

Roy'. The factory in question is therefore Locré's. Toulouse must have known his craft. Did he fail because he had wished to expand his establishment 'to extend it further and give this factory all the benefits and the splendour that would match the expenditure that it had necessitated' (the factory had been moved to Rue Amelot), or was it because, having bought it, could he not afford to maintain it? Whatever the case, Toulouse filed his petition of bankruptcy on July 11th 1789. On September 7th he turned the factory over to his creditors. The Archives de Paris contain his very detailed balance sheet, published by Chavagnac and Grollier. The liabilities amounted to 101,172l. 8s. 11d. In the assets, totalling 78,178 *livres,* were entered 'a house and factory for faience' *(sic)* valued at 15,000 *livres,* the plant and the finished and unfinished merchandise worth 25,000 *livres* and the implements 'from both factories and any structure on the owner's site ... 18,000 *livres*'. Are we to believe that Toulouse had also been manufacturing faience on Rue Amelot? Many faience makers do appear on his balance sheet. Rue de Boulets had by that time been abandoned in favour of Rue Amelot: a payment of 6l. 13s. was made on December 2nd 1786 'to the bailiff, to indicate the annulment of the rent agreement on the house in Rue des Boulets'. The white ware had probably been moved out, for in the two invaluable ledgers of receipts and expenditure which have come down to us, an entry of December 30th 1786 shows payments 'for gold, for gilding wares from the Rue des Boulets'.

On August 6th 1786 Toulouse had secured the protection of the Duc d'Orléans.

Who were Toulouse's immediate succes-sors? A table of porcelain factories kept in the Archives de la Manufacture de Sèvres gives Montansier, then 'Werstock who went bankrupt'. Another list in 1815 also mentions Werstock, followed by Lemaire.[10]

Lemaire's presence on Rue Amelot is beyond doubt. Pierre Lemaire had bought the building on Pluviôse 19th, Year VI at a cost of 66,000 francs 'in metallic tender'. He had been in partnership with Josse since Pluviôse 4th, Year IV. Julien's report speaks of the experience of those two porcelain craftsmen who 'have raised their establishment to a higher level, the first by his knowledge of the composition of porcelain bodies, the control of kilns and the supervision of throwing, moulding, etc; the second, whose knowledge is no less valuable, has turned to the chemistry of colours which he has brought, unaided and by his sustained efforts, to the forefront of perfection as we know it'. Lemaire died in Year IX. The partnership was thereby dissolved and Josse specialized in making colours. In 1786 he was works manager in the Faubourg Saint-Denis.

Madame Lemaire continued running the factory but on Floréal 27th Year X sold it to Toussaint Caron, together with the implements, kiln, muffles, wares and raw materials, for the sum fo 12,815 *livres* 17 *sols,* according to the schedule drafted by Deuster and Lefebvre. On the same day she granted Caron a nine-year lease on the house at 9, Rue Amelot.

Toussaint Caron went into partnership with Jacques Lefebvre for three years as from November 26th 1806 'for the purpose of jointly continuing the porcelain factory and its business, conducted until now by Sieur Caron alone: henceforth the responsibilities will be shared

[10] The man in question might be a certain Baverstock.

equally between him and Sieur Lefebvre'. Caron put up the capital for the business on Rue Amelot, and 'the manufactured goods' stored in Rue Amelot, in a warehouse on Rue Feydeau, and for the rents. Exempted from contributing funds, Lefebvre 'devotes himself to the business with wholehearted concern and diligen-

152 Darte Brothers. see caption page 206.

ce'. Jacques Lefebvre had previously been the factory manager at 92, Faubourg Saint-Denis on behalf of the Bernard-Hébert-Le Cointre partnership and had gone bankrupt.

The Caron-Lefebvre company, originally projected for a term of three years, went on to last for six and was dissolved on July 7th 1812. Lefebvre was left alone. Like a lot of porcelain factories this company suffered from severe handicaps caused by the economic situation, since its exports were principally intended for dispatch to Russia and Spain. It was granted a loan of 30,000 francs in 1807. The survey of porcelain factories in 1815 states that Caron & Lefebvre collapsed owing to losses inflicted by the war. They amounted to 793,700 francs, although no balance sheet has been discovered.

A bill head of 1818 bearing Lefebvre's name reveals that his factory was once again under the protection of the Duc d'Orléans, the son of the factory's first patron. On March 23rd 1819 Lefebvre sold his establishment to Thomas Antoine Edme Hulm, known as Hall, and to Joseph Louis Merlin de Failly, both dwelling at Montereau-faut-Yonne, for 130,000 francs. These purchasers were none other than the descendants of the first owners of the creamware factory at Montereau, and Hall was actually one of Lemaire's sons-in-law, having married his daughter Marie Françoise Louise.

The following year, on May 16th 1820, Hall and Merlin concluded a two-year sleeping partnership with the Baronne de Plessen of Strassburg, the company name being Hall et Co. Each partner put up 33,600 francs. At the exhibition of 1823 Hall displayed faience ware from Gien for which he was sole agent.

Many factories were by then moving their manufacturing workshops into the provinces, and Hall signed agreements with Jacques François Jeanne on November 23rd 1825, giving him half-ownership of the porcelain factory at Noirlac near Saint-Amand (Cher) and bringing the two of them into partnership for eleven years and six months. Jeanne died the following year (August 7th 1826), and Hall then applied to auction off Noirlac as an indivisible unit. A lawsuit ensued between Hall and Jeanne's widow. The seals were affixed at Noirlac and in Rue Amelot and, following a ruling between Hall and the remarried Madame Jeanne given by the court of arbitration on November 6th 1826, a second ruling, of bankruptcy, was recorded on June 11th 1828. It was only in 1832 that the porcelain stored in Rue Amelot and Rue Feydeau could be valued; the total was 33,312 francs.

Louis André, already the owner of the Foëscy factory in Le Cher took over the factory at Noirlac.

Various marks were used by the successive owners of the Duc d'Orléans' factory.

The mark which was registered in 1786 is formed out of the initials of Louis Philippe, originally Duc de Chartres but recently made Duc d'Orléans. Later a crown was set above these initials. The mark usually appears in underglaze blue, although sometimes painted in gilt.

Chaffers agrees with Chavagnac and Grollier in ascribing to Delamarre de Villiers the earliest mark of a monogram formed from the letters MVI. A further device with the letters OM signifies Outrequin de Montarcy. These two monograms are usually painted in red. Lefebvre used to sign in full, with or without the address. As to Jeanne's mark it would be tempting to attribute to him the one which gives his name accompanied by an outline, if we did not find in the same period another Jeanne in Rue Saint-Louis who by 1827 was investing himself with the title of 'Faience maker by special appointment, and supplier to H.R.H. Monseigneur, Duc d'Angoulême' *(Fayencier breveté et fournisseur de S.A.R. Monseigneur, Duc d'Angoulême)*. This second Jeanne sold porcelain as well. In the early stages output consists mostly of table pieces of which relatively few specimens are known, and of biscuit ware, known solely from texts. This porcelain is less than excellent in quality, as it is slightly muddy, often shows 'sanding', and has sub-standard decorations.

The items bearing Lefebvre's mark are frequently most original in shape, such as this cup in the shape of a human head. The miniatures which adorn some of them are of good quality.

Ill. 106, 107

Ill. 108

Factories and decorating Workshops

ANDRÉ

In 1810 there was a Paris porcelain dealer named Maurice André, who had set himself up at 8, Rue Notre-Dame-de-Nazareth. He was also known as a painter. He dwelt at that address until 1823, when he settled at 21, Rue Vendôme.

Maurice André was, from 1827, the sales agent for Coussac-Bonneval white ware. However, the decorated porcelain which he exhibited in the same year had come, in its plain state, from the factory of Boilleau Gauldrée at Magnac-Bourg (Haute-Vienne), which had its own warehouse at 26, Rue de Bondy.

At the exhibition of 1823 Maurice André displayed a porcelain candelabrum with bronze mounts and won an honourable mention for his good taste, sound gilding and moderate prices. At the next exhibition, in 1827, he displayed many Gothic pieces and a shell-shaped compote dish, the model for a service made for the King of Spain. In 1834 he exhibited numerous *Rocaille* pieces, including trinkets, some 'Etruscan' vases, clocks, 'a table with bronze legs, ormolu mounts and a porcelain top showing six figures from the *Histoire de l'Amour* after Fragonard, with ornaments and a buff ground'. This table was priced at 2,500 francs. André went bankrupt in 1841.

The Musée des Arts décoratifs in Paris contains a plate painted in his workshop by M. Juin in 1820.

Dominique André—whose kinship with Maurice remains unconfirmed—became the owner of the porcelain factory at Foëscy (Cher) in about 1825. In the *Almanach du Commerce* of 1825 the owners of the Foëscy factory are entered as the winners of a bronze medal at the exhibition of 1823.

This factory at Foëscy had been founded by Benjamin Klein and Jean Pierre Devilleaux who had been joined by Pillivuyt in a partnership deed of May 25th 1818. The next partnership, concluded in the name of L. Pillivuyt et Cie., was itself annulled on April 6th 1822. Pillivuyt was, incidentally, the manager and not the owner. In 1827 the factory, in Pillivuyt's name, won another bronze medal.

On November 23rd 1832 a deed of partnership was signed between Louis André, who was Dominique's son and the co-manager, of 40, Rue des Petites-Ecuries in Paris, and André and Cottier, bankers and sleeping partners, at a cost of 100,000 francs. The aim of this company was to run the factory at Foëscy, to sell its wares and to transact any business connected with porcelain. The official name of the firm was Louis André et Cie. Under Louis André's management the concern bore fruit. In 1834 the *Almanach du Commerce* shows that he owned both Foëscy and Noirlac. His warehouse was on Passage Violet (Faubourg Poissonnière), then, from 1836 onwards, at 41, Rue des Petites-Ecuries. Louis André died in 1840, leaving his son Charles to run the business. Yet again the warehouse changed its address: in 1844 it moved to 46/50, Rue Paradis Poissonnière. The factory was by then employing a labour force of three hundred, plus two hundred in Paris, and its turnover rose to a million francs in 1844.

Louis André died in 1861 and Charles Pillivuyt went off to found a new factory, also in Le Cher but at Mehun-sur-Yèvre, whose company headquarters and warehouse remained at the old address in Rue Paradis.

For the same reasons that Brongniart and Honoré, both in charge of important factories, were questioned, Louis André assisted in an inquiry conducted by the Ministry of Commerce in 1834. He stated that he took only wholesale orders at the factory but sold retail in his Paris salesroom. Indeed, he was working hard at exports, particularly for the United States.

It is difficult to find pieces which definitely come from this factory, firstly because the export consignments were often of plain wares, and secondly because the white wares left in France mainly bore the decorators' marks alone. Nonetheless the Musée national de Céramique de Sèvres contains a very interesting double-lidded sugar-bowl, bearing the marks both of Perche, painted in green, and of the *Manufacture de Foëscy, Passage Violet No 5, R. Poissonnière à Paris.*

Ill. 229

BLANCHERON   MAUBRÉ
BARUCH WEIL   CLAUSS
The report by Julien in 1798 gave Blancheron's address as 'rue Crussol'.
After Etienne Jean Louis Blancheron had

succeeded Potter on Rue de Crussol, he moved a short distance away, to Rue des Trois Bornes where he bought a building from Monsieur and Madame Bailly on Messidor 5th, Year VI. He went bankrupt and the factory was adjudged on Germinal 18th, Year X to Joseph Maubré, a painter at the factory. He in his turn declared himself insolvent in 1807, but he had long before concluded the sale of the implements and manufactured items.

In 1817 Baruch Weil bought the building after a lawsuit against Maubré and resold it on March 4th 1822 to Pierre Louis Alexandre Dodé and his second wife, Louise Désirée Bully who lived at 2, Rue Fontaine-au-Roy.

153 Denuelle.
Antique vase copied from Etruscan ware. Black ground with ochre-red decoration. In 1834 Denuelle exhibited some of these Etruscan vases, which look rather odd against the normal products from his factory. Vases showing the same influence were reproduced in Stéphane Flachat's work on French industry, along with porcelain by Jacob Petit and Clauss. Other Parisian factories also turned them out. This specimen was given by Mme Denuelle to the Musée Adrien Dubouché. Limoges, Musée Adrien Dubouché. Ht. 17 cm. (6^7/$_{10}$ in.).
Unmarked.

154 Deroche.
Drug-jar. Polychrome and
gold. The names of Deroche
Pochet and Gosse are in-
scribed in the upper panel.
Circa 1839.
Sèvres, Musée National de
Céramique. Ht. 46 cm.
(19$\frac{1}{3}$ in.).
Mark 91.

Dodé, whose first marriage had been to Madeleine Eléonore Russinger, had spent a year (from May 1813 to May 1814) as the partner of Russinger's brother-in-law, Antoine Laurent Béhier. Their business had been the decoration and sale of porcelain at 2, Rue Fontaine-au-Roy. Dodé went bankrupt in 1824. In 1828 we

come upon him at Fours, with the Pouyats, then in 1844 as a workshop overseer at Mayer et Cie., decorators, of Rue des Marais Saint-Martin.

However, from the faience manufacturer Jean Marc Clauss, Dodé had rented in 1824 the factory in Rue des Trois Bornes on a lease extending until October 1st 1829. When this fell in, Clauss set himself up in a building that stood on Rue Pierrelevée, which he was not to purchase till 1852.

Jean Marc Clauss was a shoemaker's son from Traben near Treves, where he had been born in about 1778. He had married Odile Seeger, the daughter and sister of porcelain painters, settled in Paris in

1821, and died in Rue Pierrelevée on July 9th 1846. Two brothers of his, Louis Daniel and Jean Etienne, were porcelain throwers in Paris. Jean Etienne had a son, Louis, who became a painter on porcelain.

From his marriage Jean Marc had five children, including a daughter Louise Adèle who married the porcelain painter Camille Flers, and a son, Marc Alphonse who succeeded him on Rue Pierrelevée and died on October 27th 1868, likewise leaving the business to his son, Marc Eugène. Marc Eugène ran the factory until 1887, when he went into partnership with Léon Bourdois and Achille Bloch, the company being entitled Clauss et Cie. By 1900 only Achille Bloch was left. Thereafter the factory remained in the hands of his descendants.

Blancheron's mark consists of his initials EB. This mark, which Chavagnac and Grollier are at a loss to explain, is found painted in gilt underneath a cup and matching saucer having a *trompe-l'œil* decoration of prints on a ground of simulated wood. Now, the prints bear the inscription *Fait chez Blancheron*. His wares are of a respectable quality. Chavagnac records some biscuit busts of Voltaire and Jean-Jacques Rousseau as being poorly made and bearing the seal in relief *E. Blancheron à Paris*.

We might note that Jean Marc Clauss took part in various exhibitions. In 1834 he exhibited a tea service which met with enormous success. We know of one specimen of this, decorated with green *Rocaille* escutcheons heightened with flowered scrolls in gilt relief, and accompanied by roses from nature bearing Schoelcher's mark alone.

155   Deroche.
Large ribbed cup and its saucer. Pseudo-Chinese polychrome decoration on nankeen ground. *Circa* 1820. Paris, Coll. Guy Passerat. Ht. 8.5 cm. (3³/₁₀ in.). Mark 90.

Ill. 111

Ill. 169

Ill. 170

156 Discry.
Two identically shaped vases with oriental decoration. Both exemplify the technique perfected by Discry, of producing high-temperature grounds by dipping. Its main characteristics were the option it offered of reserving panels, hence the low cost price. On the left a speckled blue ground with reserves decorated with sample-patterns; on the right a celadon ground with relief blossoms in reserve. One of the objectives in making these wares was to compete with oriental exports. Both vases were exhibited in 1839. Sèvres, Musée National de Céramique, Discry Bequest. Ht. 22 cm. (8³⁄₅ in.). Unmarked.

Clauss won a honourable mention at the 1839 exhibition, being looked upon as one of the best manufacturers left in Paris. Besides his porcelain and some biscuit ware he exhibited muffle-kilns for firing porcelain which took three hours to work instead of eight, and which he sold to decorators.

When, at this same exhibition, Talmours and Discry won a gold medal for their high-temperature grounds with reserved panels, Clauss gave vent to his indignation in a letter addressed to the members of the jury. He claimed to have forestalled Discry's research by a whole year and to have entrusted the decorator Peylier with his first tests in March 1836; he accused Discry of imitating his high-temperature greens late in 1837. In conclusion Clauss stressed that he had been the first to market porcelain wares coloured in the mass, mostly blue and celadon. The exhibition of 1844 was marked by the confirmation both of Discry's gold medal and of Clauss' honourable mention for his 'statuettes of biscuit, which are worthy of the highest praise'.

Clauss was principally employed by decorators to work on export wares. He seems not to have had any mark. His grandson Marc Eugène registered two in 1876: one of a trident and the other consisting of two crossed tridents.

BROILLIET ADVENIER
& LAMARRE

It seems that the so-called Gros-Caillou and Vaugirard factories originally made up no more than a single establishment consolidated under the management of Broilliet.

On the strength of the letters patent issued to him on June 7th 1762, Jacques Louis Broilliet from Switzerland established a 'factory for china' *(manufacture de Chine)* at Vaugirard. In their report of August 2nd 1772, Macquer, Rouelle and d'Arcet declared that they had examined 'items of earthenware, also cups and saucers marked L.B. which they told us were of porcelain manufactured by Sieur Broilliet at Vaugirard'. They concluded that the pieces were of such mediocre quality as not to warrant the name of porcelain, nor of faience either.

Some murky incidents alienated Broilliet and his sleeping partners, to whom he had falsely alleged that he had visited China and Japan. M. de Provigny amongst others had supplied him with more than 100,000 *livres* for his factory at Le Gros-Caillou and was reproached by Monsieur de Clare for hanging blindly upon Broilliet's promise 'to invest in his two ventures and especially in the two companies which he has set up at Le Gros-Caillou'. In another document of the same year (1772) the banker Fernier

157 Discry.
Tea- or coffee-service with
scroll-work and scallop-
motifs. Plain, undecorated.
It was exhibited in 1834.
This model was very successful throughout the 19th
century and was turned out
in large numbers by many
factories. Inspired from the
comfortably rounded
'English' services, it
resembles some contempo-
rary wares by Jacob Petit
(ill. 169). In its absence of
straight lines it stands in
opposition to the last of the
neo-Classical (antique)
influence which was still in
evidence.
Sèvres, Musée National de
Céramique, Discry Bequest.
Teapot: Ht. 18 cm. (7 in.).

recounted how, having bought a derelict
porcelain factory at Vaugirard, he had
been introduced to Broilliet who undertook to start it up again. Broilliet won
him over by showing him some Sèvres
porcelain as having been manufactured
by him, and the banker 'reappointed him
in his factory at Vaugirard, to the post of
leading freelance craftsman,' also supply-
ing him with capital. Squabbling soon
set in and it became a truly dismal story
of a daughter seduced, elopement, thrash-
ing and trumped-up privileges... The
first batch having aborted, Broilliet buri-
ed the whole lot, 'conducting himself at
Le Gros-Caillou just as he had done at
Vaugirard'. But while he was away

looking for clay at Orleans the concealed porcelain was dug up and it was
realized that a goblet marked LB which
he had been showing off as his own
handiwork had really been stolen from
the home of the Duc de Brancas-Laura-
guais. A trial ensued but a decree restored
him in triumph to his post. He duped
more victims in his attempt to set up a
factory making mortars of porcelain
and soap-stone at Vaugirard. Bertin considered him 'a danger to Society'. For his
part 'Louis Broilliet, *entrepreneur* of the
royal factory at Vaugirard making chemists' utensils and mortars,' complained
about Fernier to Bertin; he claimed to be
in an awkward situation 'having taken
the order for a set of kitchen implements
for the household of Madame la Marquise
du Barrie, which is about to undergo
firing...'

Broilliet probably went into partnership with Noël Claude Chervise 'a dealer
and manufacturer at Vaugirard near
Paris' who declared himself insolvent on
May 19th 1775. His balance sheet states:
'Sieur Chervise is positively suffering
losses, along with Sieur Broyer, Sieur
Desvergères and others, his partners for
the full duration of these partnerships.'

Meanwhile, the factory at Le Gros-
Caillou was being operated by Advenier
and Lamarre who registered their mark,
AD, on July 26th 1773. In Buhot's report
(1774) we read: 'this factory, although
very old, is still in the cradle, having
until now been in very bad hands. It has
given rise to more court cases than were
ever made porcelain pieces inside it.
Monsieur de Magnanville, Garde du
Trésor Royal, has lately been discussing
it with Sieur Provigny'. He added that
only common wares would be made
there. The decree of 1784 was commu-

nicated to Advenier & Lamarre. The previous year a craftsman at Sèvres had been asking for leave to go to Le Gros-Caillou 'to work on monochromes'.

These factories do not appear in Julien's report (1798).

This amusing and complicated story, which is somewhat reminiscent of the career of Pierre Antoine Hannong, closes with the observation that only one single piece marked AD is known today. It came to light at the Lejeal sale in Valenciennes in 1880.

CHANOU

The short-lived factory owned by Chanou was the venture of a craftsman from Sèvres who wanted to try his luck by setting up his own business in Paris but who was lucky enough, after his failure, to be readmitted to the royal factory.

Henri Florentin Chanou was one of a family which had fifteen members entered in the staff lists of Sèvres between 1745 and 1829. He himself had joined the factory as a modeller in 1767. Believing himself to be underpaid, he resigned ten years later to go to Paris. A statement of November 1780 disclosed that he took six fellow-craftsmen away with him who, had likewise been working in other factories: 'He did not last long as the employee of private factories: he has been seen signed on as a supernumerary actor in travelling shows, which does not point to his being a modeller of merit as he claims.'

By the time that he had registered his mark with the Lieutenant général de Police on May 1st 1784, he had a factory on Rue de Reuilly. When, shortly afterwards, the decree of 1784 was issued, Chanou gave up and, in April 1785, applied to be reinstated at Sèvres as a

modeller. A memorandum of July 31st 1785 to the Comte d'Angivillers confirms his return to Sèvres. He asked the Baron de Breteuil for a formal three-year deferment in repaying 5,000 to 6,000 *livres*' worth of debts which he had incurred at the Reuilly factory. According to a later document his factory had been pulled down owing to the considerable losses borne by a *fermier général* (tax-farmer). Chanou stayed on at Sèvres until 1792.

Because of its short lifespan, few pieces were made in this factory. It may be assumed that by the time that the mark was registered on May 1st 1784 wares were already being regularly turned out.

158 Escalier de Cristal. Round-based cup and deep saucer. Pink ground, polychrome decoration. Imitation of old Sèvres ware. *Circa* 1850. Sèvres, Musée National de Céramique. Ht. 4.5 cm. (1³/₄ in.). Lahoche, Escalier de Cristal

It is, however, unlikely that production was continued beyond the end of the year. By 1785 Chanou was, as we have seen, reinstated at Sèvres, which therefore allows us to date his porcelain very precisely. The wares of which we know are exceptionally well-finished table pieces embellished with landscapes, figures, borders in the style of Salembier, simulations of brown marble or pebbled decorations.

The mark CH is painted on the back in red or gold.

CHAPELLE CASSÉ-MAILLARD CHAPELLE-MAILLARD

By his own account the painter and gilder Chapelle set himself up in 1806. By 1821 he was at 168, Rue Quincampoix and in 1822 we find entered under the name of Chapelle Fils, a factory and a salesroom for either plain or painted and gilded porcelain ware, at 19, Faubourg Saint-Denis. It does, however, look as if Chapelle was only a decorator. By 1834 he had twenty-five to thirty craftsmen in his huge workshops and he won an honourable mention at the exhibition where he was merely displaying white ware by Jacob Petit which he had decorated.

About 1840 Chapelle went into partnership with Maillard of 19, Boulevard des Italiens. Since 1827, Madame Maillard had been living at this address where she kept a salesroom for porcelain and crystal glass. The *Almanach du Commerce* of 1831 listed Cassé-Maillard, a dealer in 'porcelain, crystal glass, faience, glass ware, bronzes, clocks and fancy goods, [who] hires out wares for balls and banquets, or dispatches them abroad'. The 1840 issue of the *Almanach du Commerce* additionally mentions Chapelle

Maillard of 19, Boulevard des Italiens, and Chapelle of 19, Faubourg Saint-Denis. From 1841 onwards the same almanach only includes Chapelle Maillard on Boulevard des Italiens and a Chapelle fils, decorator, at another address. Chapelle Maillard was still in existence in 1850.

Chapelle received an award at the exhibition of 1844, at that time he had an address at Belleville, 7, rue de Lilas.

Various marks relate the phases in the history of this firm (Chapelle, Cassé-Maillard and Chapelle-Maillard) and supply the address.

The meticulously finished products are made up of table pieces and ornaments following the fashion of the period with Flemish figures and *chinoiserie* influenced by the 18th century.

CHEVALIER FOURMY TRÉGENT JULLIEN MARGAINE

From the end of the 18th century two porcelain factories were being set up near to one another, at Roule, outside the traditional quarters of the ceramics manufacturers. The first was successively in Rue de la Pépinière, Rue des Grésillons and Rue de Laborde. But these last two addresses are one and the same, the street having changed its name in 1837. The second factory stood in Rue du Rocher.

In Year VII Julien's report refers to the factory of Chevalier frères at 650, Rue de la Pépinière. Chevalier won a gold medal for his sanitary fitments in Year XII, whilst in Year IX Fourmy, operating from the same address in Rue de la Pépinière, had won a silver medal. Were they perhaps partners? Whatever the case may be, it was Fourmy who was then named as occupier at this address until 1806, when the *Almanach du Commerce* also gives Fourmy and then Trégent (or Tréjean) at the same address. Trégent was employing a labour force of twenty by 1809. Like his colleagues he was subjected to the consequences of political events and applied in 1811 for a loan which was refused him. Along with the other Parisian manufacturers, he signed the petition of 1814 about ways of safeguarding their industry.

The documents of the exhibition in 1819 mention, one after the other, at the same address: Trégent Senior, another Trégent; the widowed Madame Lalouette and P. S. Jullien, her successor. Madame Lalouette exhibited a magnificent tea service, and Jullien was no less warmly complimented on two pictures with their frames bearing porcelain, palmettes, one of which showed Henri IV painted by Constant, after Gérard.

In fact, Trégent must already have left Rue des Grésillons, since he was at 3, Rue de la Feuillade when he went bankrupt on June 8th 1820.

As to the confusion between Madame Lalouette and P. S. Jullien, some genealogical records have recently enabled us to clear it up.[1]

By 1816 Jean Jacques Nicolas Lalouette was a porcelain manufacturer on Rue des Grésillons; on October 9th he married Marie Antoinette Héloïse Dodé, born on August 30th 1799, the daughter of Pierre Louis Alexandre Dodé and of Marie Eléonore Russinger. Lalouette died on June 20th 1818 and 'Veuve Lalouette', *née* Dodé, 'a porcelain maker' remarried at barely twenty on August 12th 1819. Her husband was Pierre Simon Jullien, born in Paris on October 18th 1795.

Jullien had to leave the factory on Rue des Grésillons in about 1827 to go and manage the one at Conflans where he went bankrupt on March 27th 1829. About 1840 Jullien took up the management of the factory in Saint-Léonard (Haute-Vienne). Madame Jullien died there in 1881.

In 1828 a certain Chazaud, also known as a manufacturer at l'Isle-Adam, made his appearance on Rue des Grésillons. He went bankrupt on February 9th 1832 but in 1836 was still entered in the *Almanach du Commerce* as a factory manager at l'Isle-Adam.

In 1833 we still find Margaine & Cie. at this address. Under this trade name Victor Désiré Margaine and Léonard Victor Laquintinie had signed a deed of partnership on August 30th 1833 setting up a business in porcelain; the partnership was dissolved the following year. In January 1835 Margaine joined Eugène François Reboulleau, the latter being the sleeping partner for 25,000 francs. Margaine contributed the factory funds together with the manufactured goods and raw materials. The partnership was dissolved two years later. Margaine went bankrupt in 1837. Two years later, in 1839, he was in partnership with Paul Dubois and had settled at 7, Rue de la Boule. Their partnership funds amounted to 100,000 francs and they were by then employing a labour force of forty on their premises and ten outside. Pérémé, a decorator who kept a shop at 10, Faubourg Montmartre, acted as sales agent for both Margaine and for the factory at Villedieu. We encounter Margaine once again, now a wholesale merchant at 12, Rue de l'Echiquier and in business with a certain Salmon; then, in about 1850, partnering Gibus and Redon of Limoges. In 1867 he was still there.

159 Feuillet.
Lobed plate adorned with a blue ribbon and small polychrome flowers. This piece is an exact copy of a Sèvres plate dated 1782. Many manufacturers and decorators of the mid-19th century applied – sometimes directly – to Brongniart, the manager of the Sèvres factory, asking for models of earlier wares. It is thus rather curious to observe how, at that time, any Parisian porcelain-makers who imitated Sèvres were interested only in its earlier soft pastes. *Circa* 1830.
Sèvres, Musée National de Céramique. Diam. 24 cm. (9²/₃ in.).
Mark 109.

[1] Genealogical information passed on by M. X. Védère, Keeper at the Musée des Arts décoratifs, Bordeaux.

Fourmy's products and his research into stoneware-porcelain were much acclaimed in the early 19th century, but this is beyond our scope. In the absence of specific information about the marks used by his successors we cannot at present ascribe any wares to them.

On the other hand, since Margaine personally donated some porcelain marked MA in underglaze blue to the Musée de Sèvres, we definitely know of various pieces of his table services with undulating edges and relief decoration, and plates with scalloped and pierced rims. These wares had been shown at the 1839 exhibition. Margaine supplied porcelain to many decorators and dealers, notably Rihouët and the 'Escalier de Cristal'.

DAGOTY & HONORÉ

We have identified several factories with the joint name of Dagoty and Honoré, but their histories are often so similar that it is difficult to discuss them separately without risking constant repetition.

The oldest of these establishments does seem to be the one owned by François Honoré at 5, Petite Rue Saint-Gilles, Boulevard Saint-Antoine. According to various schedules of factories, he had taken over a factory whose successive owners had probably been Lortz, Rouget, Savoye, Lebon and Latourville. The founder and Lebon went bankrupt and the other three gave up after incurring losses. The *Almanach du Commerce* gives 'Bon, petite rue Gilles 93' in Year VI, then in Year VII Lortz by himself as well as Bon and Lortz at the same address.

The partnership between Bon and Lortz is only recorded from Year VIII to Year X. In the course of that last year

Savoye emerged, to be replaced in the ensuing years by Bertrand, Hubert & Cie., or Bertrand, Henry & Cie. (from 1802 to 1805). In 1807 the name 'Vendish & Cie.' (Windisch) appeared, while Honoré is entered at the same address.

In fact, François Maurice Honoré and Jean Baptiste Windisch, both porcelain

manufacturers, had gone into partnership by signing a private agreement dated October 28th 1806. This partnership was annulled on September 8th 1810, but the dissolution was not due to come into force before March 6th 1811. This did not pass off without friction, because in their ruling of June 25th 1811 the Tribunal de Commerce de la Seine appointed two arbiters, Léonard Pouyat and Marc Schoelcher. To confuse matters, the latter found themselves at odds over the form in which Windisch should be refunded his capital outlay. The complication derived in part from the fact that Honoré owned another factory at La Seynie (Haute-Vienne) which had been

160 Feuillet.
Punch-bowl. Polychrome and gold. Swiss landscapes.
Circa 1820.
Geneva, Musée de l'Ariana.
Diam. 20 cm. (7³/₄ in.)
Mark 109.

running since 1808. A third arbiter endorsed Schoelcher's opinion, which won the day for Honoré.

In October 1807 Honoré applied to the imperial administration for a loan. This was refused him even though he had made his request more attractive by submitting the 'monogram of Their Impe-

161 Feuillet.
Fluted cup and its saucer.
Band of strawberry-plants in black and gold on pink ground. *Circa* 1830.
Sèvres, Musée National de Céramique. Ht. 8 cm. (3 1/10 in.).
Mark 109.

rial and Royal Majesties executed in porcelain flowers'. A new application for a loan, drafted in 1812, was also rejected. However, another porcelain maker called Dagoty had been awarded several loans, including one of 80,000 francs on March 19th 1807. Dagoty had stressed the losses that he had been suffering, pleading that

political events had prevented him from exporting porcelain wares. In addition he received commissions for the palaces of Versailles and Compiègne. In the files recording the loans we read that this factory 'occupies the forefront at Paris'. It won the title of the Empress's factory. It was the board of this factory, which became so popular under the Empire, that Honoré was later to join as a partner under the Restoration, in 1816. By then in fact, François Maurice Honoré was no more than sleeping partner to his son Edouard.

Just as the name of Honoré refers to two members of same family, so the name of Dagoty covers three brothers. The one known best is Pierre Louis, who was born in Paris on February 7th 1771 and died in Paris in February 1840. He was the son of the portraitist to Marie-Antoinette and grandson of the anatomist Gautier Dagoty. As they had lost their fortune on a commercial venture and had also been the pupils of Guérhard & Dihl, the three brothers tried their luck at manufacturing porcelain. Pierre Louis, Jean-Baptiste Etienne and Isidore Dagoty moved into cramped lodgings on Boulevard Poissonnière. As success came their way they had to expand and buy a proper factory. Their choice fell upon Roger's, in Rue de Chevreuse at Montparnasse.

Isidore soon died, so Jean-Baptiste Etienne and Pierre Louis may be regarded as the true founders of the Dagoty factory. When he married on Frimaire 19th, Year VII 'Jean-Baptiste Etienne Gauthier Dagoty' the porcelain painter was still living at the salesroom on Boulevard Poissonnière where, with his elder brother, he carried on his craft. His separate property included half the factory estimated at the modest sum of 3,000 francs.

162 Fleury.
Handleless cup and deep
saucer. Gold. *Circa* 1810.
Lisbon, Museu Nacional de
Arte Antiga. Ht. 6 cm.
(2¹⁄₃ in.).
Mark 113.

By the time he died two years later, in Year IX, he was living on Rue de Chevreuse, in a building on which he had just taken a nine-year lease (Germinal 20th, Year VIII). Since Jean-Baptiste left only an infant son, the factory was put up for auction by his widow and his brother Pierre Louis. The expert valuation was carried out by Russinger on Madame Dagoty's behalf and by Deuster who acted for Pierre Louis.

Pierre Louis Dagoty bought back the factory on Thermidor 8th, Year XII for 11,339 francs. It quickly rose to fame and, as we have seen, by 1807 it was a prominent Parisian factory. 'In 1806 there came out of this factory 350,000 francs' worth of merchandise, two-thirds of it for export;' one hundred to one hundred and twenty craftsmen were by then being employed. It was 'the done thing' to buy elegant gifts at Dagoty's. For a baptism, for instance, the newly-delivered mother would be given a silver-gilt *veilleuse* from Odiot's salesroom and a 'porcelain basin from Dagoty's'.

From *L'Hermite de la Chaussée d'Antin,* published in 1813 we quote this extract: 'Fine porcelain wares still number among the items most commonly given as New Year presents, and M. Dagoty's salesroom on Boulevard Montmartre is one of the most richly stocked; it is here that those beautiful table services are found, combining elegant shapes with beautiful colouring and exquisitely finished painting; those vases costing a hundred *louis* and destined to hold a fifteen-*sou* windflower; that elegant apparatus for making coffee without boiling it, and so greatly refined by chemical, physical and pneumatic techniques that one may, at half-past nine at night, hope for half a cup of coffee simply by troubling, three hours beforehand, to adjust the spirit-lamp, the holder, the cap, the rammer and other components beside which Wolf's apparatus is just child's-play. Among the people who were examining these brilliant gewgaws I spied Madame...; she had just bought a *Patrouille d'amours en biscuits* [squadron of putti in biscuit].

163 Flamen-Fleury. ▶
Veilleuse. Unrolling polychrome landscape.
Circa 1830.
London, Victoria & Albert
Museum. Ht. 23 cm. (9 in.).
Mark 114.

This chimney set, very expensive and rather vulgar, is at least in keeping with the well-known preferences of this lady, who does not conceal the especial esteem in which she holds uniformed youth.'

It was from January 1st 1816, then, that the partnership of Dagoty and Honoré took effect. With a projected

lifespan of twenty years, its objective was to manufacture and sell porcelain. In this deed it was specified that 'all the private porcelain works and factories of MM. Honoré Senior and Dagoty shall be united and amalgamated into the two factories, the first established at Paris, Boulevard du Mont Parnasse and belonging to M. Dagoty; the second at St.-Yrieix, in the Département of Haute-Vienne: this factory belongs to M. Honoré Senior. The treasury and salesrooms shall be set up, the first-mentioned at Paris, Boulevard Poissonnière, on the premises occupied by Sieur Dagoty whose leasehold tenure of both his factory and the said premises become the common responsibility of the partnership... Sieur Dagoty shall retain the use of his rooms on the first floor in their present state, plus a shed and stable for three horses'. Both Edouard Dagoty and his brother Théodore must also have had their rooms on the first floor. Thus Dagoty laid at the disposal of the partnership anything that there might be, either in his factory or on Boulevard Poissonnière and Honoré contributed his factories, one at St.-Yrieix (whose manager at that time was Anstett), and one in Petite Rue Neuve Saint-Gilles with its own salesroom. The capital outlay was fixed at 280,000 francs, half of it from Dagoty and half from Honoré Senior and Junior.

The firm of Dagoty & Honoré did not last longer than four years. It was dissolved on January 1st 1820. Edouard Honoré succeeded Dagoty. He took over the salesroom on Boulevard Poissonnière and the factory at Montparnasse. This factory had been kept in contravention of the 1816 contract. Dagoty retained the factory at La Seynie and resold it to

Denuelle in 1823. In 1824 Honoré decided to move his porcelain production to Champroux (Allier) where kaolin was available *in situ,* leaving behind in Paris only his painting and decorating workshops.

His production costs dropped by thirty-five per cent during the ensuing years and he consequently received many orders from abroad. He was by then employing a labour force of two hundred at Paris and Champroux, without counting twenty to sixty more, working 'outside'.

After 1820 Honoré played a pre-eminent role in the society of his day: he was a member of the Conseil Général des Manufactures, that is, one of the sixty hand-picked company managers who were appointed with the King's approval. He had the stature of an industrial magnate who had to be decorated with the *Légion d'honneur;* he took out patents, went bail for one of his relatives, a dealer in foreign exchange, and saw his labours elicit eulogistic comments from Brongniart in his *Traité des Arts céramiques.* He was consulted on question of economy such as the raising of Customs duty on English ceramics imported into France. Edouard Honoré died in 1855, succeeded by his son Oscar who, in 1865, handed the factory over to Ernest Raingo.

Various marks punctuate the phases in Dagoty and Honoré's careers. Although one sometimes finds these marks hand-painted in gold or red they are usually stencilled on in red.

Dagoty's factory began by taking his full name as a mark, or *P.L. Dagoty,* or, quite often, *Dagoty à Paris* painted in gilt or red cursives, or stencilled in red or black. Somewhat scarcer is the mark

164 Gonord.
Cup mounted on three paws. Black transfer-printed decoration. Borders and inside gilded. Gonord worked for Sèvres, where he decorated more particularly some plates with maps of France or of the *départements,* in gold or black. One of these plates actually appeared in the Emperor's personal service. Here he takes up the sentimental theme which became popular in the late 19th century. This note from the 'Bank of Friendship' bears Gonord's signature further down. At the time he was in Rue Moreau.

Circa 1820.
Sèvres, Musée National de Céramique. Ht. 11.5 cm. (4½ in.).
Unmarked.

165 Gaugain.
Plate. Polychrome and gold, raised rim with nankeen ground.
Child playing. *Circa* 1810.
Sèvres, Musée National de Céramique. Diam. 22.5 cm. (8⁴/₅ in.).
Mark 117.

P.L. Dagoty Maintenant à Paris rue Grange Batelière, N° 2. This was undoubtedly the address of some short-lived salesroom. Different marks recall Joséphine's patronage *Manufacture de S.M. l'Impératrice, P.L. Dagoty à Paris* or the same inscription accompanied by the address *Fbg Poissonnière N° 2*. Wares bearing these marks were sold between 1804 and 1814 for it is probable that Marie-Louise also bestowed her patronage upon Dagoty.

Porcelain marked *P.L. Dagoty – E. Honoré, à Paris* was produced within the four year duration of the partnership, 1816 to 1820. In the same period we notice: *Manuf^re de Madame Duchesse d'Angoulême P.L. Dagoty – E. Honoré.*

Left alone in charge of the factory once the partnership had been dissolved, Honoré used various marks. Some are worded thus: *Ancienne Maison Dagoty, Ed. Honoré à Paris, N° 4 boulevard Poissonnière,* whilst others only give the name Honoré, by itself or with the address on Boulevard Poissonnière.

The marks *Honoré et Cie* or *H & C* are still found, but the second cannot definitely be attributed to Honoré.

From 1824 onwards Honoré adopted another mark: *Ed. Honoré, boul. Poissonnière N° 4 à Paris, Manufacture à Champroux Allier*. This inscription is often written on an unrolled parchment and is transfer printed in black or red.

Attention must also be drawn to the mark *F.M. Honoré* which is seldom encountered but corresponds to the period before his partnership with Dagoty.

The output of the Dagoty family was considerable, as was Honoré's later on. Although Dagoty temporarily took over the factory at La Seynie, we think that items bearing his marks are to be attributed to the period previous to his partnership with Honoré, in other words before 1816.

The texts relating to these establishments give us only a little information: no post mortem inventories, no sale by court order, no bankruptcy.

On the other hand a compilation of the designs used by Dagoty and Honoré does exist. This document, which provides an excellent study of a factory's output, is composed of sixty illustrations hand-painted in gouache and kept in the Bibliothèque du Musée de l'Union centrale des Arts décoratifs, at Paris. We have reproduced some of these illustrations. Both this album and the actual objects which have been preserved reveal a

Ill. 117, 120, 121

wide variety of shapes and decorations. They are mainly carefully finished items: dessert, tea and coffee services, or single cups in traditional or more modern shapes—cylindrical, flared, with rounded base, mounted on three paws, having a raised or a low pedestal-foot, etc. Other pieces are in the shape of a swan or a shell supported on a branch of coral which forms the handle. The handles evince a great deal of imagination in looped volutes, winged females, eagles' or dogs' heads, etc. The album also displays rose- or tulip-shaped cups painted from life—a sort of *trompe-l'œil*. The three-dimensional pieces are usually ovoid, having—in the case of the sugar-bowl and teapot—a collar rising from the shoulder. The lids have charming knobs sometimes simulating a butterfly, and the spouts are in general magnificently modelled to look like animals. The milk-jugs readily assume the appearance of an antique helmet with an overarching handle.

Ill. 120

Ill. 124

Some *cabaret* items of a different type are low and oval, but others retain the traditional cylinder shape.

The album also contains a certain number of Classical vases, both ovoid and 'Medici'.

The decoration is absolutely meticulous and very varied. The richest pieces are lined with gold. The most frequent decoration is perhaps the one which arranges the big flowers painted from life inside a medallion with a ground of brown or grey that stands out against the item's overall colour, which may be pastel or bright—pink, nankeen, water green, buff, chrome green, red or mauve. Matt grounds (particularly black) are used by Dagoty to set off stylized motifs in brilliant polychrome. Traditional decora-

Ill. 120

tion remain: sepia monochromes for the landscapes, with figures, scenes from Antiquity, hunts, and polychrome landscapes, which usually unfold around a three-dimensional piece or entirely cover the bottom of a plate.

Tradition also manifests itself in the Chinese-style decorations, such as this gold-painted cup with a vermilion red ground that is reminiscent of Chinese lacquer.

One of the commonest decorations consists of figures in Antique style, painted, without modelling, in blue, red or green monochrome outlined in black.

Joséphine's account-books record various estimates and invoices from Dagoty in 1805 and 1807, and the Musée national de Céramique de Sèvres owns plates simply edged with a gilt band, bearing in the centre a cursive N surmounted by the Imperial crown, likewise painted in gold. All these objects are, of course, very well finished, but fail to attain the originality of pieces which ally modelled biscuit with glazed porcelain. A case in point is an extraordinary *cabaret,* the larger components of which have handles and spouts in the shape of swans with spread wings, and bodies adorned with a band of swans and palmettes in relief. The base of every piece is decorated with rosettes and palmettes, certain details of which are picked out in gold.

The decorator's sometimes extravagant imagination was given free rein on items on which modelled embellishments predominated, for example, egg-cups supported by cupids★, writing sets similarly adorned with cupids★, shell-shaped writing sets, etc.

Pieces bearing the mark of the short partnership between Dagoty and Honoré are obviously scarce and are hardly any

Ill. 129

Ill. 130

Ill. 124

Ill. 117, 118

★Ill. 121, 122, 127

166 Halley. Hemispherical cup on pedestal-foot, and its saucer. *Circa* 1815. Geneva, Musée de l'Ariana. Ht. 12.5 cm. (4⁹/₁₀ in.). Mark 120.

different from previous items. At the exhibition of 1819 the two partners had won a silver medal for some bas-relief vases in the Wedgwood style and for a model of the Fontaine des Innocents.

Honoré's production methods started to become really industrialized as soon as he had settled at Champroux in 1824. Some pieces resembling Dagoty's bear his mark, for instance vases adorned with antique figures. Honoré exhibited more of them in 1827.

As early as 1822 Honoré had taken out patents firstly for applying coloured grounds suitable for high-temperature firing and secondly for adapting lithography to porcelain decoration, but it was only later that he was destined to exploit them on a large scale.

Honoré won a mere honourable mention at the exhibition of 1834. The jury had disliked a Rococo clock and some vases that were 'snail-shaped... in the worst taste'. That same year, however, he made a very beautiful service for the dowager Queen of Sardinia. Objects that are probably datable to this period include the writing sets with snails or in Russian style, cassolettes and *veilleuses*. At that time Honoré declared that he was no longer making anything but 'rich ware' which was more sought-after by foreign countries, flooded as they were with cheap English goods.

Exports, especially to the United States and the Near East, were stepped up. In the case of the United States, shapes, after 1830, were produced in accordance with designs sent in by American clients. The White House contains no fewer than three services from the factory of Dagoty & Honoré. The first two bear Dagoty's mark although the dates given for the second coincide with his partner-

ship with Honoré who signed the third one. The service belonging to President Madison (1809–17) is entirely covered with a fine green mesh★. The second was owned by President Monroe (1817–25). The spread eagle, symbol of the United States, completely covers the bottom of the plates whose raised rims of brownish red are decorated with trophies in panels. The last service was made for President James Polk (1845–48). The plates, which are moulded and adorned with interlocking relief scrolls, are painted in the centre with a gigantic polychrome flower. On the rim a pale green band is interrupted by a shield emblazoned with the arms of the United States.

167 Halley.
Plate. Rim divided into alternating orange and grey grounds. Gold edging and rosette. *Circa* 1800.
Geneva, Musée de l'Ariana.
Diam. 23.5 cm. (9⅕ in.).
Mark 120.

★Ill. 120

Ill. 139

230

Another—very curious—feature of Honoré's output was that the manufacture of objects for dispatch to the Near East followed, both in shape and in decoration, designs that had been specially worked out for these countries. It is very interesting, incidentally, to compare Meissen or Vienna porcelain made for the same

168 Halley.
Plate. Rim divided into grey, pink and marbled grounds. Gold edging and rosette. *Circa* 1800. Geneva, Musée de l'Ariana. Diam. 23 cm. (9 in.). Mark 120.

Ill. 138

destination, with this tall jug embellished with spiralling bands which are themselves decorated with roses or vine shoots. The lipless shape and the decoration are very similar.

At the exhibition of 1844 Honoré displayed pieces that were scalloped, pierced and profusely ornamented in relief, and vases of Oriental inspiration. Jules Burat who reproduced them in a contemporary publication stated that they 'have kept their simplicity'. He must probably have been comparing them to the particularly exuberant wares from other factories. Everything is relative.

Ill. 80 Edouard Honoré had the talent for running his venture on the scale needed to

turn it into one of the most important businesses in the ceramic field in the mid-19th century.

DARTE
We must associate this name with not one but several factories.
The Darte family originated in Namur, at that time in the Netherlands, but one of the three brothers who set up the porcelain factories, Louis Joseph, born in 1765, was naturalized by 1786.

Joseph, Louis Joseph and Jean François joined forces on Floréal 3rd, Year III to buy a porcelain factory located at 3, Rue de Charonne, for 70,000 francs including 30,000 in promissory notes which were redeemed in cash. The factory had belonged to André Massonat and his wife who had been running it themselves and who were now selling off the kiln, implements, moulds and wares, whether they were finished or half-finished. Louis Joseph and Jean François were described as porcelain manufacturers, and Joseph as a retailer of footwear. On the same day the Dartes took over the lease granted by the cabinet maker Cosson, the landlord of the property.

The three brothers jointly ran the factory and opened up a warehouse at the Palais du Tribunat (later the Palais Royal). On Thermidor 13th, Year XI they expressed the wish that 'each should have his own establishment' and arranged to part company. These arrangements were annulled by a deed dated Messidor 12th, Year XII (1804), which made provisions for a division in kind, and from then on there were two distinct factories bearing the name of Darte.

Darte Senior

Joseph Darte began by leasing a shop at 159, Rue Saint-Honoré, for the considerable rent of 8,000 francs a year. Next, on Nivôse 7th, Year XIII, he bought the porcelain factory that Maurice Cœur Dassier had been running at 26, Rue de Popincourt. Joseph Darte must have settled there previously, for although he was giving 10,000 francs to buy 'buildings serving as a porcelain factory... consisting of four blocks divided into suites, rooms, stores and other premises necessary for manufacturing porcelain...' it was clearly stipulated in the deed of sale that 'the goods, kilns implements and other items necessary to the said porcelain factory of porcelain belong to the said *S. et D^e Darte,* and do not enter into the sale'. As for Cœur Dassier he had become the purchaser on Floréal 23rd, Year XI, of the buildings in which he was running his factory. Joseph Darte had work estimated at more than 50,000 francs carried out, and in 1805 actually had to mortgage his property. One of the witnesses is none other than Discry, who was still a tobacco manufacturer. It was 'Discry the elder' who succeeded Joseph Darte in 1823.

In 1837 Victor Discry went into partnership with Jules Charles de Talmours, a wholesale merchant. He obtained the title of supplier to the Duc d'Orléans (the Crown Prince) and the Duc de Nemours. Their partnership was dissolved on May 30th 1841 and Talmours, taking over the factory, took Adolphe Joseph Hurel into partnership as from June 7th 1841. The latter had been able to put up a capital of 80,000 francs, thanks to a 40,000-franc loan from the Discry family. Hurel already had a workshop

169   On this illustrative plate from a work published assembled various porcelain-designs specially selected for their novelty-value.   The pieces shown are respectively a tea-service by Clauss of which we know one example, decorated by Schœlcher (ill. 170), some teacups and breakfast-cups by Jacob Petit, a tea-service in the English style, which was becoming increasingly fashionable (ill. 171), and some 'Etruscan shapes' produced by Denuelle (ill. 153).   The price-list for the undecorated pieces by Jacob Petit (e.g. a teacup, fig. 5, costing 2 fr. 50) points to the separate existence, on the one hand of factories making porcelain in the white, and on the other of decorators who embellished it. We should not, however, infer from this that the manufacturers did not own decorating workshops as well. When Jacob Petit went bankrupt in 1848 his balance-sheet listed a sizeable labour-force.

From *L'industrie, description pittoresque de l'industrie française,* published by Stéphane Flachat in 1834. See opposite page.

producing terracotta at Le Petit Mont-rouge. In 1844 we come upon Discry again, at 8, Rue du Temple, Passage du Jeu de Boules, as a manufacturer of vitrifiable colours.

The porcelain which Darte exhibited in 1823 was deemed to be very indifferently and clumsily made, and second-rate in its decoration, although two vases painted by Paris were regarded as fairly good. By 1827 the quality had improved and the soundly prepared bodies and well-chosen shapes found favour. At that time he had a labour force of one hundred and thirty and by 1834 his prices were thought to be commendably reasonable for such well-finished articles: for this he won

an honourable mention. At the exhibition of 1839 Discry was awarded a gold medal for his high-temperature colours for decoration in reserves, using a dipping technique which was faster than the process of his competitor Halot. In particular Discry-Talmours exhibited a blue table service, made in ten hours and fired once only. Talmour & Hurel's gold medal was confirmed in 1844 for their application of the Discry processes. The factory had a labour force of one hundred and fifty yielding an annual output worth 300,000 francs, which was considerable.

It is to Discry that we owe those agreeable pot-bellied tea services with relief fes-

Ill. 156

toons such as our grandmothers once owned: he exhibited the prototype in 1834. We also have him to thank for some excellent imitations of Chinese porcelain. The factory was taken over in 1863 by Ch. Ménard.

Darte Frères

Louis Joseph and Jean François Darte, former partners of their brother Joseph, opted for a common destiny as ceramists. They bought 90, Rue de la Roquette, known as the Hôtel Montalembert. It was only on June 12th 1808 that they recognized the need to ratify this state of affairs in a deed of partnership. They then assumed the trade name of *Darte Frères*. The partnership assets consisted of the property in Rue de la Roquette along with everything that was necessary for making and selling porcelain, plus the salesroom at the Palais du Tribunat. On the occasion of the marriage of his son Auguste Remi, Louis Joseph Darte took him on as a partner, in a deed of July 23rd 1824. The father's capital outlay was estimated at 90,000 francs and the son's at half that figure. On the one hand Auguste Remi was the heir to one-sixth of his mother's estate, and on the other Louis Joseph settled on him a marriage portion of 20,000 francs, to be paid into the partnership. The young bride, the daughter of the hatter Lemaire, brought a dowry of 30,000 francs plus her rights in respect of her mother's estate. Louis Joseph kept his depot at 16, Rue Vivienne. One year later—July 9th 1825—the partnership was pronounced, by common consent, dissolved. Louis Joseph was left alone. Did his son carry off his capital? It is certain that Louis Joseph was declared bankrupt on September 26th 1828. The seals were affixed both to the

factory and to the salesroom which at that time was at 8, Rue du Faubourg Poissonnière. Marguerite Darte, the widow of Jean Baptiste François Darte (perhaps Jean François?) who looked after the salesroom, stated that the goods belonged either to her personally, or else to Baignol Cadet & Cie. of Limoges, except for a few pieces entrusted to her by her brother, 'Darte, the elder'. Parenthetically let us recall that Pierre Tharaud was in charge of Darte's factory after being apprenticed at Baignol's. It was he who took over the erstwhile royal factory of Limoges in 1817. By 1828, however, Louis Joseph was specially appointed to the Duc de Bordeaux. His salesroom, kept by his son Auguste Remi, was in Rue des Vinaigriers. Finally, on April 1st 1829, a settlement was concluded between Darte and his creditors and Darte continued production until about 1833. He died in 1843. He had been decorated with the *Légion d'honneur* in his capacity as battalion commander in the *Garde nationale* of Paris in 1816.

Other members of the Darte family were involved in selling or manufacturing porcelain—François, a decorator at the Palais Royal (1831–33), another—Jean Joseph—on Quai Carême-Prenant (1831) and Auguste Remi who moved to Rue Fontaine-au-Roy. Finally Marie-Thérèse Darte and her husband Remi Conrut had gone into partnership with Lhoste of Rue Meslay in Year V.

As early as the exhibition of 1806 the Darte brothers received awards, firstly for their pleasantly embellished porcelain for everyday use, and secondly for the large-scale pieces, which were decorated and painted in Caron's or Dagoty's workshops. The silver medal of 1806 was followed by another in 1819, in recognition of some fine wares which were remarkable for their size and beautiful colours. It is probable that the death of Madame Darte with its financial repercussions, including the partnership with Auguste Remi and then his departure, dealt this factory a severe blow. Besides the stock of dessert services and large ornamental pieces, we find contemporary fancy goods such as a *veilleuse*, spill holders, or the perfume 'cottages' *(chaumières à parfum)* mentioned in 1828, clocks, and portrait cups. The mark is *Darte Frères*, often accompanied by this address: *Palais Royal, Nº 21* or by that of Rue Vivienne.

Darte Frères was well known for its

trade with foreign countries. By 1807 it was employing a labour force of one hundred and fifty.

DEROCHE   POCHET-DEROCHE   GOSSE

Deroche, a ceramic dealer, never had a factory but only a decorators' workshop. By 1776 Deroche 'the younger' had set himself up as a faience maker on Rue Saint-Martin. In Year XII Deroche's addres was 336, Rue Coquillière where he resided until about 1810. An announcement in the *Almanach du Commerce* of 1815 spoke of 'a large shop selling porcelain and crystal glass, also making flasks, chemical containers, and every-

Ill. 148–152

171 Jacob Petit.   Ill. 145
'English' tea-service. Polychrome and gold, with bright-blue borders.
Circa 1834.
Geneva, Musée de l'Ariana.
Sugar-bowl: Ht. 15 cm.
(5⁹/₁₀ in.).
Mark 25.
See page 233.

thing that relates to the pharmacist's or perfumer's needs. Hôtel Plâtrière, Rue J.-J. Rousseau, number 16'. Later, in about 1830, Deroche took his son-in-law Pochet as his partner, who went on to succeed him under the name of Pochet-Deroche.

By 1834 their establishment, and Rousseau's, were regarded as the two most important Parisian concerns in the porcelain business.

In 1839 Gosse, Pochet's cousin, came to join him and then took over from him. In addition to the salesroom in Rue J.-J. Rousseau he had a second one at 5/7, Rue des Lombards. An advertisement of 1844 stated that, besides porcelain and faience, he sold articles for grocers' shops, restaurant and cafés, lighting requisites, lavatory pans, bottles, etc.

Gosse gave up this establishment in 1849 to take over the porcelain factory at Bayeux. His successors were Vignier, who had married Mademoiselle Pochet and who was supplanted first by Henri Pochet, the son of Pochet-Deroche, and then by Georges Pochet who was still the owner in about 1900.

We know of various items belonging to table services and breakfast sets from this workshop, in particular a service with a coloured ground bearing the arms of Portugal and also a few pieces decorated
Ill. 155 in the Chinese manner. We must principally mention the drug jars which stand out by virtue of their beautiful colours
Ill. 154 and their widely varied decorations.

The marks give the names of the successive owners, with or without the address.

DESPRÉZ

Amongst the Paris porcelain makers we must pay special attention to those who concentrated on manufacturing biscuit

cameos set in crystal glass. These objects are called *sulfures* ('sulphides').

One of the specialists in this art was Barthélemy Despréz who had been a modeller at the royal factory of Sèvres from 1773. He was appointed its chief modeller in 1780, but in 1783 some curious charges were laid against him. He was accused, among other misdemeanours, of sharing a carcase of pork with a certain Sebin and of paying him for it with salt belonging to the factory. This Sebin, the owner of a windmill at Sèvres, had been using his waggon to transport into Paris some porcelain supplied by Despréz. Despréz himself had been sleeping away from home every

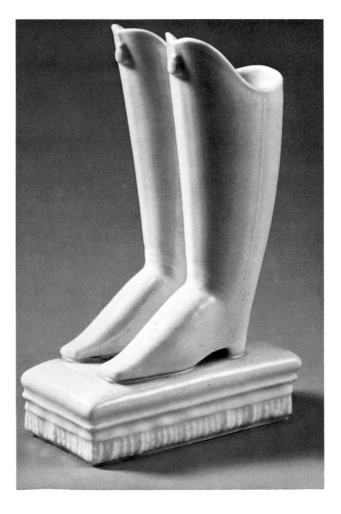

172 Jacob Petit. Match-holder. Undecorated. Appeared in the Exhibition of 1834. Sèvres, Musée National de Céramique. Ht: 12 cm. (4³/₄ in.). Mark 125.

173   Jacob Petit.
Pair of flasks. Gardener and
female companion.
Circa 1835.
Paris, Coll. Guy Passerat.
Female gardener:
Ht. 26.5 cm. (10²/₅ in.).
Mark 125.

night in order to go and sell in Paris both his porcelain and also the cobalt which he used to hand over to a painter from the Comte d'Artois' factory.

Expelled from Sèvres on May 16th 1783 and then detained at the Hôtel de la Force, Despréz—although protesting his good faith—admitted that he had been making porcelain body to a new formula of his own invention, and that he had caused 'around one hundred of these medallions or plaques' to be fired in the Sèvres kiln.

In the course of the interrogation of Despréz and his accomplice, the kiln charger Gérard, the word 'cameo' was pronounced several times.

Meanwhile Despréz was sadly missed at Sèvres. A memorandum of appraisal stated that he had assured them he had discovered the secret of making blue body, removing stains from porcelain and eliminating the gloss on overfired biscuit ware: 'There is no modeller with as much knowledge as he.' A petition from the craftsmen in the modellers' workshop brought about his return to Sèvres, where in 1786 he was even able to rise to the important post which Milot had previously occupied, supervising the preparation of bodies. He seems to have left Sèvres for good in about 1792.

Sure enough, we find Despréz already set up in Paris, at 2, Rue des Récollets, by Year IV. Julien's report mentions him as being in Rue de Lancry, but this might only be a reference to a salesroom. The *Almanach du Commerce* subsequently lists Despréz Junior who must have succeeded his father *circa* 1815. In about 1825 his address was 25, Rue des Morts, Faubourg Saint-Martin. He was still there in 1834, the street then being called Rue des Ecluses Saint-Martin.

It is important to emphasize that the cameos by Despréz are of biscuit. In this respect one is convinced by his admissions about his experimental firings and his purchases in Paris of die-stamps.

The same is true of the application which he submitted in Year IV to the Commission des Arts, requesting a cart-load of clay from Viroflay, which was annexed to the Sèvres factory.

Following in his father's footsteps, Despréz Junior likewise experimented with porcelain bodies and took out a patent 'for a new body suitable for making porcelain, and for a method of making a suitable glaze for this porcelain'.

The output from the Despréz factory was

174 Jacob Petit.
Mantelpiece-set. *Circa* 1840.
Geneva, Musée de l'Ariana.
Ht. 46 cm. (18 in.).
Mark 125.
See page 241.

sufficiently large to occasion an official debate about launching competition against England, so low-priced were his wares. He won a silver medal which was conferred at the exhibition of 1806 for blue-ground medallions, plain figures, and for cameos in porcelain body to be used for decorating vases and jewellery. An honourable mention at the 1819 exhibition was awarded for some well-executed cameos and objects set in crystal glass. By 1821 *Le Bazar parisien* was announcing that Despréz Junior sold cameos for decorating furniture, mantelpieces, clocks and gems and that he set cameos of different coloured clays in crystal glass and used them for decorating

flasks, sweetmeat containers, vases, clocks, etc. He also sold decorated glasses of French and foreign make, and collections of antique and modern medals portraying eminent men and all the sovereigns of Europe.

But although the popularity of Despréz is connected with his 'cameos inserted into crystal glass', it is no less true that he Ill. 219 sold 'all articles of painted and gilded porcelain' and that he was also the inventor of 'a porcelain which goes on the fire'. We might add that he had his rights to this invention vindicated when he signed an agreement with Pigory and Vallée of Chantilly whereby Despréz was the sell the details of his discovery in return for a three-percent commission on sales. The matter under discussion was the 'making of hard-paste porcelain which may be worked like pipe-clay'. This compact was signed on July 1st 1811. From the Despréz factory we know of crystal-glass plaques set with porcelain cameos showing members of the Imperial (and, later on, the Royal) family, often copied from medals by Andrien and Gayrard; religious objects as well, such as the modelled head of Christ. Sometimes these medallions are supported by a

crystal-glass stand or set in the bottom of a cup. Other cups of solid porcelain are embellished with a cameo at the bottom. Reproductions of original medals are always characterized by a few changes in detail and by the omission of the medallist's signature which should normally have been shown on the truncation of the bust or arm. This observation leads us to suppose that the medallists' copyright dues had been 'forgotten'.

Despréz probably worked for other dealers as well. Chavagnac and Grollier record a cup by Despréz whose saucer bears the mark of Darte Frères. Feuillet undoubtedly sold Despréz's wares.

The mark consists of the name Despréz written out in full, often accompanied by the complete address: *rue des récollets, N° 2, Paris*. It is incised on the back of the cameos.

Further manufacturers and sellers of cameos set in crystal glass were recorded at Paris. There was the dealer Acloque Junior, Rue de la Barillerie, from 1815 to 1830 (he handed over to Vimeux and Cocheteux in 1833) and Dihl, whose signature is found underneath a medallion showing Napoleon and Marie-Louise in profile and dated 1810. Also, the 'Escalier de Cristal' sold work by Dartigue of Rue du Mont-Blanc, Martoret was a dealer, around 1820, while Paris, a jeweller, gemsetter and goldsmith of 13, Rue Croix des Petits-Champs exhibited in 1819 and lastly Schmitt at 43, Palais Royal was in business between 1813 and 1830.

DUBOIS

One of the porcelain factories on Rue de la Roquette had a sign-board which read 'Aux Trois Levrettes' ('The Three Leverets') and was set up in the former Hôtel des Arbalétriers (Cross-bowmen's Hostelry). This probably explains why it is attributed with the mark of the two crossed bolts which may be confused with the torches of La Courtille. They are painted in underglaze blue.

Vincent Jérôme Dubois, who does not seem either to have registered himself officially or taken out any trade mark, claimed to have been the factory's owner since 1774. It probably manufactured faience, for on May 31st 1785 Dubois filed his petition of bankruptcy as a *manufacturier de fayance*. He protested against the decree of 1784 and in 1790 applied for a loan of 30,000 francs to re-

174a   Jacob Petit.
Mantelpiece-set. *Circa* 1840.
Geneva, Musée de l'Ariana.
Ht. 46 cm. (18 in.).
Mark 125.
See page 239.

175 Jacob Petit.
Terrine in the form of a
guinea-fowl, *au naturel*.
Reviving the practice of the
18th-century faiencemakers,
notably those in Eastern
France, Jacob Petit created
some models for *terrines* in
trompe-l'œil. The two rabbits
are painted from life, in shades
of brown and beige, one
being darker than the other.
The guinea-fowl, likewise
painted in life-like colours,
stands on a bright-orange
hillock. *Circa* 1845.
Sèvres, Musée National de
Céramique. Ht. 30 cm.
(11¾ in.).
Mark 127.

start 'his factories making faïence and porcelain'. His porcelain wares consist of standard items and products in biscuit, a certain number of which are kept in the collections of the Hermitage Museum at Leningrad.

The 'Escalier de Cristal' was one of the best-known salesrooms of the Palais Royal, if not of Paris itself. It was founded in 1802, and Madame Désarnaud owned it, on Galerie de Valois.

Marie Jeanne Rosalie Désarnaud, *née* Charpentier, was born in 1775 at Châlons-sur-Marne where her father was a goldsmith. By 1818 she was supplier by appointment to the King and Crown. Originally Madame Désarnaud sold only

crystal glass, but in every shape and form, from 'sulphides' right up to furniture. In 1819 she even exhibited a mantelpiece and won a gold medal. The *Almanach historique et commercial du Palais Royal* of 1827 gives this description: 'In this shop the glitter of all the most magnificent things that art can offer are seen, such as porcelain vases of the most sumptuous craftsmanship, porphyry, etc., etc., not forgetting the renowned crystal staircase which is the envy of foreigners: it is one of art's masterpieces.'

Her successors were: in 1828, Boin, an engraver on crystal glass and semi-precious stones, in 1839 Lahoche and in 1854, Lahoche-Pannier. The establish-

176 Jacob Petit.
Pair of *terrines* in the form of rabbits *au naturel*.
Geneva, Musée de l'Ariana.
L. 27 cm. (10⅓ in.).
Mark 125.
See caption opposite page.

ment was then moved to 6, Rue Scribe and 1, Rue Auber.

At the exhibition of 1844 Lahoche displayed some vases, a clock, some Louis Quinze candelabra and some dessert services. All of them found favour with the public. The turnover at that time stood at 150,000 francs, half of it in export earnings. There were ten craftsmen 'inside' and forty to fifty 'outside'.

The marks consist of the name of the salesroom *L'Escalier de cristal,* often accompanied by the name of one of its successive proprietors: Désarnaux, Lahoche or Pannier. They are painted in red or gold, or stencilled.

The products are extremely well finished. They consist of ornamental pieces, table services, and *cabarets.* Decoration follows the general pattern of evolution. Let us mention the services decorated with views of famous cities enclosed in reserve panels on a dark blue ground: or in the style of the old soft-paste wares from Sèvres.

Ill. 79

Ill. 158

FEUILLET

Feuillet was one of the best decorators in the Restoration period. By 1817 he was already in business at 18, Rue de la Paix and had been specially appointed to the Prince de Condé and the Duc de Bourbon.

He went into partnership with Boyer in about 1834. That year he exhibited a picture on porcelain 'set into a Louis Quinze sideboard', reproducing the *Cruche cassée* ('Broken Jug') by Greuze. He was cited as the specially appointed supplier to the aristocracy. His successors were Boyer, later joined by Jacques, and then Paul Blot and Hébert (*circa* 1900).

From 1834 onwards we find one 'Feuillet, the nephew', likewise a painter and

177 Jacob Petit. 'Catherine de Medici's *veilleuse*. The spout is disguised in the mouth of the lap-dog. This model is entered in the inventory taken after Jacob Petit's bankruptcy in 1848. Heaume-les-Messiers, Coll. Broulard. Ht. 38 cm. (15 in.). Mark 125.

decorator, who lived first in Rue Saint-Denis and then Passage Sandrié in 1837. He himself had a nephew, Hippolyte Manoury, who succeeded him in 1846. Manoury was a painter and gilder, decorating not only hard-paste porcelain but items in soft paste as well. He sold pieces 'of old Sèvres, mounted in bronze or left unmounted'.

We shall confine ourselves to the pieces by the first Feuillet, whose mark was spelt out in full, in red or gold, with or without the address of Rue de la Paix. This was also the practice of his successor

178   Jacob Petit.
Bulb-vase. Polychrome and
gold on black ground.
Circa 1840.
New York, Metropolitan
Museum of Art.
Ht. 28 cm. (11 in.).
Mark 125.

Boyer. Some items bear the additional mark of the Darte brothers who were probably responsible for obtaining the white ware.

Feuillet turned out many pieces with the arms or monogram of Bourbon-Condé (Musée Condé at Chantilly), whilst others bear the arms of Marmont, Duc de Raguse. Decorations of polychrome coats of arms, birds and flowers of dazzling craftsmanship are amongst the most numerous. We must mention, too, the imitations of old Sèvres ware, the Alpine figures and landscapes, and the very high-quality hunting scenes. Some of the floral decorations display an appealing originality.

Ill. 159, 160

Ill. 161

FLEURY   FLAMEN-FLEURY

Since Year II Jean Pierre Hoffmann had been living in the Faubourg Saint-Denis and had rented a site and four houses

on a nine-year lease, for the purpose of setting up a porcelain factory. He spent huge sums on constructing one kiln in particular, 'an item costing more than 80,000 livres, as far as can be ascertained at present'. His partner was Lalouette. His porcelain was of high quality with a fine white texture.

It seems likely that his successor was Jacques René Fleury, in 1806 the highest bidder for a house in the Faubourg Saint-Denis, which at the time was number 72, but was subsequently renumbered 168. The year after, he increased his property by purchasing a garden at number 192 of the same street. This explains the different addresses attributed to Fleury. His widow succeeded him, and in 1814 complained bitterly of the losses that she had suffered when her possessions had been burnt in the Fire of Moscow. Two years later she sold off the porcelain factory, along with the salesroom at 3, Rue Vivienne, to Placide Félicien Flamen who married her daughter Marie Françoise Elisabeth Fleury a few days afterwards.

Flamen came from the Lille region where he owned numerous properties and had joined his father in running a wire factory. In 1824 he concluded a sleeping partnership with the bankers André and Cottier. Shortly afterwards (1826) Madame Fleury died and the factory passed into her estate, the couple having contracted at marriage to bequeath one another half their respective possessions. The establishment continued to turn over, but at a slower pace, even though Flamen had been awarded the title of Supplier to the Steward of the Royal Household *(fournisseur du Garde-meubles de la Couronne)*. Finally the concern was declared bankrupt at the end of 1827 and the seals were affixed both to the factory in the Faubourg Saint-Denis and to the salesroom in Rue Vivienne. A legal settlement between Flamen and his creditors was concluded in July. In spite of everything, wares continued to be manufactured and sold, at the request of one of the creditors, the banker Collon, who had joined his colleagues André and Cottier in financing the business. The inventories list a considerable amount of painted and decorated porcelain.

Despite these arrangements Flamen soon found himself forced to go into liquidation once again, on August 10th 1831. The official account of the circumstances leading up to this second bankruptcy states especially: 'transactions with merchant adventurers from the colonies and a few, perhaps rather irresponsible, sales to Parisian buyers who gave him some compensation, only worsened the situation... Flamen-Fleury faced the difficulties for a time, but exhausted himself, and when the events of July overtook him they aggravated the situation terribly, for his clientele had consisted almost entirely of members of the defunct Court, and the figure fetched by the sale of his shop was extremely low'. On the credit side are entered the goods dispatched to Constantinople, Madrid and Philadelphia. We shall see later that Flamen's brother travelled through the Near East selling porcelain, and the factory exported it as far afield as China.

The few identifiable wares bearing Fleury's name are attractive and probably antedate 1816.

Ill. 162

Flamen-Fleury was renowned for the elegance of his products. He principally made items for export: by 1826 he had no fewer than seven muffle-kilns and by 1827 was employing a labour force of sixty to seventy.

179   Jacob Petit.
Tall covered 'snowball-
vase'. Imitation of Meissen
ware.
Circa 1840.
Limoges, Musée National
Adrien Dubouché.
Ht. 34 cm. (13 in.).
Mark 125.

Besides the pieces belonging to dessert services and tea- or coffee sets a good number of fashionable fancy goods appear. For 1828 we picked out some match-holders, *corbeilles bijou* (miniature baskets), cold-cream jars, sconces, tobacco jars, shell-shaped candlesticks, flower holders, but also cups for 'lemonade sellers' *(limonadiers)*, jam-pots, holy-water stoups and other religious objects. We find, too, lamp shades, a wide range of vases, and *veilleuses* of various types. The Musée national de Céramique de Sèvres owns a sample set of plain cups bought direct from the Flamen-Fleury factory in 1827. They are undecorated and unmarked.

Ill. 163

Flamen-Fleury's mark consists of his name in full, often enclosed in a square, and stencilled on in red.

GILLE

The factory owned by Gille was most famous in the 1850's or thereabouts.

A gem-setter, Gille had founded a porcelain factory in 1837, at 28, Rue Paradis-Poissonnière. He died in 1868 and his successors, Vion and Baury, moved it to Choisy-le-Roy in 1875. Charles Baury had been one of Gille's best modellers.

By 1844 Gille had four kilns and was employing a hundred and sixty men in his workshops, plus sixty 'outside': his yearly output was calculated at 500,000 francs – 100,000 of it for exportation.

In that same year he exhibited a porcelain mantelpiece, 'charming for boudoirs'. In 1849 he received a bronze medal for some plaques mounted in furniture and some Dresden-style figurines.

At the international exhibition in London in 1851 he won a first-class medal for some statuettes and groups in biscuit, and

by 1855 Gille was regarded as the best decorator in Paris. He had been exhibiting a mantelpiece with caryatids and also some tall groups in biscuit. These life-size of half life-size statues. The Bernard Palissy which is kept in the Musée du Conservatoire des Arts et Métiers in Paris measures no less than 1m. 82cm.

The marks are: *Gille J^{ne} Fcant à Paris*, impressed, or else a seal with the monogram GJ, either impressed (on biscuit ware), or marked in blue—as for example underneath a vase simulating old silver.

GONORD

By 1800 a decorators' workshop had been

set up in Rue Courty and François Gonord, a miniaturist and overglaze painter, was on the staff. Born in 1757, he was the son of the engraver Pierre Gonord. He died in 1822.

Gonord in 1805 had asked various favours of the Minister of the Interior who re-

181 Jacob Petit. *Veilleuse*. Polychrome and gold. The unusual is definitely one of the mediums in which Jacob Petit gives of his best. This young, seated woman holding a teapot of a design which we have already identified with the same period (ill. 170) is in fact a drink-warmer: the receptacle is hidden beneath her graceful exterior. In the inventory drawn up when Jacob Petit went bankrupt in 1848 we notice in particular thirteen 'marquise' drink-warmers, two more called 'Catherine de Medici' and thirteen 'Virgin and Christ-child'. *Circa* 1848. Rouen, Musée des Beaux-Arts et de la Céramique. Ht. 35.5 cm. (13³/₅ in.). Mark 125.

180 Jacob Petit. Pair of pagoda-shaped flasks. Polychrome and gold on green and orange grounds. *Circa* 1840. London, Victoria & Albert Museum. Ht. 20 cm. (7⁹/₁₀ in.). Mark 125.

quested Brongniart to give him his opinion about a transfer printing process for use on porcelain which Gonord had perfected.[2]

Gonord's technique was particularly ingenious since it enabled one to make enlarged or reduced positives from the same engraved plate, but its application in the early years appeared most complicated. The process was based on the properties of a slab of gelatine which expands when dipped in cold water and contracts in alcohol. Brongniart describes it in his *Traité*.

After a certain amount of fumbling, Gonord in 1808 printed the map of France onto five plates from the Sèvres factory, both in gold and in black. Their raised rims differed; some were of contrast-burnished gilt, others of *beau bleu* with a gold border. One of the plates from the Emperor's service, having a chrome-green rim, showed a transfer-printed map of France.

Meanwhile Gonord went on working in Paris, and in 1806 won a silver medal. The gold medal would have been conferred upon him if the volume of his output had been greater, for his method, kept secret until the patent was registered in 1818, had much impressed the jury.

Gonord offered to print any subjects that enthusiasts might suggest to him provided that they were 'of a pleasing nature', and that he could set aside a few proofs for himself. Following his success at the exhibition of 1806 Gonord received large official commissions, notably (in 1807) twenty-four plates decorated with the maps of the Départements, intended for the Minister of the Interior. In 1810 orders came in for prints from Chanlaire's atlas, and some views of the monuments of Paris. Being at the time well-nigh

[2] In the national factory of Sèvres there is a voluminous file on Gonord which Marcelle Brunet has studied in *Le procédé d'impression de Gonord à la manufacture impériale de Sèvres*. Archives de l'Art francais, vol. XXIV 1969.

impoverished, Gonord himself had canvassed these orders.

At the exhibition of 1819 Gonord, who was displaying 'a fine assortment' of wares, was awarded a gold medal. His address at this date was 17, Rue Moreau. In 1813 he had been at 96, Rue Popincourt.

After his death in 1822 Madame Gonord who held 'her husband's secret' continued managing the workshop, which she transferred in 1827 to 92, Faubourg Saint-Martin. In 1830 she moved it to 350, Rue Saint-Denis, Cours du Grand-Cerf, where it remained until 1843.

At the 1844 exhibition, Perrenot-Gonord, the successor to the widowed Madame Gonord, displayed various objects. By then he was decorating thirty thousand items annually for pharmacists and perfumers, as well as a thousand thermometers. His premises were at 34, Rue Grange-aux-Belles, and later at 6, Rue des Petites-Ecuries.

We are now far removed from the 'artistic' wares of the early years of the century. Apart from the plates that Gonord decorated for Sèvres, and a cup Ill. 164 embellished with a 'note' from the 'Bank of Friendship' bearing his signature on the design we know nothing either of his products or of his mark, if any.

HALLEY   LEBON-HALLEY

It is a pity not to be better informed than we are about the history of this decorators' workshop, for its creations are particularly well finished and interesting. Strangely enough, this workshop did not display anything at the exhibitions; its very existence is only known to us thanks to the *Almanach du Commerce* and to invoices.

Authors have placed Halley variously in England, at Lorient or at Caen. He may indeed have had either a factory in one or other of these places, or else a contract with one of the porcelain works there, and no more than a salesroom in Paris. Whatever the case, we find him in business on Boulevard Montmartre by 1800. In the same period Lebon was also a porcelain dealer, at 5, Rue Neuve Sainte-Eustache. The two concerns were joined by marriage, Lebon marrying Halley's daughter. In 1818 we find Lebon-Halley, the son-in-law and successor to Halley, living at his father-in-law's address at 182, Rue Montmartre. He had by then been specially appointed to Monsieur, the future Charles X. We lose track of him in 1822.

An invoice from the Chavagnac collection, dated Year XII, tells us that Halley was responsible for the painting, gilding and monogramming of all bespoke wares. We also know of a card of Lebon-Halley's specifying that, besides plain and decorated porcelain, the 'factory' (*manu-*

183   Jacob Petit. Pitcher. This object allies the techniques of biscuit and of glazed porcelain. In imitation of an antique bas-relief, fauns and Silenuses disport themselves amid a decoration of vines. A vine-stock also forms a sturdy handle. Gilded scrolls adorn the base and outer rim of the pitcher. This type of jug was very fashionable in Great Britain, and this specimen resembles an item of Minton creamware with figures in relief and in reserve on a dark-blue ground, reproduced in brown stoneware as well. The decoration originated in England from the Hanley artist, Charles Meigh's, rendering in 1844 of 'Bacchanalia' by Poussin, kept in the National Gallery. (London, V. & A. Museum). A pair of large cups by Jacob Petit showing the same influence is kept in Lisbon, in the Museu de Arte Antiga. (1840–45). Geneva, Musée de l'Ariana. Ht. 15 cm. (5⁹/₁₀ in.). Mark 125.

182   Jacob Petit.
Sleeping child. Biscuit.
Traces of lace. *Circa* 1850.
Paris, private coll.
L. 16.5 cm. (6¹/₂ in.).
Mark 125.

crown of Prince of the Blood. This mark resumes the tradition of the 18th century and is reminiscent of Clignancourt's. But under the *Ancien Régime,* 'Monsieur' had referred to the Comte de Provence, the future Louis XVIII, whereas when he ascended the throne the title of Monsieur was invested in the Comte d'Artois, who became Charles X. This mark dates the objects as belonging to the reign of Louis XVIII.

The wares bearing the mark of this sales-room stand out by virtue of the very high workmanship of their body, shapes and decoration. We should stress that the body is consistently of perfect whiteness, and we may deduce from this that Halley must have been wise in his choice of white ware suppliers. Incidentally, Nast's mark is quite often found next to his own. The exceptionally attractive colours sometimes display surprisingly bold contrasts and are invariably well glazed.   Ill. 166

It is ornamental pieces—vases with finely modelled handles—that are mainly seen, together with pieces from dessert services and tea- or coffee sets.

The Musée de l'Ariana at Geneva owns a collection of superbly decorated cups and plates; their marbled grounds, for instance, are made up of components assembled like mosaics, giving a complex polychrome colour scheme. Many decorations are antique in inspiration, while others consist of ruins, birds or charming scenes of children playing.   Ill. 168   Ill. 167

facture: sic) also sold crystal glass, 'bronze gilt clock-cases, sconces and table centre-pieces'.

The first marks used are Halley's name painted on in red or in gold cursives, and later two stencilled marks denoting Lebon-Halley, which show his name accompanied by an M surmounted by the

HALOT

In 1823 F. Halot, a painter and gilder, had a workshop at 14, Rue d'Angoulême du Temple. He won a bronze medal at the exhibition of 1839 for his high temperature grounds, achieved by a technique which he had had patented. At that time he owned a factory in the Parisian suburb of Montreuil-sous-Bois. His bronze medal was confirmed in 1844, but his factory had by then transplanted itself to Mehun-sur-Yèvre (Cher) where he had a kiln and a labour force of forty. In Paris he kept four muffles and from ten to twenty craftsmen. His yearly output was estimated to be worth 60,000 to 80,000 francs. In about 1845 he went into partnership with his son Eugène who went on in 1855 to partner Charles Pillivuyt. In 1846, however, F. Halot announced that his factory now stood by the Gare d'Ivry. He sold 'special fittings for lamps, bronzes, high-temperature *bleu de Sèvres* wares, table- and dessert services, fancy goods, novelties changing every fortnight'. His shop was at 40, Marais Saint-Martin from 1846 to 1849, and then in the Faubourg Poissonnière.

We do not know of any mark of Halot's but in 1838 and 1847 the Musée national de Céramique de Sèvres was presented with some gifts from M. Halot. They consist of polygonal cups with grounds of buff, green or blue and gilt borders, and a globular vase having a high-temperature blue ground with an undecorated reserve panel.

JACOB PETIT

Jacob Petit died a little over a century ago—in 1868—yet his works still give rise to fierce controversy.

He was born in Paris in 1796. Of his real name, Jacob Mardochée, he kept only the Christian name to which he attached the maiden name of his wife, Anne Adélaïde Petit. After studying painting by himself and frequenting Gros' studio which Lami and Bonnington also visited, Jacob Petit made a number of journeys, to Italy, Switzerland and Germany. He stayed even longer in England, studying various industries while painting decorations. On his return to France in about 1830, he published a *Recueil de décorations intérieures* and launched himself into porcelain making.

He rented a small house at Belleville where he spent 50,000 francs on installing equipment and creating the first models; then, lacking a sufficiently large site, he 'was forced to take over the factory of Fontainebleau in order to turn out flat ware and table services' some time before June 1834. Four years later he was no longer manufacturing 'either plates, dishes or commonplace implements', but exclusively ornamental pieces. When the exhibition was held in 1839 mention was made of only one of his porcelain works, the one at Fontainebleau, but a warehouse of his was recorded, at 26, Rue de Bondy in Paris. The company funds amounted to 300,000 francs and Jacob Petit was employing a hundred and fifty craftsmen in his workshops and more than sixty 'outside'. Shortly afterwards, in 1845, and in partnership with Nicolas Moriot, a painter at the royal factory of Sèvres, he attempted to set up a private factory actually within the *commune* of Sèvres. But he did not succeed; the Préfet de Police recorded the abolition of the kiln in 1850.

Jacob Petit's products met with a great deal of success, which encouraged many fraudulent imitations. He won lawsuits against shameless adversaries who had been stealing his pupils, but he also experienced many setbacks. A warehouse which he owned in Hamburg was burnt down in the city fire, and finally a clerk whom he had sent over to England embezzled 30,000 francs' worth of porcelain which had been entrusted to him.

All this, along with other losses (including the outlay tied up in the Sèvres venture) obliged him to file a petition of bankruptcy on March 24th 1848. On the balance sheet were entered the warehouse on Rue de Bondy in Paris, the factories at Fontainebleau and Sèvres and a warehouse in London. In a legal settlement of October 5th following, his creditors agreed to overlook seventy per cent of all debts due to them and they allowed him a thirteen-year respite in which to repay the rest.

In 1862 one of Jacob Petit's employees, Jacquemin, was supposed to have bought up the Fontainebleau factory. However, Jacob Petit re-emerges in Paris, in Rue du Paradis-Poissonnière, until 1866. He died at the Hôpital Beaujon two years later.

Before discussing Jacob Petit's wares we should, at this point, say a word or two about the factory at Fontainebleau. Many authors, including Chavagnac and Grollier, state that it was founded in 1795 by Benjamin Jacob and Aaron Smoll *(sic)* who were succeeded by Baruch Weil, Schmolle's son-in-law. According to these authors Jacob and Mardochée Petit bought it in 1830. We have not yet managed to prove or disprove these assertions. Here is what we have ascertained so far. Firstly, it is evident, from various deeds executed and authenticated by the notary, that Schmolle and Baruch Weil were related. Baruch Weil, however, was definitely not Schmolle's son-in-law since the women whom he had married were called respectively Hélène Schoulbach and Marguerite Nathan. The Benjamin family, including Jacob Benjamin and his brother-in-law Aaron Schmolle, had purchased in Year IV the formerly privileged factory of the Faubourg Saint-Denis and had resold it to Schoelcher in Year VI. At that time the Benjamin family was living in Paris. From 1801 to 1804 Benjamin is entered in the *Almanach du Commerce* as a factory owner at Fontainebleau, with an address in Paris at 187, Rue Chapon. It is in 1805 that we see the appearance of the name Baruch Weil, as a manufacturer of porcelain at Fontainebleau, and at 101, Rue du Temple in Paris. From 1809 to 1815 the warehouse was at 23, Rue Boucherat, then from 1816 onwards at 16, Rue de Bondy. It was at this second address that Baruch Weil died on April 8th 1828, leaving a difficult estate to administer because of the numerous children born of his two marriages.

The factory of Fontainebleau, the warehouse of plain and decorated porcelain in Rue de Bondy, and a salesroom for decorated porcelain in Passage de l'Opéra, entered his estate. The salesroom was considered to be one of the main outlets of the Fontainebleau factory.

The elder daughter of Baruch Weil, together with her husband Benoît Léon Cohen, bought up the salesroom in Rue de Bondy on January 9th 1829, for 12,550 francs. On March 2nd following, Cohen became the partner of his brother-in-law Godechaux Baruch Weil in running this porcelain salesroom.

As for the factory at Fontainebleau (10, Rue de Bourbon), the buildings for which had been bought by Baruch Weil from the Comte Durosnel in 1810, it was not sold until April 8th 1833 after various family lawsuits. Priced at 50,200 francs in 1829, the premises and goodwill were finally auctioned off for 30,000 francs. The purchase was transacted on behalf of François Lheureux, a building contractor at Fontainebleau, who paid the last instalment on November 3rd 1835. The

disparity between the price fixed in 1829 and the actual price reached in the sale of 1833 seems to indicate that the factory had by then fallen idle.

What did Lheureux do? Perhaps he did not immediately sell it to Jacob Petit who claims to have set up his business there in 1834—though he does not explain whether he was not merely the tenant. Incidentally, it is rather annoying to observe that both the Parisian salesrooms stood on Rue de Bondy, Baruch Weil's at 16, Jacob Petit's at 26.

We shall end this digression about Baruch Weil by pointing out that his business was a large one and that his wares kept up

a high standard. In 1820 he had taken out a patent on a new glaze. His factory and products were sufficiently prominent to earn Baruch Weil the *Légion d'honneur,* conferred by Charles X in person at the exhibition of 1827. By then he was employing a labour force of eighty, and his prices were regarded as modest. He ex-

185 Legros d'Anisy. Cylindrical cup and saucer. Transfer-printed decoration in black, brownish-red, beige and gold. Views of Paris. On the cup 'Place des Vosges, formerly Place Royale, near the Boulevard St. Antoine in Paris'. On the saucer: 'View from outside of the Lycée Bonaparte, formerly Capucines, in Paris'. (today the Eglise Saint-Louis d'Antin). *Circa* 1810. Lisbon, Museu Nacional de Arte Antiga. Ht. 6.5 cm. (2¹/₂ in.). Mark 137.

186   Legros d'Anisy.
Plate. Transfer-printed
polychrome decoration of
mythological subject.
Circa 1810.
Sèvres, Musée National de
Céramique. Diam. 23.5 cm.
(9¹/₅ in.).
Mark 136.

hibited two tall vases 'covered in *œil de Sèvres* blue', a breakfast set *(déjeuné)* with a buff ground, etc.

Baruch Weil had been specially appointed supplier to Louis XVIII and counted the Dauphine and the Duchesse de Berry among his customers.

We shall close this aside on Baruch Weil the porcelain maker by adding that his mark is, unfortunately, still unknown to us at present. But let us return to Jacob Petit who was an inventor. As such he excelled in the field of decoration. His drawings and his porcelain are seething with ideas; he combined Gothic, Rococo and neo-Classical styles. As a ceramist he registered patents relating variously to moulding, the application of gold, the manufacture of dolls' heads and 'the assembly of night lights showing the time'. Even the sale of his factory to Jacquemin in 1862 did not check his creative fantasies and in 1864 he registered no less than three patents dealing with 'a

Ill. 171

sort of ship' as well as some systems for stopping railway trains and vehicles. His wares consist chiefly of luxury items. The service pieces—apart from dessert services and tea- or coffee sets—are scarce and probably belong to the earliest phase of his career as a manufacturer.

Ornamental pieces, especially, reveal the superb craftsmanship of Jacob Petit: a mantelpiece entirely of porcelain made for the 1834 exhibition indicates an excellent technique as well as an inventive talent on the part of the decorator. Nonetheless, Baron Dupin, reporting on the exhibition, wrote: 'We are bestowing the honourable mention upon M. Jacob Petit not for the weird and difficult outlines with which he endows most of his pieces, but for the boldness of execution with which these difficulties are overcome.' And Baron Dupin added resignedly: 'All the decorators admit that M. Jacob Petit's innovations have given a new uplift to the porcelain business.' Stéphane Flachat on the other hand was full of admiration for this 'spirited and enterprising artist', and, marvelling at the design, shape and relief of the objects, he saw in them, 'vigour and thoughtfulness'. Jacob Petit won only a bronze medal at the exhibition of 1839 because of 'the extravagance of the shapes and grotesque adornments'. By then he was exhibiting baskets that were not moulded but 'woven' from porcelain osiers. Although he is missing from the trade fair of 1844, he did exhibit at the one in 1849 (in spite of his recent bankruptcy) and won a silver medal. Drafting the report, Ebelmen recorded that the manufacturer had given a certain impetus to the porcelain business, especially to exports, and had helped to promote national prosperity. The skill of Jacob Petit manifested itself pre-eminently in tall *Rocaille* vases, vases with flowers in relief and statuettes embellished with porcelain lace.

This silver medal was confirmed at the exhibition of 1855 at which Jacob Petit displayed two groups: *Si jeunesse savait* and *Si vieillesse pouvait*. His ingenious range of techniques found favour, partic-

Ill. 78

Ill. 179

187 Le Plé.
Flared *(jasmin)* cup with Paisley pattern and polychrome landscape on nankeen ground.
Sèvres, Musée National de Céramique. Ht. 11 cm. (4¹/₃ in.).
Mark (in red): *Mture de / Plée frères / à Paris.*

188 Locré.
Rocaille salt-cellar. Corn-
flowers and gold. *Circa* 1775.
Geneva, Musée de l'Ariana.
Ht. 4.5 cm. (1³/₄ in.).
Mark 142.

ularly his lace-clad drapery, his admirable 'embroideries' and his flowers which were fashioned leaf by leaf.

Jacob Petit excelled at making ornaments such as mantelpiece sets (clocks, vases and candelabra), toilet sets, *jardinières* (flower stands) and the thousand and one boudoir items that Balzac describes so well in *Deux jeunes mariées*. We come upon infinitely fantastic designs for the match Ill. 172 holders, perfume burners, ring stands, tubs, *veilleuses* and vases. Especially the flasks called for a creator's imagination: their shapes range from the most Classical (rectangular with chamfered corners) to Ill. 181 the most surprising: figurines whose Ill. 173 *coiffure* disguises a stopper or a pagoda. 'There is always something new emerging from his kilns' wrote a contemporary of his. It may be legitimate to accuse him of an exorbitant imagination, but we cannot but admire his technical feats such Ill. 179, as his imitations of gems or his flowers in 183, 184 relief.

Two strong trends may be discerned in Jacob Petit's work: firstly, the influence of previous styles, in particular the neo-Classical (ovoid and 'Medici') vases and bas-relief decorations. Also in evidence is a certain vagrant Romanticism in the 'Cathedral style' decorations and statuet-Ill. 184 tes of pilgrims or of chatelains; the flagons and the 'Catherine de Medici' design for a *veilleuse* hark back to the Renaissance. Secondly, Jacob Petit was very sensitive to certain foreign influences which he had absorbed on his travels. In Saxony, at Capo-di-Monte and at Derby he had been able to study *Rocaille* styles such as France failed to equal in exuberance, but from which he was to draw a great deal of inspiration. One of his successes was the 'snowball' (guelder rose) Ill. 179 decoration which had been the pride of

Meissen between 1730 and 1750. It was Saxony again that inspired his Oriental figures. Contrary to Meissen practice the statuettes of Jacob Petit have a utilitarian purpose, being flasks, tobacco jars or *pots-pourris*. As a final touch he marked his imitations with the two crossed swords of Ill. 173 Meissen.

Jacob Petit's decorations use gay, bright colours, which not only hark back to the palettes of the 18th century but also reflect the influence of Gros, who had been the first painter in the 19th century to readopt these colours. Animated scenes, flowers and fruit, in particular, are set off by *Rocaille* escutcheons reserved in plain grounds of a vivid colour (acid green, Ill. 174, 178 amaranth purple or turquoise), or even in black grounds. The contrast is further accentuated by a thick gold used in flower-strewn rock-work.

Finally we must mention Jacob Petit's biscuit ware, which has hitherto been Ill. 182 little known. Such pieces are often adorned with swags of lace, like those very fragile statuettes of brides. The Musée national de Céramique de Sèvres contains a bird's nest in biscuit, made up of slender branches on a basically rounded hollow shape.

It is always sensible, even in the case of items bearing the famous initials JP in underglaze blue, to remember that only the designs—the actual shapes—are the work of Jacob Petit. Indeed, he had handed over his moulds, designs and marks to Jacquemin who subsequently sold them all to Raingo and Vialatte. Neither should we forget that Jacob Petit supplied special plain wares to decorators or dealers, who often held exclusive rights to them, not only in France but also abroad. Therefore it comes as no surprise to find, side by side with Jacob

Petit's marks (still in underglaze blue), other underglaze marks, for example Schoelcher's, who was then a porcelain dealer in Paris, or Paneel & Chappel's, decorators at Brussels. A further note is that Jacob Petit had the use of warehouses in London and Hamburg. Finally—and this does nothing to simplify the problem—it seems likely that white wares for Jacob Petit were made at Limoges.

We therefore find ourselves confronted with nothing less than a 'holding' in trade and industry. It is very tempting to compare the JP mark to a stamped signature or a trade-union label, with all the economic ramifications which this involves.

Jacob Petit had many imitators. Amongst them one may readily cite Bastien and Bugeard of 95, Faubourg Saint-Martin who were active between about 1830 and 1850. The only document relating to them is the record of a gift to the Musée des Arts décoratifs at Paris in 1922, made by M. Charles Bastien. A certain Bastien, a dealer in crystal glass at Galerie Vivienne, 5/7, Passage des Petits-Pères, is entered in the 1830 issue of the *Almanach du Commerce*.

LACHASSAIGNE

The decorator F. Lachassaigne, in evidence from 1825 to 1851, had these successive addresses: 4, Rue de la Marche, 24, Rue de Poitou and 2, Rue Corbeau. We are indebted to him for some very

189 Locré.
Venus and Cupid (*Vénus et l'Amour*). Biscuit.
Circa 1780.
Model repeated by the La Courtille factory throughout its career.
Sèvres, Musée National de Céramique. Ht. 30 cm.
(11⁴/₅ in.).
Mark 149.

fine decorations which are vividly coloured and well glazed. In particular we might mention two tall vases showing the Adoration of the Magi and the Adoration of the Shepherds which bear the Perche mark as well; and a table, the top of which shows the apotheosis of Ferdinand VII, King of Spain. It was commissioned in 1830 and finished five years later. Today it is kept in the Palacio de Oriente at Madrid.

LASSIA

Jean Joseph Lassia was a Strassburger and childhood friend of Pierre Antoine Hannong, with whom he organized a few swindles.

Lassia is supposed to have come upon the secret of Dresden porcelain at the home of a German innkeeper in La Courtille who had received it from a compatriot, a craftsman working at Sèvres. Lassia is described as an uninteresting character; he was even imprisoned in the Châtelet. Lassia registered himself officially and took out his mark on October 26th 1774. He set himself up on Rue de Reuilly in the Faubourg Saint-Antoine. Bachelier depicted him thus: 'without talents, without possessions and without occupations; he is gorgeously dressed and indulges in luxury whenever he has found a dupe...' It is not, then, surprising to see him wind up his business as early as January 22nd 1776. Like his friend Honnong, Lassia gaily squandered the capital of his sleeping partners. In spite of the surety of Count von Klasten, Chamberlain to the Duke of Bavaria, who served to pay off the fourteen to fifteen men at the factory, Lassia's debts totalled more than 80,000 *livres*. He explained them away as 'a run of bad luck'.

The decree of 1784 was communicated to

him. At the end of 1785 a memorandum stated that Lassia had been using coal to fire some very fine porcelain and that he intended to make stoves, mantelpieces and saucepans.

Lassia meant to set up a factory for his operations with the help of two friends and 200,000 *livres* provided that he was

granted exclusive rights. In his support he produced an adulatory report signed by Cadet, Guéttard and Fontanieu, dated August 16th 1781. It recounted some experiments with cooking in porcelain over a high fire. Calonne refused him the exclusive privilege on February 14th 1768. On October 17th 1788 Lassia

190 Locré.
Figurines of huntsmen.
Circa 1780.
Sèvres, Musée National de Céramique. Ht. 17 cm. ((6⁷/₁₀ in.).
Mark 148.

191 Locré.
Plate, *fleurs jetées,* without
gold. *Circa* 1775.
Sèvres, Musée National de
Céramique. Diam. 24 cm.
(9½ in.).
Mark 142.

renewed his application to make stoves and mantelpieces. Julien's report did not mention this factory.

The mark registered is the letter L painted in black, red or gold.

The products from this factory are few, and rather mediocre in quality.

LEGROS D'ANISY

The transfer printing works owned by Stone, Coquerel and Legros d'Anisy occupy an important and special place in the history of ceramics at the beginning of the 19th century.

These three men took out a patent on February 26th 1808 for transfer printing all sorts of designs and engravings onto faience, pipe-clay, porcelain, ivory, crystal glass, sheet-metal, varnished wood, gold, silver, tortoiseshell, cloth, etc. On December 30th 1809 this patent was complemented by a certified codicil and on March 30th 1818 by a patent of refinement.

The process was based upon removing from the engraving a 'pull' made on a specially coated filter-paper, which was pressed onto the object to be decorated; this object itself was covered with a film. Firing took place in a muffle-kiln. In fact, Legros d'Anisy was the sole inventor.

Stone and Coquerel had already been partners at the creamware factory in Creil, before Saint-Cricq arrived. John Hurford Stone represented the English board of sleeping associates in the first company founded at Creil in Year VII. Athanase Marie Martin Coquerel was involved in the second partnership, formed some months later. Incidentally, he was Stone's brother-in-law.

François Antoine Legros d'Anisy joined them to create the Stone-Coquerel-Legros d'Anisy partnership which took

effect the same day that the patent was registered, that is on February 26th 1808. Legros d'Anisy, born in 1772 at Anisy-le-Château (Aisne) had been employed at the imperial factory of Sèvres since Nivôse, Year XI. He carried out some transfer printing there, following his own technique.

192 Locré.
Lidded jug. Polychrome and gold. Band with violet ribbons on pink, *œil-de-perdrix* ('partridge-eye') ground. *Circa* 1775. Geneva, Musée de l'Ariana. Ht. 21 cm. (8¹⁄₅ in.). Mark 143.

193 Locré/Russinger.
Tomb-shaped flower tub.
Polychrome, heightened
with broad green lines.
Circa 1780.
Sèvres, Musée National de
Céramique. Ht. 18 cm.
(7 in.).
Mark 142.

In the tripartite partnership Stone was responsible for management and general supervision, whilst Coquerel was just a signatory. As for Legros d'Anisy, the technician, his tasks were to select suitable subjects for reproduction, fix prices, and to choose and manage the painters and engravers. The transfer printing was performed in a factory at 9, Rue du Cadran in Paris.

When the partnership expired in 1818 Legros d'Anisy continued to run the transfer-printing factory by himself. He received a silver medal at the 1819 exhibition for being the first man in France to have exploited transfer printing techniques on a large scale for decorating faience and porcelain. We might add that he won another silver medal for machine-made tiles. Legros d'Anisy was by then operating from 11, Rue du Faubourg Montmartre. By 1825 he had moved to 13, Rue Merry; next he went to 14, Rue Charlot and in 1834 his address was 9, Rue de Poitou.

Legros d'Anisy's decorations are remarkable for their delicacy and clarity. All items which have been embellished using this method bear a transfer printed mark with the initials SCL enclosed in the circular inscription: *Manuf^re d'impression sur faïence, porcelaine, & Par brevet d'invention*. Another mark with the initials of Legros d'Anisy alone is encircled by the inscription: *Manufacture de décors sur porcelaine et faience, rue du Cadran, N° 9 à Paris*. A third mark bears the names of the three partners in full: *Stone Coquerel et Legros*, inserted in the circular inscription: *Par brevet d'invention, manuf^re de décors en porcelaine, faience*.

The *Almanach du Commerce de la Ville de Paris* of 1808 enumerated in its second supplement the themes which the factory stocked:

Fables of La Fontaine,
Portraits of great men, both ancient and modern,
Picturesque views, castles and country-houses in different lands,
Highlights from French and Roman history,
Monuments of Paris and its environs,
Engraved stones,
Military service,
A porcelain set intended specifically for the Masonic Order, etc.
All these decorations could be turned out in black or in colour, and this applies equally to any subjects that might be requested: monograms, armorial bearings, family portraits, etc. 'Engravings are now being made of the most outstanding pictures and statues in the Musée Napoléon. These precious objects will appear forthwith…'

At the exhibition of 1819 Frémont, at that time the factory manager, had exhibited an inexpensive service in white porcelain, transfer printed in blue.

Fifteen years later, at the 1834 exhibition, 'M. le Chevalier Legros d'Anisy' displayed porcelain wares transfer printed in gold to imitate brush strokes. They were intended for Sèvres services to be dispatched to the stately residences of Saint-Cloud and Compiègne.

He exhibited some more porcelain, this time decorated in colour, together with creamware from Creil and a dial made of glazed Auvergne lava.

On several occasions between 1803 and 1848 Legros d'Anisy worked at Sèvres. Various experimental models which he produced there, notably in 1804 and 1823, are kept in the Musée national de Céramique de Sèvres. He died in 1849.

Relatively few examples of porcelain decorated by Legros d'Anisy are left. Ill. 185 These are items from table services of coffee services. It is, however, certain that the output of transfer-printed creamware Ill. 186 was very considerable.

LOCRÉ RUSSINGER POUYAT

Although it changed hands several times, the factory at La Courtille, in Rue Fontaine-au-Roy, is normally known by the name of its founder Locré, who ran it for fourteen years.

It was on July 14th 1773 that Jean-Baptiste Locré de Roissy obtained permission to set up a factory for 'German porcelain'

194 Locré.
Plate with floral decoration in the centre, accompanied by a 'picoted' ribbon on the raised rim. Decoration copied at Nyon.
Circa 1780.
Sèvres, Musée National de Céramique. Diam. 24 cm. (9½ in.).
Mark 142.

at La Courtille and registered his mark of two crossed torches.

Locré was born at Paris in 1726. His father was an officer *(juré)* of the guild of merchant fringe-weavers and had made his fortune as a dealer in braid. Jean-Baptiste spent some time in Germany, where he married Christina Caritas Hoffmann, their first son was born in Leipzig in his mother's homeland. Soon after his father's death he rented a house on August 12th 1772 in Rue Fontaine-au-Roy where he made the necessary preparations for fitting out as a factory. This venture of his proved very costly and on April 2nd 1777 Locré went into partnership with Martin de Bussy, the

first and foremost as a modeller at Höchst-am-Rhein. In the terms of this agreement Russinger 'binds and commits himself: to remain attached to the said factory in the capacity of manager for the span of twelve years as from May 1st; to give it his undivided attention; to employ his talents in the sound management of manufacturing operations; to supervise the craftsmen; to continue making colours for paintings... he renounces the faculty of communicating to anybody and under any pretext whatsoever, his knowledge of anything relating to porcelain manufacture, be it a matter of its composition, grounds, firing or colouring'. In return Locré undertook to pro-

196 Locré. ▶
Pair of *pots-pourris*. Pure-white porcelain imitating Chinese white-ware but less costly. They are enhanced by ormulu mounts of exceptionally high quality, attributed to Gouthière. *Pots-pourris*, mistakenly called perfume-burners, came into fashion in the 18th century: they were used for blending different sweet-smelling flowers and also fragrant powders which, when steeped in water, gave off scents that were greatly enjoyed. Locré turned out quite a number of plain or blue bowls and vases of extremely simple shapes, which were designed to be mounted in ormulu, either as *pots-pourris*, ewers, or else as vases for adorning mantelpieces or precious items of furniture. *Circa* 1780. Paris, Musée du Louvre, Coll. Thiers. Ht. 30 cm. (11$\frac{4}{5}$ in.). Mark 142.

195 Locré.
Bowl with four lobes.
Decoration of pansies:
violet, yellow, green and
gold. *Circa* 1780.
Paris, private coll.
L. 25.5 cm. (9$\frac{3}{5}$ in.).
Mark 143.

doyen des substituts to the Attorney General at the Grand Council. De Bussy contributed 36,000 *livres* in exchange for the promise of a quarter-share in the profits. This partnership was planned to last for twelve years. Next, a few weeks later, Locré signed an agreement with Laurent Russinger who was known

vide Russinger with housing and heating, and to give him an annual salary of 3,600 *livres* plus ten per cent of the net profits.

Russinger, with wife and children, had been lured to Paris by Chapelle in 1768, to work at the Sceaux factory for 'enamel-painted faience' *(faïence japonnée)*. Fol-

lowing some notorious clashes over fi-nances with Jacques Chapelle, Russinger had been forced to sue. He had then attempted to enter Sèvres, but finally in 1777 he had been appointed manager of the factory in Rue Fontaine-au-Roy. Ten years later, on August 10th 1787, he purchased it 'with the mark of the

said Locré who solemnly promises not to set up any other establishment in the same line of business'. The deal was transacted for 110,000 *livres*. In addition Locré let the house on Rue Fontaine-au-Roy to Russinger until 1792.[3]
On February 10th 1780 a search followed by confiscations had taken place at La

[3] Russinger was not the only member of his family to make or market ceramics; we shall see further on that his daughter Madeleine Eléonore had married Pierre Louis Alexandre Dodé, a porcelain painter who, from 1813 to 1814, was a dealer at 2, Rue Fontaine-au-Roy. Dodé bought the factory on Rue des Trois-Bornes in 1822 and leased it to Clauss afterwards.

Furthermore, by his first marriage to Madeleine Russinger, Dodé had a daughter, Marie Antoinette Héloïse Dodé. The latter's first husband, Nicolas Lalouette, owned the factory in Rue des Grésillons, and her second, Pierre Simon Jullien, later shared the management of this factory with her.

ment for subsidies which were denied him. A partnership with the wholesale porcelain merchant François Pouyat of Limoges (on Fructidor 2nd, Year v) brought him 50,000 francs, before it obliged him to surrender his factory to Pouyat altogether, on Nivôse 18th, Year VIII. The dissolution of the Pouyat-Russinger partnership did not come about until December 15th 1808. The three Pouyat sons thereafter took charge as managers of the business before they became its owners on January 24th 1810. Six years later they took on Guillaume Le Bourgeois as a partner; he was the new owner of the glass works at Fours (Nièvre), where the production of white ware was also started. Le Bourgeois dropped out in 1820, leaving Fours under the management of the Pouyats. The brothers sold the Paris premises in 1823 to Pierre Saucède, termed the 'owner', although they actually retained them until 1824 in order to dispose of their goods. Pouyat-Duvignaud, one of the three, who had meanwhile been specially appointed to the Duc de Berry, continued selling porcelain at 137, Rue du Temple, styled the sole agent of Fours.

The history of the La Courtille factory may have a few more surprises in store for anyone who follows up the study of the texts and objects.

Léonard Pouyat bought up the factory at Fours in 1827, after the death of Pouyat-Duvignaud. After Léonard's own death had occurred in 1845 it was taken over under the name of Pouyat-Lebrun and did not close down until around 1865.

Another curious fact about the factory at La Courtille is that a deed of partnership was signed by Remi Auguste Darte and Pierre Louis Lemaire whereby they were to run a porcelain factory standing on the

197   Pouyat.
Milk-jug. Poppies and corn-flowers painted from life and heightened with gold.
Circa 1800.
Geneva, Musée de l'Ariana.
Ht. 17 cm. (6⁷/₁₀ in.).
Mark 143.

Courtille on the instigation of the royal factory of Sèvres. But, as with the other Paris factories, this event does not seem to have had any troublesome consequences, even though La Courtille was the only sizeable factory that had not availed itself of any influential protector. The absence of any patronage no doubt explains why, unlike many others, the factory was not exempted from the annual concourse for which the decree of 1787 provided.

Russinger laid out considerable sums of money on the construction of new buildings on a further site bought in the same street, and the Revolution did not make matters easier. He applied to the Govern-

198 Locré.
Covered broth-bowl and its
tray. Polychrome and gold.
Allegories of Cupid, Venus
and Vulcan. *Circa* 1775.
London, British Museum.
Ht. 10 cm. (4 in.).
Mark 142.

same site at 39, Rue Fontaine-au-Roy. This partnership, which took effect on December 15th 1825, was planned to last for six years, but was extended for another three commencing on December 15th 1831. Darte went bankrupt in 1835. Lastly, in 1844 we find a certain Mirabal operating from 39, Rue Fontaine-au-Roy where he was running a painters' workshop.

By 1779 this factory ranked among the three most important porcelain works in Paris, the others being Rue Thiroux and Clignancourt. Many documents described it as a 'factory of German porcelain' and stated that the wares were heat-proof. It seems, incidentally, that Rus-

singer tried to exploit this special feature in order to launch himself into the production of more utilitarian objects for the laboratory, such as crucibles and retorts 'in the Hessian manner'. Russinger displayed them at the industrial exhibitions of Year IX and of 1806, when he was breaking away from the Pouyat partnership.

Even before Russinger arrived on November 24th 1773, M. de Sartine the Lieutenant général de Police in Paris had been writing to Bertin: 'the porcelain from Locré's factory at La Courtille could, by virtue of the beauty and strength of its body, and the brilliance of its colours and gilding, bear comparison with the wares of Saxony'. The body in question was being made at the factory itself, in accordance with the declarations by Locré and Russinger of November 23rd 1787. The clay came up from Limoges, and it was due to the excessively heavy transportation costs between there and Paris that Russinger shortly afterwards had the idea of using the clay he had discovered near Cherbourg and Valognes in Normandy. He even expressed the wish to buy up the area and in Year III procured for this purpose a recommendation from the Minister of the Interior, for the Administrator of the Département of La Manche. When the planned journey proved impossible Russinger attempted a second in Year V. Meanwhile the compacts signed by Russinger and Pouyat on Fructidor 22nd, Year V were based on the understanding that Pouyat should invest 50,000 francs in the factory, including 12,000 in the form of clay and materials for porcelain-manufacture. In Year VI the Pouyats were still delivering to the factory and found themselves among the creditors when it came to balancing Russinger's main ledger on Brumaire 14th, Year VI. We might add that this same book-balancing showed up some debts to the *négociant* Alluaud, an important wholesale merchant of clay in Limoges. By about 1822 Pouyat of Limoges was the official supplier to the factory on Rue Fontaine-au-Roy which the Pouyat brothers were managing. Besides the factory they kept a warehouse there for storing unrefined kaolin from the same source.

Depending on the period, two or three kilns and a number of muffles were used for porcelain firing in Rue Fontaine-au-Roy. The labour force stood at fifty to sixty during Year II and was already up to between seventy and eighty by the following year. By 1807 Pouyat claimed to be employing ninety men and to be producing 260,000 francs' worth of goods *per annum*. Once again, this classes the factory amongst the most important.

Some of the craftsmen mentioned in Year VI are well known in other factories: Frederik, probably the painter who had been working at The Hague in 1780; or Marx Senior, whose family had started up the faience factory at Nürnberg. Sébastian Marx had been a painter at Frankenthal from 1763 to 1780; Cantagrelle was the name adopted by a modeller at Aprey as far back as 1752; and lastly the painter Weydinger's family yielded eight artists for Sèvres. The particular member employed by Pouyat is very probably Jean Léopold Weydinger, a letter of whose, dated January 26th 1819, is kept in the archives at Sèvres. He wrote it from 'Rue Fontaine-au-Roy, on the premises of Messieurs Pouyat Frères, at the porcelain factory of His Grace the Duc de Berri'.

199 Pouyat.
Theriomorphic rhyton.
Matt polychrome in imitation of antique bronze.
Early 19th century.
Paris, Coll. Le Tallec.
Ht. 12 cm. (4³/₄ in.).
Mark 143.

200 Pouyat.
Cup and saucer. Transfer-printed decoration: calendar for 1810. Saumur, Musée des Arts Décoratifs. Ht. 9 cm. (3½ in.).
Mark 143.

What did Rue Fontaine-au-Roy produce? The *Almanach Dauphin* of 1777 stated that Locré kept a shop on Rue Michel-Comte and sold 'complete table services which withstand perfectly the most scalding liquids and even the fire without any trouble'. An advertisement printed in the same year specified: 'any wares to do with coffee- or table services, whether they be white, blue-and-white, in Chantilly style, or white and gold, they are painted and gilded to suit all tastes; [also] figures in biscuit for embellishing drawing-rooms and for dessert settings; vases with blue grounds; breakfast sets on trays of every kind, also having blue grounds, and cups for *limonadiers*...' All

this appears in the inventories of the period, and in particular the confiscation records of 1780.

In the 18th century, shapes are mostly similar to those used by the other factories and are often influenced by goldsmiths' work. They are mainly table pieces including—besides the most commonplace items—round or oval baskets, and various triangular pieces such as jam pots, dishes and salt cellars. The last-named items may simulate baskets with one or with two compartments. Fewer toilet articles have come down to us: water-jugs and basins, spittoons, round or oval chamber pots, barbers' shaving-dishes and *jattes de bidet*. ('bidet bowls').

Ill. 188

271

201   Pouyat.

Current prices for porcelain from the factory of 'Pouyat Brothers and Col., Rue Fontaine-au-Roi, 39 Faubourg du Temple in Paris, and at Fours, near Decize, *départment* of La Nièvre.' This especially interesting document itemizes the pieces, giving prices for first, second and third quality, the cornflower decoration with gold band, and the thin, medium and broad gold band. This page is devoted to table- and dessert-services and to *cabarets*. Thus, a tall oval soup-tureen costs from 12 to 22 francs depending on the quality, 32 francs with cornflower decoration, and from 38 to 45 francs according to the width of the gold band. Amongst the components of *cabarets* the term 'sugar-jar' *(boîte à sucre)* persists: it goes with six, eight or twelve cups, and may be fluted, in 'new Etruscan shape with gems, glazed lid' or 'Etruscan, with woman's head'. In the largest size and decorated with a wide gold band it costs 5 francs.
Circa 1820.
Sèvres, Archives de la manufacture nationale.

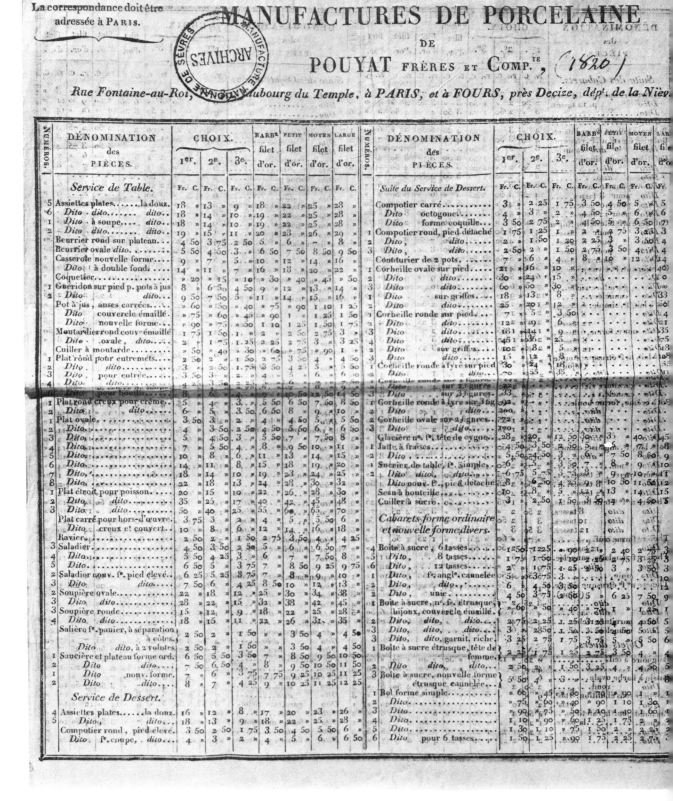

202 Pouyat.
Sketch for a plate-decoration
of aquatic themes, ascribed
to Leloy. *Circa* 1815.
Bordeaux, Musée des Arts
Décoratifs.

once again a lot of pieces referred to as 'of old-fashioned design' (*d'ancien modèle*) entered next to a number of fluted objects. The articles for the table and the toilet are then joined by holy-water stoups, drinking horns, writing sets, labels for bottles, footed cake trays and pipes with bowls shaped like heads (*pipes à tête*). Let us not forget the *veilleuses* and the apothecaries' display bottles, either ovoid or 'Medici' type.

All contemporary decorations were reproduced by Pouyat's factory. Beside the unchangeable cornflower the big flowers are to be found, and also the *trompe-l'œil* fruit, the cavaliers, regional costumes and views of cities. Next come the reproductions of Flemish or contemporary pictures, domestic or allegorical scenes: *L'Amour maternel, La Toilette de Psyché, Le Temps fait connaître la Route, L'Espérance,* etc., and miniature portraits.

The coloured grounds and contrast burnished gilt borders emphasize landscapes set in escutcheons. One new feature is the matt finish to coloured grounds. But the most surprising aspect is the variety of these grounds: blue, nankeen, yellow, red and even pure gold.

Some drawings from this factory have been discovered. It is probable that they are partly the work of Leloy 'Painter, arranger of ornaments, and draughtsman' who worked at Sèvres from 1816 to 1844. We find, with variations, sketches employing the same themes for a *petit gibier* ('small fry') service and a *forestier* ('forester') service; to wit 'Famous Frenchmen' or 'Views from Overseas'. Other designs are inspired from Classical or Egyptian Antiquity. Lastly, from about 1810 onwards, the new technique of transfer printing made it

Ill. 202

Ill. 206

Under another heading let us list the writing sets ('perpetual' or otherwise), the mortars, tobacco-jars, square tubs, sconces, cold-cream jars and pomade jars, and a *vase à bougie* ('candle-vase'). Next to these more or less refined pieces we still see a large number of cups and bowls for *limonadiers* and pomade- or rouge- jars designed for perfumers.

Later on, shapes multiplied and became complex, witness the cups decorated with beading and mounted on paw feet. They became square as well, or assumed the appearance of a snail-shell. The Etruscan and English styles enjoyed a wide popularity, but in the inventory taken after Pouyat's death (1826) we see

Ill. 207

273

possible to turn out more commonplace articles—some even carried advertisements—which were decorated with views of cities and with ordinary cal-
Ill. 200 endars.

Biscuit ware appears to have been one of La Courtille's specialities. Even in the early days Locré and Russinger had been boasting of its superiority over the products of their Parisian colleagues. Russinger had been a modeller at Höchst and was bound to harbour a preference for the art for which he was best trained, and indeed he surrounded himself with able assistants. The rivalry between this factory and Sèvres centred mainly on the modelled work; Boizot's moulds were stolen in 1777 and used at La Courtille, then there arose the affair over the bust of Madame du Barry, which has already been discussed. The day-to-day output consisted of either single or grouped figures made from a fine body and pleasingly modelled. Throughout
Ill. 189 the factory's productive life, mythological subjects were much in evidence, and
Ill. 190 so were many family and hunting scenes. Figures after Boucher made their own contribution towards portraying contemporary life, witness the touching groups *Dites: s'il vous plaît* or *La Piqûre douloureuse* (1826). The allegories of the sciences and virtues occupy an important position as well. Groups demanding great skill were displayed at the exhibitions of Year VI and 1806. Other biscuit figures or groups adorn baskets and clocks. Another noteworthy aspect of La Courtille's output from the Revolutionary period until the Restoration is the imitation of Wedgwood's blue-and-white jasper ware.

The output is so copious as to suggest that a number of pieces executed in the 18th century may well have been deco-

rated as much as thirty or forty years later. A similar hypothesis is equally valid for biscuit and ordinary porcelain alike: the moulds may have been used long afterwards, either in Paris or the provinces.

Lastly we should observe that plenty of porcelain in the white from La Courtille,

Fours or Limoges was not decorated in France at all. In 1793 Russinger was asking the Comité du Salut Public (Committee of Public Safety) to release the equivalent of the 30,000 crowns contained in the bill of exchange from the banker Perrégaux, which was for the delivery of porcelain to England.

MIGNON

Adrien Pierre Mignon registered himself officially with the Lieutenant général de Police on March 10th 1777 as a porcelain manufacturer and filed his mark, a fleur-de-lys. This mark was actually the same as the one used by Mignon's predecessors for marking the faience ware which they had been making in the Faubourg Saint-Antoine since 1740. It is also a fleur-de-lis which is found on the faience made at Sceaux by Jacques Chapelle before he partnered Mignon in Paris. In 1743 Mignon was just a silent partner in the factory on Rue de Charenton (where he was a timber merchant at

the time), but from 1759 until he died in 1788 he was its sole master. In 1749 the factory had been moved from Rue de Charenton to Rue Saint-Sebastien opposite the Pont-aux-Choux.

The 1784 decree was communicated to Mignon. The factory was destroyed in 1789.

It seems likely that Mignon supervised the production of faience and porcelain simultaneously. The inventory that was drawn up after his death lists many items of faience. It also records the existence of a register in which are entered the craftsmen 'who have worked on porcelain production'as well as the painters. The inventory mentions another book, entitled *Recueil et traité de couleurs tant de terres d'Angleterre que de porcelaine couverte par les mêmes terres, analise et dissolution de toute manière utile et éprouvée, avec des recettes de dorure et composition de porcelaine dure à l'épreuve du feu.* ('Treatise on a

collection of colours both of English clays and of porcelain with a covering of those clays: a thoroughly useful and proven method of analysis and solution, with directions for gilding and preparing hard-paste fire-proof porcelain').

We know but one item of porcelain from this factory, to wit a butter dish with truncated rim, decorated with a band and flowers in pale underglaze blue. The mark is likewise in underglaze blue (Musée national de Céramique de Sèvres).

MONGINOT

Monginot, regarded as one of the best flower-painters, had worked under Le Perre at Lille in 1784 and 1785. On the strength of his experience there he suggested to Brongniart that he should carry out tests with coal firing at Sèvres in 1811. He was then a porcelain craftsman living at 103, Faubourg Saint-Denis. We come upon him in 1825 as the painting overseer

204 Pouyat.
Design for a decoration:
Pegasus. Lavis. *Circa* 1810.
Bordeaux, Musée des Arts
Décoratifs.

276

205 Russinger, Pouyat.
Teapot, cylindrical cup and
saucer. *Circa* 1800.
Paris, private coll. Teapot:
Ht. 13.5 cm. (5$^1/_3$ in.).
Mark 143.

at the factory of Hall & Cie. in Rue Amelot. Next, he set himself up as a dealer in porcelain at 20, Boulevard des Italiens, but he went bankrupt in 1837.
By 1832 Monginot was the supplier to the King's Household (la Maison du Roi); to Madame Adélaïde and to the princesses Louise and Marie: he was selling table-and dessert- services, vases, *cabarets* and trinkets. He was well known 'for the perfect imitation of old-style Sèvres'.

All the porcelain in his salesroom was auctioned off on December 13th 1837 and January 2nd 1838, after he had wound up his business. All the fashionable fancy goods appear: baskets, sweetmeat dishes, ice-cream 'shells', match holders, card holders, flasks, ink-wells, candlesticks, *veilleuses* and 'imitation Saxon' *cabarets*. He signed in full, giving the address of his salesroom: *Monginot boulevard des Italiens Nº 20, à Paris.*

MORELLE
Morelle registered himself officially on July 16th 1773 and filed his mark MAP which is interpreted as *Morelle à Paris*. Buhot's report in 1774 recorded that, after producing porcelain in the round on Rue de la Roquette for several years, Morelle had moved his factory to Saint-Denis and claimed 'not to be concerned [with porcelain] any longer except for his own amusement, nor to be selling any'. Certain rare pieces have tentatively been ascribed to this factory.

NAST
Jean Népomucène Hermann Nast was born at Radwesburg in Styria (Austria) in 1754. His father was a master saddler and his maternal grandfather, Johann Georg Wollenben, earthenware manufacturer and a burgher of that town. Jean Népomucène arrived in Paris in about 1780. Previous to that he had been a harness maker at Versailles, then a craftsman in the Vincennes porcelain factory. There, he devoted his leisure hours to drawing classes and in 1783 took over a small Parisian factory founded by Lemaire in 1780, on Rue Popincourt, Faubourg Saint-Antoine.

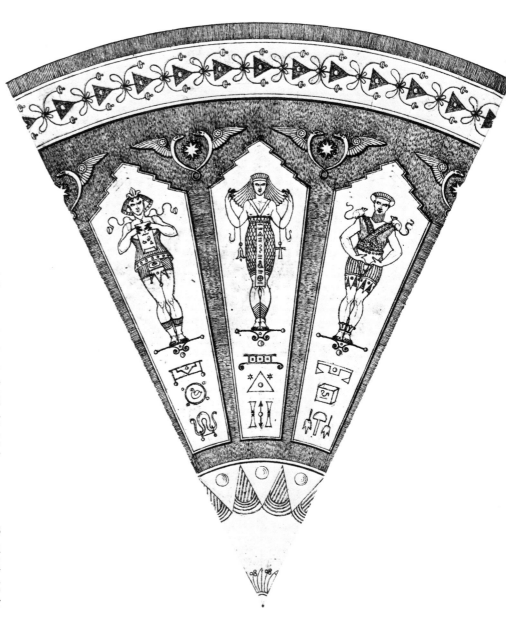

206 Pouyat.
Plate-design, Egyptian decoration. Pen-and-ink drawing.
Circa 1810.
Bordeaux, Coll. Dr. Charles Lasserre.

207 Pouyat.
Cup in the form of a shell
and its scallop-shaped saucer.
Gold and coral. *Circa* 1820.
Lisbon, Museu Nacional de
Arte Antiga. Ht. 10 cm.
(4 in.).
Mark 143.

When Nast had been working at the factory of Vincennes its manager was a certain Lemaire, and we subsequently see Pierre Lemaire in partnership with Josse, on Rue Amelot. It is tempting to imagine that the small establishment which Lemaire kept on Rue Popincourt was nothing other than a salesroom for Vincennes.

Whether or not this was so, Nast set himself up in constricted ground-floor quarters where he was simultaneously the manager, designer, thrower, moulder and kiln charger. Nast was not to be disheartened by the testing experience of two fires, and his early products attracted general attention, and in particular the notice of the chemist Proust. Proust recommended him to the Spanish Ambassador whose mission it was to organize the setting up of a hard paste porcelain factory in his own country. The unimpressive appearance of the factory made the offer a low one (1,500 *livres* plus travelling expenses) and Nast turned it down. He moved shortly afterwards to within a stone's throw of Rue des Amandiers Popincourt and when he married Marguerite Edmée Lecoutre, a master baker's daughter, in 1789, his property was valued separately at 84,000 *livres*. He was just entering a state of prosperity when the Revolution overtook him. Although commercial transactions were almost completely halted he kept on his staff, ensuring them a supply of bread at three *sols* per pound. Nonetheless the Revolutionaries wanted to hang him and the noose was already at his door when his courage disarmed the wretches. In order both to continue his work and to purchase further sites close to his factory, Nast had to resort to borrowing. Loans to him between 1792 and 1794 amounted to 55,000 francs.

Nast's wife had borne him two sons, Henri in 1790 and François in 1792. When Henri married Adèle Bevy in 1815 he brought with him a quarter-share in the factory – his mother having died – plus sizeable properties in the Paris region. His bride was no less wealthy, since her dowry came to the considerable sum of 100,000 francs. Just before Jean Népomucène died in 1817 he had reached an unwritten agreement with his two sons. The two brothers continued the business under the name of Nast Frères until

March 1st 1831. As from that date Henri took control of the whole concern. Economic conditions, however, no longer allowed him to retain so large an establishment in Paris, and rather than leave for the provinces he shut down the factory in 1835.

In 1807 there was a labour force of eighty-

208 Pouyat.
Basket and stand in imitation wickerwork. Early 19th century. Paço Ducal de Vila Viçosa, Fundação Casa de Bragance. L. 27 cm. (10²/₃ in.).
Mark 143.

280

209 Marceaux.
Veilleuse. Polychrome with
pink and pale-green ground.
Circa 1835.
Paris, Coll. Le Tallec.
Ht. 35 cm. (13²/₅ in.).
Mark 152.

three turning out annually 200,000 francs'
worth of wares; by 1819 the Nast
brothers were employing one hundred
men and the output was valued at
300,000 francs, making their factory one
of the largest. Following their father's
principles the Nast brothers concentrated
on improving their wares while bringing
down the production costs. The best
artists collaborated with the Nasts: Pajou
and Klagmann the modellers, the painters
Schilz, Flers and Cabat, and chemists such
as Cadet de Vaux and Vauquelin. Until
his death in 1828 this latter held the post
of permanent director of the factory
laboratory. There he discovered chrome
green, it is said.

Nast took out two patents in 1810, the
first concerning a mechanical method of
producing borders in relief ('rouletting')
and the second on a special porcelain body
intended both for these borders and for
medallions and figures in relief.

The greatest awards were conferred upon
Nast at the national industrial exhibitions. He received a silver medal in 1806
for the busts of the Emperor and Empress,
which he displayed together with two
vases of one and a half metres, embellished with bas-reliefs. The jury deemed
his factory to be the most important in
Paris. The 1819 exhibition established the
reputation of the Nast brothers by granting them a gold medal. Praise was bestowed upon their fine manufacture, the extraordinary size of their pieces, the beauty of
the shapes and the excellent taste shown
by the design and ornaments. The King   Ill. 76, 77
personally encouraged them. Further
gold medals were awarded them in 1823,
1827 and 1834. Such was their renown
that at the first international exhibition,
held in London in 1851, (seventeen years
after the factory had closed down) a tall

bowl by Nast was exhibited by France next to the porcelain from the factories that were still operating.

Two documents permit us to date a few of the original shapes and *décors*. These are the inventories taken after the deaths respectively of Madame Nast in 1811 and of Jean Népomucène in 1817.

From the first of these we may pick out—besides the common wares—the following items, distributed between the factory's nine salesrooms: dials, footed trays, *marronniers* (dishes for hot chestnuts), gravy boats *(jussières)*, bidets, candlesticks, pipes, mortars, and wine- or liqueur-labels. A lot of biscuit ware is entered, too, particularly clocks with Ill. 213 mythological or allegorical subjects. Along with the decorations using flowers and landscapes many matt *décors* are listed: *jaune jonquille* ('daffodil yellow'), matt-green ground on matt gold, matt yellow or green grounds with figures. We should also observe the wreaths of hay, a pair of vases showing Egyptian Ill. 225 figures on a chrome-green ground, cel-

lular patterns, zigzags, and gold or black embellishments. Gothic arches appear, whilst a dessert service is decorated with birds after Buffon. A 'tall vase in biscuit with a coloured ground having very beautifully gilded bas-relief ornaments' is valued at 2,000 francs.

1817 sees the appearance of 'Arabian coffee pots', coffee measurers, 'coffee jugs for journeys', rice dishes, openwork plates, tea infusers, snuffers, snuff boxes, alembics, curtain pulls, 'bed finials and attachments', thermometers, Antique lamps, epergnes, handles and drip pans. Like many big manufacturers the Nasts would sell their white ware to the decorators. Nast's clients included the dealers and decorators Duhamel, Feuillet, Perdu, Duban, Leplé, Gaugain and Deroche, all operating in Paris; Verneuil in Bordeaux; others in Rotterdam, London, Coblenz and Aachen; the clockmaker Lepautre (who bought dials and clock cases), and perfumers such as Frageon and Houbigant. All of them guaranteed regular orders from him.

210 Nast.
Factory's plaque of sample-patterns. Polychrome and gold. The whole decorative repertory in current use on porcelain is assembled here. The special emphasis is on borders, most of which consist of more or less stylized plants, of trophies, sways and friezes.
The two landscapes may be adapted either for a border, for a panel in reserve or even for a continuous design unrolling around three-dimensional pieces. Lastly, two geometric patterns, one derived from the heraldic butterfly-motif and rendered in contrast-burnished gold, the other gilded on white and made up of cross-hatching, are found as the secondary or principal decoration on three-dimensional pieces.
Early 19th century.
Limoges, Musée National Adrien Dubouché.
L. 32 cm. (12³/₅ in.).
(The other half of this plaque is illustrated page 290.)

colours, decoration and gilding are well-nigh perfect.

This is exemplified by the service which King Ferdinand VII of Spain ordered when he married Isabel of Braganza in 1816. The magnificently modelled shapes are enhanced with a matt gold and a purple ground heightened with a lustrous gold.

Ill. 220

NICOLET AND GREDER REVIL

The Petite Pologne district (the present-day quarter of Saint-Augustin) harboured, in Year VII, the factory of Antoine Greder which stood at 477, Rue du Rocher.

Nicolet had been a craftsman there since 1791. Julien's report, also in Year VII, recorded the factory of Battazerd on Rue du Rocher. Perhaps it was during that year that Nicolet purchased it. By 1805 Nicolet and Greder had settled not far away, in Rue Neuve des Mathurins. Their old Rue du Rocher address was now occupied by Revil. He applied for a loan in that very year, 1805, stating that he had 'long been established in Rue du Rocher' and had a salesroom on Rue Neuve des Capucines, in the elegant quarter nearby. By 1807 Jean Charles Revil kept a labour force of fourteen in his factory on Rue du Rocher, and the following year he went into partnership with his two sons Jean Etienne and Dominique Narcisse, under the company name of Revil & Fils. This partnership was dissolved on August 31st 1813, and in the same year the two brothers took a third, Alexandre Louis, as their partner, under the trade name of Revil Frères. The capital of the partnership amounted to 240,000 francs. A new application for a loan in 1814 was turned down like the previous ones. The saleroom was kept

211 Portrait of Nast (and one of his daughters-in-law). He was a talented draughtsman. Painting by Joseph Abel, an Austrian painter and engraver (1764–1818). Paris, private coll.

The porcelain which has come down to us is marked with Nast's name written in full; it is painted in gold onto pieces bearing gilt decoration, otherwise in red, either in cursives or stencilled. The rouletted items usually show the mark: *Nast par brevet d'invention*. Both the quality of the body and the beauty of the by Mademoiselle Revil-Signoret, sister or aunt to the Revil brothers. In 1819, still in the salesroom of Boulevard des Capucines, she married the faience maker Jacques Lepère and was herself styled *fayancière*. Thereafter we lose track of the Revils.

The Revils' porcelain wares are marked in red, the name being spelt out in full. They are of an attractive quality and the pieces of which we know are decorated with vivid colours or with plain coloured grounds; for example a brown cup from the Musée national de Céramique de Sèvres, whose only decoration consists of a monogram painted in gold on an escutcheon.

LE PETIT CARROUSEL

When the factory of the Faubourg Saint-Denis was sold by the Marquis de La Salle to de Leutre on January 24th 1778, it had two salesrooms in Paris, one of them being at Le Carrousel, under the management of *sieur* and *dame* Houdeyer. The inventory showed that 21,841 *livres, 1 sol*'s worth of goods were stored there, indicating it was the bigger of the two. It took the place of the warehouse on Rue Plâtrière which Hannong had used as far back as 1774 and which had been kept by Madame Boutet de Monvel. This lady was none other than the wife of Jacques Marie Boutet de Monvel, one of the factory's ephemeral partners. Monvel was famous for his comedies, which were performed by the King's standing troupe of actors, and for an historical novel *Frédégonde et Brunehaut* which was to be found 'at the author's home, the porcelain salesroom in Rue du Petit Carrousel'. As the novel appeared in 1775 it is likely that this was the date when the warehouse on Rue Plâtrière was moved. The

inventory of April 18th 1775 mentions merely 'the salesroom in Paris', in the following year it is sited 'at Le Carrousel', and when Barrachin left the Faubourg Saint-Denis factory on June 18th 1776 he surrendered to the partners 'the two compacts concluded with Dame de Monvel in respect of the Carousel [*sic*] salesroom... three sales ledgers from that shop at Le Carousel, with entries until June 18th 1776'. On that very day Boutet de Monvel ceded to his co-partners his sub-lease of the third-floor rooms, and his shares. He then retired from the company. Nonetheless, Madame Boutet de Monvel went on managing the shop on the strength of agreements signed

212 Nast.
Plate. Sepia and pink.
Rebus (picture-puzzle) giving the motto: *A l'amour tout doit flechir* ('All must yield to Love'). Late 18th century.
Sèvres, Musée National de Céramique. Diam. 24 cm. (9²⁄₃ in.).
Mark 172.

213 Nast.
Clock in white and blue
biscuit, copied from
Wedgwood ware. Figure of
Urania. *Circa* 1800.
Boulogne-sur-Seine, private
coll. Ht. 44 cm. (17^1/$_5$ in.).
Unmarked.

Her resignation was accepted on August 19th 1776 and Monvel took his capital away to the new factory which was being prepared on Rue Thiroux. From his affair with Jeanne Marie Salvétat, Monvel had a daughter who became the celebrated Mademoiselle Mars.

The salesroom was moved a little further down the same street, to the junction of Rue de l'Echelle and Rue du Carrousel. The lease agreement was signed on October 29th and Houdeyer, the comptroller at the factory of the Comte d'Artois, became its manager. He was living there as early as 1777. This salesroom consisted of a shop and a back-shop together with living-quarters, the whole complex being attached to a house that belonged to Sieur Trémeau, embroiderer to the King. The annual rent was 1,500 *livres.* Houdeyer was posted there as a clerk, housed and salaried by the factory; but subsequently, after he had offered a security of 20,000 *livres,* a contract of July 24th 1778 changed the administrative structure. Houdeyer was thereafter in charge of the saleroom and warehouse, to receive porcelain exclusively from the factory. On behalf of the Faubourg Saint-Denis factory, Deleutre undertook firstly to grant him 'the privilege of being called a *maître fayencier* to save him embarrassment' and secondly, as an essential proviso, to 'supply the said depot and salesroom with assorted goods as best [he] can and to keep them constantly stocked, more particularly with soup tureens, dishes, plates, cups and other common items, both painted, gilded, in white and gold, and in plain white; and [he] promises lastly to attend to the execution of all orders which may be transmitted to him by Sieur Houdeyer'. As a matter of fact it was the Marquis de

with Barrachin, who also withdrew from the Faubourg Saint-Denis factory, whereupon his successor Chaussard revealed that Barrachin's agreement with her was too onerous and that she had refused alternative proposals. She did, however, offer to retire provided that her heating and lighting were paid until October.

La Salle who loaned Houdeyer the 20,000 *livres* of security.

This new administrative arrangement lasted less than a year. On April 13th 1779 the merchant haberdasher Charles Barthélemy Guy, residing in Rue Berthisy, succeeded him and La Salle granted him a nine-year lease. Guy collected 300 *livres* a year, plus a commission of fifteen per cent on the goods sold annually, for the first 15,000 *livres,* and twenty per cent on sales in excess. In return Guy was at liberty 'to conduct whatever trade he may see fit, be it in haberdashery, in jewellery, hosiery or anything else, provided that he does not in a way rearrange the decoration and the established order in the said salesroom'.When the inventory of April 30th 1779 was taken, the salesroom contained more than 32,000 *livres'* worth of goods. Finally La Salle surrendered it to Guy on August 20th 1780. Charles Barthélemy Guy, the son of a merchant haberdasher, had married in 1770 Geneviève Eulalie Santilly, the daughter of a merchant and burgher of Paris. Before moving on to Le Carrousel he had gone bankrupt after partnering a merchant haberdasher of London, one Harrison. They went into voluntary liquidation on March 7th 1774. Both of them gave power of attorney to an advocate at the Parlement, Jean-Baptiste Chaussard. Now, Chaussard had married Charles Barthélemy's sister, Marie Thérèse Guy, and two years later he actually became an overseer in the factory of the Faubourg Saint-Denis. Then, by taking over a portion of Boutet de Monvel's stock, he entered the partnership on June 18th 1776. Meanwhile, on October 4th 1777, Guy had once again wound up his business as a merchant haberdasher, this time in Rue Saint-Martin.

Guy, however, continued to keep the salesroom on his own account. He sold porcelain not only from the Faubourg Saint-Denis, but also from Clignancourt, Lemaire, Chevalier Frères Lefebvre, Pétry, Rue Thiroux and Perche. He also sold pipes back to the goldsmiths Biennais and Odiot. His ledger which begins in Year II is especially interesting. This was the year in which Charles Barthélemy Guy took his son Charles into his business as a wholesale and retail manufacturer, as stipulated in a contract of marriage with Marie Adélaïde Cahours. The object was that Charles should inherit his due share of his mother's estate, which was tied up in the capital of the business. The inventory following Madame Guy-Santilly's death was taken by Alexandre Moitte and Nicolas Pétry.

Slightly later, Guy went into partnership with Houzel in order to buy the factory in Rue Thiroux, on Pluviôse 30th, Year V. He died shortly afterwards, on Germinal 9th, Year VI. This time the post mortem inventory of the saleroom was taken by Jean Mathias Lortz, a porcelain manufacturer of Petite Rue Saint-Gilles, and Etienne Jean Louis Blancheron of 'Rue Crussoles'; while Moitte and Jean François Darte were responsible for the factory in Rue Thiroux. In the meantime Charles Guy Junior had gone into partnership with his cousin Brière, of Toulouse, to set up a salesroom in Madrid. Brière's disorderly ways led to considerable losses and a compromise settlement had to be offered to the creditors. Charles Guy departed for Madrid and his father, left in Paris, died while he was away. The banker Récamier, a creditor in Madrid, had the Paris establishment seized and the house in the Spanish capital closed down. The young Madame Guy, *née* Cahours,

214 Nast.
Cup supported by three
eagles. Gold on white.
Rouletted decoration.
Profile of Napoleon in
biscuit on matt-gold ground.
Circa 1810.
Sèvres, Musée National de
Céramique. Ht. 11 cm.
(4¹/₃ in.).
Marks 172 and 175.

was authorized to carry on the business.
On Fructidor 24th, Year VI the two sons
of Charles Barthélemy Guy, having
forsworn their father's estate to enforce
their claims to their mother's, which had
been sunk into the enterprise, put half
their father's factory on Rue Thiroux up
for sale. It was valued at 17,156 francs

33 centimes, but Houzel acquired it for
17, 350 francs.
The petitions of bankruptcy for the
partnerships respectively of Guy Senior &
Junior, and of Guy Junior & Brière were
filed on Frimaire 28th, Year VIII.
Le Petit Carrousel, then, was just a salesroom. Initially it was exclusively wares

from the Faubourg Saint-Denis that were sold there, but as soon as Guy assumed responsibility for the shop he reserved himself the right of using it to sell whatever he saw fit. From 1789 onwards, long before he purchased the factory in Rue Thiroux, Guy was its sales agent, and we have seen that his *Journal* between 1791 and 1793 lists business ties with many Parisian factories, some of them well known and others obscure. In this document, one entry deserves particular attention: it refers to an important payment of 30,000 *livres* to 'Perche, our manufacturer'. Moreover, Perche was receiving monthly payments. Does this mean that Le Petit Carrousel had a contract with that mysterious character Perche? We only know some later porcelain wares of his marked with the fish of that name in underglaze blue or green; or else his name spelt out in full and stencilled on in red. Usually these marks are accompanied by

Ill. 230
Ill. 37
Ill. 229

those of a decorator or dealer—Lachassaigne's or Schoelcher's. A mark is also found on a sugar bowl from the Foëscy factory. Chavagnac and Grollier recorded a mark painted on in cursives: *Perche, Petit Carousel, à Paris*.

Strictly speaking, then, no wares may be called characteristic of Le Petit Carrousel. Nonetheless, some pieces are particularly meticulous in design: this is shown by a finish that points to a luxurious taste. For example, a teapot-handle bears *trompe-l'œil* studs, a dense diaper of delicate leaves

Ill. 236

in a lovely, lustrous gold, and a fine border, likewise gilded. Witness also a sepia rosette spread right across the bot-

Ill. 237

tom of a plate or saucer—gay colours and elegant shapes.

In the inventories drawn up after the death in Year VI of Charles Barthélemy Guy many toilet items and ornamental

pieces may be found. We have picked out a large number of bowls with different decorations: with cornflowers, roses, golden dots★; with green or yellow grounds, figures, ornate panels, a crown of roses and arabesques, trophies, etc. Ordinary pieces are also listed, (plates, dishes, soup tureens, and *compote* bowls), but so are many individual cups. There are breakfast sets with *cailloux* (pebbled ground) or a buff ground, with Greek fret, or a yellow ground adorned with bouquets and arabesques, with gilt ground, or with decorations of birds. The vases are ovoid, 'dolphin' or 'Medici'. Flower tubs, trumpet vases and *pots-pourris* are recorded as well, along with

215 Nast.
Cylindrical cup and saucer. Blue scarabs and gold-painted hieroglyphics on a beige or brown ground. *Circa* 1810.
Musée National de La Malmaison. Ht. 6 cm. (2²/₅ in.). Mark 173.

★Ill. 235

Ill. 233

216 Nast.
Medici vase. Chrome green, the high-temperature decoration used here as the ground-colour, was invented in 1802 by the chemist Vauquelin – some say for Sèvres, others say for his friend Nast. Chrome green was used on the most sumptuous pieces, more particularly (at Sèvres) on the Emperor's personal service. It was of course one of the most costly colours. Nast's craftsmanship is displayed in the reserves, notably the simulated gadroons on the belly, and by the application of a particularly subtle pink.
Circa 1810.
Paris, private coll.
Ht. 35 cm. (13²⁄₅ in.).
Mark 173.

lozenge-shaped writing sets and yellow-ground sconces. Other objects absolutely typify the 'little gift'—snuff boxes, pipes, tobacco jars and tea caddies.

The most frequently mentioned decorations are coloured grounds, either green, yellow, pink, black or gold. The objects' only embellishment is this coloured ground edged with a delicate gilt border in reserve. The commonest painted decorations are grisaille (for flowers) and figures, rose wreaths, cornflowers, butterflies, gold dots, and Greek frets. We might add the polychrome decorations in vertical panels, ribbons and lozenges.

The marks used by Le Petit Carrousel are as follows: originally the letters CPG which may be interpreted as the combined initials of Charles Philippe (Comte d'Artois) and of Guy. These three letters are normally accompanied by another mark: *Manufacture du Petit Carousel, Paris,* either spelt out in full or abbreviated. It is stencilled in red or painted in gold. Any items bearing these marks are therefore datable to between 1779 and approxi-

mately 1790. It is a reasonable assumption that pieces marked solely with the name of the salesroom, without the initials CPG, were sold during the Revolutionary period, but this remains unconfirmed. Finally, we have encountered some exceptional marks. The oldest ones are: the crowned CP of the Faubourg Saint-Denis accompanying the initials CPG; the crowned A of the Queen's factory with *Manufacture du Petit Carousel;* next, a mark in the name of Guy, *Petit Carousel à Paris;* and lastly the abovementioned mark of Perche with the address: *Petit Carousel Paris.*

PÉTRY AND RONSSE

Two manufacturers, Nicolas and Pierre Romain Joseph Pétry, whose exact kinship is unknown to us, are among the Paris porcelain makers.

Nicolas Pétry had been a thrower at the Queen's factory in 1778 but had actually become a manufacturer by 1793, on a site at the bottom of Rue de Belleville. According to a document of Year IV he

217 Nast.
Second part of the factory's plaque of sample-patterns illustrated page 282.

produced 'English-style porcelain and faience'. When his two partners seemed to be 'losing interest', he applied in Year IV to the Ministry of the Interior for assistance. It was refused, even though he had offered to repay them 'in supplies of faience for the alms-houses'.

Julien's report (1798) locates this factory at 'Ménil-Montant'. A list of factories dated 1815 sites it at the 'Butte de Belleville' and specifies that 'Pétry and Guy have stopped [production], after incurring losses'. We have no further information.

Pierre Romain Joseph Pétry and Jean Joseph Ronsse had first gone into partnership as bankers in 1829, but concluded a new partnership in 1836. The company, still styled 'Pétry & Ronsse' was to 'manufacture, buy and sell both plain and decorated porcelain'. The headquarters were at 11, Rue Vendôme in Paris whereas the factory was at Vierzon. Founded in 1815, this Vierzon factory had been bought up in 1829 by Pétry and Ronsse. A further deed of partnership was signed on December 31st 1842 by the same parties, who were joined by Pierre Adolphe Hache Pétry. The headquarters were now at 26, Rue des Petites-Ecuries, Paris. This company was dissolved in 1845, but was taken over jointly by the Hache family and Pépin-Lehalleur.

By 1836 the factory was employing a labour force of three hundred, and by 1844 the figure had risen to five hundred at Vierzon, plus one hundred decorators in Paris. The decoration was carried out at Paris and the yearly output was estimated at 850,000 francs plus 50,000 francs' worth of exports. The company won a silver medal in 1844 for the low prices and sound quality of its products. These products consisted of table services, *cabarets,* baskets, vases, holy-water stoups, sconces, etc.

We do not know of any mark associated with this factory as managed by Pétry & Ronsse.

POTTER NEPPEL DENUELLE

In 1789 M. de Tolozan made representations to the Council of Commerce 'that Sieur Potter, an English gentleman, requests an exclusive seven-year concession in order to set up a factory in France for painting and transfer printing on glass, porcelain and faience'. After deliberation it was decided 'that if Sieur Potter wishes to carry out his techniques of transfer printing and of applying designs onto glass, we shall see what can be done'. A favourable report from Berthollet and Desmarets of July 22nd 1789 failed to secure for him the desired privilege, for the National Assembly had first to pronounce its verdict on exclusive privileges. On June 18th the Mayor of Paris, Bailly, endorsed Potter's application in the presence of the President of the National Assembly, but Glot, the administrator of the Département of Paris, holding power of attorney from the manufacturers of porcelain and faience throughout the country, made some virulently unfavourable remarks about Potter to the *députés*. He contested his plans, particularly the setting up of a factory which was to employ a work force of five hundred.

It seems, then, that the privilege was not granted, but the factory nonetheless operated for a few years and was known as the 'Factory of the Prince of Wales'. Chavagnac owned some token-money dated 1792 which this factory, standing in Rue de Crussol, had issued. In the same year Christopher Potter bought the factory at Chantilly from Antheaume de Surval, and went on to found other centres at Forges and Montereau. In 1802 he took out a patent to have his transfer-printing techniques officially recognized and won a gold medal for his faience ware from Montereau. In 1805 he was to 'crash' spectacularly in Chantilly.

But let us return to Paris, when Julien's report gave Blancheron's address as Rue de Crussol (1798). Blancheron did not stay there long and moved to Rue des Trois Bornes in Year VI (see p.212).

In 1804 the *Almanach du Commerce* cites the name of Constant as the factory manager in Rue de Crussol. The porcelain works then passed into the ownership of Pierre Neppel who won an honourable mention at the exhibition of 1806, and took out a patent on a method of underglaze transfer printing in 1809. By then he was employing between one hundred and fifty and two hundred men.

On April 16th 1816 Neppel purchased the former glass bottle house at Nevers and set up a porcelain factory which he managed on his own until 1834. Thereafter his son Louis and son-in-law Louis Guérin assisted him. In 1839 the annual output reached a value of 160,000 francs and was composed of plain porcelain, fire-proof porcelain and bricks. His Paris warehouse was at 34, Rue de l'Echiquier. As for the factory on Rue de Crussol it had been taken over by Benjamin Cadet de Vaux and Dominique Denuelle who in 1819 won a silver medal for some superb shapes, meticulous execution and, above all, 'a matt gilding which has arrested the attention of connoisseurs'. They wound up their business on September 1st 1819 and their partnership was dissolved in 1820. Denuelle took part in the exhibition of 1823 by himself. His

most notable exhibits bore tortoise-shell grounds, and a bust of the Duchesse de Berry to whom he was a supplier by special appointment. He was awarded a bronze medal. In the same year Denuelle bought the factory at La Seynie from Dagoty.

In 1834 the jury ruled that Denuelle's porcelain was not of a high standard. From 1834 till 1848 he had his business at 18, Boulevard Saint-Denis and bore the title of supplier to the Queen. From 1849 to 1852 he ceases to appear in the *Almanach du Commerce* except as a maker of porcelain bodies and enamels, at 39 bis, Rue des Petites-Ecuries.

Potter's mark usually consists of his name *Potter* or *Ch. Potter* or again *Potter à Paris*. The surname is often accompanied by letter B and a number which possibly indicates a given shape, as was the case with Strassburg ceramics, but not in so precise a manner, it would seem. This mark is generally painted in underglaze blue, but it may be painted in red or gold. On a handleless cup decorated with butterflies we have the mark in underglaze blue: *B Potter 42,* whereas the matching saucer is signed with the initials EB, for Blancheron.

Potter's porcelain is of decent quality. We know of hand-painted service pieces Ill. 239 adorned with flowers, ribbons, butterflies, Ill. 238, 239 landscapes, cupids, *trompe-l'œil* motifs, etc. Neppel used to mark his name in full, either painted in gold or stencilled in red. His products include table services, normally bearing transfer-printed decora- Ill. 228 tion.

Denuelle spelt out his signature as well. His early—and much prized—wares were followed by pieces which, except for his tortoiseshell grounds, were second-rate. He manufactured principally table

218 Nast.
Pot-pourri. The knob is in the
form of Janus. Gold on
purple ground. *Circa* 1810.
Paris, Private coll.
Ht. 28 cm. (11 in.).
Mark 173.

services, tea- or coffee-sets, and ornamental items. In 1834 he exhibited some 'Etruscan' vases.

RIHOUËT

Louis Marie François Rihouët set himself up at Paris in 1818, at 49, Rue de l'Arbre Sec—a street in which a number of dealers and decorators of porcelain were already established. He was born in 1791 at Perrier (Manche), into a family which was in the service of the Duc d'Orléans; one of his uncles was the steward *(administrateur général)* to the dowager Duchesse d'Orléans. He himself had been enfranchised since 1818, implying that he received the requisite income from his land. Already specially appointed to the Duc d'Orléans he was awarded the title of faience maker to the King in 1824.

Once success had come his way, Rihouët moved shop in about 1830 to 7, Rue de la Paix, where he sold crystal glass as well. He went into partnership in around 1856 with Lerosey who succeeded him and was still working in 1900. By 1867 Lerosey was exhibiting porcelain from Margaine Frères.

Ill. 240
The porcelain wares sold by Rihouët are mostly table services and tea- or coffee-sets. They are carefully made. Besides the pieces merely bearing a monogram, coats of arms or just a decorative border on a coloured ground, there is an important dessert service showing polychrome views of Philadelphia, taken from American Ill. 241 painters and engravers of the first half of the 19th century.

Rihouët's mark consists of his name in full, sometimes with the address, painted in red or gold. A stencilled mark is also found, proclaiming his title of supplier to the King.

ROUSSEAU

In 1838 Francisque Rousseau opened up a decorating- and gilding-workshop at 108, Rue de Ménilmontant, where he also sold colours.

The very next year he won a silver medal for wares decorated with a number of magnificent coloured grounds fired at medium temperature, and for some exquisite gilding. He boasted that he could imitate English porcelain, notably the very fine sheen of their colours. His company funds now stood at 70,000 francs; he was employing nineteen craftsmen on the actual premises and fifteen 'outside'.

He moved his workshops and salesrooms to 49, Boulevard Saint-Martin and 54, Rue Meslay in about 1844, when he also won a gold medal for 'his very hard-wearing and inexpensive gilt ornaments in relief; his gilding on both plain and coloured body or glaze in relief; and his economical and durable gilding of ornamental components'. The number of men in his workshops had risen to twenty-five, but only ten were left 'outside'. The report-drafter for the exhibition recorded that he had been stocking 'the whole of Europe with colours' for five years. Shortly afterwards he invented a 'new silvering for use on porcelain, which is genuinely untarnishable, imitating the high lustre of silverware without ever turning black'. He became supplier to the King in 1847.

Various items decorated by Francisque Rousseau are to be found in the Musée national de Céramique de Sèvres. In particular there is a porcelain vase from Sèvres which Rousseau has embellished with bunches of gilded grapes and red, white and turquoise beading on a green Ill. 243 ground.

Simultaneously, the *Almanach du Commerce* from 1831 to 1839 listed an A. Rousseau of 77, Rue des Fossés du Temple, who became Rousseau et Cie in 1840. He, too, was renowned for his gilding and his 'high-temperature muffle-fired grounds'. He set himself up in business at 19, Rue Pierrelevée, in about 1850. Lastly, a third Rousseau was recorded at 43, Rue Coquillière.

SOUROUX
Souroux registered his mark on June 23rd 1773. Buhot's report (1774) claims that this factory 'is very old as a faience works, the output of which he has reduced, thereafter using porcelain to make his three-dimensional items, which had either a biscuit or a glazed finish'. The decree of 1784 was communicated to him at his address in Rue de la Roquette. A schedule of factories in 1815 stated that Souroux had pulled down his works and yet was appointing a successor, Olivier, who is said to have surrendered the business to Pétry after incurring losses.

The Souroux mark is an S. We know of few pieces from this factory.

TINET
Pierre Charles Tinet kept a salesroom for porcelain and crystal glass, at 29, 32 or 38,

219 Despréz.
Biscuit cameo set into cut crystal-glass ('sulphide').
Portrait of the Duc de Berry.
Circa 1820.
Paris, private coll.
Diam. 7.5 cm. (3 in.).
Mark 97.

Rue du Bac, its sign-board reading 'Désespoir de Jocrisse' ('Hen-Pecked Husband's Despair'). Chavagnac and Grollier think that he had settled there in about 1815. The heading on their invoice gave the date 1824.

In 1839 he exhibited some 'imitations of old China ware and old Sèvres, crystal glass and a new patented type of stopper'. His company funds were put at 100,000 to 150,000 francs, and he was employing six craftsmen in his workshop and twenty-five outside.

Also in 1839 Tinet set up a factory at Montreuil (Seine) where, by 1844, he had two kilns and a labour force of sixty, plus twenty more outside. The value of his annual output at that time stood at 150,000 francs, half of it in exports.

As from 1845 he had a second salesroom at 6, Rue d'Enghien. Both the Montreuil and Rue du Bac branches of his factory may be traced until 1873.

Several marks of Tinet's are known; some give his name and address in full, in varying scripts, whilst others have been ascribed to him by Chavagnac and Grollier. These consist firstly of four crossed swords which are easily confused with the ones which Jacob Petit used, and secondly of counterfeited Far-Eastern marks, found on pseudo-Chinese or -Japanese items.

Tinet made good imitations of Sèvres, Meissen, Chinese and Japanese ware. Besides the service pieces, some glazed statuettes of his are known; they resemble Jacob Petit's work and are influenced by the previous century.

Ill. 242

VION

August Victor Vion founded a decorators' workshop at 12, Faubourg Saint-Denis in 1818. Some time after 1831 he moved it to 10, Impasse de la Pompe. This cul-de-sac was entered from Rue de Bondy, between numbers 80 and 83. He was still there in 1850.

He exhibited wares in 1839, when he stated that he employed a labour force of twenty actually in his establishment, with another ten working outside. He again displayed objects in 1844 and specified that his yearly output was worth 50,000 francs, including 10,000 francs' worth of exports. Together with Baury, Vion took over Gille's factory.

The mark which should probably be attributed to him is the anchor, as affixed to a tall biscuit statuette, the *Cruche cassée* which is kept in the Musée du Conservatoire national des Arts et Métiers in Paris.

The above notes concerning the factories and decorating workshops are not exhaustive, which would occasionally be irksome. They have been selected according to historical interest or the production of these factories. It is particularly interesting to see porcelain techniques being used in little-known forms, such as, for instance, the incrustations of porcelain cameos in blocks of cut glass (see Ill. 219), or again, the much neglected industrial production of buttons and of religious objects.

The repertory of factories, decorating workshops and store-houses at the end of this book gives a longer list of these establishments as well as a large selection of the marks in use between 1770 and 1850, in production and decoration.

TRADE

The expansion of trade in Paris during the 18th century was promoted by a thriving consumer market and by a huge influx of capital.

The market for luxury goods, and notably for porcelain had—despite its earlier depression—become remarkably buoyant in Paris: the factory managers who had no trouble in finding locally available funds for running their businesses, also had a ready-made outlet to an enormous and wealthy clientele.

Before the end of the *Ancien Régime* and in spite of regulations that tended to restrict manufacture, the Paris region was one of the most important, if not the leading, centre for the production and sale of porcelain in France.

But the Revolution was going to deal a very severe blow to this flourishing trade. The political and economic upheavals which it brought in its wake, and above all the almost total disappearance of the moneyed customers, had disastrous repercussions on the factories, which wellnigh closed down altogether.

Nonetheless, once the turmoil was over, a new clientele soon came forward. The trade in porcelain now benefitted from such clients and underwent a revival which was only accelerated by the fact that the creation of new establishments was favoured both by the abolition of privileges and by a new influx of capital.[1]

Several of the older factories had withstood their trials quite well. This was so for Guérhard & Dihl, whose business, according to a memorandum of Year V, 'has soared to become, by virtue of its beautiful artefacts, the rival of Sèvres itself, to which factory it is now superior in terms of the volume of its sales'. In that same year Madame Guérhard gave her daughter a dowry of 130,000 francs in 'metallic tender'—a considerable amount for that period.

Parisian trade, which had already been making a perceptible recovery during the Directory, rose to a new level in 1802 thanks to the Peace treaty of Amiens which brought about a resumption of commerce on an international scale.

This is not the place to recapitulate the historical and economic events—notably the eruption of several crises under the Empire—with which we have already dealt above (cf. p. 86), but it should be emphasized that these crises came as a heavy blow to improvident industrialists. For it is not enough for a porcelain factory to have good moulds, excellent models and competent craftsmen; it also needs a strong financial structure, otherwise it cannot withstand the economic backlash from certain political events and finds itself driven into bankruptcy, as has previously been demonstrated.

In 1801 the regional military commanders were instructed to carry out investigations, and the *préfets* (administrators of

[1] We should specifically mention the re-emergence in 1797 of the 'Caisse des comptes courants', later (in 1800) to become the Bank of France. It concentrated its activities in Paris, thus offering facilities that were available nowhere else.

the Départements) had the task of answering the economic questions. General Lacuée, the commander of Paris, and Frochot, the Préfet de la Seine, supply us with invaluable information.

After analysing the situation over the previous years (the discredit of the promissory notes, the Terror driving away capital investment, the war hampering exports and depressing inland consumption, and the workers rising in revolt), the observers recorded a resurgence of commercial activity after Brumaire 18th.

The *préfet* Frochot in 1801 discerned three sectors in Parisian trade:

a) Inland business, stimulated by Parisians and travellers coming to Paris.

b) Trafficking between Paris and the Départements.

c) Exports.

These headings will serve as a schema for the eighty years studied in this book.

1 Parisian Trade

The Parisian porcelain factories mainly worked to order. They had their models for shapes and decorations, but the customer assembled his service from whatever items he wished. He could even commission 'replacers' for Sèvres, Meissen and other services, particularly if they were in common production.

In the 18th century the clients of the privileged factories were their main patrons, followed by the courtiers. In their wake they brought a large number of buyers, who were attracted as much by the princely liveries of the porters as by the quality of the porcelain. It was sometimes difficult to extract payment; Denuelle had to commence legal proceedings against the Marquis de Louvois before his outstanding debts were paid off.

But the customers also included tradesmen, in particular the *limonadiers* and perfumers who were concerned with the appearance of the porcelain wares used in their business. There was additionally a traffic between manufacturers and dealers: the merchant faience maker Duban resold porcelain from many factories, even from those which had their own salesrooms or depots. The merchant haberdashers ('Le Petit Dunkerque', for example), also made regular sales of porcelain from various sources, even occasionally commissioning exclusive decorations, and generally served as middle-men between customer and manufacturer. Finally, trade between white ware makers and decorators, principally in the 19th century, greatly expanded even before the factories had moved out into the provinces; by 1819 Legort, a painter and gilder on porcelain, was exhibiting two vases from Lefebvre's workshops, which he had painted with landscapes. By 1834 Discry was the official supplier to the decorators Perdu and Parcheminier; and as for Chapelle, he decorated nothing but Jacob Petit's wares. In addition, there were many professional bodies regularly buying porcelain; the goldsmiths and bronze-founders mounted vases; the inlay-workers used porcelain trimming on their travelling cases *(nécessaires:)*; the cabinet makers set plaques and medallions into their most exquisite pieces of furniture and clock makers fitted the porcelain clock cases with works or perhaps put in Nast's porcelain dial-plates. The picture framers and glass blowers also dealt with the porcelain makers. When, in the inventory taken after Nast's death (1817), we survey the whole range of his products —from labels for liqueur bottles, via the most standard items, to curtain pulls and

Ill. 114

Ill. 196

Ill. 74

Ill. 103
Ill. 104

Ill. 76, 213

220 Nast.

Teapot. Gold on purple ground. This object unites all the elements that go to produce a sumptuous effect: the shape is enriched with moulded or modelled devices representing the sum total of Restoration craftsmanship: a lyre, winged lions, lion's paws, etc. The *fleurons* and palmettes arranged in bands are rouletted – a technique which Nast had patented in 1810. All these ornaments are coated in a bronze-like matt gold, to contrast with the painted decoration of lustrous gold on a purple ground. This piece, an example of Nast's luxury wares, belongs to the service of King Ferdinand VII and Queen Isabelle of Braganza, who were married in 1816 and whose initials F and I appear on all the items. Since Queen Isabelle died in 1818 the service cannot be dated with sufficient accuracy.

Madrid, Museo Arqueologico Nacional. Ht. 26 cm. (9⁴/₅ in.).

Mark 176.

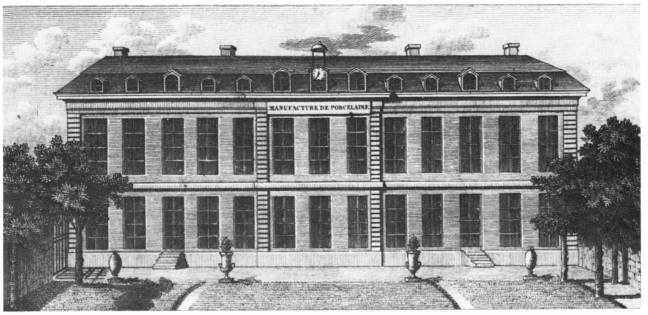

221 Honoré.
View of the factory,
50 Boulevard St. Antoine.
Circa 1820.
Paris, Archives Nationales.

thermometers—we are bewildered at the diversity of the intermediary customers. In any case, the porcelain manufacturers did not sell porcelain exclusively: Pouyat made his clay available, Clauss offered muffle kilns, Dihl his famous mastic and sagger-clay which came from his estate at Houdan.

The trade in colours was brisk. Dihl stocked his colleagues and decorators with them, but Desfossés, Mortelèque and Colville later turned this trade into an industry in its own right.

Paris attracted numerous travellers, many of them eager to educate themselves; for sundry reasons relating both to Art and Industry, many such people visited the factories and bought their wares.

The most frequented factory was Guérhard & Dihl. The Baronne d'Oberkirch, escorting the Comtesse du Nord[2] to Paris in 1782, was accompanied by the Duchesse de Bourbon. In his diary Governor Morris, a member of the colonial aristocracy and United States representative in Paris, noted down his visits to the 'factory of Angoulême' in 1789. He toured it with Madame de Flahaut and he bought porcelain with Washington in mind. 'We find that the porcelain here is more elegant and and cheaper than it is at Sèvres'. The next year he sent Washington a biscuit group of a woman in Antique style with cupids, for which he had paid around one hundred *louis*. We have already recounted the amusing visit of the Prince de Clary.

2 The traffic between Paris and the Départements.

Beginning back in the 18th century, the trade between Paris and the provinces expanded a great deal. The big factories of the *Ancien Régime* owned salesrooms and warehouses in the provinces; the Comte d'Artois' factory had set them up at Avignon, Marseilles, Caen, Bordeaux and Lyons, and organized public auctions at Orleans.

The exhibition of 1819 revealed the scale on which Parisian factories were emigrating into the provinces. As early as 1816 the Pouyats had set up their business

---

[2] Maria Feodorovna, wife of the future Paul I of Russia.

at Fours in the Nièvre district. Gradually, porcelain production in Paris petered out, and only decorators' workshops were left behind. Hence, white wares from the provinces flowed continuously towards Paris to be decorated. The companies kept warehouses in Paris and entitled them 'factories'. The real porcelain works, however, were mainly situated in regions that were rich in kaolin deposits—Limousin, Allier, Cher, Nièvre and Haute-Marne. The labour available there was less expensive than in the capital, but less skilled. Other factories and decorators were simply quartered in the suburbs and kept just a salesroom in Paris itself: Tinet, a manufacturer at Montreuil-sous-Bois, kept one salesroom on Rue du Bac and another Rue d'Enghien.

222 Nast.
Cup with flattened belly and saucer. Red, blue and gold.
Circa 1820.
Paris, private coll.
Ht. 7.5 cm. (3 in.).
Mark (type 173): *Nast à Paris.*

3 Exports

By the 19th century there was nothing new about exporting Paris porcelain. Under the *Ancien Régime* a two-way current of commerce, due in particular to a trade agreement, had sprung up between France and England. In 1787 the banker Perrégaux, as Josiah Wedgwood's representative, signed a contract with Dominique Daguerre, a merchant haberdasher in Rue Saint-Honoré: 'to sell in Paris, through the good offices of Monsieur Daguerre, the artefacts which are made daily in Sieur Wedgwood's factory'. The shipping costs to Rouen and Le Havre were defrayed by Wedgwood who, moreover, allowed Daguerre a twenty-percent commission. Contrariwise, Guérhard and Dihl signed a compact on March 31st 1789 with the Flight brothers of London, whereby they guaranteed them for six years an annual supply of porcelain to the minimum value of 50,000 *livres tournois,* carrying a twenty-percent commission. The Flights undertook not to sell any other French porcelain once their existing stocks had been exhausted.

It was similarly with a view to extending his business that Guy opened up a salesroom in Madrid affiliated to Le Petit Carrousel, in about 1793.

When the Hamburger Nemnich came to France in 1809 he noted in his diary that Spain and Russia purchased the most valuable wares produced by Parisian factories, adding that jammed or hampered communications with these countries had been causing a lot of embarrassment to the managers of these companies. One entry in his diary, incidentally, is rather amusing on the subject of Nast's factory, where Boizot had decorated two four-foot vases which simulated bronze so

which had been ordered from England and Russia.

Once peace and freedom had returned to the high seas, the Parisian porcelain makers starting exporting their wares outside Europe. In 1819 Flamen-Fleury dispatched his brother to the Levant in order to organize competition against Saxon and Austrian porcelain. He entrusted him with a 'complete collection of all the porcelain pieces for use by the Turks and Levantines', but 'the disastrous war between the Greeks and the Divan' cut off these new outlets. Flamen-Fleury's exports were not confined to the Near East; he boasted of receiving an order from the Government of Peking for 'a countless number of pieces dedicated to the four great religious ceremonies of these peoples'. Later, in 1844, Honoré was priding himself on being as well known in Constantinople as in Paris, having for thirty years been exporting to the Levant 'beautiful large-size jugs decorated with flowers, fruits★, emblems and painted or modelled birds; bardaks, [tumblers], surays, jahans and hookahs'. Marc Schoelcher, too, sent his son Jules off to the East, while in 1829 Victor went to Latin America and the United States. A report has come down to us which Clauss made in 1839 on the conditions under which export-business was transacted: 'It is the mercantile agents who establish and appreciate the extent of these markets through their connections. An agent having ties with, say, Spain, will buy the porcelain plain, have it decorated in accordance with the tastes of his consignees, and dispatch it; another agent will deal with England or Russia, yet another (and this has been the case with me) has items turned out for barter with China. It often happens that the wares

successfully that even experts were taken in; still more so were the Russian Customs officers who who let the articles in, despite the ban on French porcelain in Russia! We have already seen how Lefebvre had gone bankrupt as a result of enormous losses inflicted by the closure of the Spanish and Russian markets. The Imperial loans were in fact granted to exporters first and foremost. Dihl, Dagoty and Darte had been exporting to Russia regularly. When Dagoty applied for a loan he pointed out that in 1806 he had produced 350,000 francs' worth of merchandise, two-thirds of it for export, and Dihl complained of having 800,000 francs' worth of unsold goods on his hands,

224 Nast. ▶
Cylindrical cup and saucer.
Polychrome on black ground, and gold.
Early 19th century.
Paris, Musée des Arts Décoratifs. Ht. 6 cm. (2²/₅ in.). Mark 174.
Mark 174.

◀223 Nast.
Coffee-percolator (with drip-filter). Polychrome and gold. Paris, Musée des Arts Décoratifs. Ht. 35.5 cm. (13³/₅ in.).
Mark 174.

★Ill. 124

225 Nast. ▶
Cylindrical cup and saucer.
Tessellated (mosaic) pattern in blue and gold. Circa 1810.
Geneva, Musée de l'Ariana.
Ht. 6 cm. (2²/₅ in.).
Mark 174.

which are turned out are ordered in the market by agents: such goods are designed expressly for them and they secure exclusive rights to them, forbidding the sale or issue of any further specimens from the factory. They alone know the secret of the buyers for whom the goods are intended and they do not divulge this secret to anyone. Since the narrow range of present-day Parisian wares, reduced as it is to novelties, can justify neither the cost of freighting them abroad, nor the cost of the extremely varied decorations which foreign tastes call for, the result is that manufacturers rely on their agents for finding outlets for their factories.'

For the purpose of protecting French commercial interests, imports were subjected to regulations. An enquiry into the entry of foreign goods into France was conducted under the chairmanship of Duchatel, the Minister of Commerce in 1834. Brongniart, André and Honoré were questioned and the last two spoke mainly of their exports. André exported principally to the United States but not much to England or Belgium because of the excessive tariffs in those countries. Honoré adopted quite a severe attitude towards the importation of English porcelain: 'The English flood us with tea services of gilded, red and blue porcelain which is sold over here at between 72 and 80 francs but bought in England at between 25 and 30 shillings. Since then I have only been selling highly ornate services.' As for exports to America, Honoré stated: 'For three to four years I have been producing goods to designs which the Americans have been sending me and which resemble English designs.' He added that his prices were competitive with English prices and mentioned that he was also exporting wares to England, 'but only rich porcelain'. The services kept in the White House include, besides Nast's and Dagoty's which Governor Morris probably brought back, a service by Honoré with wide moulded designs, floral decoration and pale-green raised rims stamped with the coat of arms of the United States. It was commissioned in Ill. 139 1848 by President James Polk.

Let us now look at some figures dealing with both output and exports. Unfortunately their respective criteria vary widely and it is practically impossible to compare them.

According to Tolozan in 1788 the basic cost of producing porcelain and faience was 4 million *livres,* whereas for glass ware and mirrors it reached 6 millions. According to Chaptal the corresponding output in 1812 was given at 11 millions for porcelain and faience, whereas glass ware and mirrors stood at only 10. In that same year Chaptal stated that the thirty-five factories of France had a sales-turnover totalling 10 millions, the two hundred and fourteen faience and earthenware businesses were worth only 6,2 millions, while the ribbon trade with its one hundred and ninety-four premises realized a turnover of 9,2 millions.

Moreau de Jonnès in his *Tableau statistique du commerce* gives the following figures:

In 1823 porcelain exports rose to 3,816,000 francs. They moved up by 687,000, to 4,503,000 francs in 1824, while over the same two-year period exports of glass ware and mirrors had climbed to 3,127,000 and to 2,643,000 francs respectively.

In 1844 porcelain exports reached 9 millions before redoubling in 1851.

Some further statistics, notably the figures recorded in 1834 by the Ministry of Commerce, show the same rapid progress made by exports. Unfortunately they are expressed in kilograms of porcelain, which hardly enables us to correlate them with the other data. We shall exemplify this by giving a few figures to demonstrate that (despite minor ups and downs) the overall pattern of exports is an ascending one:

1816	373,131 kgs.
1819	559,406 kgs.
1825	603,751 kgs.
1829	835,525 kgs.
1833	904,574 kgs.

In the report on the 1827 exhibition Auguste Blanqui said that porcelain exports for 1826 were valued at 2,998,165 francs for 599,633 kgs. and imports at a mere 8,505 francs for 1,701 kgs.

By an order of January 11th 1829 the exported and imported porcelain wares had been valued at 5 francs per kilo as against 40 centimes for faience. By 1851 this unit price had gone up to 7 francs for porcelain but stayed at 40 centimes for faience.

305

The enquiry of 1834 moreover gives a few figures that enable us to draw comparisons—however fragmentary—in the international porcelain trade. For instance, the exportation of porcelain and earthenware from France to the United Kingdom reached 290,000 francs in 1831, then 220,000 in 1832 and 282,000 in 1833, although German exports to the United Kingdom during the same years were worth no more than 52,000, falling to 36,000 and finally rising to 38,000 francs. Still in the years 1831, 1832 and 1833, French imports of English pottery and porcelain had jumped from 20,000 to 43,000 and then to 48,000 francs. On the other hand British exports to the United States were fetching large sums of more than 6 millions in 1831 and 1832, dropping by a million in 1833 to give the figure of 5,541,525 francs.

If we take the year 1832, exports from France were going (in descending order of importance) to the United States, the Hanseatic towns, England, Portugal, Mexico and the French colonies.

Even in the foregoing decades one cannot overlook the fact that prices were being lowered, but by 1839 for example it was stated that the prices of common domestic porcelain had fallen by between twenty and twenty-five per cent since 1834. Decorated items, however, are not priced.

In 1860 the Paris Chamber of Commerce issued the following figures: the value of Paris porcelain exports alone totalled 5,500,000 francs of which 4,500,000 had been earned exclusively by the decorators, who had been exporting mainly to America (332,000 frs.), England (237,000), Russia (174,000), Germany, Switzerland and Spain. To demonstrate how big these export orders were, one needs to supply figures of the total output from Parisian porcelain works in the same year: 1,127,000 francs for the manufacturers and 5,373,000 for the decorators. Foreign demand eventually accounted for a considerable quantity of Paris porcelain wares. Some companies, indeed, hardly worked on anything but

228–228ᵃ Neppel.
Plate. Transfer-printed decoration consisting of a thick wreath of white roses shaded in beige or grey and with yellow centres, on a matt-gold ground studded with contrast-burnished dots. On the back we find, besides the manufacturer's mark, a

exports. This is borne out by particulars of the decorator Corbin, an exhibitor at the trade fair of 1844: out of a turnover of 200,000 he exported 180,000 francs' worth. Clauss recorded that he was working principally on commission, but this could refer to French as much as to foreign orders. It is interesting to note the

shield bearing the arms of
Portugal, surmounted by a
pelican as crest and accompanied by the motto *Pela leg,
Pela grey*. These armorial
bearings belong to the
Portuguese family of the
Counts of Louza. Around
the mid 19th century, the
threefold consideration of

discretion, identification and
thrift – since this method of
making did not necessitate
modifying the decoration
– caused many different
table-service items to display
their owner's mark in this
way. Such a mark may be
(as it is here) a coat of arms or
else a monogram combining

the initials of two families.
It is worth recalling that the
Sèvres services ordered at
about the same time by
Louis-Philippe for his
divers residences had the

name of each them stamped
on the back. *Circa* 1830.
Lisbon, Museu Nacional de
Arte Antiga. Diam. 24 cm.
(9²/₃ in.).
Mark 181.

figures which other exhibitors in 1844 had personally supplied for gauging the relative size of their exports.

Gille   100,000 francs' worth of exports against a turnover of 400,000 frs.
Lahoche   75,000   150,000 frs.
Mayer   30,000   60,000 frs.
Talmours   50,000   200,000 frs.
Tinet   75,000   150,000 frs.
Vion   10,000   50,000 frs.

Unfortunately we do not know the volume of André's exports, but his turnover had reached the huge total of a million francs by 1844.

By 1848 the turnovers realized by the manufacturers and the decorators of Paris porcelain totalled 559,500 and 4,392,100 francs respectively. These two figures doubled between 1850 and 1860.

Lastly, we should not ignore one other feature of Paris porcelain exports—white wares. We have seen how the English painter Billingsley decorated porcelain from La Courtille in London. Let us now take Belgium, for instance. There, Cretté decorated Potter's porcelain, and wares from Rue Thiroux and La Courtille; also, in the 19th century, Chapelle and Panneel or Jacquet and Nédonchelle used to buy Jacob Petit's white wares.

229 Perche.
Sugar-bowl with double lid, one of them perforated. In its undecorated state it comes from the *Foëscy* factory (André). Underglaze-blue decoration touched with red and gold. *Circa* 1835. Sèvres, Musée National de Céramique. Ht. 16 cm. (6³/₁₀ in.). Mark 1.

230   Perche/Lachassaigne.
Tall vase. 'Adoration of the
Shepherds', signed by
Lachassaigne. Its companion-
piece is decorated with the
'Adoration of the Magi'.
Circa 1830.
Geneva, Musée de l'Ariana.
Ht. 49 cm. (19³/₁₀ in.).
Mark 191.

PRICES

Obviously, porcelain prices varied with the period or with the object in question. Decoration could as much as centuple the price of a piece in its plain state.

In this connexion only fragmentary data is available for the time being. We must not, of course, judge by the estimated value of the confiscations which Sèvres inflicted upon the Parisian factories, nor by the values entered in the post mortem inventories or in written bankruptcy proceedings. These prices can only serve as points of comparison between the products in any one evaluation. We intend in this section to record only the retail prices.

In 1773 Pierre Antoine Hannong proclaimed in an advertisement published in the *Mercure de France* that the price of his porcelain was 'more or less the same as for Strassburg faience ware'. Now, Joseph Hannong would sell an undecorated plate for 9 *sols,* But the same item painted with India flowers was worth 13 *sols* 4 *deniers* and with high-quality painting 1 *livre* 10 *sols*. A teapot could cost up to 4 *livres*. When, on February 2nd 1779, the Marquis de Montesquiou bought four dozen plates 'with scattered bouquets' from Monsieur's factory they were invoiced at 48 *livres* per dozen and the matching monteiths at 60 *livres* a piece. In Year XI (1803) Schoelcher was asking 120 francs for a 'breakfast set of twelve cups and four larger pieces, decorated in gold'. Thanks firstly to the growing fashion for transfer printed creamware and secondly to new mechanical techniques of production and decoration, the price of plates in the early 19th century dropped a great deal and on a more impressive scale than other items. In the report on the exhibition of 1819, Costaz wrote that since 1806

Ill. 55

Ill. 21

231 Petit Charrousel. Cylindrical cup and saucer. Piped ribbon in green, brown and yellow. Gilded frieze. *Circa* 1790. Paris, private coll. Ht. 6.5 cm. (2³/₅ in.). Mark 196.

the labour costs for plates had sunk by twenty-five per cent, chiefly because kilns were being used more efficiently. He noted that a wholly hand-made plate cost 10 francs whereas Legros d'Anisy, adapting the lithographic technique to gilding, sold plates at one franc apiece. As we have seen, one of the preconditions of participation in industrial fairs was that the prices of the exhibits should be stated. Again in 1819 Legros d'Anisy was charging 30 francs for 'a dozen plates plus an oval soup-tureen and its tray, in blue-and-white porcelain that is much superior to Japanese ware'. Conversely, the Prince de Clary was amazed at the price of four *louis* for a cup at the Dihl & Guérhard works in 1809, although it seemed quite normal for that factory. When in 1815 Madame Jacquotot at Sèvres painted a cup bearing the portrait of Ninon de Lenclos, it was sold for 750 francs. But to return to commoner wares, in 1827 Baruch Weil exhibited a complete seventeen-piece breakfast set having a buff ground decorated with a 'rich border' in gold, for 42 francs. This was regarded as very inexpensive. The report on the exhibition also praised his 'opalescent cups at five francs [whose] small size is

certain to stimulate a heavy demand'. At this exhibition Honoré displayed two polygonal *cabarets:* one of them, at 195 francs, had a turquoise ground and white relief work in imitation of jasper ware, while the other, at 350 francs, had the same design and turquoise ground, but copied 'old Sèvres ware' in its decoration of 'sprays of assorted flowers'. The prices of his cups varied between 20 and 95 francs. Still at this trade fair, a dozen plates in Creil creamware were selling at 2 fr. 20, and in opaque porcelain with blue transfer printed decoration at 3,75. However, the comparable price of 'corn-flower' porcelain was between 10 and 12 francs, and from 13 to 15 for embellishment with green and gold streaks. The price of plates by Pétry & Ronsse ranged from 11 up to 100 francs per dozen. A further noteworthy feature is the price of Jacob Petit's white ware: a clock, likewise a pair of sconces, 250 francs; a breakfast cup, 10 francs and a teacup, Ill. 69 2 fr. 50 c. The prices of porcelain exports are equally interesting: Honoré, who won orders of between 10 and 15,000 cups at a time from the United States, had greatly reduced his prices: his teacups and saucers of American design were being sold at 65 francs per hundred in 1830 but at only 45 francs by 1834.

The cost of ornamental pieces was much higher since prices were fixed chiefly on the basis of decoration. The two blue-ground *vases hollandais* which the Comte d'Artois ordered from his factory in 1784 cost him 300 *livres* apiece. At the exhibition of 1819 Darte displayed 'two 22-inch high vases painted with coloured figures. Subjects: firstly the Holy Family, secondly multicoloured animals. Rich incised decoration of matt gold'. They were priced at 3,000 francs. Ill. 192

232 Nast.
Group in biscuit: 'Baccha-nalia.' The prototypal model for this group is attributed to Lemire, who worked mainly at Niderviller where he actually started a school of moulding and drawing in the porcelain- and cream-ware-factory, managed at that time by Lanfrey. Lemire distinguished him-seld principally through his neo-antique creations. The piece complementing this group is of Cupid and Psyche. Exemplars of both, repro-duced in biscuit at Nider-viller, are now kept at the Hermitage Museum, Leningrad.
Paris, Coll. Le Tallec.
Ht. 39 cm. (15²/₅ in.).
Mark 179.

INFLUENCES

The history of ceramics, and of porcelain in particular, is studded with discoveries, propagated by man and by the objects themselves, thus giving rise to further inventions or new refinements, against the background of a constant exchange of artistic ideas.

In this context we must emphasize the important role played by a work such as *Art de la Porcelaine* by the Comte de Milly, published in 1771. Guided by the desire to produce a comprehensive study he made a survey of the techniques being employed at the time, whose dissemination was promoted by its simultaneous appearance in French and German.

But the exchange of ideas was usually due to the ceaseless peregrinations of craftsmen such as we have already observed on several occasions, occurring not only within any one country but also from state to state. Alone or accompanied by their families the craftsmen and artists of ceramics would emigrate—sometimes for good—to another production centre. Such displacements were never very great, but it is nonetheless worth recording that after the factory at Niderviller had been shut down fifty or so of its craftsmen came to ask Dihl for work, and all were signed on.

It was thanks to these deserters that the techniques for making the first hard-paste porcelain in Europe, which was originally manufactured in Meissen a-lone, had found their way into France despite the jealous precautions taken to keep them secret. Moreover, it is not irrelevant to recall that Paul Hannong had conducted the earliest experiments (at Strassburg) using German kaolin. Following upon his successes a decree from the King's Council in 1752 had reserved for the Vincennes factory the exclusive privilege of producing 'porcelain wares of the same quality as those made in Saxony'. This had precipitated Paul Hannong's exile to Frankenthal.

It is Pierre Antoine Hannong, however, who takes the credit for the appearance of hard-paste porcelain in the Paris region. Under the pretence of manufacturing faience, Pierre Antoine set up two factories close to Paris, one at Vincennes and one at Vaux, and was not slow to test his methods for making porcelain. When in 1772 he and his passive associates signed the deed of partnership founding a porcelain factory in the Faubourg Saint-Denis, Paris, he immediately set about exploiting the secrets from Meissen and Frankenthal.

In addition to the methods and formulae of the Germans, Pierre Antoine Hannong introduced the style that characterized their porcelain ware. In the first inventories of the factory in the Faubourg Saint-Denis there are many entries of flat-ware items which are referred to as 'of Saxon shape', with an indented edge extending in ridges down the cavetto, in the Meissen style. Flowers, poultry  and insects are likewise in the tradition of Meissen and of German factories in general.

Other Parisian factories played upon their German origins. Locré, who was French but had lived and married at

ager, a Frenchman, specialized in matching up 'replacers' to Saxon porcelain. Hence the influence of Meissen upon early Parisian wares was overwhelming. This influence was subsequently eclipsed by Sèvres, but it later returns with added exuberance, in Jacob Petit's work. *Ill. 179* Other Eastern regions similarly had their

233 Petit Carrousel. Monteith. Polychrome and gold decoration in the style of Salembier, also called 'Greek fashion' *(à la grecque). Circa 1785.* Sèvres, Musée National de Céramique. L. 40 cm. (15³/₄ in.). Mark 196.

Leipzig, had a sign-board at La Courtille reading *Manufacture de porcelaine allemande* and as we have seen, Madame du Barry alluded to him as 'the man from the German factory'. Nor should we forget that Russinger, first Locré's partner and then his successor, hailed from Höchst. The Clignancourt factory whose man-

effect on Parisian porcelain makers. An early demonstration of this is the appearance of *trompe-l'œil* decorations, consisting of a monochrome print applied to an imitation wood ground. These decorations first found favour at Vienna and in the Strassburg and Niderviller factories of Eastern France. *Ill. 111*

Ill. 112

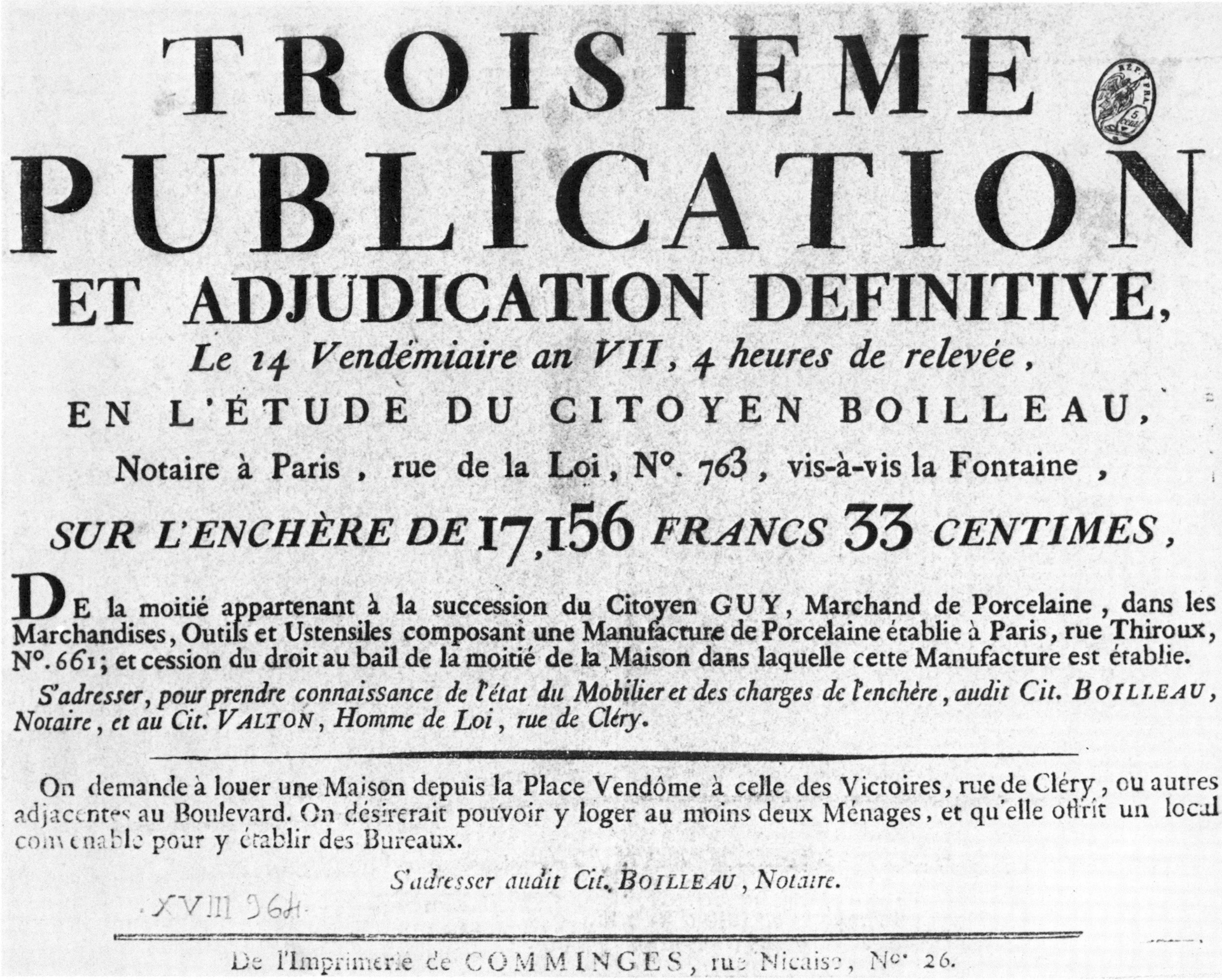

TROISIEME PUBLICATION

ET ADJUDICATION DEFINITIVE,

Le 14 Vendémiaire an VII, 4 heures de relevée,

EN L'ÉTUDE DU CITOYEN BOILLEAU,

Notaire à Paris, rue de la Loi, N°. 763, vis-à-vis la Fontaine,

SUR L'ENCHÈRE DE 17,156 FRANCS 33 CENTIMES,

DE la moitié appartenant à la succession du Citoyen GUY, Marchand de Porcelaine, dans les Marchandises, Outils et Ustensiles composant une Manufacture de Porcelaine établie à Paris, rue Thiroux, N°. 661; et cession du droit au bail de la moitié de la Maison dans laquelle cette Manufacture est établie.

S'adresser, pour prendre connaissance de l'état du Mobilier et des charges de l'enchère, audit Cit. BOILLEAU, Notaire, et au Cit. VALTON, Homme de Loi, rue de Cléry.

On demande à louer une Maison depuis la Place Vendôme à celle des Victoires, rue de Cléry, ou autres adjacentes au Boulevard. On désirerait pouvoir y loger au moins deux Ménages, et qu'elle offrît un local convenable pour y établir des Bureaux.

S'adresser audit Cit. BOILLEAU, Notaire.

XVIII 364

De l'Imprimerie de COMMINGES, rue Nicaise, N° 26.

Furthermore, Vienna was justly renowned for its colours and Julien's report states that 'Citizen Dihl makes colours following the methods of Z. Winger, Chemist of Vienna in Austria, the most learned who ever lived in those parts, judging by the manuscript which [Dihl] bought from his widow'. Finally, it was in Vienna once again that the lapidary wheel was first used in a porcelain factory, for erasing defects.

The influence of Berlin appears to have come later. In 1826 we detect it in the *forme Berlin* cups which are mentioned in the inventory taken after Pouyat-Duvignaud's death: they were probably cy-

234 Notification that half the porcelain-factory in Rue Thiroux, belonging to Guy's estate, is to be auctioned off on Vendémiaire 7th, Year VII. Paris, Archives Nationales.

314

235 Petit Carrousel. Water-jug and basin. Decoration of polychrome butterflies on patterns of gilt foliage. *Circa* 1790, Sèvres, Musée National de Céramique. Ht. 26 cm. (9⁴/₅ in.). Mark 196. By kind permission of the factory of the Petit Carousel, Paris.

lindrical, surmounted by a raised collar. Lastly let us recall that Cotteau, an enameller of clock dials at Geneva, imparted to the porcelain of the Faubourg Saint-Denis the influences both of Switzerland and of a technique related to enamelling.

Ill. 15

But France also sought inspiration else-where than in Eastern Europe. Like many other countries she was attracted by the originality of Wedgwood's jasper ware and copied it shamelessly. Desprez boasted of his imitations, and we know that as early as 1783 he had discovered the secret of the blue body. Nast, Guérhard and Dihl produced clock cases and vases

Ill. 213

closely resembling Wedgwood. Indeed, a wave of Anglomania was about to sweep across France under Louis XVI, and the porcelain group from the Faubourg Saint-Denis called *L'Anglais à Cheval* bears witness to this (1778). As we have observed, the Revolution failed to halt this trend: the inventory taken after Madame Russinger's death in Year VI lists '9 English [-style] breakfast sets with minute decoration'.

Moreover, Paris porcelain is indebted to England for two techniques: her coal-firing which had been put into operation ★Ill. 156 back in the 18th century and her transfer printing processes, in common use half a ★Ill. 112 century before the Parisian specialists registered their patents. It is also significant that an Englishman, Stone, belonged to the board which Legros d'Anisy set up to exploit his patent.

Finally, the reopening of the Continent to English trade caused English designs and Ill. 169 especially 'English tea services', to be speedily copied by a number of manufacturers such as Honoré and Jacob Petit, although the latter was also influenced by previous English products, notably Derby ware.

A separate mention must be accorded to the Oriental—and especially Chinese—influence which was continuously in evidence, though more or less prominently depending on the period. From the outset of porcelain making in Paris the most official documents such as the decrees from the King's Council refer to plain or blue-and-white Chinese porcelain, and the earliest products of the Faubourg Saint-Denis are clumsy copies of Far-Eastern porcelain. Decorations *au* Ill. 5 *chinois,* which actually are more akin to lacquer-work than to porcelain, were particularly esteemed from Louis XV's

reign until the Restoration. One decoration, with fairly large figures surrounded by vegetation and Oriental architecture is painted in blue and gold with touches of red. It was employed at Clignancourt as early as 1780 or thereabouts, but recurs in about 1830 on a bulb vase of Jacob Petit's which Schoelcher decorated, and on a double-lidded sugar bowl bearing the marks of Perche and Foëscy. These decorations, which became classics, are half-way between an almost perfect copy of China ware (witness the celadon-ground vase by Discry★), and a taste that relishes the exotic aura of the bazaar. A flowerpot cover by Cassé-Maillard is an amusing illustration of this★

Ill. 130

Ill. 63

Ill. 42

Ill. 229

236 Petit Carrousel. Cylindrical teapot. Diaper of fine gold foliage. *Circa* 1790. Paris, Coll. Guy Passerat. Ht. 11.5 cm. (4½ in.). Mark 196.

237 Petit Carrousel.
Cylindrical cup and saucer.
Cupid and attributes in
grisaille overhung by canopy
with pink swags of drapery.
Chains of roses painted from
life on golds bands.
Circa 1785.
Paris, Coll. Guy Passerat.
Ht. 6.5 cm. (2¹/₂ in.).
Mark 195.

But foreign influences were not the only ones affecting porcelain manufacture in Paris. By virtue of its proximity to the capital and the fame which it was enjoying at the time, Sèvres stood as a paragon which was eagerly emulated. It must indeed be acknowledged that Paris porcelain made its fortune by plundering Sèvres.

Although protected in the 18th century by strict regulations, the royal factory had nonetheless to endure the defection of its craftsmen, the theft of its techniques, raw materials and models, and even the illicit use of its equipment. The members of the royal family had no qualms about asking their private factories to supply replace-ments for Sèvres porcelain sets. Perhaps it is even permissible to speculate that the Princes, who forwarded only trifling commissions to Sèvres, were merely buying samples from the royal factory in order to have them made up by the factories upon which they had conferred their patronage.[1] The Comte d'Artois' order from the Faubourg Saint-Denis in 1784 endorses this hypothesis. Ill. 14

At the end of the *Ancien Régime* the royal factory was tottering under the double impact of the 1787 decree, granting the privileged factories almost complete free-dom of manufacture, and of its own grave crisis. Sèvres' radiating influence faded very appreciably.

[1] VERLET, Pierre. 'Sèvres, le XVIIIᵉ siècle'.

317

By the time that Alexandre Brongniart had been appointed manager of Sèvres in 1800, the factory's plight was desperate. Fortunately his clever administration gained him the support of successive monarchs and he stayed at his post through forty-seven years until he died. Brongniart's role as the head of the Sèvres factory was not just that of a manager. He also succeeded in winning the confidence of the private companies and in organizing exchanges with them which benefitted all parties concerned. Not one of the phases of manufacture was left untouched.

All the factory owners had been awaiting the appointment of the new administrator and in 1800 Deruelle Junior wrote to him denouncing the 'old habits' of the Sèvres workers who handed down their craft from father to son: 'Every craftsman, thinking himself famous in his art, did not and would not compare his wares with the best that the factories of Paris were ceaselessly turning out'.

'When the trainee craftsman from Sèvres entered a Paris factory he was forced to rid himself of the routine ways of his workshops and was obliged to undergo a sort of apprenticeship in order to acquire a skill quickly. Once he was more skilled he could not be persuaded to return to his former work…' Deruelle insisted once again on the superiority of the Parisian

238 Potter.
Handleless cup and saucer. Grisaille, mauve and gold. Cupid. as a painter and as a musician. Late 18th century.
London, British Museum. Ht. 6.5 cm. (2¹/₂ in.). Mark 205.

factories, adding further on: 'One observes in Paris porcelain a whiteness and transparency which Sèvres ware definitely lacks: the reason is that the habits of the chemists preparing the porcelain body at Sèvres obstruct its refinement. They claim that their porcelain is the best of all by virtue of being harder to fire, and that Paris hard paste buckles and warps at Sèvres' kiln temperatures…'[2]

Brongniart, displaying his customary objectivity, did not hesitate to have experiments conducted in various private factories. Probably as a result of Deruelle Junior's memorandum, he had Sèvres wares fired in the kiln at Lefebvre's factory and vice versa. In his *Traité des arts céramiques,* incidentally, he often refers to experiments of this kind and reproduces the structural plans of one of Dihl's kilns. In 1834 he had the kilns at Sèvres modified in the light of tests by Darte and Discry. However, he could not convince himself of the advantages of the coal firing which the Faubourg Saint-Denis had been using successfully as far back as 1783, and it was not before his death that it was first adopted at Sèvres, in 1849.

The instances of co-operation between Sèvres and Paris through the first half of the 19th century are frequent, with Brongniart proving himself a first-rate collaborator.[3] The manufacturers appealed to him to intervene with the Government over some awkward questions. For example Dagoty in 1802 complained to Brongniart about the work of outside craftsmen who were decorating his white ware, and he asked him to take steps towards rectifying matters.

For his part, Brongniart did not hesitate to ask Dihl for some sagger-clay which the latter mined on his lands at Houdan (1802), and when later he ran out of

239 Potter.
Square bowl. Polychrome and gold. Yellow ribbon.
Late 18th century.
Paris, Coll. Guy Passerat.
L. 20 cm. (7^9/$_{10}$ in.).
Mark 204.

cobalt he ordered it first from Darte Frères, then from Neppel. Neppel took the opportunity to remind him that one of his throwers who had signed on at Sèvres owed him money (1813).

Other manufacturers brazenly turned to Brongniart for the secrets of which they were ignorant; Dagoty begged him to divulge the method of producing a 'mazarine blue [*gros bleu*] in the muffle' which was being used in Vienna: 'I have been assured that you are familiar with their method.' In exchange he offered him high-quality clay from his mine at Saint-Yrieix (1807). Similarly, Louis André asked Brongniart to lend him the small testing-kiln at Sèvres so that he

[2] Archives de la Manufacture nationale de Sèvres, N1.
[3] PRÉAU, Tamara. *Alexandre Brongniart et les Porcelainiers parisiens, (1800–1847)'. Cahiers de la Céramique… N° 46/47.

could fire a couple of batches of grounds at a medium temperature. This wish was granted (1842). Extending the spirit of co-operation still further, Brongniart even sent Honoré one design for a plate-jigger and another for the two-tiered kiln recently constructed at Sèvres which he further invited him to watch in operation (1843).

Honoré (1841), Talmours & Hurel (1843) and Jacob Petit (1844) had no qualms about asking for drawings and even for old moulds of Sèvres wares, and they were gratified. It was, indeed, the period in which Parisian decorators were returning to earlier fashions and in particular to the Louis Quinze style. Although Sèvres was copied once more in the mid-19th century, it was not so much for her contemporary products (which were actually rather belittled, despite their technical perfection), as for the art facts which had brought her to fame. Thus, many dealers and decorators boasted of specializing in 'old Sèvres'. Furthermore, Sèvres' sales-ledgers disclose that the manufacturers of Paris did not hesitate to buy up her white wares and even her rejects in order to have the chance of decorating them—witness Honoré in 1824, Legros d'Anisy in 1834, Rihouët in 1842 and Lahoche ('Escalier de Cristal') in 1843. Finally Brongniart decided to organize some big sales of Sèvres stock, including white ware, which delighted the hearts of Parisian decorators.

Sèvres and Paris, then, are tightly interwoven, which does not mean that new shapes and decorations were invariably pioneered by Sèvres. Amongst the modelled groups, for instance, the *Tambour de Basque* appeared at Sèvres in 1779, whereas it had been known to the Faubourg Saint-Denis ever since January

240 Rihouët.
Plate. Blue, pink and gold. 'Cathedral-style' decoration, monogram of Gothic letters. *Circa* 1840.
Geneva, Musée de l'Ariana. Diam. 22 cm. (8²/₃ in.). Mark 216.

1778. In the same way, Gothic arcades are mentioned at Nast's factory in 1811, thus antedating the first Gothic *décors* at Sèvres by several years.

In its influences, then—be they received, imparted on reciprocated—Sèvres resumes the artistic history of the Parisian factories.

This did not preclude a continuous current of exchange with foreign countries. We have seen how some of them had supplied ideas to the Paris factories, especially at the outset. But they in turn were about to benefit by discoveries and creations from Paris.

Even Germany, to whom Paris porcelain owed its very existence, occasionally gained by French inventions. After he had discovered lithophanes in 1827, the Baron de Bourgoing sold the technique in the same year to Meissen, then to Berlin and lastly to the Netherlands.

This invention was equally popular in England, where the first patent on it, however, only dates from 1828. The vitality, originality and commercial suc-

241 Rihouët.
Plate. Polychrome and gold.
This plate belongs to an
important dessert-service
comprising hemispherical
sugar-bowls mounted on
pedestal-feet, *compote*-dishes
and several dozen plates. All
these items are decorated
with panels enclosing or
else monuments from all
over the world. Many of
them display different views
of Philadelphia in the
18th and 19th centuries,
taken from prints by
American artists published
some time between 1820 and
1840. This plate shows
'Christ Church' after a
lithograph by John Casper
Wild (1804–1846), from
'Views of Philadelphia, and
its Vicinity', published by
J. C. Wild and J. B. Chevalier
in Philadelphia in 1838.
This service was probably
made for an eminent Phila-
delphian. *Circa* 1840.
Philadelphia Museum of Art.
Diam. 21 cm. (8¼ in.).
Mark 215.

cess of English ceramics are factors that adequately explain why Paris porcelain exerted so little influence in England. Nonetheless we should remember firstly the exports regularly dispatched by Dihl, whose London agent, Flight, bought up the Worcester porcelain works; secondly Locré's export white ware which was painted by the floral artist Billingsley 'in the Parisian style' and finally the existence in London, about 1840, of one of Jacob Petit's warehouses in which both plain and decorated porcelain was stored.

The countries bordering on France were understandably influenced by Paris por-celain.

By 1799 the Swiss porcelain makers were lamenting the competition from Paris, whose factories 'are reputed to be setting the fashion' and whose wares 'have the loveliness of rich paintings'. They record that all they can do is to retaliate with lower prices. Two establishments are pre-eminently influenced by the Parisian style: Nyon, whose products resemble the wares of Clignancourt and Rue de Bondy;[4] and the workshop of Pierre Mulhauser, a decorator at Geneva who used to buy his white wares from Paris. In Belgium, the two factories set up in the Brabant at the end of the 18th century sometimes drew inspiration from Parisian products, as we detect in a Clignancourt

design at Montplaisir (founded in 1786). The piece in question is a sugar bowl with tray attached. Its belly and lid are wound round with ribbons which cross at the top to form the handle. Certain other decorators served as a real link between the Ile-de-France and the Brabant. Louis Cretté (born at Bourg-la-Reine in 1758) set himself up in business in 1790, painting La Courtille or Rue Thiroux white wares bought at Potter's. Charles Van Marcke, who was in business as a decorator in 1798, was one of the specialists in the pseudo-antique style copied from Paris. Another factory producing hard-paste porcelain was founded in 1818 at Ixelles near Brussels and was managed by Frédéric Théodore Faber, who went into partnership with Christophe Windisch, probably the son of Jean Baptiste Windisch, Honoré's former partner. Many decorators subsequently stocked up from Jacob Petit. Various items kept in the museums and private collections of Belgium bear the marks both of the French manufacturers and of the Belgian decorators: Rue Fontaine-au-Roy and Cretté; Jacob Petit and Panneel & Chappel of Brussels, or again Jacob Petit and Jacquet & Nédonchelle, also of Brussels.[5]

Paris porcelain had been much admired in Spain ever since about 1780 and we have already noted the offer which the King of Spain's ambassador made to Nast, that he should organize a hard-paste porcelain factory on his estates. We shall not return to the setting up in about 1795 of a shop affiliated to 'Le Petit Carrousel' in Madrid, which was jeopardized by its manager's carelessness.

The influence of Paris porcelain on Spanish wares was to make itself felt mainly in the first half of the 19th century, and in this context we should note that

243 Rousseau, Francisque. ▶
Celadon-ground baluster-vase, the shoulder decorated with a frieze of vine-shoots in gold, applied together with relief-work of translucent, opaque enamels which are red, turquoise and white. The neck and body each bear a row of beads, likewise enamel, arranged between fine gilt patterns. The undecorated 'blanc' came from the royal factory of Sèvres. Displayed by Rousseau at the 1844 Exhibition, this vase synthesizes the features which earned Rousseau a gold medal: coloured grounds fired at medium temperatures, applications of multicoloured enamels, and very durable and inexpensive relief-patterns in matt and contrast-burnished gold: *dorure de garniture économique et durable* ('decorative gilt which is economical and hard-wearing'). Rousseau was one of the most renowned stockists of colours in Paris, and he exported them to all parts of Europe. Sèvres, Musée National de Céramique. Ht. 19 cm. (7$\frac{1}{2}$ in.). Mark 219.

242 Tinet.
Statuette in the style of Jacob Petit. Plain, undecorated. *Circa* 1850. Sèvres, Musée National de Céramique. Ht. 20 cm. (7$\frac{9}{10}$ in.). Mark 225.

[4] PÉLICHET, Edgar. 'Porcelaines de Nyon'.
[5] MARIEN-DUGARDIN, A-M. Céramique. Ile de France – Brabant. Catalogue de l'Exposition, Sceaux-Bruxelles, 1962.

Vista Alegre. Because several Frenchmen were posted there, including the portraitist Victor François Chartier Rousseau (who supervised the painters' workshop from 1835 to 1851) many of this factory's wares resemble Parisian products. Sometimes they hark back to a slightly earlier period, like Schoelcher's cameos on dark-brown grounds, but sometimes they are modern, following the shapes of rectangular tea service items with chamfered corners, or the new designs introduced by Jacob Petit.[6]

The Italian factory of Vinovo near Turin, which from 1776 until 1780 was managed by Hannong after he had left the Faubourg Saint-Denis, turned out some pieces resembling those that he had been making in Paris. We have even come across a handleless cup decorated with polychrome wildflowers, bearing Hannong's Vinovo mark but matching a saucer marked with the 'Parisian' H. In the early 19th century the factory at Doccia near Florence made porcelain having shapes and decorations that bore a resemblance to Paris wares.

There was frequent contact between Parisian and Russian porcelain works. A number of Frenchmen were taken on by Russian factories. There is even every reason for supposing that Stahn, who was the painters' overseer at the Faubourg Saint-Denis before becoming its fictitious owner, was summoned to Russia in about 1781 to set up a factory there.

But it was chiefly in the 19th century that Paris contributed towards the making and decorating of Russian porcelain. Following the treaty concluded in 1808 between Napoleon and the Tsar, one of Russinger's sons was signed on by the Imperial Factory. The painter Swebach,[7] who worked at Sèvres and Paris for

Perche was posted to Buen Retiro. A branch of this factory, founded in 1817 at Montcloa, made many items of porcelain having Empire style decorations of polychrome scenes and ornaments which are very similar to Paris porcelain. The first hard-paste porcelain factory in Portugal was not founded until 1824, at

[6] PLINVAL-SALGUES, Régine de. 'La Contribution française à la Porcelaine portugaise'.

[7] SWEBACH, Bernard Edouard. (1800–1870). Son of Jacques Francois José. Painter of landscapes, historical scenes and battles.

various factories, stayed in Russia too, from 1818 to 1820: he returned loaded with honours and commissions. Finally, in 1844, Auguste Darte was called to the Imperial Factory to construct two kilns and to supervise firing. Darte worked at Kornilov's factory in Saint-Petersburg as well, before moving on to André Michlevski's at Gloukhov, where he stayed until 1851. A lot of Russian-made porcelain of the early 19th century is closely related to Parisian wares under Napoleon, with large decorations painted in quite vivid and well-glazed colours: animated scenes, landscapes and portraits, often set against rich grounds of contrast burnished gold.

Finally we should stress that French ceramic artistry enjoyed an unquestionable popularity in the United States, to the extent of seriously threatening British imports. Earlier, Governor Morris had bought General Washington many porcelain pieces from Dihl's works,[8] and we have also mentioned the sundry services commissioned from Dagoty & Honoré for the White House. Hence it comes as no surprise to learn that in 1816 Henry Mead of New York made some pieces closely resembling Parisian wares. Indeed the oldest item of porcelain manufactured in the United States is a vase from his factory, ovoid in shape, standing on a pedestal foot and flanked by winged figures emerging from a sheath.[9] Next, the famous factory of William Ellis Tucker, founded at Philadelphia in 1825, produced some items, in particular a large number of vases, that were not unlike contemporary Paris porcelain.[10]

Approximately eighty years separate the discovery of kaolin from the industrialization of methods for manufacturing hard-paste porcelain. This interval of time, although relatively short in the broader perspective of History, was enough to allow a technique to leave behind its humble beginnings as a handicraft, to progress towards a perfection that was constantly striven after, and to attain rapidly the stage of mass-production. Moreover, this phase was highlit by remarkable artistic endeavour whose many facets may be studied in the objects that survive.

Within this evolution the Parisian factories secured a constantly expanding position. Marked by the influences primarily of Saxony, from which it drew its origins, and of Sèvres which long stood as its paragon, Paris porcelain managed to acquire an original character that epitomizes Parisian taste.

It is undoubtedly the case that in the late 18th century the Parisian factories occupied the vanguard of all French hard-paste porcelain works, and that in the 19th century this supremacy of Paris was consolidated in the field of porcelain decoration, even on an international scale.

By virtue of its brilliance and diversity, Paris porcelain in its turn radiated its influence throughout the world and even as far as China—thus, after a long career, reaching back again to its origins.

---

[8] MORRIS, Gouverneur: Connoisseur of French art. *Apollo*, June 1971. Some of this porcelain is kept at Mount Vernon.
[9] Philadelphia Museum of Art.
[10] TRACY, Berry B. *The decorative arts in Classical America 1815–1845*. Exhibition at The Newark Museum, 1963.

REPERTORY OF MARKS

This repertory assembles the factories, decorating workshops and porcelain dealers, including several reputed stockists of decorators' materials.

Besides the businesses and individuals mentioned in the text, the repertoire embraces certain other manufacturers or merchants having their own porcelain marks but whom we have, for various reasons, been unable to study.

It does not, however, pretend to be exhaustive. For although the factories may be fairly easy to trace, the same does not apply to isolated decorators, workshop managers or to dealers, who are entered by the score in the successive *Almanachs du Commerce*. The 1848 issue lists sixty-six decorators, some of whom reappear amongst the sixty-nine dealers who follow.

Furthermore, although we have compiled large numbers of marks, we thought it superfluous to give all the variations on any one mark. Similarly, we have not incorporated any marks setting unsolved problems, except for the underglaze blue dot which is found either on its own or with other painted, overglaze marks from early 19th-century factories such as Nast's (mark 175) or Pouyat's.

Let us recall that marks enable us not only to identify porcelain, but often to date it with a fair degree of accuracy as well. In the 18th century, the patron's mark usually replaced the one used since the factory was first founded. The designations in the 19th century that were reserved for specially appointed suppliers (for example the factory of the Empress or the Duchesse d'Angoulême), or perhaps the inclusion of the address, likewise enable us to classify objects chronologically, which is an invaluable asset in studying stylistic evolution.

The compulsory marking of porcelain dates back to the 1766 decree issued by the Kings Council. It commanded every manufacturer 'to paint, incise or impress on the back of every item of porcelain the initials of his name or whatever other mark he may have chosen; and, before commencing production, to register himself, to wit in Paris, in the presence of the Lieutenant général de Police..., and to confine himself to using the mark of which he has filed the facsimile.' These provisions were reiterated by the decree of 1784 and the main manufacturers complied with them.

Nonetheless, some small businesses which were illicitly engaged in porcelain production did not mark their output—nor did 'outside' craftsmen who were only decorating wares in the white from various factories.

A few years later the Declaration of Human Rights set trade free, and competition in the field of porcelain became so intense that, in the Empire period, Madame Dihl asked for a return to certain

Mark 17. See p. 328

restrictions, especially to the compulsory marking of porcelain. She recalled, incidentally, that under the *Ancien Régime* only four factories out of nine had been marking their output. We have also observed that one of the instructions to participants in the industrial exhibitions of the first half of the 19th century was to affix their marks during manufacture. Many producers, however, failed to mark white wares destined for export or intended for Parisian decorators or dealers, who were then the only ones to sign them. Of course, there are exceptions: the marks of the manufacturers Jacob Petit, Nast and others are found side by side with the decorator's (or the merchant's).

The distinction between the two is theoretically a straightforward one, but in practice it runs into numerous difficulties. If the mark painted in underglaze blue is indeed the maker's, then attention must be drawn to how rare it is, especially in the 19th century. The marks most commonly encountered are painted in overglaze red, black or gold, unless they are stencilled in red, brown or black. The biscuit marks are incised, or occasionally stamped in relief.

In any case, it must be emphasized that quite often the different pieces of a given service are not all marked, only some of them.

The factory marks may be joined by other devices. Some artists added their own. Painters' initials are particularly in evidence on porcelain from the Duc d'Angoulême's factory, as are those of modellers at Locré's works, where Mô affixed his signature to biscuit ware (mark 148).

Apart from the marks peculiar to each factory, there are others denoting the families who have purchased the porcelain: thus, on the undersides of certain service pieces, we may see coats of arms more or less heraldic emblems or interwoven monograms. The latter, incidentally, are often wrongly thought to be unidentified factory marks. It is worth adding that such marks, normally painted or stamped in gold or black, may greatly post-date the actual manufacture of the porcelain.

ANDRÉ, Dominique; then Louis; then Charles, & PILLIVUYT
Decorating workshops; factory at Foëscy
...1819–1865...
45, Faubourg Saint-Martin (...1831)
5, Passage Violet (1832–1836)
41, Rue des Petites-Ecuries (1836–1844)
46/50, Rue Paradis Poissonnière (1844–1861...)

Circa 1832–1836

1 Part of the stencilled mark in black accompanying the PERCHE mark

ANDRÉ, MAURICE
Decorator
1810–1841
8, Rue Notre-Dame de Nazareth (1810–1823)
21, Rue Vendôme (1823–1841)
We have his signature dated 1820 ●

DUC D'ANGOULÊME
Factory
1781–1828
Guérhard & Dihl
Rue de Bondy (1781–1789)
Boulevard du Temple/Rue Meslay (1789–1828)

A) *Patronage of the Duc d'Angoulême*
   (1781–Revolution)

2 In red

3 In underglaze blue

4 In red
5 In red

6 Stencilled in red

7 In red or gold
8 In red or gold

9 Stencilled in red

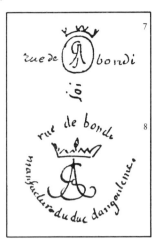

10 Incised
11 Incised

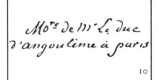

See pages 347 and 348 for the list of entries and cross-references.

B) *Marks of Guérhard & Dihl*
12 In red or gold
13 In red or gold

14 Stencilled in red

15 Stencilled in red

16 Stencilled in red
17 Mark painted in black, probably accompanying the device of some family, stamped in gold. Mark illustrated p. 326.

C) *Dihl alone (circa 1795–1800)*
18 In underglaze blue
19 In red
20 Incised

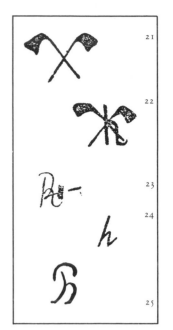

COMTE D'ARTOIS
Factory, then decorating-workshop and salesroom
1772–1810 (?) –1834
Hannong, Mis d'Usson, Mis de La Salle, Bourdon Desplanches,
Houël, Benjamin, Schœlcher
Rue du Faubourg Saint-Denis (1772–1810?)
Boulevard des Italiens/Rue de la Grange-Batelière (1804–1834)

A) *Hannong (1772–1774 or 1779)*
21 In underglaze blue
22 In underglaze blue
23 In underglaze blue
24 In underglaze blue
25 In underglaze blue

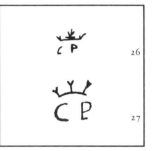

B) *Patronage of the Comte d'Artois (1779-Revolution)*
26★ In gold
27 In blue and gold

28 Stencilled in red

29 Stencilled in red

30

30 Incised

38

38 Stencilled in black

31

C) The Schœlchers
1) Schœlcher (1798–1834)
31* In underglaze blue ●
32* In sepia ●
33 In red or gold
34* Stencilled in dark brown
35 In gold ●

32

33

34

35

BAPTEROSE
Manufacturer of porcelain buttons
Circa 1849...
27–29, Rue de la Muette, Faubourg Saint-Antoine

BARUCH WEIL
Decorating workshops; factory at Fontainebleau
...1805–1828
101, Rue du Temple (1805)
23, Rue Boucherat (1809–1815)
16, Rue de Bondy (1816–1828)
Passage de l'Opéra (1828)
See also: Blancheron

BERNARD
Decorator
1824–1829
13, Rue de Poitou (1824–1826)
Rue des Fossés-du-Temple (1827–1830)
24, Rue des Marais-du-Temple (1831–1839)

39

BERNON
Decorator
1845–1850...
49, Rue de l'Arbre-Sec
See also: Jacob Petit

39 Jacob Petit's underglaze blue mark, with
     Bernon's red stencilled mark

2) Schœlcher Senior & Junior (1829–1834)
36 In gold

36

37 Stencilled in red

BLANCHERON, MAUBRÉ, BARUCH WEIL, DODÉ,
CLAUSS
Factory
Year VI–1829
Rue des Trois-Bornes
See also: Potter, Clauss
Circa 1798–1802

40

41

42

40 In red or gold
41 In underglaze blue
42 In relief

37

329

BONDEUX
Dealer in porcelain, faience and crystal glass
1800–1844
Palais Royal, 1109/1110, later 6, Cour des Fontaines
(1800–1831)
Rue Croix des Petits-Champs (1832–1835)
159, Rue Saint-Honoré (1836–1844)

43   In gold

BRINGEON
Decorator, also dealer in porcelain, faience and
crystal glass
Circa 1805
19 and 66, Rue Vivienne
44   In gold, red or black
45   In gold, red or black

46   Stencilled in red ●

46

BROILLIET, CHERVISE, ADVENIER & LAMARRE
Factories
1762–1775
Gros-Caillou (...1773)
Vaugirard (1762–1775)
47

47

BUTEUX
Porcelain colours
1838–1850
17, Rue du Faubourg du Temple (1838)
15, Rue des Marais-Saint-Martin (1844–1850...)

CHANOU
Factory
Circa 1784
Rue de Reuilly

48   In red or gold

CHAPELLE, MAILLARD, CASSÉ-MAILLARD
Managers of decorating-workshops, also dealers
1806–1850...
168, Rue Quincampoix (1821)
19, Faubourg Saint-Denis (1822–1840)
19, Boulevard des Italiens (1827–1850...)
Circa 1830–1840
49★ In red and brown

Circa 1840–1850...
50   In red, black or gold

51   Stencilled in red or black ●

51

CHEVALIER, FOURMY, TRÉGENT, LALOUETTE, JULLIEN,
CHAZAUD, MARGAINE Factory
...Year VII–1837...
Rue de la Pépinière
Rue des Grésillons, renamed Rue de Laborde
See also: Margaine

CLAUSS, BOURDOIS & BLOCH, BLOCH
Factory
1824 to the present day
Rue des Trois-Bornes (1824–1829)
Rue Pierre-Levée (1829 to the present day)
No known mark before 1850
See also: Blancheron

CŒUR DASSIER, DARTE SENIOR, DISCRY, TALMOURS,
HUREL, MENARD
Factory
Year XI–1863...
26, Rue de Popincourt
See also: Darte, Discry

1)   *Cœur Dassier (1803–1805)*
52   In blue (given by Ris-Paquot)
2)   *Darte Senior (1805–1823)*
53   Painted in gold

54

3) Discry (circa 1830)
54   In underglaze, imitating Chinese ware ●

COLVILLE
Painter and gilder, later dealer in porcelain colours
1821–1850...
138, Faubourg Saint-Martin (1821–1827)
22, Rue des Vinaigriers (1828–1850)

CORBIN
Decorator
1843–*circa* 1855
57, Faubourg Saint-Denis

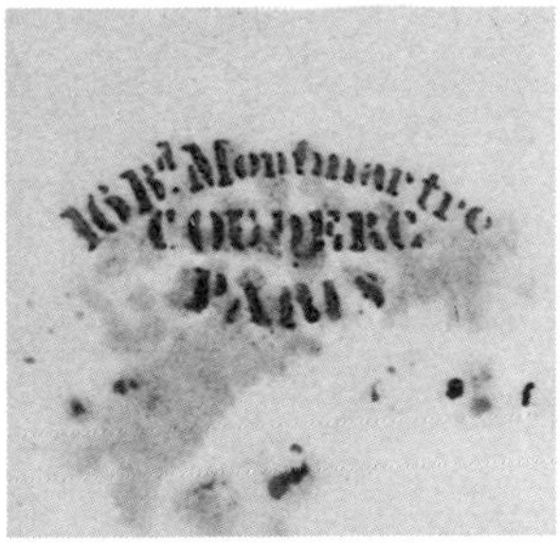

COUDERC, COUDERC-BUCHER
Dealer
1844–1850...
16, Bd. Montmartre
55   Stencilled in red

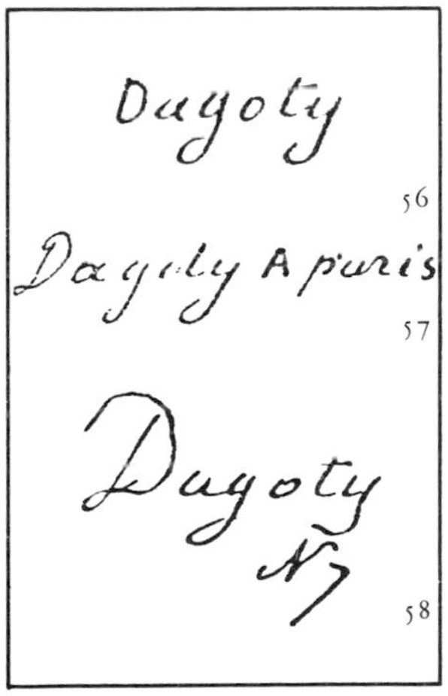

55

DAGOTY & HONORÉ
Factories
Year VI–1865...
Boulevard Poissonnière (Year VII–1865...)
Rue de Chevreuse (Year VIII–1820)
Petite Rue Saint-Gilles (1806–1820...)
See also: Honoré & Windisch

1) Dagoty (1799–1816)
56   In red or gold
57   In red or gold
58   In red or gold

Dagoty

56

Dagoty A paris

57

Dagoty
N 7

58

59

59   Stencilled in red ●

60   Stencilled in red ●

60

61   Stencilled in red ●

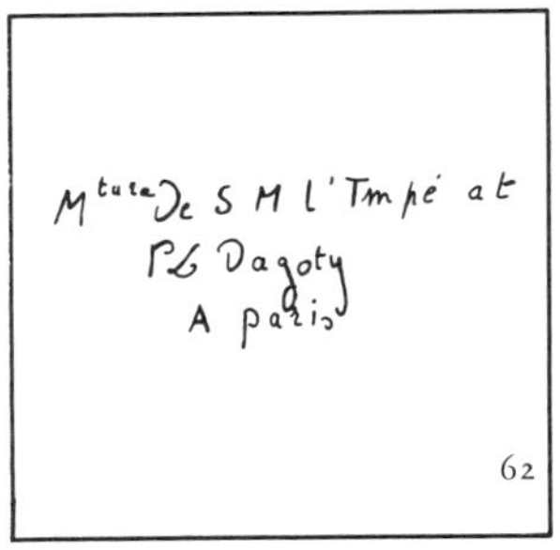

61

2) Dagoty (1804–1815)
62★ In red or gold, or incised ●

62

63   Stencilled in red ■ (60×34 mm.)

63

64   Stencilled in red

64

65 Stencilled in red

71 Stencilled in red or brown ■

3) Dagoty & Honoré (1816–1820)
66 Stencilled in red

72 Stencilled in red or brown

67 Stencilled in red

73 Stencilled in red or brown

68 Stencilled in red

74 Stencilled in red or brown

4) Honoré (after 1820)
69★ In gold ●
70★ In dark green

5) Honoré (after 1824)
75 Stencilled in brown or black

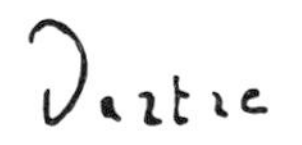

DARTE

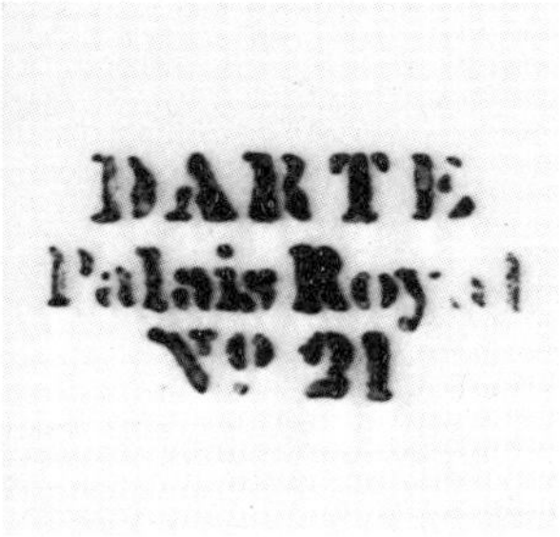

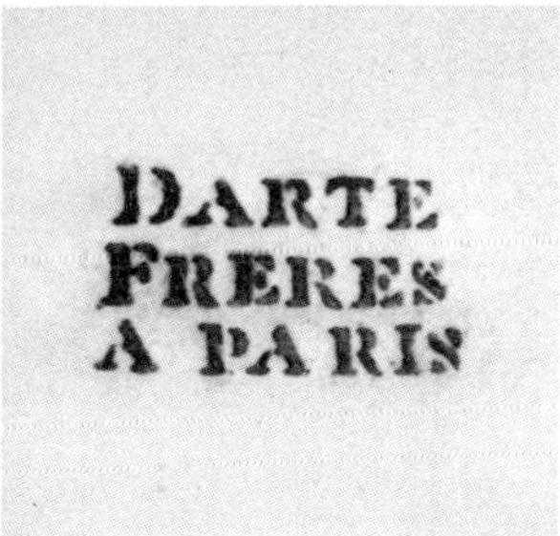

Factories

1. The Dartes (Joseph, Louis Joseph and Jean François: successors to MASSONET
   Year III–1804
   3, Rue de Charonne (Year III–1804)
   34/35, Palais du Tribunat (circa 1803)

2. Darte Senior (Joseph)
   Year XII–1823
   159, Rue Saint-Honoré (Year XII)
   26, Rue de Popincourt (Year XIII–1823)
   See also: Cœur Dassier

3. Darte Frères (Louis Joseph and Jean François, later August Remi)
   Year XII–1833
   90, Rue de la Roquette (Year XII–1828)
   Palais du Tribunat
   16, Rue Vivienne
   8, Faubourg Poissonnière
   Rue des Vinaigriers

N.B. The Dartes decorated pieces from other factories, such as Nast's.

76* In gold
77 Stencilled in red
78 Stencilled in red
79 Stencilled in red

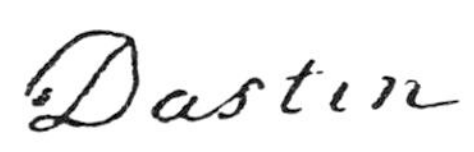

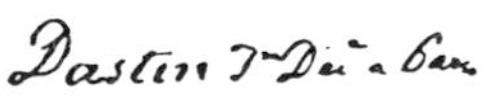

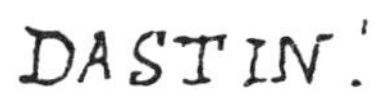

DASTIN
Porcelain dealer
1801–1818
Rue des Deux-Portes (1801–1802)
129, Rue Sainte-Barbe (1802–1806)
22, Rue de Bondy (1807–1818)

80 In gold
81 In gold
82 Stencilled in red

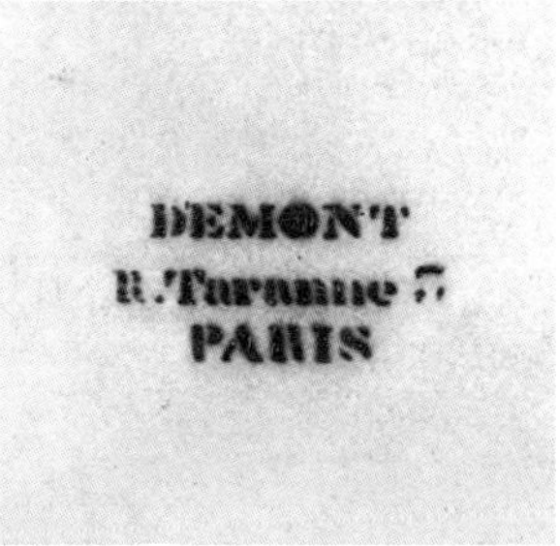

DECAEN, AUGUSTE
Decorating workshops; factory at Grigny
Faubourg Saint-Denis

DEMONT, LAVROIRE, LEROUX (successors to **SÉJOURNAND**?)
Dealers
1832–1850...

From 1835 to 1842
83 Stencilled in red or black

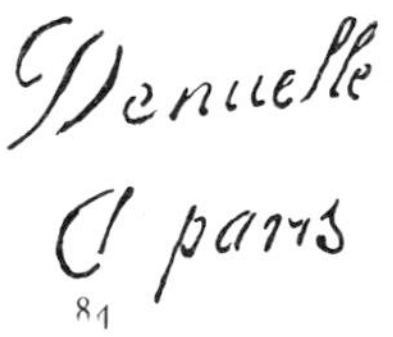

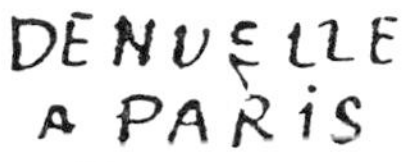

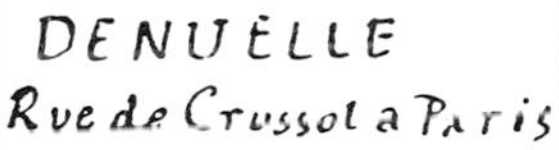

DENUELLE
Factory
1819–1852
Rue de Crussol (1819–...)
18, Boulevard Saint-Denis (1834–1848)
39bis, Rue des Petites-Ecuries (1849–1852)
See also: Potter

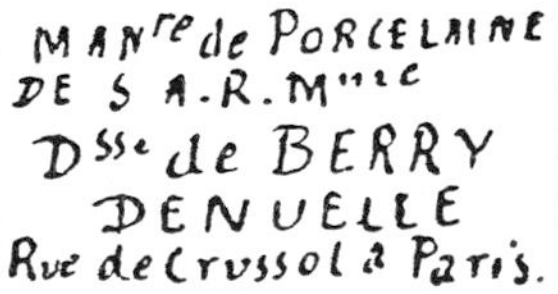

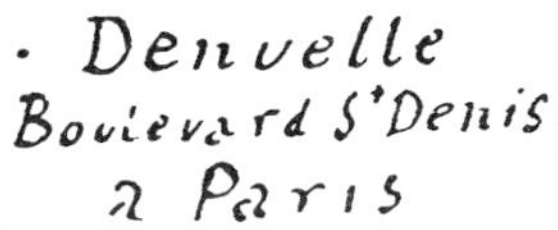

84 In gold
85 Stencilled in red
86 Stencilled in red
87 Stencilled in red
88 Stencilled in red

89

90

91

DEROCHE, POCHET-DEROCHE, GOSSE, VIGNIER
Dealer, later decorator
1776–1900...
Rue Saint-Martin (1776–...)
336, Rue Coquillière (1804–*circa* 1810)
16, Rue Jean-Jacques Rousseau (*circa* 1815–1900...)
5/7, Rue des Lombards

1) Circa 1810–1830
89 In red
90 In gold

2) Circa 1830–1839
91 In black

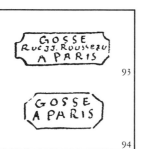

92

92 Stencilled in red

GOSSE
Rue J.J. Rousseau
A PARIS

93

GOSSE
A PARIS

94

3) Circa 1839–1849
93 Stamped pad
94 Stamped pad

VIGNIER
16 r J.J. Rousseau
a Paris

95

4) As from 1849
95 Stencilled in red

DESFOSSÉS FRÈRES
Decorators, later dealers in porcelain colours
...1838–1850...
72, Rue de Bondy

DESPREZ.

96

DESPREZ
Rue des Récollets
A PARIS

97

DESPREZ
Rue des Recolets
no 2-2 Paris

98

DESPRÉZ
Factory
... Year IV–1834
Rue de Lancry (1798)
Rue des Morts (*circa* 1825)
Rue des Ecluses Saint-Martin (1834)

96 Incised
97 Incised
98 Incised

DEUSTER, FREUND, CREMIÈRE, CREMIÈRE-GUILLEMOT
Factory
Circa 1800–*circa* 1820
Rue de la Folie-Méricourt (*circa* 1800–1807)
Rue de Ménilmontant (*circa* 1807–*circa* 1820)

DISCRY
Manufacturer, later dealer in colours and enamels
1823–1844...
26, Rue de Popincourt (1823–1841)
8, Rue du Temple, Passage du Jeu de Boules (1844)
See: Cœur Dassier for the period 1823–1841

DUBAN
Dealer in porcelain, faience, glass and crystal glass
...1776–1820
43 or 50, Rue Coquillière (1776–1810...)
14, Rue des Fossés-Saint-Germain (1818–1820)

Duban

99

99 In red

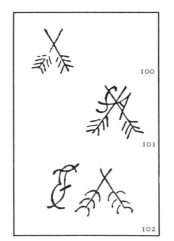

100

101

102

DUBOIS, Vincent Jérôme
Factory
1774–*circa* 1790
Rue de la Roquette, 'Aux Trois Levrettes'

100 In underglaze blue
101 In underglaze blue
102 Incised

DUHAMEL
Dealer in porcelain and crystal glass
1790 (?)–1822–1825
1, Quai de la Cité, below Pont Notre-Dame

Duhamel

103

103   In red or gold

DUTERTRE
Decorator
...1838–1860...
16, Rue Grange-aux-Belles (1839)
41, Rue des Marais du Temple (1840)
15, Passage du Jeu de Boules (*circa* 1847–1860...)

'ESCALIER DE CRISTAL' (MADAME DÉSARNEAUX,
BOIN, LAHOCHE, PANNIER)
Decorating workshop, also salesroom for porcelain,
bronzes and crystal glass
1802–1900...
Palais Royal, Galerie de Valois (1802–1854...)
6, Rue Scribe and 1, Rue Auber

*Mme Désarneaux
à l'escalier de Cristal*

104

*Désarneaux
à l'escalier de
Cristal à paris*

105

1) Circa 1802–1828
104   In red, black or gold ●
105   In red, black, green or gold

*Lahoche
palais-Royal*

108

2) 1839–1854
108   In red, black or gold

*à l'Escalier
de Cristal*
106

*l'Escalier
de Cristal
PARIS*

107

3) Marks used throughout the salesrooms existence
106   In red, black or gold
107   In red, black or gold

FEUILLET, BOYER, BLOT, HÉBERT
Decorating workshop
...1817–1900...
18/20 Rue de la Paix

Feuillet   109

*Feuillet
rue de la paix n°18*

110

*Feuillet
rue de la Paix
n° 20*

111

1) *Circa* 1817–1834
109   In red, black or gold
110★ In gold ●
111   In red, black or gold

Boyer Sr de Feuillet.

112

2) As from 1834
112   In red, black or gold ●

FEUILLET (the nephew), **MANOURY**
Decorating-workshop
1834–1846...
Rue Saint-Denis (1834–1836)
Passage Sandrié (1837–1846...)

FLEURY, FLAMEN-FLEURY (successors to
HOFFMANN & LALOUETTE)
Factory
Year II–1831
68, later 168 and 192, Faubourg Saint-Denis

Rue Vivienne
N.B. *circa* 1840, we notice Déséglises, a manufacturer, at
168, Faubourg Saint-Denis

*fleury
paris*

113

1) *Between 1806 and 1814*
113★ In gold

2) *Between 1814 and 1831*
114   Stencilled in red

114

FROMENT, Louis Pierre
Porcelain painter
1819–1825
47/49, Rue de l'Arbre-Sec

GAILLIARD or GAILLARD or CAILLARD
Dealer
Circa 1830
Passage de l'Opéra, 10, Galerie de l'Horloge

115   In red or gold

GRENON (successor to BLOTTIÈRE, 1827–1837)
Dealer
1838–1850...
12, Rue Mabillon (1838–1846)
51, Faubourg Saint-Martin (1847–1850...)

GAMBIER
Dealer in porcelain and faience
1812–1816
20, Rue de l'Arbre-Sec

116   In gold

HALLEY, LEBON-HALLEY
Decorator and dealer
1800–*circa* 1822
182, Boulevard Montmartre

1) Between about 1800 and 1817
120   In red and gold

2) Between about 1818 and 1822
121   In red and gold

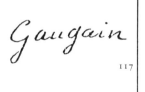

GAUGAIN
Dealer in porcelain and faience
1810–1823
76, Rue de Grenelle Saint-Germain

117   In gold

122   Stencilled in red

GILLE, VION & BAURY
Factory
1837–1868...
28, Rue Paradis-Poissonnière
See also: Vion

118   Incised
119   Bluish seal

123   Stencilled in red ●

GONORD, PERRENOT-GONORD
Transfer printing factory
1800–1844...
Rue Courty (1800)
96, Rue de Popincourt (1813–1818)
17, Rue Moreau (1819–1826)
92, Faubourg Saint-Martin (1827–1829)
350, Rue Saint-Denis, Cour du Grand-Cerf
(1830–1843)
34, Rue Grange-aux-Belles (1844...)
6, Rue des Petites-Ecuries

HALOT, F. & E.
Decorating workshops
...1823–1853...
14, Rue d'Angoulême du Temple (1823–1846)
40, Marais Saint-Martin (1846–1849)
Faubourg Poissonnière (1849...)

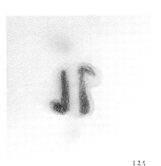

HONORÉ & WINDISCH, later HONORÉ & DAGOTY
(successors to BON & LORTZ, SAVOY, BERTRAND)
Factory
Year VI–1820...
Petite Rue Saint-Gilles
See also: Dagoty & Honoré

124   In red

JACOB PETIT
Circa 1830–1866
Factory at Belleville (*circa* 1830)
Factory at Fontainebleau as well
Salerooms:
18, Rue Basse-Porte-Saint-Denis (1834)
18, later 26, Rue de Bondy (1835–1848)
Rue du Paradis-Poissonnière (...1866)
See also: Baruch Weil

125   In underglaze blue (in different sizes)

126★   In underglaze blue
127   Pseudo-Meissen mark in underglaze blue

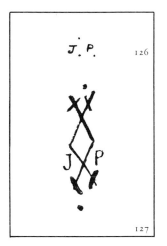

JEANNE
1) Dealer and decorator; Margaine's warehouse
1839–1842
18, Rue Notre-Dame-de-Nazareth (1839–1841)
14, Bd. Poissonnière (1842)
See also: Factory of the Duc d'Orléans

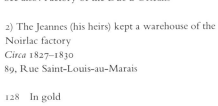

2) The Jeannes (his heirs) kept a warehouse of the
Noirlac factory
Circa 1827–1830
89, Rue Saint-Louis-au-Marais

128   In gold

JULIENNE
1) *Julienne, then Léveillé*
Dealer in porcelain and crystal glass
1825–1835, 1836–1850...
8, later 12, Rue Thiroux
2) *Julienne Junior, then Julienne-Moureau*
Manufacturer (?)
1836–1850...
50, Rue du Bac

129   In gold
130   Stencilled in red

As from 1836
131★   In gold ●

132   Stencilled in red

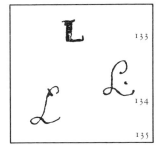

LACHASSAGNE, Alexandre (successor to BAIGNOL
JUNIOR)
Warehouse for various provincial factories
1835–1850...
55, Rue Meslay

LACHASSAIGNE, MORET and LACHASSAIGNE
Decorator
1825–1851
4, Rue de la Marche
28–30, Rue Notre-Dame de Nazareth (1835)
24, Rue de Poitou
9, Rue Corbeau (1844–1851)

LASSIA
Factory
1774–*circa* 1788
Rue de Reuilly

133   Painted in black
134   In red
135   In red

LEBON
Dealer in porcelain and faience
1800–1818
5, Rue Neuve-Saint-Eustache
See also: Halley

LEBOURG
Maker of porcelain flowers
1844–1850...
9, Rue Corbeau

LE BOURGEOIS, or BOURGEOIS
Manufacturer (?)
1799–1818
42 or 92, Rue du Faubourg Saint-Denis
(Year VII–1817)
39, Rue Fontaine-au-Roy (*sic*) (1818)
LEGOST
Painter and gilder
1819–1833
48, Rue Saint-Sébastien (1819–1822)
35, Rue de Popincourt (1823–1824)
24, Rue de Bondy (1828–1830)
35, Rue Fontaine-au-Roy (1831–1833)

LEGOST JUNIOR
111, Faubourg Saint-Denis (1845–1847)

LEGROS D'ANISY
Transfer printing factory
1808–1849...
9, Rue du Cadran (1808–1818)
11, Rue du Faubourg Montmartre (1818–1824)
13, Rue Merry (1825–...)
14, Rue Charlot
9, Rue de Poitou (1834–...)
See also: Spooner

136   Printed mark in black or sepia

137   Printed mark in black or sepia

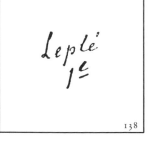

138

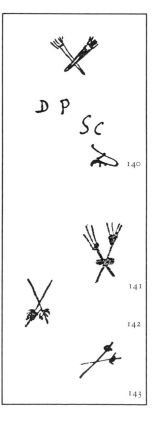

139

140

141

142

143

LEPLÉ OR LEPLÉE, probably PLÉE as well
1) Plée Frères
1818–1820
Manufacturers
42, Rue de l'Hôpital
2) Leplé (Senior), then Leplé (the elder son)
Decorator
1824–1835
49, Rue de Richelieu
3) Leplé
Decorator
1825–1826
19, Rue du Bac

138   In black or gold

Circa 1825
139   In red or black ●

LHOTE or LHOSTE
Factory (?)
...1797–1825
Rue Meslay
32, Rue Basfroy (1810–1825)

LOCRÉ, RUSSINGER, POUYAT
Factory
1773–1824
39, Rue Fontaine-au-Roy, La Courtille
140   In underglaze blue
141   In underglaze blue
142   In underglaze blue
143   In underglaze blue; the commonest motif with
      many variations.

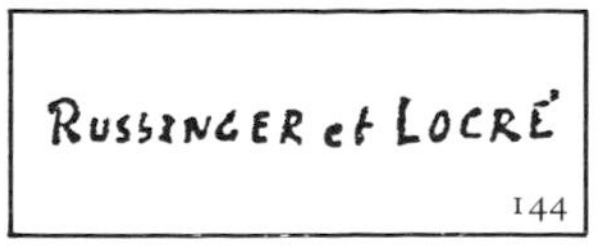

144

Circa 1780
144 In red

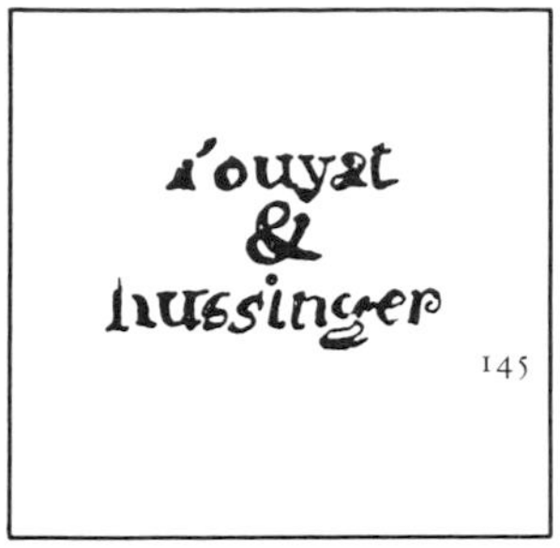
145

Circa 1797–1800
145 Stencilled in red

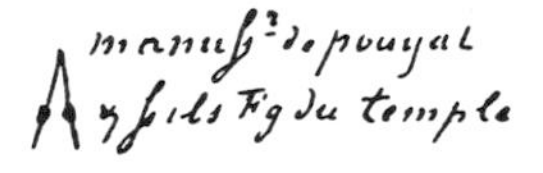
146

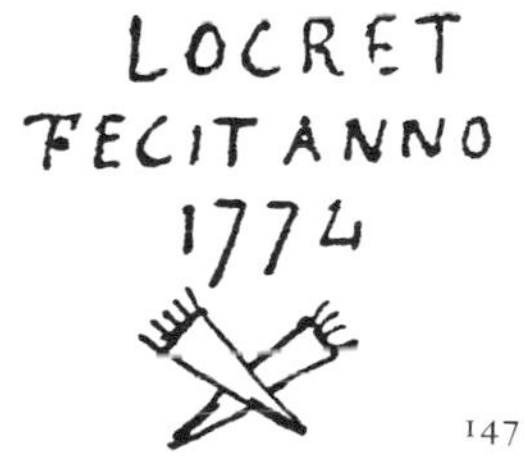

147

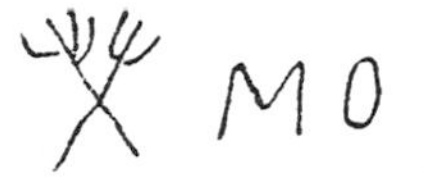

148

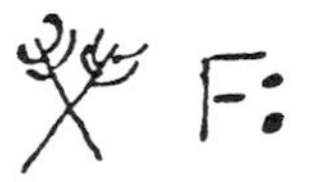

149

Circa 1824
146 In underglaze blue and painted in gold

147 Incised biscuit marks
148 Incised biscuit marks
149 Incised biscuit marks

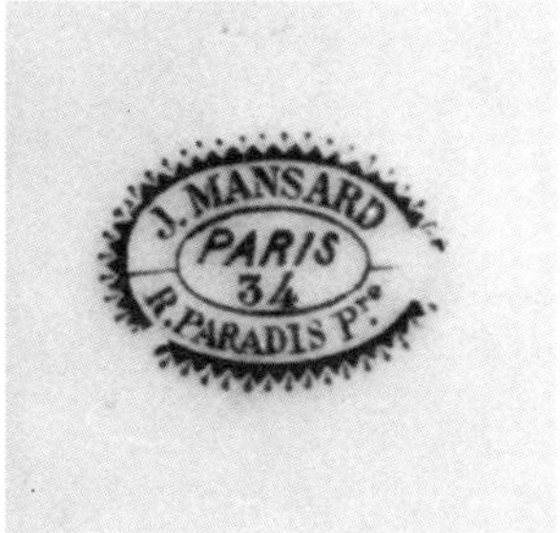

150

MANSARD
Decorator
1846–1850. . .
111, Faubourg Saint-Denis
34, Rue Paradis-Poissonnière (after 1850)

150 Stencilled in red

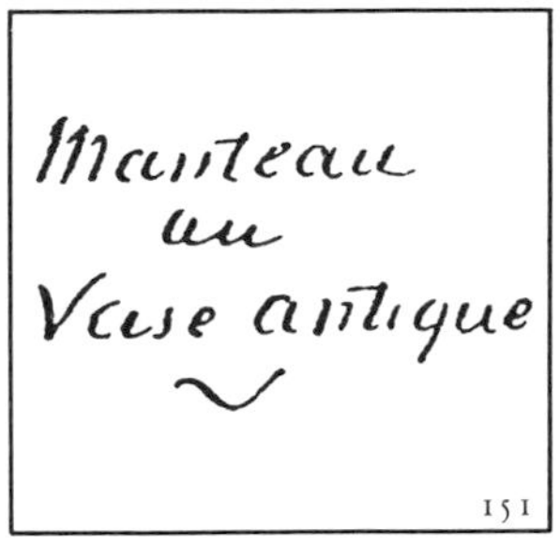

151

MANTEAU, 'Au vase Antique'
Dealer
1804–1809. . .
1, Rue de Grenelle (1804)
160, Rue Saint-Honoré (1805)
4, Rue Neuve de Luxembourg (1809. . .)

151 In black

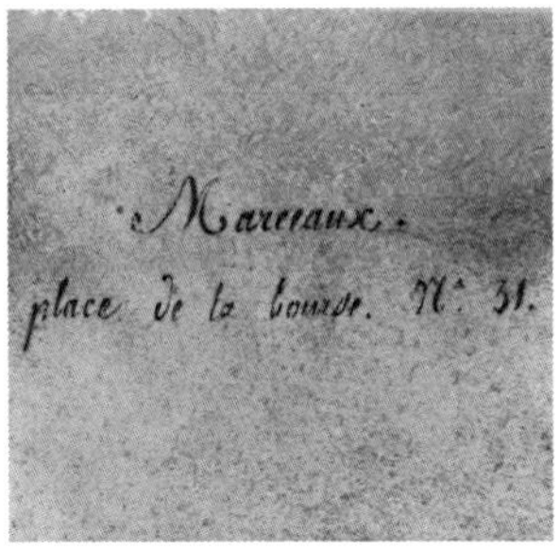

152

MARCEAUX
Dealer
1827–1837
15, Rue Feydeau (1827)
31, Place de la Bourse (1837)

152* In black ●

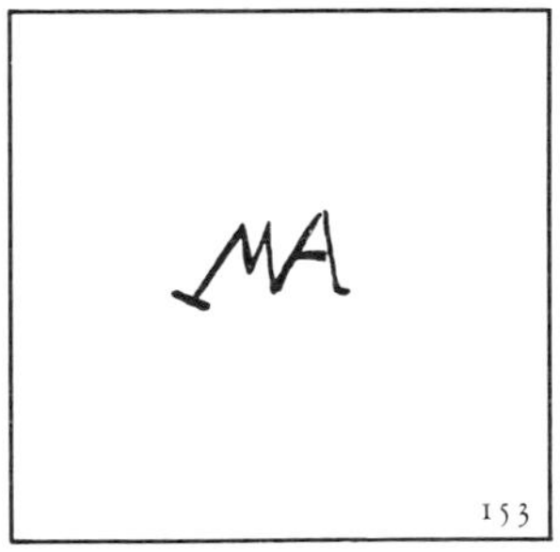

153

MARGAINE
Decorating workshop
1839–1867. . .
7, Rue de la Boule (1839–1849)
12, Rue de l'Echiquier (1850–1867)
See also: Chevalier, Jeanne

153 In green

MAYER
Several decorators having this name:
Mayer: 187, Rue Chapon (1804)
Mayer, M. 69, Rue Sainte-Avoye (1805)
Mayer, A: 15, Rue de Crussol (1819–1822)
Mayer: 50 bis, Rue des Marais-Saint-Martin (1830–1844)

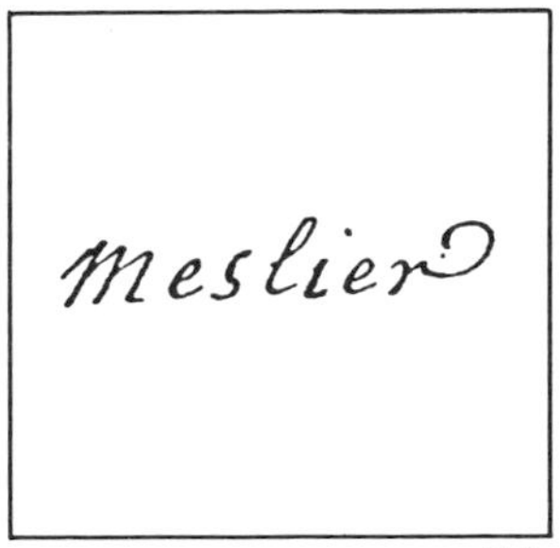

154

MESLIER
Dealer in porcelain and crystal glass
1825–1834. . .
37, Rue de l'Arbre-Sec (1825–1828)
17, Rue du Faubourg Montmartre (1830–1834...)

154 In red and gold

155

MIGNON
Factory
. . .1777–1789
Rue Saint-Sébastien, au Pont-aux-Choux

155   In underglaze blue

161

2) *Patronage of Monsieur (1775–1791, when factory was transplanted)*

161   In red

156

MONGINOT
Manager of decorating workshop, and porcelain dealer
Circa 1830–1837
20, Boulevard des Italiens

156   In gold

162

162   In red or gold

157

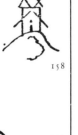

158

159

160

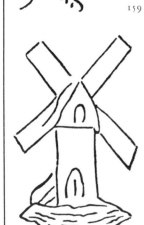

MONSIEUR, COMTE DE PROVENCE
Factory
1772(?)–1799
Deruelle, Moitte
Clignancourt

1) *Until 1775*
157   In underglaze blue
158   In underglaze blue
159   In gold
160   Incised

163

163   In red ●

164

164   In red

165

165   In red

3) Revolutionary period: Moitte (1791–1799)
166★ In gold
167 In red or gold
168 In red or gold
169 In red or gold

170 Stencilled in red

171 In underglaze blue

N.B. Different marks from this factory may be combined on a single object. For example—a) the windmill (157) plus the monogram (162), b) this monogram with the crowned M (165) (or with the crowned B, 164) and c) the word *Clignancourt* (170) and the M (171).

MORELLE
Factory
Circa 1773
Rue de la Roquette
Saint-Denis (1774...)

MORTELÈCQUE, then DUBOIS & HACHETTE
Painter on porcelain and glass, dealer in colours
1820–1850...
120 or 132, Rue du Faubourg Saint-Martin

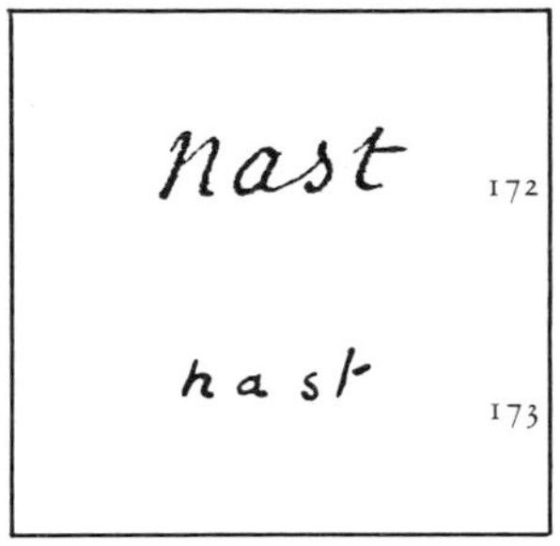

NAST (successor to LEMAIRE)
Factory
1780–1835
Rue de Popincourt (1780–1783)
Rue des Amandiers Popincourt (1783–1835)

172 In red or gold
173★ In red or gold

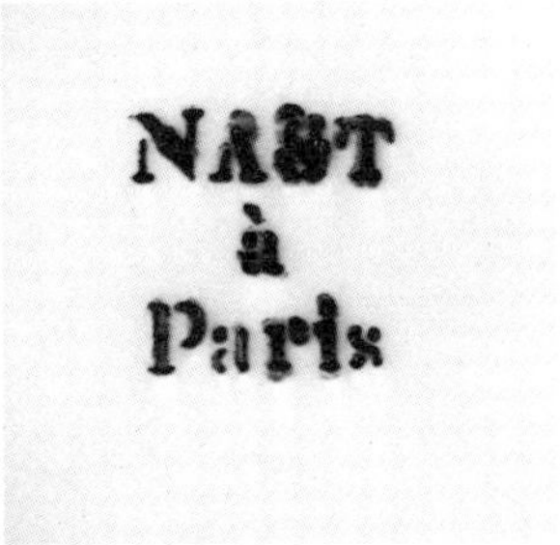

174 Stencilled in red

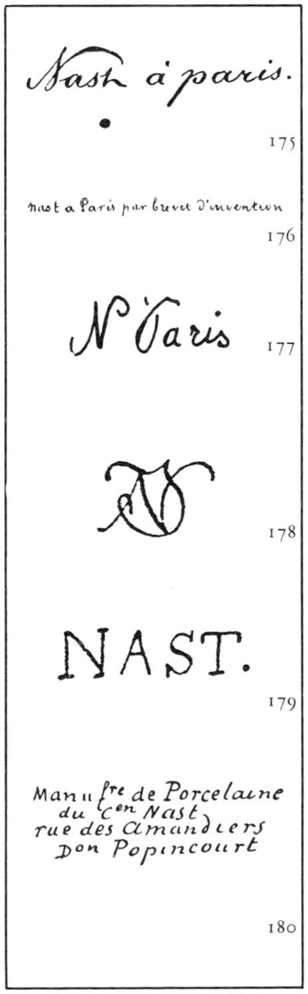

175 In gold, plus dot in underglaze blue ●
176 In gold or black (as from 1810) ●
177★ In gold
178 In red
179 Incised
180 Incised ●

Examples of labels

184

3) Patronage of the Duc d'Orléans; initials of Louis-Philippe (1786–Revolution)

184 In underglaze blue

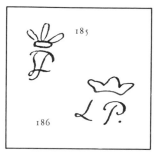

185 In underglaze blue
186 In underglaze blue

185

186

187 In gold

187

NEPPEL
Factory
Rue de Crussol, *circa* 1805–1818 (took over the factory founded by Potter)
Set up a factory at Nevers, but kept a warehouse, first in Rue de Crussol, then at 34, Rue de l'Echiquier (1823–1836)
See also: Potter
181★ Stencilled in red

NICOLET & GREDER, then REVIL (successors to BATTAZERD)
Manufacturers
477, Rue du Rocher (1792–1813)
Rue Neuve des Mathurins: salesroom (*circa* 1805)
See also: Revil

181

DUC D'ORLÉANS
Factory
1784–1828
Delamarre de Villiers, Outrequin de Montarcy, Toulouse,

LEMAIRE, CARON & LEFEBVRE, MERLIN-HALL, JEANNE
Rue de Boulets (1784–1786)
Rue Amelot (1786–1828)

4) Lefebvre (1806–1816)
188 In gold ●
189 In black or gold ●

188

189

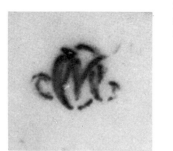

182

1) *Delamarre de Villiers (1784–1786)*
182 In red
2) *Outrequin de Montarcy, Toulouse (1786–1789)*
183 Stencilled in red

190 In gold ●

183

190

PARCHEMINIER
Master decorator
1807–1848
Rue du Faubourg Saint-Denis, 'Au Chandelier d'Or'
(1807)
6, Rue des Martyrs (1820)
68, Faubourg Saint-Denis (1830–1837)
85, Rue du Temple (1845–1848)

PERSON
Porcelain decorator and dealer
Year VIII–1812...
10, Jardin Egalité (Year VIII)
5, Boulevard Montmartre (1811–...)

193   In gold

PAU
Porcelain colours
1828–1850...
50, Rue des Marais-Saint-Martin (1828–1832)
7, Rue Albouy (1832–1841)
2, Rue Neuve Samson (1842)
2, Rue de la Douane (1844–1850...)

'AU PETIT CARROUSEL'
Manager of decorating workshop and porcelain
dealer
1775–Year VIII
(BOUTET DE MONVEL, HOUDEYER, GUY &
HOUZEL)
At le Carousel, courtyard of the Louvre

194   Painted in red, *circa* 1775

PELLETIER
Master decorator
Circa 1836–1840
2, Rue Paradis Poissonnière

195   Stencilled in red

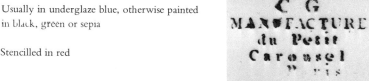

PERCHE
Perhaps the father and son were active
Addresses unknown
The marks of a) the fish, or b) the name spelt out in
full, usually accompany factory marks or those of
dealers: 'Le Petit Carrousel,' Schoelcher, Lachassaigne, Foëscy factory, etc.
(see under these names)

191   Usually in underglaze blue, otherwise painted
in black, green or sepia

192   Stencilled in red

196   Stencilled in red ●

197   Stencilled in red ●

PERDU
Decorator
1805–1837
1047, then 120, Bd. Poissonnière (1805)
10, Impasse de la Pompe (1837)

PÉRÉMÉ
Decorator, warehouse of the Villedieu factory
1840
10, Faubourg Montmartre

343

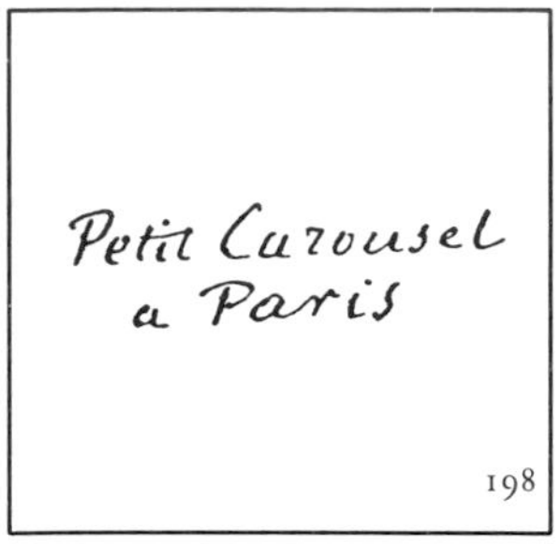

198

198 In gold ●

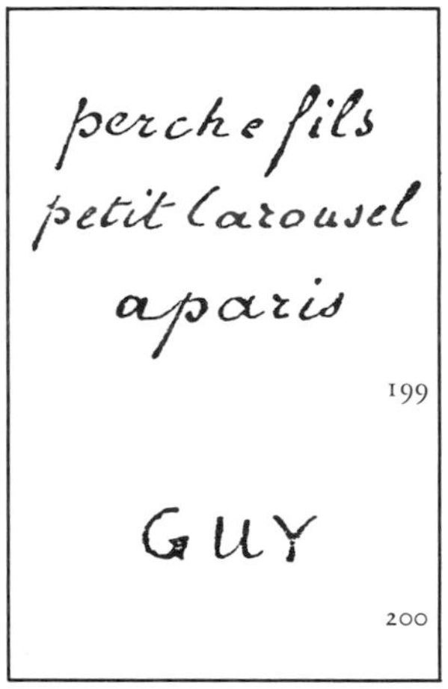

199
200

199 In gold
200 In red, pre–1797

PÉTRY, Nicolas
Factory
1793–1798...
Rue de Belleville

PÉTRY & RONSSE
Decorating workshops; factory at Vierzon
1815–1903...
6, then 11, Rue Vendôme (1815–1841)
26, Rue des Petites-Ecuries (1842–...)

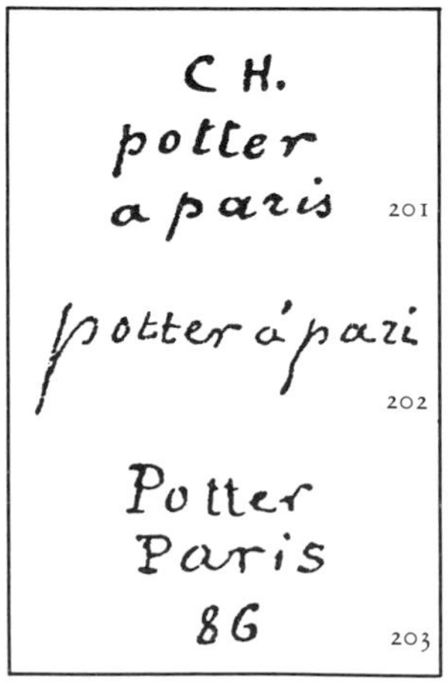

201
202
203

POTTER, BLANCHERON, CONSTANT, NEPPEL, CADET DE VAUX & DENUELLE
Factory
1789–1834 (?)
Rue de Crussol
See also: Neppel and Denuelle

1) Before 1798
201 In underglaze blue
202 In red
203 In underglaze blue

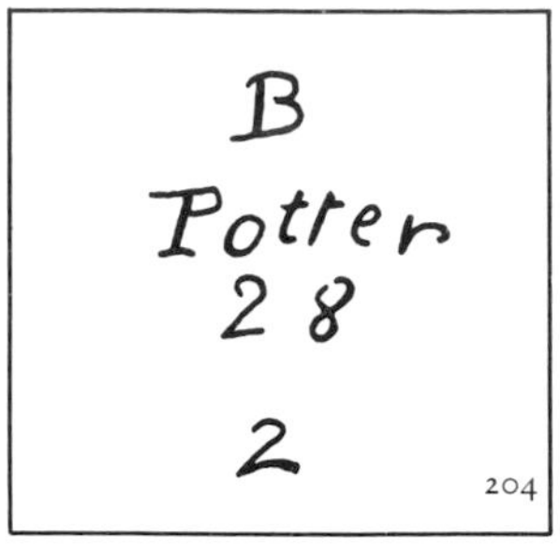

204

204 In underglaze blue, with number painted in overglaze red

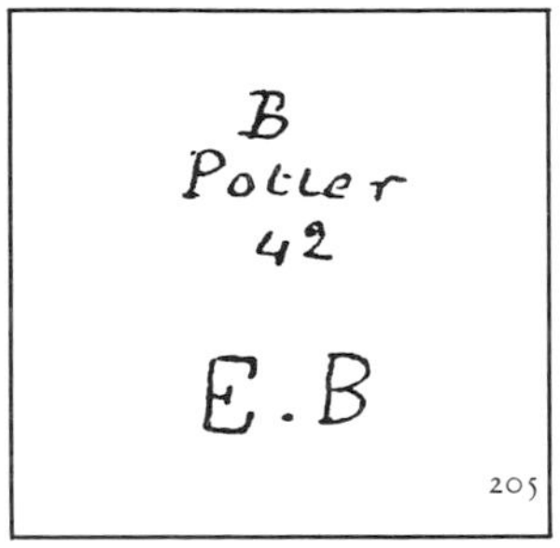

205

2) Circa 1798
205 In underglaze blue, with initials EB painted in gold

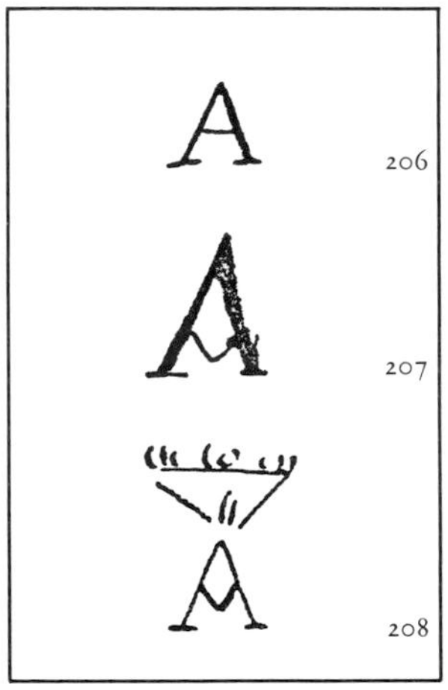

206
207
208

THE QUEEN
Factory
1776–1801 (?)
(LEBEUF, GUY, HOUZEL)
Rue Thiroux

1) Queen's patronage (1776–1792)
206 In underglaze blue
207 Painted in red
208 Painted in red

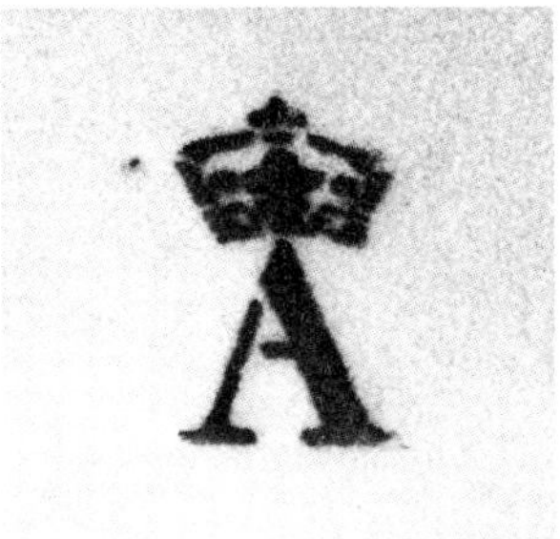

209

209 Stencilled in red

210

210   In gold

216

216   Stencilled in violet ●

G·b.
Rue Thiron
'a Paris

211

2) Guy and Houzel (circa 1797–1799)
211   In red

houzel

212

3) Circa 1800
212   In red

Lerosey
17 Rue de la paix

217

217   Various colours used

Renou

213

RENOU
Dealer in porcelain, crystal glass and faience
1820–1825
29, Rue Caumartin

213   In gold

Rousseau
43
Rue Coquillere

218

ROUSSEAU
Dealer
1844–1850
41/43, Rue Coquillière

218   Various colours

REVIL Rue
Neuve des
Capucines

214

REVIL
Initially a manufacturer
477, Rue du Rocher (1805–1815?)
Later a dealer
Rue Neuve des Capucines (1815–1819…)
See also: Nicolet & Greder

214   Stencilled in red

RIHOUËT, LEROSEY
Manager of decorating workshop, dealer in porcelain
and crystal glass
1818–1889…
49, Rue de l'Arbre-Sec (1818)
7, Rue de la Paix (*circa* 1830–…)

ROUSSEAU, A.
Decorating workshop
1831–1850…
77, Rue des Fossés du Temple (1831)
19, Rue Pierre-Levée (*circa* 1850)

219

ROUSSEAU, Francisque
Manager of decorating workshops, porcelain dealer
1838–1847…
108, Rue de Ménilmontant
49, Boulevard Saint-Martin
54, Rue Meslay (*circa* 1844)

219   In green

Rihouet.

215

215   In gold or red

SCHEILHEIMER
Decorating workshop
Before 1800
5, Cour Mandar

220   In gold ●

SOBRE & CIE.
Factory
1839–1840
32, Rue des Trois-Couronnes

SOUROUX
Factory
1773–1784 (?)
Rue de la Roquette

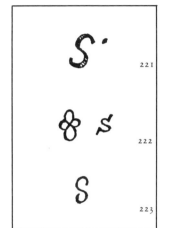

221   In underglaze blue
222   In underglaze blue
223   In underglaze blue

SPOONER
Transfer printing factory
1819–1822
9, Rue du Cadran
See also: Legros d'Anisy

TINET
Manufacturer, also dealer in porcelain and crystal glass
Circa 1815–1873
29, 32 or 38, Rue du Bac
6, Rue d'Enghien (1845–. . .)

224   Stencilled in red

225   In underglaze blue (copied from Meissen)

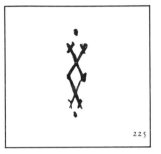

TOY, W. E.
Dealer, warehouse for English porcelain
1837–1850. . .
62ᵇⁱˢ Rue de la Victoire (1837–1839)
19, Chaussée d'Antin (1840–1850. . .)

226* In red ●

VION
Decorating workshops
1818–1850
12, Faubourg Saint-Denis (1818–1831)
10, Impasse de la Pompe, Rue de Bondy (1831–. . .)
See also: Gille

227   In green

LIST OF ENTRIES AND CROSS-REFERENCES TO THE REPERTORY OF MARKS, FACTORIES, DECORATORS AND SALESROOMS

Entries are preceded by a plus sign (+)

Advenier & Lamarre: see Broilliet
+ André, Dominique, then Louis, then Charles André & Pillivuyt
+ André, Maurice
+ Angoulême, Factory of the Duc d'
+ Artois, Factory of the Comte d'

+ Bapterose
+ Baruch Weil
    Battazerd: see Nicolet & Greder
+ Bernard
+ Bernon
    Bertrand: see Honoré & Windisch
+ Blancheron, Maubré, Baruch Weil, Dodé, Clauss
    Bloch: see Clauss
    Blot: see Feuillet
    Blottière: see Grenon
    Boin: see 'Escalier de Cristal'
    Bon & Lortz: see Honoré & Windisch
+ Bondeux
    Bourdois & Bloch: see Clauss
    Bourgeois: see Le Bourgeois
+ Bringeon
+ Broilliet
+ Buteux

    Cadet de Vaux & Denuelle: see Potter
    Caillard: see Gaillard
    Caron: see Orléans, Factory of the Duc d'
    Cassé-Maillard: see Chapelle
+ Chanou
+ Chapelle, Maillard, Cassé-Maillard
    Chazaud: see Chevalier
    Chervise: see Broilliet
+ Chevalier, Fourmy, Trégent, Lalouette, Jullien, Chazaud, Margaine
+ Clauss, Bourdois & Bloch, Bloch
+ Cœur Dassier, Darte Senior, Discry, Talmours, Hurel, Ménard
+ Colville
    Constant: see Potter
+ Corbin
+ Couderc, Couderc-Bucher
    Cremière and Cremière-Guillemot: see Deuster

+ Dagoty & Honoré
+ Dastin
+ Decaen, Auguste
    Delamarre de Villiers: see Orléans, Factory of the Duc d'
+ Demont, Lavroivre, Leroux
+ Denuelle
+ Deroche, Pochet-Deroche, Gosse, Vignier
    Désarnaux: see 'Escalier de Cristal'
    Déséglises: see Fleury
+ Desfossés Brothers
+ Despréz
+ Deuster, Freund, Cremière, Cremière-Guillemot
    Dihl: see Angoulême, Factory of the Duc d'
+ Discry
    Dodé: see Blancheron
+ Duban
+ Dubois, Vincent-Jérôme
    Dubois & Hachette: see Mortelècque
+ Duhamel
+ Dutertre

+ 'Escalier de Cristal'

+ Feuillet, Boyer, Blot, Hébert
+ Feuillet (the nephew), Manoury
    Flamen-Fleury: see Fleury
+ Fleury, Flamen-Fleury (successors to: Hoffmann & Lalouette)
    Fourmy: see Chevalier
    Freund: see Deuster
+ Froment, Louis Pierre

+ Gailliard, or Gaillard, or Caillard
+ Gambier
+ Gaugain
+ Gille, Vion & Baury
+ Gonord, Perrenot-Gonord
    Gosse: see Deroche
+ Grenon
    Guérhard & Dihl: see Angoulême, Factory of the Duc d'
    Guy & Houzel: see Petit Carrousel; also Queen, Factory of the

347

SOURCES

Introduction

Struggle against Sèvres: Archives nationales: o¹ 2059, o¹ 2060, o¹ 2061, F¹² 1493, F¹² 1494; Archives de la manufacture nationale de Sèvres: A⁴, H².

Financing: The deeds of partnership relating to the various factories mentioned, and especially: Factory of the Faubourg Saint-Denis, Archives nationales, Minutier central des notaires, Etude XV; Factory of Rue Fontaine-au-Roy, id. Etude XXII; Factory of Rue Thiroux, id. Etude XV: Factory of Rue de Bondy, id. Etude XI.

The craftsmen: Archives nationales: o¹ 2059, o¹ 2061, F¹² 1494; Archives de la manufacture nationale de Sèvres: Y³⁵bis and H³. We must also mention the various partnership-deeds referred to above (Financing), together with the works of Chavagnac and Grollier (*Histoire des manufactures francaises de porcelaine*), Verlet, Granjean and Brunet (*Sèvres*) and the introduction by R.A. Weigert to *Les porcelainiers du XVIIIᵉ siècle francais*.

The Eighteenth Century
GENERAL REMARKS

Brongniart, Alexandre. *Traité des arts céramiques.*
Chavagnac and Grollier, *Histoire des manufactures françaises de porcelaine.*
Dihl. *Rapport sur les couleurs pour la porcelaine du citoyen Dihl.*
Milly, Comte de. *L'Art de la porcelaine.*
Archives nationales: o¹ 2063, F¹² 1494: Minutier central des notaires: Etudes XV and XVI for the deeds of partnership of the factory in the Faubourg Saint-Denis.
Archives de la manufacture nationale de Sèvres: ¹, Y³⁵bis.

OUTPUT AND EVOLUTION OF STYLE

Archives nationales: o¹ 2062, R¹ 328,
Minutier central des notaires: Etudes IX, XV, XVI, XVIII, CX.
Archives de Paris 5B⁶ 2566.
Archives de la manufacture nationale de Sèvres: A4.
The precise references are given following the historical accounts 'of the factories mentioned: of the Comte d'Artois; the Comte de Provence; the Queen; Locré; Guérhard & Dihl, and the salesroom called 'Le Petit Carrousel').

Bibliothèque nationale, Cabinet des Estampes (Dept. of Prints): anonymous painter. (Portfolio of 400 cylindrical cups decorated in the eighteenth century).
Verlet, Pierre. *Une acquisition du Louvre, le nécessaire de voyage de Marie-Antoinette*, in *Jardin des Arts*, Paris, May 1955.

The Nineteenth Century
GENERAL REMARKS

Aulard, Alphonse. *Paris sous l'Empire.*
Ballot, Charles. *Les Prêts aux manufactures sous le Premier Empire.*
Bourgin, Georges and Hubert. *Le Régime de l'industrie en France de 1814 à 1830.*
Chambre de Commerce de Paris. *Statistique de l'industrie à Paris résultant de l'enquête faite par la Chambre de commerce pour les années 1847–1848.*
Gille, Bertrand. *Documents sur l'état de l'industrie et du commerce de Paris et de département de la Seine (1778–1810).*
Lanza de Laborie, L. de. *Paris sous Napoléon.* Vol. VI.
Reports on industrial and commercial exhibitions.
Archives nationales: F 3832, F¹² 2436, 2439, 3126, o¹ 2061.
Archives de la manufacture nationale de Sèvres: U¹⁵, U¹⁶bis, U¹⁹.

INDUSTRIAL AND COMMERCIAL EXHIBITIONS

Reports and documents published for each of the exhibitions mentioned. They appear in: *Bibliographie analytique des expositions industrielles et commerciales en France, depuis l'origine jusqu'en 1867*, by Régine de Plinval-Salgues.
Archives de la manufacture nationale de Sèvres: U¹⁵, U¹⁶bis.

TECHNIQUE

Brongniart, Alexandre. *Traité des arts céramiques.*
Descriptions of machines and processes specified in the patents of invention, refinement and importation.
Reports on national exhibitions of industrial goods.

OUTPUT AND EVOLUTION OF STYLE
SHAPES
DECORATION

Archives nationales: Minutier central des notaires: Etudes VI, IX.
Archives de Paris: D^5U^1, D^8U^1, $D^{11}U^3$, $D^{125}E^3$.
Archives de la manufacture nationale de Sèvres: U^{16bis}.
National industrial exhibitions, cf. p.
Chaussard, J.B. *Le Pausanias français,* Paris, 1806.

BISCUIT WARE

See the sources given under 'Output and Evolution of Style' for the eighteenth and nineteenth centuries respectively, pages 55 and 121.

Historical Account of the Factories

1 For the privileged factories in general:
– Archives Nationales: $F^{12}106$, $F^{12}107$, $F^{12}1493$, $F^{12}1494$, $F^{12}1496$, 0^12059, 0^12060, 0^12063.
– Archives de Paris: $D4^{U6}$, $D5$ ^{6}, $D11^{B3}$, DQ^{10}.
– Archives de la manufacture nationale de Sèvres: A^2, A^3, A^4, H^1, U^{15}, Y^{35bis}.
– CHAVAGNAC et GROLLIER. 'Histoires des manufactures françaises de porcelaine.'

2 Factory of the Comte d'Artois.
– PLINVAL-SALGUES, Régine de. 'La Manufacture de porcelaine du Faubourg Saint-Denis, dite du comte d'Artois.' Monograph presented to the Ecole du Louvre, Paris, June 1956.
– 'Les Schœlcher et la Porcelaine' in *Cahiers de la Céramique...* nº 6.
3 Factory of Monsieur, Comte de Provence.
– PLINVAL-SALGUES, Régine de. 'La Manufacture de porcelaine de Clignancourt, dite du comte de Provence' in *Cahiers de la Céramique...* nº 31 (important bibliography).
4 Factory of the Queen.
– Archives nationales, Minutier central des notaires, Etudes XV, XXII, LXXXVI.
5 Factory of the Duc d'Angoulême.
– Archives nationales, Minutier central des notaires, Etudes XI, XVIII, LXXVI.
– Archives de Paris: $D^{31}U^3$.
– Archives de la manufacture nationale de Sèvres: H^7.
– 'Souvenir du Prince Charles de Clary et Aldringen. Trois mois à Paris lors du mariage de l'Empereur Napoléon Ier et de l'Archiduchesse Marie-Louise.'
6 Factory of the Duc d'Orléans.
– Archives nationales, Minutier central des notaires, Etudes VII, XI, XVI, XXXIII, CI.
– Archives de Paris: D^4B^6, D^5B^6, D^8U^1, $D^{31}U^3$.
– *Almanach du commerce de Paris.*
– ARIÈS, Maddy. 'La manufacture de Creil de 1797 à 1820' in *Cahiers de la Céramique...* nº 45.

N.B. From p. 297 to p. 324 the sources are identical to the footnotes.

BIBLIOGRAPHY

1. CERAMICS

a) WORKS IN PRINT

ALFASSA et GUÉRIN. La Porcelaine française du 17ᵉ siècle au milieu du 19ᵉ. Paris. Lévy, no date.

ARIÈS, Maddy. La Manufacture de Creil de 1797 à 1820. *Cahiers de la céramique, du verre et des arts du feu,* Sèvres, Nᵒ 45, 1969.

AUSCHER, E.S. Comment reconnaître les porcelaines et les faïences d'après leurs marques et leurs caractères. Paris, Garnier, no date, 2 vols.

BIRJUKOVA, N.-Ju. Farforavaja plastika manufaktur Lotaringii vtoroj polvini XVIII. [Porcelain figures and groups from the Lorraine factories of the second half of the 18th century]. *Trudi Gosubarstvennogo Ermitaja Zapadnoevropeiskoe iskusstvo,* vol. VI, no date.

– Francuzskaja farforavaja plastika XVIII veka. [Porcelain figurines and groups from French factories in the 18th century]. Leningrad, Hermitage Publications, 1962.

BRONGNIART, Alexandre. Traité des arts céramiques ou des poteries considérées dans leur histoire, leur pratique et leur théorie. Paris, Asselin, 1877. 3rd ed., with notes and additions by Alphonse Salvétat. 2 vols. and atlas.

BRUNET, Marcelle. Le Procédé d'impression de Gonord à la manufacture impériale de Sèvres. *Archives de l'art français,* modern period, vol. XXIX. Paris, Société de l'histoire de l'art français, Nobele, 1969.

CHAVAGNAC, X. de, et GROLLIER, de. Histoire des manufactures françaises de porcelaine. Paris, Picard, 1906.

DAVILLIER, Ch. Les Porcelaines de Sèvres de Madame du Barry. Paris, 1870.

DAYDI, Olivar. La Porcelana en Europa. Barcelona, 1952.

DEMMIN, A. L'Amateur de faïence et de porcelaine. Paris, 1873.

DIHL. Rapport sur les couleurs pour la porcelaine du citoyen Dihl, fait à la classe des sciences physiques et mathématiques de l'Institut national de France, dans la séance du 26 brumaire an 6. Paris, Baudouin, Year VI.

ERNOULT-GANDOUËT, Marielle. La Céramique en France au 19ᵉ siècle. Paris, Grund, 1969.

GARNIER, E. Histoire de la céramique, poterie, faïence et porcelaine. Tours, 1882.

GAULÉJAC, B. de. Les Manufactures de porcelaine de la Nièvre. *Mémoires de la Société académique du Nivernais,* Nevers, t. 53, 1965.

GAUTHIER, Serge. Les Pouyat et leurs blancs. *Cahiers de la céramique et des arts du feu,* Sèvres, Nᵒ 13, 1959.

HANNOVER, E. and RACKHAM, B. Pottery and Porcelain, a Handbook for Collectors. London, 1925. 3 vols.

HAVARD, Henry. Dictionnaire de l'ameublement. Paris, no date.

HONEY, W.B. European Ceramic Art: Dictionary of Factories, Artists, Technical Terms and General Information. London, Faber and Faber, 1952.

– French Porcelain of the 18th Century. London, Faber and Faber, 1950.

HOSOTTE-REYNAUD, Manon. Aperçu inédit sur une manufacture de porcelaine de Paris: La Courtille, de Locré à Pouyat, 1773–1823. *Cahiers de la céramique, du verre et des arts du feu,* Sèvres, Nᵒ 35, 1964.

HOSOTTE-REYNAUD, Marie-Antoinette. La Manufacture de Pont-aux-Choux, 1743–1788. *Paris et Ile-de-France. Mémoires* published by the Fédération des sociétés historiques et archéologiques de Paris et de l'Ile-de-France, Paris, vols. XVI–XVII, 1965–1966.

JACQUEMART, A. Histoire de la céramique. Paris, 1877.

– Les merveilles de la céramique. Paris, 1877.

JACQUEMART, A. et LE BLANT, Edmond. Histoire de la porcelaine. Paris, J. Techener, 1862.

LANDAIS, Hubert. La Porcelaine française. Paris, Hachette, 1961.

LESUR, A. et TARDY. La Porcelaine française. Paris, Tardy, 1967.

MARIEN-DUGARDIN, A.-M. [Céramique] Ile-de-France – Brabant. Exhibition catalogue. Sceaux-Brussels, 1962.

MILLY, Comte de. L'Art de la porcelaine. Nyon, 1773.

PÉLICHET, Edgar. Porcelaines de Nyon. Nyon (Switzerland), Editions du musée, 1957.

PLINVAL-SALGUES, Régine de. L'Exotisme de Jacob Petit. *Art de France,* Paris, Bérès, vol. III, 1962.

– La Céramique française aux expositions industrielles de la première moitié du 19ᵉ siècle. *Cahiers de la céramique, du verre et des arts du feu,* Sèvres, Nᵒ 22, 1961.

– La Contribution française à la porcelaine portugaise. *Museu,* Ports, Seria 2, Nᵒ 2, Mayo 1961.

– La Manufacture de porcelaine de Clignancourt, dite du

comte de Provence. *Cahiers de la céramique, du verre et des arts du feu,* Sèvres, N⁰ 31, 1963.

– La Manufacture de porcelaine du Faubourg Saint-Denis, dite du comte d'Artois. Study submitted to the Ecole du Louvre, Paris, June, 1956.

– Les Schœlcher et la porcelaine. *Cahiers de la céramique et des arts du feu,* Sèvres, N⁰ 6, 1957.

PLINVAL DE GUILLEBON, Régine de. Jacob Petit. *Plaisir de France,* Paris, N⁰ 365, March 1969.

– Note sur Despréz, fabricant de camées de porcelaine à Paris. *Cahiers de la céramique, du verre et des arts du feu,* Sèvres, N⁰ 46–47, 1970.

PLINVAL DE GUILLEBON, Régine de, et LASSERRE, Charles. La Production de la manufacture de La Courtille, 18e et 19e siècles. *Cahiers de la céramique, du verre et des arts du feu,* Sèvres, N⁰ 38, 1966.

– Les Porcelaines françaises de 1647 à 1914. Exhibition catalogue, Paris, Pavillon de Marsan, 1929.

– Les Porcelainiers du XVIIIe siècle français. Paris, Hachette, 1964. Coll. *Connaissance des Arts,* «Grands artisans d'autrefois».

PRADÈRE, Jeanne. La Manufacture de La Seynie. *Cahiers de la céramique et des arts du feu,* Sèvres, N⁰ 13, 1959.

PRÉAU, Tamara. Alexandre Brongniart et les porcelainiers parisiens. *Cahiers de la céramique, du verre et des arts du feu,* Sèvres, N⁰ 46–47, 1970.

SARRIAU. Rapport du Comité d'organisation de l'exposition universelle de 1900. Saint-Cloud, Belin frères, 1905.

TILMANS, Emile. Porcelaine de France. Paris, Les Deux mondes, 1953.

TRACY, Berry B. The Decorative Arts in Classical America 1815–1845. Exhibition at the Newark Museum, 1963.

UJFALVY, Charles de. Dictionnaire des marques et monogrammes des biscuits. Paris, no date.

VERLET, Pierre. Une Acquisition du Louvre, le nécessaire de voyage de Marie-Antoinette. *Jardin des arts,* Paris, May 1955.

VERLET, Pierre, GRANDJEAN, Serge, et BRUNET, Marcelle. Sèvres. Paris, Le Prat, no date, 2 vols.

WAKEFIELD, Hugh. Victorian Pottery. London, Herbert Jenkins, 1962.

b) PORCELAIN MODELS AND DESIGNS. ORIGINAL DRAWINGS AND PRINTS Album de référence d'une manufacture de céramique, Epoque Restauration. Paris, Musée des Arts Décoratifs, Library. Modèles de porcelaine peinte et dorée, Fabrice de Honoré et Cie, Paris, Musée des Arts Décoratifs, Library. [Four hundred patterns for cylindrical cups, 18th century]. Paris, Bibliothèque nationale, Cabinet des Estampes [Department of Prints].

FAŸ. [Portfolio of miscellaneous decorative designs]. Paris, Bibliothèque nationale, Cabinet des Estampes.

II. MISCELLANEOUS WORKS

Almanach Dauphin. 1776, 1777, 1789. Paris.

Almanach du commerce de Paris pour l'an [VI–XII] [later].
Almanach du commerce de Paris, des départements de l'Empire Français [later: de la France] et des principales villes de l'Europe [later: du monde]... [Year XIII – 1838] Paris. [As from 1838 its title is:] Statistique annuelle de l'industrie. Almanach du commerce de Paris, des départements de la France...

Annales de l'industrie. Paris, 1820 (1824 ed.)

AULARD, Alphonse. Paris sous le Consulat. Paris, 1903–1913.

– Paris sous l'Empire. Paris, 1913–1923.

BALLOT, Charles. Les Prêts aux manufactures sous le Premier Empire. *Revue des études napoléoniennes,* Paris 1912. *Bazar parisien, Le,* Paris, 1821 to 1826.

BOURGIN, Georges et Hubert. Le Régime de l'industrie en France de 1814 à 1830. Paris, Picard, 1921.

BURAT, Jules. Exposition de l'industrie française, année 1844. Description méthodique accompagnée d'un grand nombre de planches et de vignettes... [Paris, Challamel, 1845].

CHAPTAL, Jean Antoine Claude. De l'industrie française. Paris, 1819.

CHAUSSARD. Le Pausanias français. Paris, [1806].

CLARY et ALDRINGEN, Prince Charles de. Trois mois à Paris lors du mariage de l'Empereur Napoléon et de l'Archiduchesse Marie-Louise. [Published by de Milis and de Pimodan]. Paris, 1912.

DALLY, Ph. Belleville. Histoire d'une localité parisienne sous la Révolution. Paris, Schmit, 1912.

FELKAY, N. In the Archives de Paris. Note sur le fonds des justices de paix 1791–1830. *Annales historiques de la Révolution française,* Paris, 42nd year, N⁰ 201, July-September 1970.

FLACHAT, Stéphane. L'Industrie, exposition de 1834. Paris, Tenré, 1834.

FRANCE. MINISTÈRE DU COMMERCE. Enquête relative à diverses prohibitions établies a l'entrée des produits étrangers, commencée le 8 octobre 1834, sous la présidence de M.T. Duchatel ministre du commerce. Paris, imp. royale, 1835.

GILLE, Bertrand. Documents sur l'état de l'industrie et du commerce de Paris et du département de la Seine (1778–1810) publiés avec une étude sur les essais d'industrialisation de Paris sous la Révolution et l'Empire. Foreword by Michel Fleury. Paris, imp. municipale, Hôtel de Ville, 1963. Documents pour servir a l'histoire économique de Paris, fascicule 1. (Ville de Paris, Commission des travaux historiques, Sous-Commission de recherches d'histoire municipale contemporaine.)

GOURNAY. Almanach général du commerce. Paris, 1788.

– Tableau général du commerce. Paris, 1789 and 1790.

GUILLAUME, Germaine. Merry Joseph Blondel et son ami Ingres. *Bulletin de la Société d'histoire de l'art français,* Paris, 1936.

JOUY. L'Hermite de la Chaussée d'Antin, ou observations sur les mœurs et les usages parisiens au commencement du XIXe siècle. Paris, Pillet, 1813.

LANZAC DE LABORIE, Léon de. Paris sous Napoléon. Paris, Plon Nourrit, 1905–1913.

LAZARE, Félix et Louis. Dictionnaire administratif et historique des rues et monuments de Paris. Paris, 1855 (2nd ed.)

LEGOUVÉ, Ernest, Soixante ans de souvenirs. Paris, no date.

MAZE CENSIER, Alphonse. Les Fournisseurs de Napoléon 1er et des deux impératrices. Paris, Laurens, 1893.

MIXELLE. Collection des maisons de commerce de Paris les mieux décorées. Paris, no date.

MOLARD, C.P. Description des machines et procédés spécifiés dans les brevets d'invention, de perfectionnement et d'importation... publiée d'après les ordres de M. le comte de Montalivet. Paris, 1811–1818...

MOREAU DE JONNÈS, Alexandre. Statistique de l'industrie de la France. Paris, 1856.

– Tableau statistique du commerce de la France en 1824. *Revue encyclopédique,* Paris, 91st instalment, tome XXX, July 1826.

MORRIS, Gouverneur. Connoisseur of French art. *Apollo,* New York, June, 1971.

PARIS. CHAMBRE DE COMMERCE. Statistique de l'industrie à Paris résultant de l'enquête faite par la Chambre de commerce pour les années 1847–1849. Paris, Chambre de commerce, 1851.

– Statistique de l'industrie de Paris résultant de l'enquête faite par la Chambre de commerce pour l'année 1860. Paris, Chambre de commerce, 1864.

PARIS, VILLE DE. Nomenclature des voies publiques et privées. Paris, imp. municipale, Hôtel de Ville, 1951. (7th ed.)

PLINVAL-SALGUES, Régine de. Bibliographie analytique des expositions industrielles et commerciales en France depuis l'origine jusqu'à 1867. Thesis for the Diploma in documentation at the Institut National des Techniques de la Documentation, Conservatoire National des Arts et Métiers. Paris, 1960.

PRONTEAU, Jeanne. Le Numérotage des maisons de Paris du XVe siècle à nos jours. Paris, 1966. (Ville de Paris, Commission des travaux historiques, Sous-Commission de recherches d'histoire municipale contemporaine, No 8).

PRUD'HOMME, Louis. Miroir historique, politique et critique de l'ancien et du nouveau Paris et du département de la Seine. Paris, 1807.

THIÉRY. Guide des amateurs et étrangers... à Paris. Paris, 1787.

TULARD, Jean. Nouvelle histoire de Paris. Le Consulat et l'Empire, 1800–1815. Paris, Association pour la publication d'une Histoire de Paris, Hachette, 1970.

VIENNET, Odette. Napoléon et l'industrie parisienne. Paris, Plon, 1947.

– Une enquête économique dans la France impériale. Le voyage du Hambourgeois Nemnich. Paris, Plon, 1947.

INDEX

The page numbers in italics indicate illustrations
A list of technical terms is given at page 361

356

Technical terms

PHOTOCREDIT

This book was printed in the workshops of Imprimerie
Paul Attinger S.A., Neuchâtel, in July 1972. Setting by
Filmsatz Stauffer & Co., Basle. Photoengraving by
Atelier Technique Atesa S.A., Geneva. Binding by
Mayer & Soutter S.A., Renens-Lausanne.
Layout by Studio S + T, Lausanne.
Printed and bound in Switzerland.

4816